MW01350208

The celebration of our Tricentennial Anniversary is an opportune time to celebrate what has transpired on this unlikely spot on the map, and recall all that New Orleans has exported across the world over the past 300 years, both literally via the port, as well as through the rich traditions and culture unique to our city.

Our fascinating histories have involved and appealed to everyone from early French explorers to current day hipsters and everything in between. This book does not attempt to recount and explain all this history. It's just too dense. Rather, we preferred to allow some of our city's most well-respected contemporary scholars tell a few stories of New Orleans' milestones, personalities, myths, and passions so that our friends and partners could discover the ones with which they most self-identify.

On reflection of all that has happened here from 1718 until now, it is impossible to exaggerate New Orleans' expansive impact. It is a city that some say shouldn't even be here, but has thrived. More than that, it has let the good times roll through three centuries, and inspired many to live their lives creatively and collaboratively with constant acceptance of diversity, sometimes through tumultuous change.

One can hardly imagine today's culinary scene worldwide without the flavors and gifts of the New Orleans kitchen. No concert hall, bar, or even reading of the Sunday paper is imaginable without the sounds and emotional call of jazz music – birthed here from the early origins of Congo Square. And then there are the people of New Orleans, descendants of a hearty lot who braved the long trip to get here and the inhospitable environment they found upon arrival - many whose next generations still call New Orleans home. Their spirit and resilience is an inspiration for capability to re-invent and move forward through change in a positive light.

The city's history would be incomplete though if it were not to recognize so many who have lived beyond its borders with the essence of New Orleans in their hearts. We are grateful for our clients, media, visitors, partners, and friends who each make their own contributions to our story and who carry New Orleans' vibrancy and character to share throughout all corners of the world. On behalf of the New Orleans Convention & Visitors Bureau, our teams, our leadership, and our hospitality community – to you we dedicate this book, and for your support and love we thank you sincerely.

Stephen Perry
President & CEO

Kristian Sonnier
Vice President of Communications & Public Relations

Louis No. 2., by John Scott, woodblock print, 2003. Courtesy of the Louisiana Endowment of the Humanities.

NEW ORLEANS & THE WORLD

1718-2018

TRICENTENNIAL ANTHOLOGY

A PARTNERSHIP OF

PROGRAM SPONSOR

The Louisiana Endowment for the Humanities
New Orleans, Louisiana

LIBRARY OF CONGRESS CATALOGING-IN-PUBLICATION DATA

New Orleans & the World:1718-2018 Tricentennial Anthology / edited by Nancy Dixon.
Includes biographical references and index.
ISBN 978-0-692-94192-4I (hardback)
1. History, United States. I. Dixon, Nancy, editor of compilation.

Copyedited by Ann Glaviano
Designed by Toan Nguyen and Cider Mill Press
Printed and bound by Pel Hughes, New Orleans, Louisiana

Frontispiece:
Eric Waters
Keith Ferdinand on Trumpet and Dr. Michael White at Danny Barker's 2nd line funeral, 1994. Black & White photograph
Courtesy of Eric Waters
Cover design by Taylor Boudreaux

Title page:
John Scott
Louis No. 2., 2003
Wood Block Print
Courtesy of the Scott Family
Collection of Louisiana Endowment of the Humanities

End paper, front:
Simon Gunning
The Big Bend, 2014–15
Oil on Canvas
Courtesy of Simon Gunning and Arthur Roger Gallery

End paper, back:
John Scott
Funeral for Louis, 2002
Wood Block Print
Courtesy of the Scott Family
Collection of William Goldring

Back cover:
J. Wells (delineator)
W. Ridgway (engraver)
New Orleans, La and its Vicinity, 1863
Hand Colored Engraving
Courtesy of The Historic New Orleans Collection

Cover design by Taylor Boudreaux

Acknowledgments

This project arose from conversations between the leadership at the New Orleans Convention and Visitors Bureau, the New Orleans Tourism Marketing Corporation, and the Louisiana Endowment for the Humanities. After comparing notes and reviewing our organizational histories, it became clear that we shared a fundamental belief: the stories of New Orleans deserve the very best storytellers. The three-hundred-year history of this "turn in the river" is as complex as any city on the planet, and the things that happened here have sent forth ripples that shaped the world. Whether you're a visitor or a lifelong resident, New Orleans has touched your life through its music, food, commerce, and the countless contributions made by the collective, persistent genius of its diverse people. If we are to truly celebrate these three hundred years, we should welcome the world with a collection of stories that shows just how important New Orleans has been to the world.

Our deepest gratitude goes to Stephen Perry, Cara Banasch, and Kristian Sonnier at NOCVB, and Mark Romig at NOTMC and the 2018 NOLA Foundation. They brought vision, resources, and enthusiasm to this project, demonstrating again and again the very best qualities of partnership—honest communication, industriousness, and generosity. We received great encouragement from Mayor Mitch Landrieu and Scott Hutcheson, Deputy CAO and Senior Advisor to the Mayor for Cultural Economy, and strong support from the membership of NOCVB. We look forward to many more collaborations with these civic leaders and the members of the 2018 Tricentennial committees. And we look forward to a full year of programs to commemorate the Tricentennial, thanks to our friends at Union Pacific.

Scholarship has been at the heart of this endeavor, as it has been for more than forty-five years at the Louisiana Endowment for the Humanities. All of us have a story—most have at least three hundred—to tell about New Orleans, but New Orleans is blessed by the attention of scholars who've worked tirelessly to research this city and its milestones, personalities, myths, and passions. We thank Richard Campanella, Robert L. Dupont, Freddi Williams Evans, Alecia P. Long, Kara Tucina Olidge, and Lawrence N. Powell for the care they demonstrated in selecting the stories, engaging in the editorial process, and holding the bar high for each sentence in this anthology. Read their books, attend their lectures, and support their institutions.

We brought Nancy Dixon onboard as executive editor because she is the embodiment of a New Orleans humanist. As a storyteller, educator, researcher, and editor, she demonstrates a rigorous love for the city that has benefited countless students, readers, and dinner party guests. On behalf of everyone at the LEH—thank you, my friend.

Every day the board of directors and staff of the LEH find new ways to rise to the challenge of delivering the humanities to people in all sixty-four Louisiana parishes. Executive Director Miranda Restovic and the rest of our team keep pushing the envelope, heading up I-49 or down Highway 90, on back roads and in classrooms, at libraries and museums. For this project, I am forever grateful to LEH managing editor Romy Mariano, designers Taylor Boudreaux and Toan Nguyen, assistant editor Ann Glaviano, and John Whalen and the good folks at Cider Mill Press for their dedication and persistence. We also tip our hat to Pel Hughes, our printing partners based here in New Orleans.

This book would not be possible without our state's great archives. We offer our deepest thanks to The Historic New Orleans Collection, the Louisiana State Museum, Tulane University, Amistad Research Center, Hogan Jazz Archive, Louisiana Research Collection, New Orleans Museum of Art, State Library of Louisiana, and the talented photographers who document the vividness of New Orleans.

As you turn these pages, know that many, many people spent many hours trying to get it right, because we believe in this city, in its importance to the world, and in the lessons found through its awesome, uproarious, heart-wrenching stories.

Brian W. Boyles

Executive Publisher
Vice President of Content
Louisiana Endowment for the Humanities

Table of Contents

INTRODUCTION

Executive Editor Nancy Dixon, PhD

As Lawrence Powell writes in his essay on the city's founding in 1718, New Orleans had to be dragged from the mud. Unfortunately, that wasn't a one-time deal. A little over ten years ago, residents were again dragging the city out of the mud left by the floodwaters after Hurricane Katrina. Many lawmakers in the nation's capital questioned the logic of spending money to rebuild the city, the majority of whose land lies below sea level, and they had a point. But this squabble itself is nothing new. Three centuries ago Bienville had to fight John Law and his Company of the Indies to settle the new port city in the hurricane-prone swamp near the mouth of the Mississippi River, and he won that fight, just as we New Orleanians did some ten years ago. In fact, we never even questioned the logic of coming back. Nor do the people from around the world who come to delight in our music, *joie de vivre*, and food—who can resist our gumbo! The three-hundred-year journey has not been easy, but few today would question its worth.

New Orleans and the World is an ideal way to commemorate the last three hundred years of the city, and as executive editor, I have been fortunate to work with an editorial board comprising some of the finest New Orleans and Louisiana writers and historians in order to create a book that paints an honest picture of the city while celebrating its rich history. Naturally, that does not mean the city's history is not complicated. It is. And *New Orleans and the World* tries to reflect the sometimes difficult nature of that history while examining the role of New Orleans on the local, national, and international stage. To that end, the book is divided into seven thematic sections: People, Space and Place, Conflict and Freedom, Spirits and Sin, Cuisine and Culture, Sounds, and Renewal.

The book opens with two essays that explain why New Orleans is situated in this crescent of the Mississippi River and describe the earliest population of the region. Richard Campanella's essay describing the region's "peculiar formation" coupled with Lawrence Powell's about the "imperial backwater" lay the ground for the ensuing thematic sections mentioned above.

From its inception as an international port, New Orleans has been a polyglot and polymorphous place; the influences are global but begin, of course, with the people, initially Native Americans, whose knowledge of the area helped keep early French, Spanish, and American settlers alive, as Dan Usner explains in his essay on American Indians. Freddi Williams Evans writes about Africans and free people of color in the city, and Laura Kelley explains that the Irish came and worked as soldiers and laborers, many digging the New Basin Canal, a portage from the Mississippi River to Lake Pontchartrain. Irish women were often domestics and many Irish opened pharmacies, restaurants, churches and schools. Finally in the section about people, Justin Nystrom writes of the Italian immigrants and their influence on the French Quarter and the produce business, dazzling early New Orleanians with the simple yet exotic lemon!

In Space and Place, Richard Campanella lays out the city's early urban rise, starting with the its geography and the creation of the French Quarter. Jack Davis looks at New Orleans centuries later during the city's short-lived oil and commercial boom in the 1980s in his essay, "Big-Time City." Naturally, Bienville strategically chose to situate the city at the mouth of the Mississippi River, and nearly one hundred years later, President Thomas Jefferson sent word to American Ambassador to France Robert Livingston concerning the city's strategic location: "There is on the globe one single spot, the possessor of which is our natural and habitual enemy. It is New Orleans. . . ." Robert L. Dupont documents the history of the Port of New Orleans and its rise and fall from world prominence.

The shipping industry figures prominently in the next section as well. In Conflict and Freedom, Jerry Strahan examines the vital role that Andrew Higgins played in shaping twentieth-century world events with the creation of his World War II landing craft that helped assure Allied victory. In fact, President Dwight D. Eisenhower would later call him "the man who won the war for us."

Nonetheless, most battles were not fought abroad but here in New Orleans, still changing the course of history. Erin M. Greenwald chronicles New Orleans as one of the largest centers of the slave trade. So it is no surprise that it was also the center of the battle for civil rights. Kara Olidge and Keith Weldon Medley write about twentieth-century Civil Rights heroes, Ruby Bridges and Homer Plessy, respectively, whose landmark Civil Rights cases played out on national and international stages.

Our rich history aside, New Orleans is perhaps better known today for its cultural laissez faire attitude, one that Alecia P. Long examines in her essay "A Wicked City?" We certainly have our share of hedonism, as tourists are bound to notice in the French Quarter, but at its center is one of the nation's oldest Catholic cathedrals, the St. Louis Cathedral. New Orleans is in fact a very religious city, as Emily Clark underscores in her history of the Ursuline nuns. What becomes apparent in this section of Spirits and Sin is the city's ability

ABOVE *View of Jackson Square, New Orleans*, by J. Dürler, 1855. Courtesy of The L. Kemper and Leila Morre Williams Founders Collection at The Historic New Orleans Collection.

to reconcile both divine and physical indulgence. Mardi Gras and Ash Wednesday are perfect examples.

The two thematic sections, Cuisine and Culture and Sounds are at the heart of today's economy, and essays in these sections examine the evolution of the city's signature cultural practices. Allison Alsup discusses perhaps one of New Orleans' greatest and certainly most celebrated customs, the cocktail. While Zella Palmer traces the origin of New Orleans cuisine to slave quarters throughout the city centuries ago, stressing the debt we owe to these African American chefs who were not here freely, something that Leah Chase also points out. Freddi Williams Evans notes that the first beats of jazz drumming and dancing can be traced back to Congo Square, where enslaved Africans and free people of color congregated to trade, make music, and celebrate their African and Caribbean culture. Musical historian Bruce Raeburn explains how those jazz beats endured and evolved as he takes us on tour with early jazz musicians Louis Armstrong, Kid Ory, and Jelly Roll Morton. By the middle of the twentieth century, Cosimo Matassa put New Orleans rock and roll on the map while giving African American artists their due, championing such legends as Fats Domino, Dave Bartholomew and Allen Toussaint. These homegrown musical giants have all been featured at the New Orleans Jazz and Heritage Festival, one of the premier musical events in the world, as have more recent local stars, Lil Wayne, Big Freedia, and Mystikal. The combination of music and food at Jazz Fest is yet another reason New Orleans continues to be a musical and culinary destination.

The book's final section, Renewal, focuses on Katrina and the ensuing flood, certainly the most critical experience in the city's recent history, but so was the city's recovery. Brian Boyles takes us back to the symbolic Saints 2010 Super Bowl victory, when the whole world was watching the city's comeback. Mayor Mitch Landrieu touts the strength and resilience of New Orleanians in rebuilding their city, something no American city had yet to endure. On that note, the most fitting way to end the book is with Dr. Michael White's "The Soul of New Orleans," a look at second lines, the city's quintessential celebrations of life and death.

New Orleans is a city that honors traditions and their significance. New Orleanians know better than to eat the delicious carnival treat, King Cake, before Twelfth Night (the first night of carnival season) or after Mardi Gras, or oysters in any months without an R in them. We enjoy satsumas in the fall and Creole tomatoes in the spring. It's true we like red beans and rice on Mondays, and seafood on Fridays. We know that second lines are a revered tradition and we honor them as they pass. We drink beer with our crawfish, we drink it on the street, and we welcome tourists to join in our fun. We truly believe in what has become our tagline—*Laissez les bons temps roulez*—and we love our city. Louisiana has the highest number of native-born residents in the nation, and that is no accident. Even those who aren't born here have trouble leaving once in the city's grip. New Orleans' storied past leaves little doubt that there is something remarkable about this little bend in the river, something that Bienville recognized three hundred years ago.

Forewords
Lessons from the Gumbo Pot

Walter Isaacson

The great cultural and political divide in our world today is between people who embrace the edgy creativity that blossoms in diverse communities versus those who recoil from it. In a globalized world that has been torn by sectarian strife and tribal wars and backlashes against immigrants, the places that thrive will be the ones where people have learned to respect—indeed value—neighbors from different backgrounds, and to realize that a vibrant cultural mix is a key to stimulating creativity.

Ever since Bienville set up a French outpost among the Chitimacha Indians three hundred years ago, our town has been enriched by waves of new arrivals: Americans and Creoles of varying hues, slaves and freed slaves and *gens de couleur libres*, Spaniards and Latinos, Irish and Italians, Germans and Greeks, Yugoslavs and Croatians, Haitians and Vietnamese. At its best New Orleans was not so much a melting pot as a gumbo pot: each group blended with the others while retaining some of its own texture and flavor. And sometimes the gumbo pot was more than a metaphor; from Antoine's to Dooky Chase's to Leidenheimer's to Mosca's to Uglesich's to MoPho to Shaya, each new ethnic influence serves to enrich our local food traditions.

The regular influx of influences also helped to create New Orleans' unique music, architecture, and festivals. Take jazz, for example. Flowing together on our street corners a century ago were the sounds of marching brass bands, funeral parades, rhythms echoing the drummers who once gathered in Congo Square, the gospel songs of the sanctified church, the sophisticated orchestras led by Creoles of color, the ragtime piano professors of the brothels of Storyville, the raggedy sounds of Buddy Bolden and his imitators at corner honky-tonks, the blues from the plantation field hands who had moved to town, and the military bands returning from the Spanish-American War who came to New Orleans and either played or hocked their horns. Plus, a kid like Louis Armstrong could learn Russian lullabies from a Jewish family in the Third Ward that took him under wing.

The cultural and ethnic interplay produced by the town's diversity—and especially the electricity that was generated by its integrated neighborhoods, such as Broadmoor, Tremé, Central City, Marigny, and the Irish Channel—has always been a source of its creativity. Valence Street near my childhood home was the location of a private club called Valencia, where teenaged white preppies hung out, and it was also the street where many old-line black people and Creoles of color lived, including the Neville Brothers, who named a New Orleans funk song after it. Nearby was Tipitina's at the foot of Napoleon Avenue, Mason's Motel Americana on Claiborne Avenue, and Sylvia's on Freret Street.

Katrina was a reminder that we New Orleanians are all, almost literally, in the same boat. The challenge of rebuilding brought back a lot of expatriates who had spent time away. Wynton Marsalis said it eloquently at a big homecoming party we threw a few months after the storm. "It's good to be home," he said. "It's especially good to be home in a time of crisis, because tough times force us to return to fundamentals. And there is nothing more fundamental than home."

ABOVE Walter Isaacson (left) with Walker Percy, 1986. Courtesy of Walter Isaacson Collection.

The storm showed how tough and resilient New Orleans is, and its aftermath brought yet another wave of immigrants, ranging from Latino workers who were crucial in the rebuilding to creative types and young entrepreneurs who wanted to be part of the revitalization of a fascinating city.

Just as New Orleans has learned so much from almost all the cultures of the world, so too New Orleans can help teach the world something. Bred deep into its genetic code is the ability to celebrate the vitality of its mélange of cultural influences. Cities like New Orleans that have a constantly renewed mix of interesting peoples are able to feel comfortable with both preservation and progress—proud of both its heritage and horizons.

Chef Leah Chase

You know, in New Orleans, a good bowl of gumbo is important to us. Food is what we are all about. We make people happy with our good food, and we think that is important. Food is a way to bring people together. It always has been.

When I think back on the seventy-five years I have spent at Dooky Chase Restaurant, and the years before when I worked in restaurants in the French Quarter, I am reminded of the important roles different groups of people have had in the evolution of our great city into a center for Creole cuisine. Our city's story around food—how it became a focal point of the lives of native New Orleanians and those who call New Orleans their second home—is worthy of being told.

New Orleans was not always known for food. We always had great food, but we had not done a great job telling our story. It wasn't really until Chef Paul Prudhomme introduced the world to Cajun food when he worked for Ella Brennan at Commander's Palace that people began to take notice of the food in our city and quality service that all legendary New Orleans family restaurateurs insist upon. At first, people were confused about the difference between Cajun and Creole. And when people came to eat Paul's Cajun food, they went around the city and learned more about Creole food too, and that was good for the city. People started paying attention to New Orleans' cuisine.

It is important for everyone to know that long before Paul and me, our city as a "gathering space" centered around food was built on the foundation laid by countless African Americans who worked in the kitchens of restaurants all throughout the French Quarter. They really made our food here, as there were very few Caucasians in the kitchen then. These African Americans were the first chefs in the city. They did not have degrees and credentials, but family recipes, determination, hard work, and a love of food. There weren't celebrity chefs back then. The name of the house was more important. These African-American chefs established the city's true culinary greatness. Rudy Lombard wrote an excellent book, *Creole Feast*, chronicling the Black chefs behind our legendary Creole dishes.

As our cuisine grew more popular, the requirements for being a chef shifted from innate skill to certification, and African Americans who had begun our food journey were moved out of spaces they had held for years and replaced with others who had degrees and formal training. Once African-American chefs were out of the kitchen, it was hard for them to get back in. I am one of the last of the female Black chefs around.

As I have said, there is so much more to food in our city than what is on the table. When I think about the role food has played in some of the most critical times of our city's history, I naturally go to the Civil Rights era. At Dooky Chase Restaurant, we really did change the course of America over countless meals. In the midst of segregation our restaurant was the only place that Whites and Blacks could meet to develop strategies for integration without being bothered by law enforcement. In the 1960s, all of the freedom riders in Louisiana met at the restaurant to determine who they were going to vote for once they had the right to vote. We fought for equal rights with the NAACP. Thurgood Marshall and the others wanted to make changes without offending people. The young people wanted to fight for things right away no matter the consequences. Thurgood Marshall sat in our restaurant and developed a strategy for integration over a bowl of gumbo and fried chicken.

We supported them by feeding them. I fed them before and after they finished organizing. When they were arrested, I sent food to the jail. I didn't know what else to do. I knew I couldn't do what they did. I still believe that the total community should work for change together. It has worked for me for the last seventy-five years. Not too bad.

ABOVE Leah Chase at her restaurant. Courtesy of Jeremy Shine, 2015.

Besides Civil Rights leaders, I wanted to create a unique experience for all Black people. Too often, they just had to eat at a bar or sandwich shop. My in-laws and I wanted to do something different. Black people deserved to have somewhere nice to sit down to dinner. When I came to the restaurant in '46, I had to change things, but change is always hard. People told my mother-in-law that I was going to ruin her business, but she even helped me, and Dooky's became a safe place to be. No one could drink too much, or my father-in-law would put them out. Black people in New Orleans realized they deserved the same fine dining experience as White diners.

When I think about our city moving forward, I believe the most important issue is our diversity. For example, we have a large Vietnamese community, who at first, did not understand New Orleanians, and we did not understand them. But over time, we learned about their food and began to embrace their unique cuisine, and we now have so many fine Vietnamese restaurants in the city.

We are learning how to learn about each other and get along in these tough times. Embracing diversity and shedding the past is hard to do. It's okay to hold on to the past, but we can't let it hold us back. We must move forward. If God wanted you to look behind you, he would have put your eyes in the back of the head!

As we work together to move forward in New Orleans and accomplish difficult changes, food will continue to be important to us. The city will continue to be a food destination. The truth is, the food may get you to New Orleans, but it's everything else that makes you realize how truly amazing this city is.

"—It is not an easy thing to describe one's first impression of New Orleans; for while it actually resembles no other city upon the face of the earth, yet it recalls vague memories of a hundred cities. It owns suggestions of towns in Italy, and in Spain, of cities in England and in Germany, of seaports in the Mediterranean, and of seaports in the tropics. Canal street, with its grand breadth and imposing façades, gives one recollections of London and Oxford street and Regent street; there are memories of Havre and Marseilles to be obtained from the Old French Quarter; there are buildings in Jackson Square which remind one of Spanish-American travel. I fancy that the power of fascination which New Orleans exercises upon foreigners is due no less to this peculiar characteristic than to the tropical beauty of the city itself. Whencesoever the traveler may have come, he may find in the Crescent City some memory of his home—some recollection of his Fatherland–some remembrance of something he loves…"

— Lafcadio Hearn

"At the Gate of the Tropics," *Cincinnati Commercial*, November 26, 1877

New Orleans from the Lower Cotton Press, by Alfred M. Hoffy and Peter S. Duval, 1852. Courtesy of The Historic New Orleans Collection.

THE COURSE OF
MISSISSIPI RIVER
from Bayagoulas
to the Sea.
Lake Maurepas
Manchac
LAKE PONTCHARTRAIN
Colapisas
NEW ORLEANS
LAKE OUACHAS
LAKE BORGNE
Low and Marshy Meadows
Ensenada de Palos
or Wood's Bay
According to the Spanish Charts
Ruins of Fort la Boulaye
the First Settlement
made in 1700
Cheneaux
I. aux Vaisseaux
Ship I.
I. aux Chats
or Cats I.
I. la Bonne Chere
I. aux Oiseaux
Birds I.
Shallow water cover'd
with many Small Islands
which are but very little
Known
Isles de la Chandeleur
Candlemas Islands
I. au Breton
East Pass
Entrance of the River
South Pass or Pass a Serigny
Cabo de Lodo or Mud Cape
According to the Spanish Charts
South West Pass
MOUTHS OF THE MISSISSIPI
GULF OF MEXICO
British Statute Miles

"The Land is of Peculiar Formation"

How the Mississippi River created New Orleans' dynamic deltaic environment

by Richard Campanella

"As you ascend, the banks appear more and more submerged, the land being scarcely visible," wrote a bewildered Frenchman sailing up the lower Mississippi in 1699. "[We see] nothing more than two narrow strips of land ... having the sea on both sides of the river, which... frequently overflows . . ."

The anonymous crewmember had reason to sound concerned. His expedition, led by Pierre Le Moyne, Sieur d'Iberville, strove to establish a French colonial society in these watery *prairies tremblantes*. Seventeen years had passed since Robert La Salle claimed the vast Louisiana Territory for France, having judged that "a port or two [here] would make us masters of the whole of this continent." Iberville arrived to establish such an outpost, lest the Spanish or British intrude. But how, amid such fluidity? And where, upon land so low? "[The] cane-brake [is] so tall and thick [and] impossible to pass through," wrote the crewmember, "beyond [which] are impenetrable marsh."

Few European eyes had ever seen a river as large as the Mississippi, much less a deltaic plain so unstable and shifting. Indigenous eyes would have witnessed even greater dynamism, prior even to the formation of those "two narrow strips of land," when open gulf waters prevailed over the future site of New Orleans.

What had converted that sea to this land was, ironically, global warming. Prior climate changes over millions of years had, in times of cooling, expanded the world's ice sheets (and thus lowered sea level, as water increasingly solidified into ice), or alternately melted them, as temperatures warmed and sea levels rose. The last of the cooling cycles reached its most frigid point about 18,000 years ago—glacial maximum, when ice sheets reached nearly to the Ohio River Valley and when New Orleans's future spot likely had gently undulating clay soils and a climate more like that of the present-day Midwest.

From that point forward, global temperatures gradually, though inconsistently, warmed. Ice sheets slowly receded, and more and more sediment-laden runoff flowed out the newly resculpted watersheds of the Missouri, upper Mississippi, and Ohio Rivers. Sea levels rose, and the future site of New Orleans became seascape.

The augmented tributaries conflowed by present-day St. Louis, Missouri, and Cairo, Illinois, to form the lower Mississippi River, which continued southward through a down-warping of the Earth's crust known as the Mississippi Embayment. Vast quantities of alluvium would fill this indentation, forming today's Lower Mississippi Valley, and the remainder disembogued into the Gulf of Mexico, which at the time lay south of present-day Baton Rouge.

Despite all the deposition, no delta yet formed, and what we know today as southern Louisiana remained open salt water. Because the gradual warming of the earth occurred with substantial perturbations, the sea level intermittently fell, rose, fell, and rose again; the uncooperatively fluctuating ocean had the effect of interrupting the land-building processes of the Mississippi and scattering its depositions offshore, rather than allowing them to accumulate and consolidate into a plain.

OPPOSITE *Plan of New Orleans*, by Thomas Jefferys and Louis Brion de la Tour, 1759. The plan shows the region as traced by Mr. de la Tour in 1720. Courtesy of Library of Congress.

This began to change around 7,200 years ago, when the pace of sea-level rise slowed but the rate of sediment deposition did not. Mucky saline marshes, known as the Maringouin Delta Complex and joined later by the Teche Complex, subsequently began to rise above the sea faster than the sea itself was rising. These deltaic "lobes" extended the coastline of the North American continent to form what is now south-central Louisiana.

The future New Orleans site, meanwhile, still comprised open Gulf of Mexico, complete with its own barrier island. Known as Pine Island, this elongated atoll was created by Pearl River sand deposits roughly five thousand years ago, which were then nudged westward by gentle longshore currents.

It was around this time that the churning waters of the lower Mississippi River broke through a bank and, finding a steeper and shorter path to the sea, lunged eastward and began creating land in an entirely new area. This would be called the St. Bernard Complex; starting four to five thousand years ago, it would be responsible for creating the land surface of modern New Orleans.

But as it did, the river encountered Pine Island. The atoll had two interrelated effects on the outflow of the Mississippi. Its latitudinal bulk steered the river straight eastward and directed its sediment deposition to what is now eastern St. Bernard Parish. Meanwhile, its north-side flank cordoned off a bay of the Gulf of Mexico. This is today's Lake Pontchartrain, really a tidal lagoon.

Sediments deposited within the St. Bernard Complex over the next 3,300 years accumulated first upon the sea floor, an undulating surface of compacted clay formed during the Pleistocene Epoch. Called the suballuvial surface, today it lies buried beneath twenty-five to one hundred feet of riverborne sand, silt, and clay particles. That alluvium eventually broke the sea surface and became saline marsh, then freshwater swamp, then a series of ridges of relatively well-drained soils.

For a while, the riverine deliveries of mud came not courtesy of the current channel of the Mississippi River, but along what is now Metairie Road, City Park Avenue, Gentilly Boulevard, and Bayou Sauvage. Later, around 2,600 years ago, the river shifted into its current channel and started building up lands to the south of that ridge.

Modern-day New Orleans was taking shape, and the hydrological forces at play would continue well after the founding of the city in 1718. "We coasted along" the eastern fringes of Orleans Parish, wrote Scottish visitor Basil Hall in 1828, "past numerous small, sandy islands[,] bars, spits, keys, and . . . shoals [typical of areas] whose Deltas are silently pushing themselves into the sea, and raising the bottom to the surface."

During the time of the St. Bernard Complex, another crevasse opened in the river channel below present-day Baton Rouge, redirecting some flow toward what is now Thibodaux, Raceland, and Golden Meadow. This would be called the Lafourche Complex, so named because early French colonials viewed the split flow as a fork of the Mississippi. Both the Lafourche and St. Bernard deltas co-existed as outflows of the Mississippi, until 1,100 years ago, when most of the discharge lunged in yet another direction, down to present-day lower Plaquemines Parish. This is the "birdfoot" delta, the river's active mouth today—but by no means the first, nor the last.

The Mississippi's ever-shifting mouth(s) and enormous volume overwhelmed the ability of the Gulf of Mexico to sweep away its sediment deposition. Those twin processes are why south-central and southeastern Louisiana, an area known as the Mississippi River Deltaic Plain, took form. To the French geographer Élisée Reclus, who visited New Orleans in 1853, the process brought to mind "a gigantic arm projecting into the sea and spreading its fingers on the surface of the water." Meanwhile, longshore currents swept some sediment westward, creating slender east-west–oriented ridges favored by oak trees—*chenier* in French, thus the Chenier Plain. Southwestern Louisiana emerged from the mud.

Smaller increments of land-building occurred more frequently, when high springtime runoff overtopped river banks and spilled laterally upon the deltaic plain. With those floodwaters came suspended sediment, the coarsest of which (sand and silt) settled in the highest quantities immediately, followed by finer particles (clay), which settled farther back. "The upper surface is a marsh mud . . . with a small mixture of sand, & below this surface are decayed vegetables, water at 3 feet," wrote Benjamin H. B. Latrobe in 1819; "[s]uch a soil [is] the result of the gradual accumulation of the deposition of the river." Repeated over millennia, the accretions yielded an inverted topography unique to alluvial and deltaic environs, in which rivers rise above the landscape

BELOW *Bird's-eye view of the Mississippi River*, by E. Molitor, 1884. Courtesy of Library of Congress.

rather than erode it down. "You will observe that the land [around New Orleans] is of peculiar formation," wrote the Jesuit priest Father Louis Vivier in 1750. "Throughout nearly the whole country, the bank of a river is the lowest spot; here, on the contrary, it is the highest." This paradoxical topography is essential to understanding the urban history of New Orleans, for it was exclusively upon these upraised natural levees, ten or so feet above the level of the sea, where builders could erect a city. The backswamp and marshes, high in water content and organic matter and nary a few inches above the sea, were all but undevelopable until the twentieth century.

Consider the distinctions of New Orleans' underlying geography. Here we have one of the world's biggest and best examples of a rare phenomenon, a river-dominated (fluvial) delta, where dynamism and disorder reign and where the resulting ephemeral land progrades far beyond the coastal bight—quite different from most deltas, which are dominated by wave or tidal action and barely protrude at all. Here, too, we have a society engaged in the ambitious, courageous, and perhaps arrogant effort to impose rigidity and order on that deltaic messiness, in the form of levees, embankments, gates, barriers, canals, and pumps.

What had converted that sea to this land was, ironically, global warming.

What has resulted is a remarkable and beautiful experiment called New Orleans, a place apart, a world city, and a key cog in the engine of global trade. But engineering interventions have also subverted the processes that spawned this land in the first place, and paradoxes and dilemmas abound. To wit:

- Levees erected along the Mississippi River have contained its springtime floods—to the benefit of urbanization, but at the cost of greatly diminished dosages of new freshwater and sediment to the deltaic plain.
- Revetments and channel-control structures, like the herculean Army Corps weirs at Old River, have successfully restrained the Mississippi's inclination to jump paths—to the benefit of all those dependent on its current channel, but at the cost of land-building elsewhere along the coast.
- Canals excavated for the convenience of shipping and extraction of oil and gas have enriched the region—but also scored and scoured delicate marshes with erosion-prone intrusions of rising seawater and ingresses for the surges of tropical storms.
- Combustion of these and other fossil fuels, meanwhile, have helped warm global temperatures to a degree not seen even when the ice sheets started melting eighteen thousand years ago. Seas will rise at a pace likely ten times higher in the 2000s than in the 1900s, and the power and frequency of tropical storms might increase.
- Outfall canals and pumps have enabled the development of New Orleans neighborhoods like Gentilly and Lakeview, not to mention nearly all of the suburban parishes. But they also lowered the groundwater, dried out the soil body, and allowed the landscape to subside by five to fifteen feet. As a result, half of New Orleans has sunk below sea level over the course of one century, making it all the more critical that the city be surrounded by well-engineered levees and floodwalls. In fact, many of them breached when Hurricane Katrina struck in 2005, and the seawater that poured in became impounded within topographic bowls inadvertently created by the very human engineering originally designed to keep the area dry.

In successfully launching a society on this fluvial delta, where previously the river "won the battle" by depositing sediment faster than the sea could sweep it away, humans have interrupted hydrological processes and inadvertently allowed the sea to regain the upper hand. If current trends continue, half the delta could be gone by New Orleans' 350th anniversary, and most by its 400th. Reversing this trend will entail the commitment of the nation, as well as the concessions of some Louisianans, to tap into the phenomenal land-building capacity of the Mississippi River by redirecting its freshwater and sediment back onto to the deltaic plain, pushing back that salt-water wedge and depositing alluvium at a pace faster than the sea is rising.

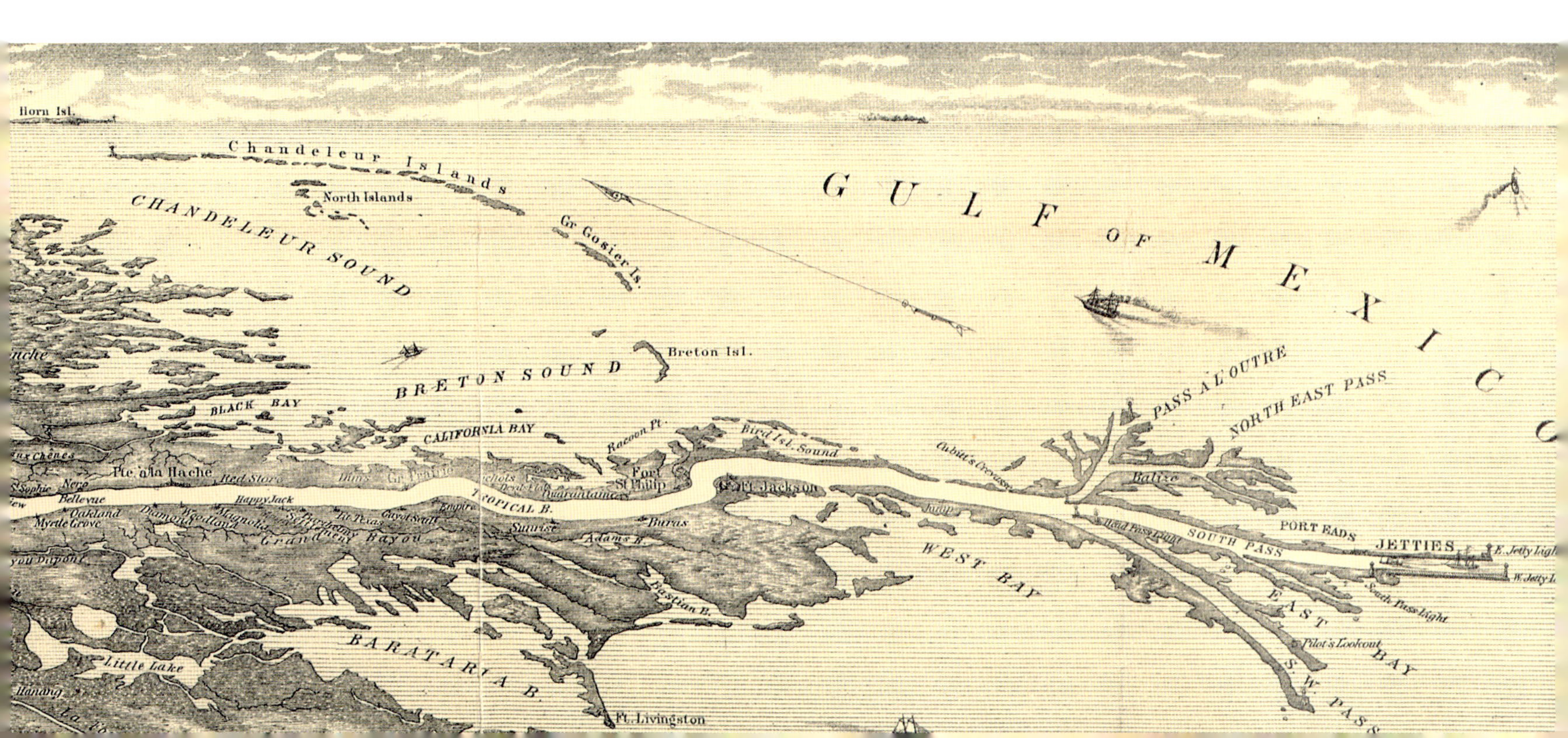

COLONIEE
FRANCOISES
1699.
Pe. Le MoyNE
SR de-IbVle
LP PL

Promethean Ambition

How an imperial backwater entered world history

by Lawrence N. Powell, PhD

Colonial New Orleans was no stranger to abrupt shifts in sovereignty. The eighty-five-year-old town changed hands three times before America took control in 1803. The original owner, Bourbon France, had used convict labor and enslaved Africans to drag the place from the mud in 1718. Paris then turned over the entirety of Louisiana to Bourbon Spain in 1763 as indemnification for Madrid's territorial losses resulting from its alliance with France during the French and Indian War. Then France, this time under the tricolor of Napoleon Bonaparte, secretly regained control of Louisiana in 1801. Bonaparte was fired by an ambition to restore France's North American Empire, quash the successful slave revolution on the once fabulously sugar-rich island Saint-Domingue (now Haiti), and use Louisiana as the island's granary. However, Saint-Domingue's former slaves, abetted by yellow fever, decimated the crack army Napoleon had sent to the island, upending the First Consul's best-laid plans. Bonaparte promptly sold New Orleans to the United States as part of the Louisiana Purchase. The cession unfurled the fourth flag to fly over New Orleans in the space of slightly more than four-score years.

To Thomas Jefferson, the real prize had always been Louisiana's creole capital. He stated his reasons in an 1802 letter to Robert Livingston, the American ambassador to Paris: "There is on the globe one single spot, the possessor of which is our natural and habitual enemy. It is New Orleans." It was all about location. New Orleans is a seaport on a river—no different from New York, say, or Philadelphia, or Baltimore—but with this huge exception: New Orleans' river system drains a continental vastness stretching from western Pennsylvania to the Montana Rockies. Its waterways penetrated practically every crop region in the country, and they all flowed south into the Mississippi, past the city's levees, the last trade stop before America's greatest commercial artery emptied into the Gulf of Mexico. Once that boundless drainage basin began to fill with towns and people, New Orleans would become the staple port for the greatest free-trade zone the world had ever seen.

This economic boon didn't materialize overnight. The site was dreadful: diseased, battered by hurricanes, flooded half the year. It was an ancient wetland, neither quite land nor quite water, but a spongy amalgam of both, and it would have to be constantly fortified with earthen levees—defenses that starved New Orleans of river-borne sediment necessary for counteracting continual subsidence. Yet the largest disadvantage was the Mississippi: its powerful currents, its sand bars and shoaling at the mouth. New Orleans sits ninety nautical miles from the river's birdfoot mouth, and in the Age of Sail, tacking shore to shore over that long upstream reach was an endurance test few mariners cared to experience. The proprietary company then controlling Louisiana—the Company of the Indies, a linchpin in the Scottish gambler John Law's corporate takeover of a kingdom—was, for this reason, solidly opposed to building New Orleans in the crook of the famous crescent meander that provides the city its nickname. The company preferred an upriver location near Baton Rouge called Bayou Manchac, because it offered, through the lakes and connecting rivers and bayous, a less arduous backdoor pathway to the sea. Bayou Manchac is where New Orleans likely would have ended up but for the stock market crash known as the Mississippi Bubble, brought on by Law's financial overreach. At the time, about the only proponent of the site on which New Orleans sits today was the founder himself, commandant-general Jean-Baptiste, Sieur de Bienville. And he got his way mainly because the Parisian board was too preoccupied with reorganizing the company's post-crash finances to notice that Bienville defied their orders to move to Bayou Manchac. Instead of pulling up roots, Bienville sank them deeper, populating and expanding New Orleans' built environment with focused energy, creating faits accomplis that not even the exasperated directors felt at liberty to reverse once they discovered Bienville's insubordination. That is how New Orleans became an accidental city.

Even so, New Orleans came squalling into the world with outsized expectations. The Company of the Indies envisioned transforming the town's hinterland into a Chesapeake on the Mississippi and making it the sole source of tobacco for French consumers. New Orleans would be the commercial hub. To that

OPPOSITE The Iberville Stone, 1699, was recovered from the site of Fort Maurepas, the first permanent settlement established by Iberville in the Mississippi Valley. Courtesy of Louisiana State Museum.

end, the company poured considerable resources, human and otherwise, into new river settlements. Early settlers included vagabonds and asylum and prison inmates given early release. Others were artisans—caulkers, joiners, carpenters. A small contingent of Ursuline nuns would end up having enormous influence on the town's religious ethos. There was a small cadre of military and administrative officials, as well as a detachment of troops. Rounding out the group was a smattering of planters (*concessionaires*, to use the French term for these proprietors), along with their supervisory adjuncts (*commandeurs*), for implicit in the company's early vision was the promethean ambition to create a full-blown plantation society de novo and to accomplish it in the blink of time.

Enslaved Africans figured prominently in these early plans. They were the indispensable labor force Louisiana's first master class depended on to clear canebrakes, fell swamp willows, dredge canals, and mound up levees. They would cultivate the colony's first cash crops—tobacco and a blue dye plant called indigo. Between 1719 and 1731, nearly six thousand slaves, most of them war captives, were transported to New Orleans and its hinterland from the West Coast of Africa. They comprised a mélange of ethnicities and different language groups every bit as various as the potpourri of European immigrants who would flood the city in the next century. And almost overnight they became the majority of the population.

ABOVE Territory map of the Mississippi River and its environs. *Partie meridonale de la rivière de Mississippi, et ses environs, dans l'Amérique Septentrionale*, by Nicholas de Fer, 1718. Courtesy of The Historic New Orleans Collection.

Yet as critically important as enslaved Africans were to the early development of New Orleans and its trading area, not even their skills and brawn were enough to vouchsafe a prosperous future. Louisiana indigo couldn't compete with superior grades grown elsewhere in the Caribbean basin, nor was tobacco suitable to the relentless summer heat and humidity of south Louisiana. Too often tobacco rotted on New Orleans' levees while awaiting transshipment to France. It only took one disaster—the 1729 uprising by Natchez Indians that wiped out the colony's major tobacco-growing operations—to induce the Company of the Indies to relinquish its charter. Thereafter, Louisiana's economy went to ground, and the crown lost interest in New Orleans' affairs.

The benign neglect turned out to be a cultural blessing in disguise. For it was when France's official gaze turned away that a distinctive creole culture began to crystallize in New Orleans. Town and country now had to fend for themselves, and so too, more or less, did most of the slaves. Staple crops having ceased to turn a profit, thousands of enslaved Africans were suddenly idled. The master class encouraged the practice of self-rental to building contractors and engineers in need of carpenters and joiners—provided the rented slaves shared wages with their owners. Soon a provision economy, stocked by slave-grown vegetable gardens, sprang up. A market emerged for the fish and game slaves caught and killed and for the firewood they had bundled in from the cypress swamps. And as this provisions-based economy found purchase, so did New Orleans metamorphose into a New World incarnation of an African market town. By the second generation, after slaves had forged a linguistic community anchored in pidgin French, New Orleans would become an Afro-creole town as well.

Meanwhile, the white governing class—a mix of Canadians and French planter-merchants and civil and military officials—began to intermarry. A white creole society took hold. It had been left in the lurch by the mother country's loss of interest in New Orleans' commercial possibilities. So New Orleans and its environs fended for itself by going rogue, thumbing its nose at the mercantilist dogma of the times that colonies were supposed to trade only with the metropole. Instead New

ABOVE *Jean Baptiste Le Moyne, Sieur de Bienvill*, by Rudolph Bohunek, 1910. Courtesy of Louisiana State Museum.

Orleans reinvented itself as a Gulf Coast crossroads in the marketing of contraband, even if that meant trading with the hated British—indeed, especially with the hated British, because at least they were able to keep the town supplied with much-in-demand textiles. Soon smuggling became the economic lifeblood of New Orleans.

Whether the result of imperial neglect or a function of life on the edge, New Orleans' early elites quarreled, to an extraordinary extent, over power, patronage, and status. First there was the fractious rivalry between frontier-seasoned Canadians, such as Bienville, and waves of self-fashioning arrivals from France dripping with condescension. Then came the friction between creoles and outsiders generally. There were safety valves for letting off steam and for lowering social barriers, as New Orleans became a place that took its sensate pleasures seriously. For the *petit blancs* (as well as footloose slaves) there were countless taverns and grog shops, and billiard halls, too, where huge quantities of cheap tafia rum were consumed. For *les grands* there were weekly balls, often masked, for New Orleans was a dance-crazed community decades before gaining fame as "one vast gallopading hall." Pierre de Rigaud de Vaudreuil, Louisiana's only aristocratic governor (1743–1753), is still celebrated for turning the creole capital into a Paris in the swamps.

The town's creole elites were thrown completely off guard when news arrived, eighteen months after the fact, that the French crown had ceded the entirety of Louisiana to Bourbon Spain in 1763. It shouldn't have come as a surprise. From the vantage of Versailles, New Orleans was unprofitable and ungovernable, notorious for its "disorders": factionalism, smuggling, social promiscuity, to say nothing of slaves who didn't know their place. The list of infractions seemed endless. New Orleans had grown comfortable with being governed from an indulgent distance. But Spain was not like France. It was an active imperial power, its international bureaucracy second to none. Where would New Orleans and its hinterland fit within this sprawling commercial empire? The town's creole didn't wait for an answer. They launched a campaign to

"There is on the globe one single spot, the possessor of which is our natural and habitual enemy. It is New Orleans." – Thomas Jefferson

persuade the French crown to take them back. In 1768 they even staged a revolt, the first colonial uprising in the western hemisphere, and expelled the new governor, Antonio de Ulloa, a world-class scientist who was gifted at just about everything except personal diplomacy. The revolt was easily suppressed the following year by General Alejandro "Bloody" O'Reilly, who dispatched the instigators but whose treatment of the rebellious town never measured up to his fearsome nickname.

In popular imagination Spain has seldom received the kudos it deserves for its stewardship of late colonial New Orleans. Although recruited from the bureaucratic second string, its governors were uniformly competent. They established the first city government (the Cabildo), gave the town its first street lights, established its first police department and fire brigade, created its first building code. Twice New Orleans nearly burned to the ground, in 1788 and 1794, and twice Spain rebuilt it by dipping into its own coffers. (The French Quarter is as much Spanish as French.) Spain enjoys the dubious distinction of revitalizing plantation slavery and reopening the slave trade—but also fostering the rise of New Orleans' three-caste racial order. The city's distinctive Afro-Creole class comprising free people of color took shape under the Spanish, thanks to a legal custom called *coartación*, or self-purchase. Slaves possessing the wherewithal could buy their freedom at prices set by Spanish authorities, which many thrifty veterans of self-hiring during the French period rushed to do. Finally, Spanish governors organized free black militias, fostering a corporate identity among this population. The militia formed the backbone of New Orleans's free colored community, which not long after Spanish rule ended exploded in size when boatloads of Saint-Domingue refugees from that island's great slave revolution arrived on the levee by way of Cuba.

Even in the area of trade, Spanish policy was flexible and pragmatic. Lucky for New Orleans that it was. Louisiana exported little that Spain wanted, and the metropole produced next to nothing New Orleans cared to purchase. Madrid's chief motive for accepting Louisiana as a sort of consolation prize was its utility as a buffer zone against British designs on Mexico's silver mines. To deal with that threat, General O'Reilly had chased British traders hovering near New Orleans back to British-occupied Baton Rouge. Shortly afterwards, the next Spanish governor let them back in, realizing rather quickly that the town's survival depended on smuggling. There was one serious attempt at a major reset: Governor Bernardo de Galvez's wildly successful military campaign during the American Revolution to drive the British away from the Gulf Coast while England was combatting the Continental Army. But driving the British from Spanish Louisiana hardly put an end to the economic penetration of New Orleans. Predictably, England blockaded Veracruz, a crucial source of foodstuffs for New Orleans. In order to victual New Orleans and fresh troops from Havana, Spanish governors were forced to purchase wheat from Maryland and Pennsylvania. Soon commerce with Americans would dwarf the contraband trade with Britain, as an economic nuisance morphed into an existential threat to Spanish sovereignty.

The drawback to Spain's helping Americans win their independence is that it removed British limitations on Anglo-American migration into the Mississippi Valley. London had restricted immigration into the Trans-Appalachian West, fearing its settlers would drive Indian nations into the arms of imperial rivals. With American independence the ban disappeared, and American demography started shifting on its axis. Farmers and town-builders from the eastern seaboard poured across the Alleghenys, presaging the torrent that would flood the Ohio Valley after 1800. Soon they were eager to get surplus produce and livestock to market. Eastern merchants had little trouble dragging finished goods across the mountains and selling them for a profit. Not so with bulky grains moving in the opposite direction. Until the canal boom of the 1830s and the completion of the east–west trunk railroad system in the 1850s, the Valley's western produce trade, as the commerce in grains, furs, and livestock came to be called, had to reach distant markets by way of the Mississippi. And that river system, as we have seen, flowed south and funneled past New Orleans, the river's only seaport and therefore the Mississippi Valley's principal transshipment center.

If there was a historical moment when New Orleans' slide into the American sphere of economic influence became irreversible, it was probably shortly after 1787. An early catalyst was Spanish diplomacy. To prevent downriver western commerce from taking over the economy and undermining Spanish sovereignty itself, Madrid offered eastern merchants preferential trading privileges with Spain in return for America's acquiescence in Spain's closure of the Mississippi to American commerce. The intent was to stir up sectional ill will between East and West, in the expectation of inducing westerners to become Spanish subjects, or at least break off into an independent and therefore more malleable confederacy. To that end Spanish officials entered into a secret agreement with an American general and Kentucky landholder named James Wilkinson, who promised to foment a western secession movement in exchange for a monopoly over the Mississippi River trade. Meanwhile, Spain began offering spectacularly large land grants to

BELOW The poster used for recruiting settlers to the colony. *Le Commerce que les Indiens du Mexique font avec les Francois au Port de Mississippi*, published by François Gérard Jollain Jr., 1719 - 1721. Courtesy of The Historic New Orleans Collection.

impresarios in exchange for settling New Orleans' hinterland with Americans, even Protestant Americans, who agreed to become Spanish subjects. It offered lucrative tobacco subsidies to Anglos who had settled in Natchez, then still a Spanish possession. The Machiavellian diplomacy and inducements were all for naught. The currents of western trade into New Orleans soon grew as overpowering as the currents that splayed tons of sediments across the deltaic plain every time the Mississippi jumped its banks.

With the burgeoning trade came an influx of merchants into New Orleans. They arrived from Philadelphia, Baltimore, New York, and Boston, to say nothing of the British Isles and France. They were, simply put, the agents of American annexation. Usually in their early twenties, many arrived as junior partners of counting houses in the East, dispatched to New Orleans so as to integrate the creole capital into trade networks that tied together the Upper Mississippi Valley, the eastern seaboard, and even the island of Saint-Domingue. By 1795, four years after the Saint-Domingue slave revolution disrupted the world's paramount producer of sugar and enabled south Louisiana to transition from indigo to cane cultivation, at the same time that Eli Whitney's cotton gin was facilitating a similar shift in Natchez from tobacco to cotton, the gravitational pull of American commerce had become practically irreversible. It was the culmination of the economic takeover that preceded the political one, and indeed made it possible.

There were countless taverns and grog shops, and billiard halls, too, where huge quantities of cheap tafia rum were consumed.

All that remained to legitimize the new geopolitical reality was the Louisiana Purchase. One can sympathize with Thomas Jefferson's alarm at learning of Spain's secret retrocession of Louisiana to Napoleon. Compared to Spain, France was the most active power of them all. Secessionist discontent was still simmering in the Trans-Appalachian West and threatened to boil over after a local Spanish official peremptorily closed the river to American commerce. The integrity of the republic depended on securing unimpaired access to New Orleans. No longer a sleepy backwater of an empire, New Orleans was suddenly thrust into the Atlantic world of commerce and intrigue, a position it wouldn't relinquish until after the Civil War.

RIGHT TOP Courtesy of Louisiana State Museum.
RIGHT MIDDLE Courtesy of Louisiana State Museum.
RIGHT BOTTOM Wikimedia Commons

COLONIAL GOVERNORS OF LOUISIANA

Five fascinating figures from early New Orleans

Jean-Baptiste Le Moyne, Sieur de Bienville

Terms: 1702-1713, 1716-1717, 1718-1724

Born in Montreal, Bienville was twelve years old when joined the French navy. He and his older brother, Pierre Le Moyne d'Iberville, established a permanent French settlement in Louisiana, Fort Maurepas in 1700. Bienville chose the site for New Orleans, named for the French Duc d'Orléans, in 1718.

Etienne de Périer

1727-1733

Périer worked to improve the infrastructure of the colony, deepening the main channel of the Mississippi River and constructing levees and a park in New Orleans. However, his lack of respect for the Natchez Indians, up until then a key partner for the French, led to a massacre near present-day Natchez in 1729 that left 236 settlers dead. He was recalled when the French Crown took back control of the colony from the Company of the West.

Louis Billouart, Chevalier de Kerlérec

1753-1763

Prior to his time as governor, Kerlérec had been wounded off the coast of St. Domingue and served time as a prisoner-of-war in England. In New Orleans, his intense rivalry with colonial administrator Vincent de Rochemore resulted in his imprisonment in the Bastille.

Alejandro O'Reilly

1769–1770

An Irish mercenary, O'Reilly joined the Spanish infantry at the age of ten. He arrived in New Orleans in the wake of the Insurrection of 1768, a coup attempt that followed the transfer of Louisiana from France to Spain. O'Reilly brought with him an army of two thousand men. He ordered the execution by firing squad of five of the insurrection's leaders, giving "Frenchmen Street" its name and inspiring his nickname: "Bloody O'Reilly."

Bernardo de Gálvez

1776-1786

A veteran of conflicts against the Apaches, the Portugese, and Ottoman forces in Algiers, Galvez led Louisiana militiamen against the British during the American Revolution. His forces included people of French, Spanish, Acadian, African, Native American, Swiss, German, and Mexican descent. Galvez was also responsible for the increased importation of enslaved Africans to the colony.

Part I:

PEOPLE

Two Jacksons

When General **Andrew Jackson** arrived in New Orleans in December 1814, the nation was at war with the British. Louisiana had entered the Union just two years earlier; Jackson and his superiors in Washington had reservations about the loyalties of the locals. Would the city's French creoles, Spaniards, and free blacks stand with the Americans? Faced with rumors of dissent and civilian spies, Jackson declared martial law. Anyone breaking a 9:00 p.m. curfew would be considered a spy. Martial law also allowed Jackson to impress men into military service. The fighting force he assembled reflected the diverse population, with Native Americans, African Americans, free men of color, Jews, and Jean Lafitte's Baratarian pirates joining with the Louisiana militia to support the army. After several skirmishes downriver, the British attacked the earth works protecting the east bank of New Orleans on January 8, 1815. As the fog lifted, the Americans unleashed their muskets and cannons, overwhelming the invaders. By the end of the fighting, the British had suffered more than two thousand casualties, including 278 dead, compared to just 39 killed on the American side. The War of 1812 had officially ended weeks earlier, but the victory confirmed for the nation that New Orleans truly was an "American" city. Though fêted in a public ceremony in the *Place d'Armes* that included a triumphal arch, Jackson kept martial law in place for another two months, earning the ire of many New Orleanians and a one thousand-dollar fine for contempt of court. (In 1844, Jackson demanded and received a refund from Congress.) The *Place d'Armes* was renamed Jackson Square in 1851, and the sculpture of Jackson on horseback was installed in 1856.

LEFT *Andrew Jackson*, by John Vanderlyn. Courtesy of the City of Charleston.

Mahalia Jackson grew up in the churches of Uptown New Orleans. "Everybody in there sang and they clapped and stomped their feet and sang with their whole bodies," she wrote in *Movin' on Up*, her 1966 memoir. "They had a beat, a powerful beat, a rhythm we held on to from slavery days, and their music was so strong and expressive it used to bring tears to my eyes." Born in 1911 into a family that included her formerly enslaved grandparents, Jackson was surrounded by music in the Black Pearl neighborhood. She moved to Chicago around 1928, where she worked as a maid while singing in churches and recording gospel songs distinguished by the "bounce" of her jubilant vocal style. Her 1948 breakout hit, "Move on Up a Little Higher," brought her national renown and led to European tours, television appearances, and increasing wealth. Jackson performed at Carnegie Hall in 1950, the inauguration of President John F. Kennedy in 1961, and at the March on Washington in 1963, singing "Buked and Scorned" just prior to Dr. Martin Luther King Jr.'s "I Have a Dream" speech, which she is said to have prompted with her comment, "Tell them about that dream, Martin." Her activism during the Civil Rights movement led Harry Belafonte to praise her as "the single most powerful black woman in the United States." Upon Jackson's death in 1972, Coretta Scott King said that "the causes of justice, freedom and brotherhood have lost a real champion whose dedication and commitment knew no midnight." Renamed by the New Orleans City Council in her honor in 1993, the Mahalia Jackson Theater for the Performing Arts is located in Louis Armstrong Park.

ABOVE Mahalia Jackson. Courtesy of The Hogan Jazz Archive, Special Collections, Howard Tilton Memorial Library, Tulane University.

TUSTENNUGGEE EMATHLA
OR JIM BOY
A CREEK CHIEF.

American Indians in New Orleans

Native communities were integral to the city's foundation

by Daniel H. Usner, PhD

The ceremony began when a delegation of about forty Chitimacha Indians landed in several dugout canoes at the Mississippi River's bank fronting New Orleans, a colonial town that had just begun to be cleared and surveyed. A chief the French called Framboise and his wife were among them. Singing to the cadence of gourd rattles and waving a calumet pipe toward the sky, the Chitimachas marched solemnly to the makeshift cabin of Jean-Baptiste Le Moyne, sieur de Bienville. Once his retinue was seated on the ground, the chief lit the pipe and presented it to Louisiana's governor. After a decade-long war with the French had ravaged his people, Framboise expressed joy over Bienville's acceptance of peace. "Our hearts and our ears are filled with it," the chief declared, "and our descendants will preserve it as long as the ancient word shall endure." He then presented gifts of deerskins to the governor and further elaborated on the causes and consequences of the costly war. With a brief speech, Bienville received the chief's promise of peace, along with the pipe itself as a gift. He commanded the Chitimachas to return all colonists taken captive during the war, but he refused to return any Chitimacha people captured and enslaved by the French. Bienville then closed this ceremony by insisting that Chief Framboise relocate his village closer to New Orleans, a city that would henceforth take its rituals very seriously.

The origins of New Orleans depended intricately on French relations with American Indians throughout the Mississippi Valley. Exploring the Mississippi River in early March 1699, Pierre Le Moyne d'Iberville had been shown by a Biloxi Indian guide "the place through which the Indians make their portage to this river from the back of the bay where the ships are anchored." Situated between a chain of estuarine lakes and the Mississippi, the crescent-shaped bend that would become New Orleans had long been used by Indian people for short overland travel between waterways as well as for seasonal gathering of food sources.

Over the millennia, American Indians in this alluvial lowland had developed a seasonal pattern for exploiting its rich array of animal and plant resources. As the Mississippi River's delta jumped directions every several centuries, Native communities easily shifted their uses of old and new channels. During summer and autumn, people occupied natural levees formed by the waterways' spring deposits of sediment, hunting game, fishing in backwater lakes, and gathering fruits and nuts. In winter these communities dispersed into camps along bayous and lakes, harvesting fish, fowl, clams, and oysters. When spring flooding began, the nearest bluffs bordering this floodplain became centers of occupation. This was the season for group-oriented hunting, for engaging in longer-distance trade and warfare, and for intensifying production of domestic crops. Several centuries before French colonization began, the Pontchartrain Basin had become prime habitat for this seasonal round of activity. East-to-west ridges left by abandoned channels of the Mississippi provided ground for occupation and travel above the floodplain, and a sizable bayou entering the lake offered convenient access to the banks of the Mississippi.

Indian commerce and conflict generated by French colonizers shaped New Orleans' future in countless ways. Closest to the site chosen for the colonial town were villages of Chaouacha, Ouacha, and Acolapissa people, but the disruptive effects of European imperial rivalry between France and England had also caused groups of nearby Houma and faraway Natchitoches Indians to take refuge along bayous and ridges between the Mississippi River and Lake Pontchartrain. Once the Company of the Indies began sending settlers and slaves to develop plantations along the lower Mississippi, steady relations with American Indians became

OPPOSITE
Tustennuggee Emathla, Creek Chief. From *History of the Indian Tribes of North America, vol. 2.* Courtesy of The Historic New Orleans Collection.

essential. Thus the destructive war between Chitimachas and Frenchmen finally reached its end within months of New Orleans' founding.

Although Indian diplomatic delegations became an important feature of public life in New Orleans, the city's survival and early growth depended more upon goods and services provided by American Indian people. A frontier exchange economy began to channel deerskins for exportation and food supplies for urban consumption. Acolapissas on the north shore of Lake Pontchartrain, as Governor Bienville reported, "furnish us almost all the fresh meat that is consumed in New Orleans without however their neglecting the cultivation of their lands which produce a great deal of corn." Within no time, Indian people regularly delivered grain, game, bear oil, and peltry to New Orleans and worked as guides for travelers and as fugitive-catchers for slaveowners. Most Indian work in the colonial town, however, was provided by those captured and enslaved in early conflicts. During the 1720s Indian people formed a substantial part of the city's slave population. The 1721 city census listed more than fifty Indian slaves living in and around New Orleans, many of them women working at domestic tasks and some even marrying non-Indian men.

The presence of enslaved Indians, marked by early episodes of their rebellious collaboration with enslaved Africans, heightened apprehension among slaveowners over the possibility of violent resistance from oppressed groups. In New Orleans this fear spiked after November 29, 1729, when Natchez Indians launched anti-colonial warfare 250 miles away. Within a matter of days, a large delegation of Choctaws approached the city to offer military assistance to a rather nervous Governor Étienne Boucher de Périer. Needing their allegiance but worrying about their intention, he dispatched an officer to meet them outside the city with a supply of trade gifts. Although a plot by slaves in New Orleans was discovered, rumor of a simultaneous conspiracy by local Indians caused the governor to recruit and arm enslaved black men for a downriver attack against the Chaouachas. Despite persistent anxiety among colonial officials, Indian attacks only came near New Orleans when Choctaw civil war spilled onto upriver settlements in 1748. Even then, however, settlers driven from the German Coast by hostile Choctaws found sanctuary among neighboring Indian villagers. Peaceful exchange between American Indians and town residents remained the norm throughout the eighteenth century, and Indian interaction contributed immeasurably to that now famous cultural gumbo into which future groups of immigrants would add their own influences.

When Louisiana was transferred from France to Spain and Florida from Spain to England in the 1760s, unusually large delegations of Indian people frequented New Orleans. In July 1763, Jean Jacques Blaise d'Abbadie, newly appointed Director-General of Louisiana, was visited by chiefs of the Biloxi, Chitimacha, Houma, Choctaw, and Quapaw nations—all of whom were "friendly and devoted to the French" but came to New Orleans, as recorded by d'Abbadie, "to sound out rumors circulating among them concerning the cession of fragments of Louisiana to England and, they say, to Spain." A pan-tribal Indian war was raging against British garrisons and settlements north of the Ohio River, and Spain's newly acquired possession of Louisiana would not be officially announced for months to come. Some of New Orleans' most elaborate Indian ceremonies occurred during the autumn months of 1769, as delegates were summoned by General Alejandro O'Reilly once he firmly established Spain's possession of Louisiana. Several communities were

BELOW *Louisiana Indians Walking Along a Bayou*, by Alfred Bouisseau, 1847. Courtesy of the New Orleans Museum of Art, gift of William E. Groves.

represented at a single council held in late September inside O'Reilly's house, where emissaries pledged alliance to Spain and beseeched Spanish authorities to "grant us the same favors and benefits as did the French." After Spain entered the American Revolutionary War against Britain several years later, Governor Bernardo de Gálvez was able to recruit fighters from these allied Indian nations for his successful campaigns against British forts on Mississippi River and Gulf Coast.

Most Indian retinues visiting colonial New Orleans on a routine basis came from communities that the French called *petites nations*—Native nations drastically depopulated by epidemic diseases but still inhabiting banks of the lower Mississippi and its distributaries. Altogether by the 1770s this population numbered about a thousand people, living in at least eight villages interspersed among colonial plantations. Paddling their dugout canoes down the Mississippi River or along the shore of Lake Pontchartrain and into Bayou St. John, they brought foods and furs to New Orleans and occasionally worked as hunters, rowers, and patrollers for neighboring colonists.

Indian trade in and around New Orleans remained important and by the end of the eighteenth century, some Choctaw Indians from present-day Mississippi established communities on the north shore of Lake Pontchartrain. Commerce with the populous Choctaw Nation from New Orleans had persisted during the 1760s and '70s, to the dismay of English officials in West Florida. One merchant in Mobile urged the legislature of that colony "to have a stop put to the trade that's carried on by the inhabitants of New Orleans with the Indians on the English side . . . to the great prejudice of this Province and particularly those concerned in the Indian trade." But Bayou St. John and Lake Pontchartrain provided convenient passage for goods and skins, so Choctaw men spent more time hunting on the north shore of Lakes Pontchartrain and Maurepas. Reinforced by the return of West Florida to Spain after the American Revolution, communities that later became known as St. Tammany Choctaws began to take shape.

The city's survival and early growth depended more upon goods and services provided by American Indian people.

At the same time, however, the *petites nations* in the orbit of New Orleans confronted severe pressure to sell their land to encroaching white planters and to relocate away from the Mississippi River's banks. Biloxis and Tunicas migrated northwestward to the lower Red River, Alabamas left for the Opelousas district farther west, Houmas moved southward along Bayou Lafourche, and Chitimachas concentrated their population westward along Bayou Teche. These widening distances from New Orleans reduced the frequency and scale of Indian visits, but a significant Indian presence continued to be made on the urban landscape. Stickball games played by Indians, for example, became a source of entertainment for non-Indian residents as well as a means of cultural persistence by Indian participants. The earliest documentation of Indian lacrosse being played at the city dated back to June 1764, when a delegation of Biloxis and other Indians from the Gulf Coast, as recorded by Director-General d'Abbadie, "assembled near New Orleans to play ball and for diversions, attracting there numerous spectators." At the time of Louisiana's transfer to the United States, French prefect Pierre Clément de Laussat witnessed one Sunday "Negroes and mulattoes, in groups of four, six, eight—some from the city, others from the country"—playing "*raquette des sauvages*" against each other. Native products like basketry, woodcraft, and wild plants also persisted as a form of Indian adaptation to a growing and diversifying city. Although their political and economic importance to New Orleans was slipping, American Indians engaged local resources for their own livelihood and survival.

Land along Bayou St. John, and the road leading from it, became familiar campgrounds for Indians regularly visiting New Orleans, while the city's physical environs encouraged their open exchange with residents. "The inhabitants, sailors, Indians, and slaves run around freely inside as well as beyond the town," as one mid-eighteenth century visitor from France put it. "They meet in the thick and intruding woods that border the town almost all around." Well into the next century, wetlands around New Orleans provided optimal space for what city elites and officials considered illicit and dangerous activity. Drinking, gambling, bartering, and dancing back-of-town brought diverse people together in ways that especially troubled slaveowners, who came to expect stronger prohibitions and police action in a city rapidly approaching a population of thirty thousand by its centennial year. There is only a scant record of Indians seriously disturbing the peace or being arrested for vagabondage during these years. Remembering Choctaws in camps along Bayou St. John and in various New Orleans markets before the Civil War, life-long resident Henry Castellanos wrote in the 1890s that "the police never arrested them for misdemeanors or crimes, but turned the offenders over to the chief of their tribe for punishment, the exemption, it was claimed, being based upon treaty stipulations or immemorial usage."

Behind this continuing Indian presence in New Orleans was a wider network of exchange and travel. Many Indian people moved through a seasonal round of hunting, fishing, gathering, and trading activities that brought them into regular contact with other Louisianans. Some even picked cotton on plantations during harvest season. In many cases, itinerant groups of Indian people forged strong personal relationships with non-Indian families. Most Indians who developed such close ties to non-Indian households and communities were people resisting pressure to leave their homeland, now a city rapidly growing in population and expanding in size. Development of New Orleans into the nation's second largest port as well as point of entry for immigrants was based largely upon work demanded from tens of thousands of African-American men and women producing cotton and sugar on the region's plantations. It also derived, however, from the millions of acres of land being expropriated from the country's American Indian people.

The removal of nations from their homelands in the East brought the largest formal parties of Indian people through New Orleans after the Louisiana Purchase, a time when delegations seldom visited the city. Driven from their remaining territory in Alabama and awaiting transportation to Indian Territory, a large number of Creeks were encamped for three months in 1837 at Pass Christian. Stickball games played by these prisoners of war became an attraction for New Orleanians who took boat rides over Lakes Pontchartrain and Borgne. One of their leaders, Tustennuggee Emathla (called Jim Boy), visited the city on October 16 to attend a performance at the St. Charles Theatre. That same day, 160 Delaware and Shawnee Indians arrived from the West, staying in military barracks below the city before heading to Florida as auxiliary soldiers in the US war against the Seminoles. The following March, Seminole prisoners of war were encamped at those same barracks.

When some of their leaders attended two different theaters, they were themselves regarded contemptuously as an entertaining spectacle by city residents. During a play called "Holland Barrett" at the St. Charles, according to the *Daily Picayune*, these Seminole chiefs "broke forth in boisterous whoops and yells, as amusing to the pale faces as were the performances on the stage."

By the mid-nineteenth century, New Orleanians' image of American Indians was becoming more a product of entertainment than of understanding, and consequently, nearby Indian people were increasingly viewed as only pathetic remnants of a once nobler race. When George Catlin's tour of Plains Indian portraits and landscapes came to No. 78 Chartres Street in the spring of 1835, the artist told visitors that he hoped "to give the world, a work on a race of men who will cease to exist in a few years, and who if not totally destroyed, must sink into vice and thus lose every vestige of those ennobling virtues which their ancestors once possessed." Later demonstrations of vanishing "Indianness" in Wild West shows and ethnological exhibits would further popularize belief that "real" Indian people belonged only to a remote and romantic past.

While American Indians were being exiled to distant places and confined to distant times, groups still near New Orleans continued nonetheless to adapt their customs and innovate their roles in the city. Urban development encroaching on wetlands between New Orleans and Lake Pontchartrain certainly made an Indian presence harder to maintain. But for at least another half century following the Civil War, Choctaw families living just north of the lake made New Orleans' French Market an integral part of their income and identity and became something of a tourist attraction. While Choctaw women sold baskets, filé powder, and other signature items, promoters of tourism advertised their routine presence in the French Market as a sight to behold. A special opportunity to feature them in publicity about New Orleans came with the World's Industrial and Cotton Centennial Exposition in 1884. Visitors to the world's fair were encouraged to see Indian women at the market selling medicinal and culinary plants alongside beautifully woven baskets. Yet other than some boarding-school students working for the Smithsonian exhibit at the US government building and western Indians performing in Buffalo Bill's Wild West show outside the fairgrounds, there was hardly any American Indian participation in this international exposition.

While American Indians were being exiled to distant places and confined to distant times, groups still near New Orleans continued to adapt their customs and innovate their roles in the city.

By the late nineteenth century, women in prominent New Orleans families began to mobilize and organize on behalf of American Indians, motivated by a blend of philanthropic, aesthetic, literary, and scientific pursuits. Driven by an interest in unique basketry produced by Choctaw and Chitimacha women as a means of economic uplift and also by a desire for general reform of Indian policy, some of these women befriended local Indian people and even facilitated anthropological and governmental attention to their badly neglected communities. Mary Avery McIlhenny Bradford and Sara Avery McIlhenny, daughters of the Tabasco pepper company's founder, helped the Chitimachas save their land and acquire federal protection. Josephine Ellis, widow of US Congressman E. John Ellis and friend of north shore Choctaws, presided over the New Orleans chapter of the Women's National Indian Association until her death in 1912.

In a very different form of attention, African Americans in New Orleans were organizing what would become known as "Mardi Gras Indian tribes." Appropriating the popular image of dangerous yet free-spirited Indian warriors, as displayed in Wild West shows and other kinds of entertainment, black workers began to disguise their own defiance and prowess in Jim Crow New Orleans behind an acceptable mask of "wild" Indian behavior. As early as the 1880s, the Creole Wild West Tribe began dressing in fancy Indian costumes every Carnival season and channeling African-American song and dance into a new ceremonial practice. Black New Orleanians' collective memory of fugitive slaves seeking freedom among nearby Indian nations certainly influenced their association of "Indianness" with resistance.

During the first decade of the twentieth century, most Choctaws living north of Lake Pontchartrain were relocated to Indian Territory by the federal government. This left the Chitimacha Tribe of Louisiana to become the federally recognized Indian nation closest to New Orleans, although distance from their Bayou Teche reservation did not encourage any regular presence in the city. Persistence and growth by Houma Indians in adjacent areas, however, set into motion the twentieth-century chapter of American Indians in the Crescent City. Today, the thousand or so American Indians residing in New Orleans include members of south Louisiana tribes as well as migrants from more distant Native American nations who work in and around the city. And the tradition of vendors from local Indian nations selling basketry and other crafts in New Orleans does persist, most notably at the New Orleans Jazz and Heritage Festival.

Stickball games continued to be played occasionally by black and white New Orleanians into the twentieth century. By the city's bicentennial, however, baseball and football would replace this ancient Indian sport on the urban landscape. Meanwhile, in the late summer of 1897, a traveling troupe of Choctaws from Mississippi, called Chief Philup's Band, came to play a weekend of "Indian Ball" at New Orleans's Athletic Park. Two teams, each with sixteen players, competed on the field for three consecutive afternoons and performed "war dances" after every match, on an evening program of music that included the Chicago Marine Band—all for an admission price of two bits. Excitement over this spectacle of Indian sport and dance, however, became quickly overshadowed by news that Chief Philup's Band was stranded in the city, because their manager had been robbed of their train fare back to Meridian. After staying overnight in a city jail, the athletes spent the next day on Lafayette Square, where according to the *Daily Picayune* "they naturally attracted a large crowd" and waited for New Orleans citizens to donate sufficient funds for their return home. Although a far cry from that Chitimacha peace ceremony back in 1718, this sequence of events dramatically showed that American Indians would not stop improvising their presence in New Orleans—a city famous for cultural improvisation.

RIGHT Members of the Turnverein of New Orleans at a convention in Milwaukee in 1893. Courtesy of German Cultural Organization, Deutsches Haus.

German Turners: Healthy in Body and Mind

A few hundred German peasants arrived in Louisiana in 1722, recruited by John Law's Company of the West. They settled on Governor Bienville's property thirty miles upriver from New Orleans in an area eventually referred to as the German Coast. By the 1840s a diverse German community had developed in the city, including merchants, planters, farmers, mechanics, and later brewers, bakers, silversmiths, lawyers, doctors, architects, journalists, and musicians. The new immigrants formed clubs, benevolent organizations, orphan asylums, and singing societies to preserve the traditions of home.

Refugees from the failed German revolution of 1848, known as the Forty-Eighters, brought with them the "Turner" movement, a social and political philosophy of a healthy mind in a healthy body that became popular in Prussia during the nineteenth century. Led by Friedrich Ludwig Jahn (1778–1852), a controversial German nationalist who advocated for a constitutional monarchy, the movement sought to "bring [each member's] body to a uniformly strong development" through physical activity that included tumbling, parallel bars, horse-vault, and pyramid-building. As a rule, Turners were anti-clerical and freethinkers, and the members of the organization were boys and men between the ages of 18 and 30.

Turnvereine (German for athletic clubs) were organized throughout the United States, and New Orleans was home to one of the earliest and southernmost in the country. About forty people assembled on November 16, 1851, at Louis Stein's establishment on Orleans Street for the purpose of founding a Turnverein. Dr. Benjamin Maas became the club's president. A physician in New Orleans for forty-one years, Maas was a socialist and a Unionist who supported the Republican Party. At the first meeting, Maas proposed to apply for membership in the national Turnerbund and to accept the statutes of the Socialist Turnverein of New York. By February 1852 the club had 140 members.

In 1867 the turnverein purchased two lots in order to build Turners' Hall at 938 Lafayette Street. Designed by German-born architect William Thiel and finished within the year, Turners' Hall was a spectacular building, featuring a library full of the club's collection of artifacts and sheet music, a large hall for physical exercise, and an auditorium for theatre performances and other gatherings that generated rental income to pay off the club's sizable debt. According to historian Sally Reeves, "if the Turnverein of New Orleans was true to form, one suspects that the Lafayette Street hall was indeed the site of drinking and good times, even on Sunday, and even in Reconstruction-era New Orleans."

Financial issues plagued the Turnverein, however, and in 1877 the club moved to a new building. Turners' Hall passed through several owners, serving as a machine shop, a furniture warehouse, and the offices of a medical supplier. The many German social clubs in the city unified to form the Deutsches Haus in 1928. In 2000, the Louisiana Endowment for the Humanities purchased Turners' Hall; the building continues to serve as the organization's headquarters and the home of the Louisiana Humanities Center.

-Brigitta Malm

ABOVE This wood engraving by E.W. Kemble depicts dancers performing the "Bamboula" at Congo Square. The image accompanied an article by George Washington Cable in Century Magazine in 1886; Kemble himself never witnessed a performance. Courtesy of The Historic New Orleans Collection.

A Window to Africa

Enslaved Africans perpetuated cultural and commercial practices at Congo Square

by Freddi Williams Evans

Congo Square, a public gathering place located on North Rampart Street, hosted hundreds, some say thousands, of enslaved and free African descendants on Sunday afternoons during the eighteenth and nineteenth centuries. Gatherings occurred in the area intermittently under French, Spanish, and American rule. Although similar events were hosted at other public locations, including Washington Square in Philadelphia, Pennsylvania, which once also carried the name "Congo Square," such gatherings existed in New Orleans' Congo Square over a longer span of time and at later dates in time. Dena Epstein's extensive research and documentation of African music in the New World led her to conclude that, regarding the mainland of North America, "[o]nly in *Place Congo* in New Orleans was the African tradition able to continue in the open." A study of the cultural practices perpetuated at those gatherings provides a window to the past, reveals Louisiana's connections to countries in Africa and the Caribbean, and unearths cultural commonalities and continuums.

At the gatherings, to varying degrees over time, people of African heritage operated a thriving market, played African-derived rhythms on African-styled musical instruments, and engaged in African and African-based religious practices, songs, and dances. The cultural practices that they perpetuated mirrored those found in the parts of Africa and the French and Spanish West Indies, particularly Haiti and Cuba, where large numbers of the gatherers originated or resided before landing in New Orleans.

The research of historian Gwendolyn Midlo Hall identifies the geographical and ethnic origin of those enslaved Africans who populated the territory. Under French rule, 1682–1762, traders brought Bambara, Mandinga, Wolof, Fulbe, Nard, Mina, Fon, Yoruba, Chamba, Ado, and Kongo-Angola people to Louisiana. These ethnic groups landed directly from Africa between 1719 and 1731. Two-thirds of them originated in the Senegambia region, and others originated in the Bight of Benin and the Kongo-Angola region.

During the Spanish period, 1763–1802, the Africans whom traders brought to the colony originated in four main areas of the continent, including the three locations involved under French rule and the Bight of Biafra. Among them were also Africans from Sierra Leone, the Windward Coast, the Gold Coast, and Mozambique. The additional nations included the Caraba, Ibo, Mobo, Kissy, Canga, and more. Hall's research shows that during this period, Africans were primarily transshipped to Louisiana from the Caribbean and came less often directly from Africa. Voyages were initiated and carried out, for the most part, by independent planters and included ports in Jamaica, Martinique, Saint-Domingue, and, after 1790, Cuba. Records show, however, that the Africans on those voyages were not likely to have been born or socialized in these Caribbean countries. The clustering of African nations during this transshipment period, from 1770 to 1803, shows that the Kongo represented the largest single African ethnic group in New Orleans.

Such heavy presence of Kongo descendants in New Orleans remained true after American rule in 1803, and by 1820, the overwhelming majority of enslaved Africans in Louisiana were of Kongo-Angola origin. Not only did they comprise the largest single ethnic group brought to Louisiana, they were the largest nation that remained in New Orleans. Without indicating the time period, writer George Washington Cable also referred to the Africans of the Kongo coast as the most numerous in the state, pointing out, "These are they for whom the dance [Congo dance] and the place [Congo Square] are named."

Political circumstances and historical events such as the Haitian Revolution, Louisiana Purchase, and domestic slave trade affected who could have attended the gatherings. With American rule, settlers from other states increasingly migrated to Louisiana, and many of the enslaved people who accompanied them were American born. With the 1808 US constitutional ban on the importation of captives from Africa, the domestic slave trade increased sharply and New Orleans was a main port. This intercoastal trade introduced enslaved blacks from other slave holding states, particularly Virginia, Maryland, South Carolina, and Washington D.C. Africans from those locations brought their creolized languages, cultural practices, and musical influences to the city and to Congo Square.

At the same time, traders continued to introduce Africans directly from the continent by smuggling them through the Louisiana swamps and bayous. This activity continued throughout almost the entirety of the period of the Congo Square gatherings. An 1879 *Daily Picayune* article noted that many of the Africans who had been smuggled into the territory attended the Sunday meetings in Congo Square. Their participation in the gatherings contributed to the strength of the African cultural practices that persisted. Even with the increase in American-born black people and the introduction of European-derived activities, newspaper articles and eyewitness accounts attest to the ongoing presence of African-based culture.

Adding to the diverse population at the meetings were refugees from Saint-Domingue who began entering the city beginning in the 1790s as a result of the revolution that led to the country's independence and to the establishment of the Republic of Haiti. Another wave of Haitian immigrants, approximately nine thousand in total, entered Louisiana via Cuba from 1809 to 1810, and the majority remained in New Orleans. Among them were approximately three thousand enslaved Africans and an almost equal number of free people of color. Along with increasing the population of African descendants, these Haitians reinforced African-derived dances, songs, food, food-ways, and religious practices in the city.

Many African practices continued at Sunday gatherings, which took place at several locations in the city before 1817, ninety-nine years after the city's founding. During that year, Congo Square became the sole designated location for enslaved black people to congregate. As a popular Sunday attraction for white tourists and locals, the gatherings drew numerous eyewitnesses who wrote about what they saw and heard. Those accounts enable scholars to identify and explore specific cultural practices and connect them to their ethnic groups and countries of origin. The accounts also enable scholars to explore the influence of those cultural practices on contemporary New Orleans culture.

Traveler Christian Schultz provided an example of a continued cultural practice in 1808 when he witnessed enslaved Africans congregated in circles dancing and performing what he called "their worship." He observed that the principal dancers or leaders adorned themselves with "wild and savage fashions, always ornamented with a number of tails of the smaller wild beasts, and those who appeared the most horrible always attracted the largest circle of company."

LEFT Wood and iron figurine of a musician with a drum, Dogon peoples, Mali. Courtesy of New Orleans Museum of Art, bequest of Victor K. Kiam.

Historian Robert Farris Thompson discovered that in the Democratic Republic of the Congo, the tradition of wearing tails of small animals, often hanging from the waistline, represents *nkisi*, spirits or objects that contain spiritual properties and medicines. Ritual specialists, who are also known in the Democratic Republic of the Congo as diviners, use those spirits and medicines to heal, protect, predict the future, counsel, and advise. Thompson further explained that when diviners dance and spin around, the animal tails fly out and vaunt protection for the diviners as well as for those who stand around the circle.

Thompson's findings explain why the largest circle of followers surrounded the principal leaders and dancers and provide evidence that a consistent and intact belief system of Kongo origin existed in Congo Square. This revelation also sheds light on the role of the Kongo nation and its system of medicines in the emergence and resilience of the Vodou religion, a new world religion that blended tenets of Catholicism with beliefs and practices from several African nations, including the Kongo. Many ritual experts from the Kongo surfaced as conjurors, roots-people, and Voodoo Queens and Kings in New Orleans and throughout the South. Their knowledge of herbs and creation of *nkisi* (in this case amulets, *wanga*, *gris gris*, and charms) for healing, protection, and other purposes continued to influence local culture and gained recognition by the dominant commercial culture as a major part of the New Orleans tourism industry, even today.

Such appropriation and the trend to sensationalize and commercialize Vodou started in the 1800s as the religion grew in followers and transcended economic, social, and racial lines. A national firm manufactured, advertised, and sold charms and powders or commercial *nkisi*, and local newspapers announced some ceremonies as public events. Failing to distinguish between the New World religion and those public spectacles along with associated behaviors, local writers interchangeably used the words Vodou, the religion, and Voodoo, public meetings. By the mid-1880s, the line between the two had disappeared and the mythology of Vodou had become institutionalized. Today, Voodoo goods and services are at the center of the city's tourism brand and are advertised through all forms of media. Offerings include readings, rituals, and consultations as well as material goods such as oils, *gris gris* bags, dolls, and other crafts. There are Voodoo tours, Voodoo music, a museum, and a plethora of Voodoo practitioners who daily position themselves around the main square of the city, Jackson Square.

Continued cultural practices were also prevalent among the rhythmic patterns, songs, and dances that gatherers perpetuated in Congo Square. The most written about and perhaps the most popular dance during the American period was called the Congo dance. Some writers used the name Bamboula when describing it. An equally popular song, "Quan Patate–Lachuite" (also spelled "Tant Patate-là Tchuite" and "Quan' Patate La Cuite"), or "When the Sweet Potato Will Be Cooked," accompanied the dance and was among several popular Creole slave songs that originated in Saint-Domingue (Haiti). The song's fame extended to free people of color and white residents as well.

Composer Louis Gottschalk learned "Quan Patate–Lachuite" as a child from Sally, the enslaved woman who took care of him and who migrated from Haiti with the family. By 1845, at age sixteen, Gottschalk had completed his world famous composition "Bamboula – Danse des Nègres, Op. 2," which he based on the popular song. His sister, Clara Gottschalk Peterson, who also learned songs from Sally, wrote and published the musical notation to a collection of those songs and included "Quan Patate–Lachuite." The song and the dance continued to influence New Orleans popular culture decades beyond the gatherings in Congo Square. In the early 1900s, New Orleans native Alice Dunbar Nelson claimed that every child in New Orleans could sing the melody to the Congo dance, "Quan Patate–Lachuite." In 1911, Afro-British composer Samuel Coleridge-Taylor also interpreted the song's melody and named his composition "The Bamboula, Op. 75." Taylor placed the song's melody at the beginning of the composition and credited the West Indies as its place of origin.

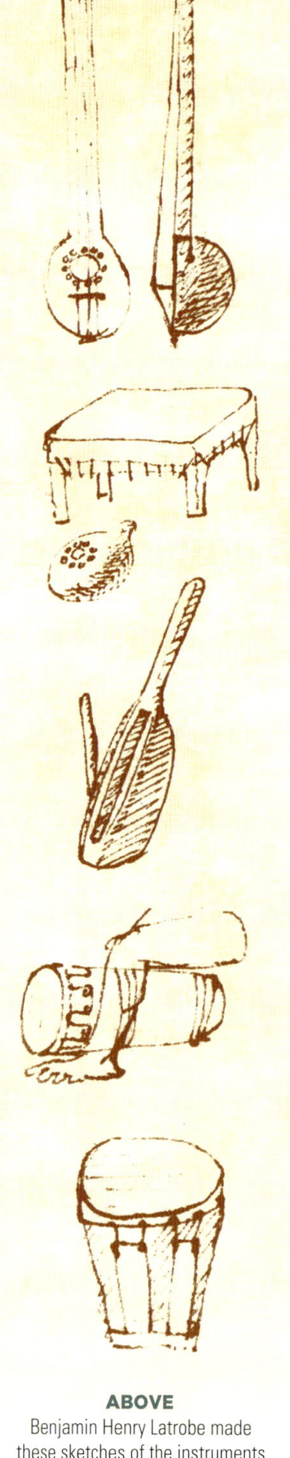

ABOVE
Benjamin Henry Latrobe made these sketches of the instruments played at Congo Square in 1819. Wikimedia Commons.

Several versions of the Congo dance exist today in parts of Haiti, in both religious and social forms. Anthropologist Harold Courlander found that the names for some of these dances include Congo *Paillette*, Congo *Franc*, and Congo *Mazonne*, also known as Congo Creole. Courlander found that the latter version existed in Cuba, Martinique, and New Orleans. Danys "La Mora" Perez Prades, a native of Santiago who specializes in traditional Afro-Cuban dances and songs of Eastern Cuba, provided additional names, including the Congo *Layet*, the social dance that writers observed in New Orleans, the Rhumba *Guaguancó* and the *Yuca*. Versions of the dance presently exist in other parts of the African diaspora, including Panama, where it carries the name "The Congo." The influence of the Congo dance family was extensive. While dances that carried the name "Congo" did not have identical descriptions throughout the diaspora, the ethnic origin, choreographic features, and cultural practices—including drumming styles and rhythmic patterns—revealed commonalities and family ties.

The Habanera Rhythm

The African-derived rhythm embodied by the song "Quan Patate–Lachuite," as well as many other songs that accompanied dances, received the name *habanera*. Another name was the tango bass line, and Jelly Roll Morton, regarded as the first jazz musician in New Orleans to write and publish jazz music, referred to the rhythm as the "Spanish tinge." Morton stated that this rhythm, the *habanera*, had to be present if the music was to be called jazz.

Today, a three-beat derivative or variation of the *habanera* rhythm is at the foundation of New Orleans indigenous music. In Cuba, that three-beat variation is called the *tresillo*. In New Orleans, the name for the rhythmic pattern is the second-line beat. It is also known locally as the parade beat, *bamboula* beat, street beat, and the New Orleans beat.

The Second-line Beat

The African-derived rhythms called for African-styled musical instruments, which were visual representations of continued African cultural practices in Congo Square. Engineer Benjamin Latrobe, who witnessed a gathering in 1819, sketched some of those musical instruments and described the music and dance. When exploring Latrobe's sketches, professor Kazadi wa Mukuna, ethnomusicologist and Democratic Republic of the Congo native, realized that all of the musical instruments were familiar to his homeland. The string instrument that Latrobe sketched, a *banza*, was the precursor to the banjo. It was made using a gourd and animal skin, and enslaved Africans in other locations in the country also played versions of it.

In addition to showing various kinds of drums, Latrobe depicted a style of drumming when sketching a drummer playing while sitting astride his drum. A special feature of the style is that the drummer presses the heel of his foot against the head of the drum intermittently in order to change the tone. Some drummers call this technique "giving heel" to the drum. Throughout the African

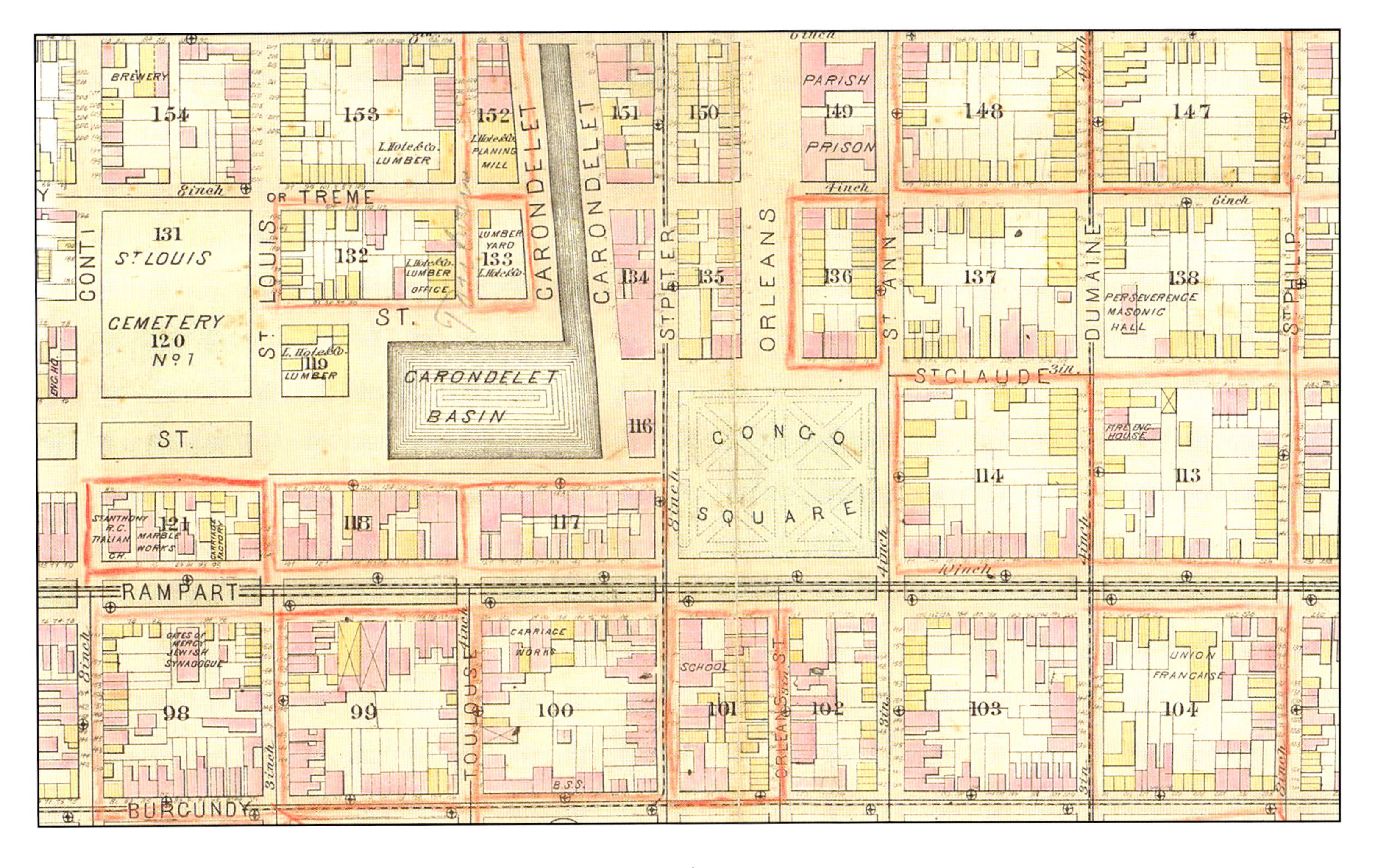

ABOVE From Robinson Atlas, 1880, published by Elisha Robinson and Roger H. Pidgeon. The maps are believed to have been drawn by city surveyor John F. Braun in the late 1870s. Courtesy of the Orleans Parish Clerk of District Court.

diaspora, this style of drumming is associated with people of Kongo/Angola heritage and is prevalent in sacred as well secular practices. The numerous locations include Haiti, Martinique, Virgin Islands, Cuba, Brazil, Puerto Rico, and Jamaica, where the drums played in this manner carried a variety of names.

By 1817, Congo Square became the sole designated location for enslaved black people to congregate.

Professor Mukuna explained that drummers used their foot in a different way to alter the tone of the stool-shaped drum that appears in Latrobe's sketches. When seated on the ground, the drummer placed the drum with his foot underneath the head so that his big toe could intermittently touch the head to alter the tone as he played with his hands. In New Orleans, drummers in spasm bands employed similar concepts when using their foot to alter the tone of buckets, boxes, and other objects. Spasm bands, groups of children who played music on the streets using instruments made out of found objects, gained attention around the 1890s, also the developmental years of jazz.

One of the dances that Latrobe described involved two women, each holding a handkerchief by the corner while dancing. Other writers in New Orleans and Louisiana at that time also reported women holding handkerchiefs or the corners of their aprons as they danced the Congo. Robert Ferris Thompson explained that in the Democratic Republic of the Congo, waving handkerchiefs while dancing is an act of cleansing or purifying the air of evil spirits. Waving handkerchiefs while dancing, particularly second-line dancing, is a popular New Orleans tradition today.

Cultural continuums also existed in the area of marketing and reflected West and West Central African practices where Africans bought, bartered, and sold what they harvested, hunted, gathered, and made. Commonalities existed among food items as well as the way some foods were prepared. One of the items was *calas*, deep-fried rice cakes covered with powered sugar. *Calas* were also popular throughout the week, particularly at breakfast time. Market women customarily walked the streets with baskets full of the freshly prepared cakes balanced on their heads while chanting, "Belle *Calas*! Tout chaud!" (Beautiful *Calas*! All hot.) Customers often ate them with café au lait (half coffee and half hot milk). Today, popular items are beignets, a very similar fried pastry made with flour instead of rice, and café au lait. Food historian and cookbook author Jessica Harris found that the calas originated in Liberia, where, as was true in New Orleans, women street vendors traditionally sell the fried cake. There the rice fritter is called kala, or rice in the Vai language of Liberia.

As shown in these examples, an examination of the African practices witnessed in New Orleans' Congo Square exposes much about the city's history and past international relations. It also highlights the influence of African culture on New Orleans popular culture and reveals that many once marginalized practices are now mainstream traditions. This ongoing study, discovery, and discussion of African cultural continuums in New Orleans significantly contribute to the multi-disciplinary and multi-dimensional story of "New Orleans and the World."

Les Cenelles

Destin donnein toi
L'ouvrage de ramasser encore
Les cenelles pour garder ye fleurs
Pour tout le monde.
Pour longtemps ye reste en
ténèbres
Comme le noble Cœur de
La Louisiane Française.
Ça sera to courage-la
Qui va guider nous l'histoire
A champs plus fertiles.
Les cenelles. Ye repousse
Ferme et beau, comme
to fidèle, amour Créole.

The Mayhaws

Fate gave you
The work of gathering again
The mayhaws to keep their
Flowers for all the world.
For a long time they lay
In darkness like the noble
Heart of French Louisiana.
It will be your courage
that will guide our history
to more fruitful fields.
The mayhaws. They grow
Once again, strong and beautiful
Like your faithful Creole love.

-Armand Lanusse

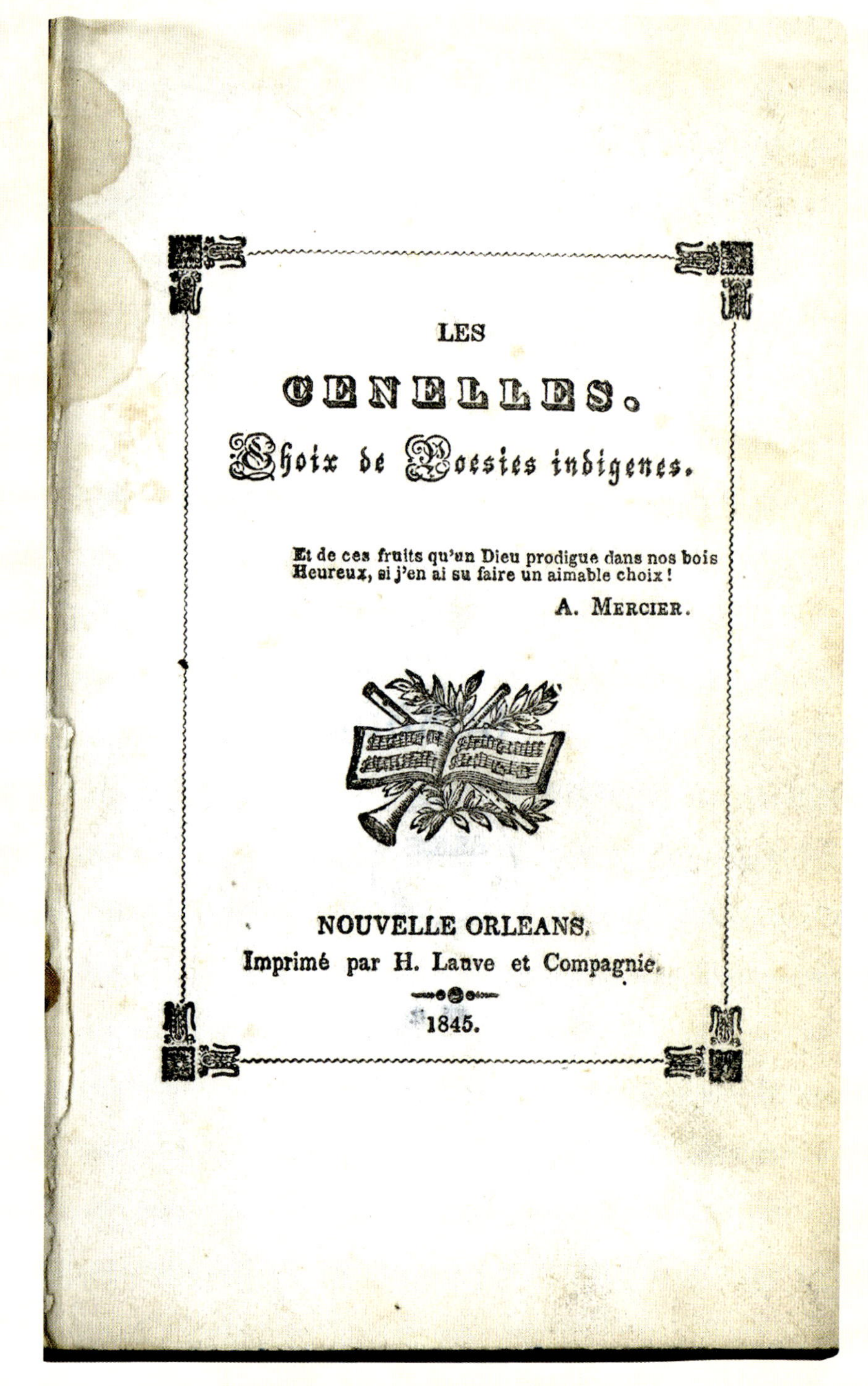

LES

CENELLES.

Choix de Poesies indigenes.

Et de ces fruits qu'un Dieu prodigue dans nos bois
Heureux, si j'en ai su faire un aimable choix !

A. MERCIER.

NOUVELLE ORLEANS.
Imprimé par H. Lauve et Compagnie.

1845.

ABOVE Title page from an original copy of *Les Cenelles*. Courtesy of State Library of Louisiana.

RIGHT Victor Sejour from an illustration in *La Presse Illustrée, No. 341, Journal Hebdomadaire.* Courtesy of The Historic New Orleans Collection.

The Poets of *Les Cenelles*

by Nancy Dixon, PhD

Armand Lanusse (1812-1867), a free Creole of color in New Orleans, was a writer and educator who published the first collection of poetry by African Americans in the United States in 1845, *Les Cenelles (The Mayhaws). Les Cenelles* was also the name of a group of seventeen free Creoles of color, a unique class of educated and often wealthy Creole men who contributed to the collection. Of the seventeen contributors, Haitian-New Orleanian, Victor Sejour went on to become the most prominent as a very popular playwright in Paris and the author of the first American short story penned by a person of color, "*La Mulâtre.*" In 1860 Napoleon III named Sejour, Chevalier of the Legion of Honor, Belles Lettres. Included here is the dedication to the collection, *Les Cenelles*, written by Lanusse.

From Famine to Influence

The Irish community had a formative impact on the city

by Laura D. Kelley, PhD

When speaking about the Irish Diaspora in the United States, New Orleans is not a place that first comes to mind. We perceive the city as a savory gumbo of Spanish, French, Creoles, Afro-Caribbean and Africans, yet pay little attention to the attraction this strategically placed port city might have had on an island with a long history of outward migration. The Irish have been coming to New Orleans since the early French colonial era and continued to arrive through the Spanish colonial and subsequent American period following the Louisiana Purchase. However, Irish immigrants to New Orleans in the eighteenth century differed substantially from those who contemporaneously immigrated to the British colonies on the Atlantic coast. Irish immigrants to the thirteen colonies were primarily Presbyterian and would become known as "Scotch-Irish." Those coming to Louisiana were Catholic and arrived not directly from Ireland but through a circuitous route known as the path of the Wild Geese: their families left Ireland for France and Spain, traditional enemies of England, to escape religious persecution and discrimination due, in large part, to the Penal Laws. Enacted between 1689 and 1749, these laws reflected intentional government discrimination based solely on sectarian differences, with the intent to exterminate the Irish "race." Safely abroad, many Irish pursued mercantile or military careers—two well-established avenues of advancement that relied upon professional and social networks to take advantage of opportunities offered in the new world.

Most of the Irish who came to New Orleans during the colonial period had arrived there via these two routes; initially as members of the military, and subsequently, seeking the opportunity that a frontier post had to offer.

Arguably the most famous (or infamous) Irishman from the colonial period was Alejandro "Bloody" O'Reilly, so called because of his swift handling of the 1768 revolt among the inhabitants of New Orleans against the first Spanish Governor of Louisiana, Antonio de Ulloa. O'Reilly, at the height of a brilliant military career in the service of the Spanish crown, had been dispatched from Cuba to reinstate Spanish control of the Louisiana colony. After a spectacular entrance into the city, accompanied by cannon fire and two thousand troops, O'Reilly invited the leaders of the rebellion to an elegant dinner, during which he arrested thirteen, subsequently executed six, and expropriated the conspirators' property. Within his yearlong stay in the city, he also abolished the French Superior Council, established the Cabildo in its place, and instituted the Spanish version of *Code Noir*, regulations governing the rights and treatment of slaves.

Nineteenth Century Arrivals

The end of the eighteenth century was a tumultuous time in the Western Hemisphere. Both the French Revolution in 1789 and the Haitian (Saint-Domingue) Revolution in 1791 precipitated wars among the nations of Europe. Ireland also witnessed revolution on her shores, and the failed 1798 Rebellion resulted in many exiles fleeing Ireland to Europe and America. New Orleans was among the places to which these refugees came. Arriving at the dawn of the new century, they encountered a fast-growing town in a state of rapid change. The sudden purchase of Louisiana by the United States in 1803 surprised most people inside and outside of New Orleans. The local Creole population was unhappy about yet one more change in territorial masters and suspected the newly arriving, non-French-speaking American Protestants of various dubious motives. The transition was fraught with uncertainty but just as rich in opportunity. New Orleans had become the main exchange for all goods travelling down the Mississippi and her tributaries. By 1812, the first steamboat, aptly called the New Orleans, would begin plying its trade up and down river. The golden age of the Crescent City had begun.

The new American period was marked by a pronounced expression of Irish ethnicity. In 1806, the first recorded public St. Patrick's Day Celebration in New Orleans occurred, and it would become an annual celebration. It was followed in 1813 by the formation of an Irish militia, the Republican Greens, and in 1817 by the Hibernian Society, the first Irish charitable and social club in the city.

The European-wide depression at the end of the Napoleonic Wars and a period of poor harvests, periodic famines, and outbreaks of disease, exacerbated by the high population density in Ireland, initiated a second wave of Irish immigrants to Louisiana during the 1820s and 1830s. Their arrival changed the racial demographic of the city from a population of predominantly African descent (free and enslaved) to one of mainly European origin. The booming cotton trade—"King Cotton"—reduced the cost of the trans-Atlantic voyage as ships filled with cotton looked for cargo, human or otherwise, to fill their holds on the voyage back to New Orleans, and, as a result, many more Irish immigrated to the United States. In Louisiana, Irish labor and enterprise helped dig canals, hew roads and build railroads. In New Orleans, for example, the Irish provided the bulk of the labor to build the Pontchartrain Railroad and the New Basin Canal, respectively finished in 1831 and 1838. Moreover, two Irishmen, Maunsel White and Charles Byrne, held major stakes in the New Orleans Canal & Banking Company, which owned and financed the building of the canal.

The difficulties and dangers of clearing swamps, attacks of yellow fever, cholera and other diseases, caused numerous deaths among the nascent immigrant community. How many is unknown. Speculations range from 2,000 to 20,000. Documentary evidence, however, does not substantiate these high numbers.

The flow of Irish immigrants to the city turned into a virtual flood when the Great Famine struck Ireland in 1845 and continued its assault on the island for ten more years. The potato, subject to a devastating blight, had been the staple crop for the vast majority of Irish. By 1855, the island would lose nearly one third of its population to death or

By 1850, New Orleans had emerged as the largest Irish city in the American South.

emigration. A well established direct shipping route from Liverpool to New Orleans facilitated the transportation of waves of Famine refugees. Ticket prices were increasingly affordable as a result of the booming cotton trade, as freighters carried immigrants to offset the costs of the return trip to New Orleans. Other Irish immigrants, after arriving on the East Coast of North America, chose an overland route to Louisiana. The buoyant economy in New Orleans offered a great variety of employment at excellent wages; housing was significantly improved over Ireland; and food was plentiful and in reliable supply. Furthermore, the city's primacy of Catholicism allowed the Irish to practice their faith as well as establish and benefit from church-sponsored institutions.

OPPOSITE Workers at the New Basin Canal construction site. Photo by George Francois Mungier. Courtesy of the Louisiana State Museum.

ABOVE A doubloon from the 1977 Downtown Irish Club parade. Courtesy of The Historic New Orleans Collection.

By 1850, New Orleans had emerged as the largest Irish city in the American South. Contrary to popular belief, the Irish were not only employed as common laborers. Half of the Irish men listed in the 1850 census had other occupations, from doctors to druggists, policemen to undertakers. The Irish soon dominated the port and the commerce associated with it by working as mechanics, draymen, (drivers who transported goods to/from businesses and the port) screwmen (skilled men operating jackscrews to store the greatest possible number of cotton bales into a ship's hull), steamboat men, engineers, and pilots. Irish "clannishness" extended economic opportunities to family and other Irishmen, which also led intermittently to collective action that would be used as an effective industrial bargaining tool. The first strike occurred in the 1830s, during the building of the New Basin Canal. Several times in the 1850s, Irish steamboat men shut down the port with their refusal to work or allow anyone else to cross the picket lines. Captains and factors (middlemen/brokers) were forced to negotiate and to grant higher wages.

The Irish also helped to organize the first proto-union, the Independent Screwmen's Benevolent Society, in 1851 in New Orleans. By restricting the number of screwmen to less than five hundred, the organization kept wages high. Screwmen successfully managed to negotiate a pay increase twice, while having to strike officially only once prior to the Civil War.

Irish women similarly took advantage of existing work opportunities, using them to achieve not only economic but also family-oriented goals. Most worked as domestics or in the service industry. A prevailing disequilibrium of supply and demand in the domestic labor market helped many of these Irish women to define their terms and conditions of labor to accommodate family and community needs. They demanded better work conditions and a schedule that would allow them to attend wakes, baptisms, communions, and other important family events. It is worth noting that the second public statue erected to honor a woman in the United States was a statue of a New Orleans Irish woman, Margaret Haughery, to commemorate her philanthropy and business success.

The Irish of New Orleans built cohesive communities throughout the city, far beyond the traditional "Irish Channel." Usually they clustered around the neighborhood church, often built through personal efforts by its parishioners. As it grew, the New Orleans Irish community frequently petitioned the Roman Catholic Diocese of New Orleans for permission to establish their own neighborhood parishes. St. Patrick's Parish was established in 1833. By 1848, the Irish Catholic population had grown dramatically, and many of the recent Irish arrivals lived in other neighborhoods beyond the parish boundaries; one church was no longer adequate for the Irish congregation. Bishop Antoine Blanc (1851, Archbishop), ardent supporter of the Irish, sanctioned the building of St. John the Baptist Church, St. Alphonsus Church, and Sts. Peter and Paul Church. He recruited Irish priests and Irish female religious orders, such as St. Mary's Dominican Convent at Cabra, directly from Ireland to serve in these new parishes. Soon after the completion of the new churches, Irish families successfully petitioned for the establishment of their own schools. Within five years after their founding, St. John the Baptist and St. Alphonsus Parishes were served by parochial schools. St. Patrick's also operated a "free school" run by the Congregation of Christian Brothers, and Sts. Peter and Paul had a parochial school maintained by the sisters of the Marianites of Holy Cross.

The local church community also served as a safety net for the Irish during times of crisis. Yellow fever and cholera were common in New Orleans, especially during the summer months, and the Irish fell victim to these outbreaks more than any other immigrant group. In 1850, for example, Charity Hospital admitted 18,476 patients, of whom 11,130 (60%) were Irish. To mitigate the effects of this high mortality, the Irish frequently utilized Catholic orphanages to provide temporary shelter for half orphans and, if necessary, a long-term home for full orphans.

Echoing other cities around the country, New Orleans' Irish became an important voting bloc loyal to the Democrats. Already in the 1828 presidential election, Democrats actively wooed the local Irish community and rewarded its members after a good showing at the polls. Local lawyer and politician John Slidell took advantage of this political development; he arranged to have Irish immigrants quickly naturalized and then on election day moved them to whatever location he felt votes that served his interests were needed. One of the more infamous examples occurred in 1844, when Slidell sent boatloads of Irish immigrants to

LEFT A parade goer at the Irish Channel Parade, ca. 2012. Courtesy of Laura D. Kelley.

Plaquemines Parish to "vote early and often" for Democratic Presidential candidate James K. Polk.

The Irish in Louisiana generally supported slavery but were reluctant to support secession during the period leading up to Lincoln's election. After the 1860 presidential election, however, the Irish firmly supported the secession of the South, partly from fear of a black majority threatening their employment and position in society. New Orleans' Irish provided the largest number of Irish recruits to the Confederate Military. They were represented in all the volunteer militias and comprised almost the entirety of the Sixth Louisiana Infantry Regiment, which fought in many of the major battles of the Civil War.

The Civil War arrived early in New Orleans. The city was captured in 1862 and remained occupied until the end of the war. A well-known anecdote illustrates New Orleanians' attitude during this time. St. Patrick's Father James Mullon had refused to comply with the city's Union commander, General Benjamin Butler, who gave an order to seize all of New Orleans' bells and turn them into Union cannons. Butler then ordered Father Mullon to appear before him and accused him of refusing to bury any Union soldiers. Mullon replied, "The charge is false, General. I'd be delighted to bury any Yankee, including yourself."

Immigration from Ireland to New Orleans slowed significantly during and after the Civil War. King Cotton no longer reigned, and railroads were replacing steamships. The South, still reeling from the effects of the war, would lag behind the rest of the nation for generations. The

> In Louisiana, Irish labor and enterprise helped dig canals, hew roads and build railroads.

immediate post-bellum period thus exposed the local Irish to experiences and challenges that were quite different than those of their Northern counterparts. The contraction in economic opportunities resulted in fewer Irish immigrants to New Orleans. This period is best described as a time when the local Irish community consolidated and solidified its foundation. For example, Irish Americans formed the Hibernia Bank in 1870; new demonstrations of Irish heritage also manifested themselves. In 1874, the first chapter of the Ancient Order of Hibernians (AOH) was formed, quickly followed by three more chapters. As in the early 1800s, Irish-Americans again formed militia groups, this time affiliated with the AOH, the Irish Rifles, and the Mitchell Rifles. Some members from AOH joined the Fenian Brotherhood and later Sinn Féin, radical Irish nationalist groups with the aim to free Ireland from British rule. In addition, the AOH collected and sent funds to help Ireland's struggle for freedom.

Twentieth Century and Beyond

As the Irish rose through the ranks of the Democratic Party in the nineteenth century, the role of tax assessor was where they made the biggest impact. An assessor's job simply entailed assessing and assigning a value to a property for the tax rolls. Starting in the 1930s, certain Irish-American families came to dominate several such offices in New Orleans. The first was James E. Comiskey, known as "Big Jim," who served as assessor for the First District from 1934 to his death in 1972. Every Wednesday night, Comiskey made himself available to meet with the residents of his district. These famous weekly meetings became affectionately known as "confessionals." As his brother Larry described, "He never turns one away without a hearing. Sometimes I've known him to come home at five o'clock in the morning, staying up to listen to them." Big Jim explained further, "Everybody in the ward that have any trouble is here, and if they don't be here, they should be here . . . When I hear what they want . . . I process it to its final completion." This seemingly innocuous political office had become a potent source of help for his constituents in times of need. The assessor became the all-powerful patron and benefactor of his district, best exemplified by Comiskey and, subsequently, the Burkes for the Fourth District. It is noteworthy that the rise of the assessor occurred during the Great Depression. With bills mounting and jobs scarce, a helping hand was considered god-sent. Political expediency and economic necessity resulted in a happy marriage for all parties concerned.

Irish pride in New Orleans continued throughout the twentieth century and is ever-present today. In 1947, Assessor Richard Burke created the Irish Channel St. Patrick's Day Parade Marching Club, the organization responsible for the large Uptown parade that still rolls in New Orleans every March. Quintessentially Irish, the parade is unique on several counts. It is the only New Orleans parade that officially starts at a Catholic Church, St. Alphonsus. Perhaps more famously, it is known for throwing to parade watchers everything needed for an Irish stew—potatoes, cabbage, carrots, onions—except the meat. Other organizations also parade or hold festivities, among them the Downtown Irish Club, the Algiers Irish Rebels and Friendship Club, and the Old Metairie St. Patrick's Day Parade.

In 1990, concerned citizens of the city founded the Friends of St. Alphonsus (FOSA). In 1996, as a result of their efforts, St. Alphonsus Church, an architectural and historic marvel in the Irish Channel, became an official National Historic Landmark. The church now functions as the St. Alphonsus Art and Cultural Center and contains a museum about the Catholic religious order, the Redemptorists as well as the Irish Channel. In addition, FOSA offer tours and host special events, often pertaining to the Irish heritage of the city. In the 1990s, the American Irish Cultural Society helped erect a Celtic Cross in New Orleans, maintained by the AOH, to commemorate the Irish workers who died digging the New Basin Canal. In 2011, a chapter of Irish Network USA was formed in New Orleans. Irish Network–New Orleans promotes the city's Irish heritage and encourages ties with Ireland. In 2012, the Irish Cultural Museum of New Orleans opened, with artifacts and interactive displays illustrating the history of the Irish in the city. In 2014, the Republic of Ireland chose New Orleans as the International Famine Commemoration City for that year, in recognition of the sanctuary offered here to the many Irish Famine refugees.

The lives, labor, and culture of Irish people in New Orleans exerted a formative influence on the city that is still vibrant today. Irish people continue to immigrate to New Orleans, and Irish immigrants and their offspring constitute one of the largest European ethnic groups in New Orleans today. When asked "Why New Orleans?" many Irish often reply, "Because it reminds me of home." The friendliness of our city's people, our strong sense of community, the importance of spending time with family and friends, the sounds of church bells ringing in the morning: on many different levels, New Orleans continues to offer the Irish a familiar sense of place in a new world.

ABOVE A 1905 postcard shows a typical Italian fruit stand in the French Quarter. Courtesy of The Historic New Orleans Collection.

The Power of the Sicilian Lemon

Italians shaped the culture and commerce of New Orleans

by Justin Nystrom, PhD

"One Hundred and Fifty Boxes of Sicily Lemons, in fine order," announced an 1838 advertisement by the Magazine Street auction house of Thomas Spear. Citrus remained a rare luxury in most American cities in 1800, but the explosive growth of transatlantic trade during the *Pax Brittanica* enabled the Sicily lemon to become a global commodity by the 1830s for trading houses like Spear's. It was, thus, the once lucrative trade in Mediterranean citrus that was responsible for bringing the founding generation of Sicilians to the principal port cities of America—including New Orleans, the riverine gateway to the growing nation's vast interior.

Awash with Germanic and Irish immigrants, New Orleanians living through the boom years of the 1830s and '40s might not have fully appreciated the significance of barquentine rigged schooners full of lemons arriving at the levee. Yet in the space of two decades, the industry of this comparatively small enclave of Sicilian fruit merchants evolved from selling cargoes on the levee to operating major importing and wholesaling houses along the city's commercial thoroughfares. The growing prosperity of this tightly knit community allowed it to wield an increasingly disproportionate influence along the wharves fronting the old French Quarter where fruit cargoes typically arrived. Citrus also enabled New Orleans to develop an early reputation as a desirable destination for Italians.

Emblematic of the Sicilian ascent in New Orleans was the path of Palermo native Rosario Tramontana, who, despite being not yet thirty years old, had by 1860 established a thriving wholesale produce trade of "foreign fruits, green and dry" at 14 Fulton and 4 Front Streets. Perhaps most noteworthy about Tramontana's enterprise was his diversification into tropical goods imported by kinsmen from the Caribbean and Central America, including coffee, coconuts, and pineapples, as well as bananas, a fruit whose lucrative destiny awaited a future generation.

Migrants from Ustica, a tiny island located about thirty miles north of Palermo, comprised a second large contingent of antebellum Italians in New Orleans, and their legacy still can be seen today. While some members of the Usticese colony also engaged in importing and wholesaling, a greater number entered into seafood distribution, oyster saloons, catering, and the restaurant trade. Unlike many of the migrants from Sicily proper, the Usticese settled in the Faubourg St. Mary and in the old Magazine Market area. The most recognizable names among them today are the Commander (born Camarda) brothers Emile and Charles J., who founded the restaurants Commander's Palace and The Delmonico respectively. Other families, like the extended Tranchina clan, operated noteworthy clubs and restaurants at West End and Spanish Fort, resorts that were crucial in the development of early jazz. The Usticese descendants, more numerous in New Orleans today than any other place in the world, maintain an active social presence through the auspices of the San Bartolomeo Society.

Sicilians, like many of the city's recently arrived Germans and French, did not greet the coming of the Civil War with enthusiasm. Weak local ties and the fact that they engaged in international commerce largely divorced from the region's slave-based agricultural economy attenuated the devotion that Italians harbored toward the cause of southern independence. Those who did not return to Italy enlisted in local militia groups comprised of foreign-born soldiers generally characterized by low expectations of their martial value.

Italian New Orleans in Late-Nineteenth-Century Politics and Commerce

In contrast to its halfhearted service during the Civil War, the growing Sicilian community played an active role in the far less abstract struggle over Reconstruction-era politics. They had aligned with the immigrant-friendly "Ring" faction of the Democratic Party since the "Know Nothing" violence of the 1850s. By 1870, Italians constituted an important bloc in the city's fifth and sixth wards, anchored in the French Quarter. The *Innocenti*, a fabled Italian street gang drawn from fruit wharf stevedores, prowled the French Quarter on behalf of the Democratic Party during the bloody presidential election of 1868. When the White League later emerged in 1874, it included a company of Italians led by the Maltese-born produce importer and ascendant shipping magnate Joseph P. Macheca. While an erstwhile expression of southern patriotism, Italian participation in political street violence of Reconstruction also fueled speculation about the presence of the Mafia on the waterfront.

The rapid modernization of the immediate postbellum era also transformed the sort of global commerce in which the city's Sicilian enclave engaged. The wealthy fruit and commodity importers of Decatur Street invested in a fleet of steamers capable of more reliably and inexpensively transporting citrus and other goods from the Mediterranean. With this expansion in capacity came increased diversification in other seasonal commodities, most notably tropical fruit. Importers who blazed trails to Central America in the late 1860s like Macheca and Santo Oteri (the first to convert to steam) ultimately sold their operations to larger fruit conglomerates by 1890. The market for banana imports was so capacious, however, that relative latecomers like Joseph, Luca, and Felix Vaccaro and their partner Salvador D'Antoni were able to form Standard Fruit, the antecedent of Dole Foods, in New Orleans as late as 1898. The advent of refrigeration on the banana boats and in railcars during the 1890s made possible the distribution of bananas to every corner of the nation and brought enormous fortunes for the men who imported them.

As late as 1885, the Sicily lemon remained the third most valuable import at New Orleans, only slightly ahead of the rising trade in bananas. Yet aspiring growers in California sought to topple Sicily as the world's leading producer, and at the beginning of the twentieth century, the California Fruit Growers Exchange, known today as Sunkist, enforced industry discipline on its members, negotiated favorable rail rates, and ultimately used xenophobic tactics to get a tariff in 1921 that made Sicily lemons uncompetitive in American markets. These efforts all but destroyed the sinews of commerce that had first brought Sicilians to America.

Although few people today remember the citrus trade, without it the Sicilian poor, facing ecological collapse and the grim social prospects in their homeland, would not have found such affordable transit to New Orleans. Those who rode the citrus fleet between 1885 and 1914 came from every corner of the island, representing diverse geographic and ethnic qualities. Notable among them are the ethnically Albanian "t'Abresche" from the hamlet of Contessa Entellina.

The postbellum South's white planter class looked upon Sicilian immigrants as an attractive alternative to black labor and actively recruited in Sicily for agricultural workers. Labor agents in New Orleans, known as *padroni*, encouraged by planter-sponsored immigration initiatives, arranged contract wage labor with Sicilian peasants in exchange for their passage to Louisiana. Many of the *padroni* were already engaged in importing citrus and other commodities from the Mediterranean and merely branched out into labor. The inexpensive regularity of the citrus fleet made possible the seasonal commuting of the region's all-male sugar harvesting labor force between Sicily and New Orleans from the mid-1880s through the 1890s. But as the twentieth century approached, these peripatetic "birds of passage" gave way to immigrants more intent on permanent settlement, including family units. This shift reflected in part the US federal government decision in 1905 to make the often abusive *padrone* system illegal.

Most Italians came to Louisiana before the advent of World War I in 1914. By that time, roughly 45,000 Italians, about 90 percent of whom came from Sicily, had entered through the port of New Orleans. These immigrants fanned out across the Gulf South, often tracing the route of the Mississippi River or the steel arteries of the region's railroads, opening groceries and bars, engaging in truck farming, logging, and other forms of labor. Others remained in or drifted back to New Orleans. Far more numerous than the earlier merchant class, this cohort ultimately came to shape what we today imagine Italian immigration to mean.

Social tension in Italian New Orleans between 1890 and 1919

As the Sicilian enclave grew in the late 1880s, two distinct sub-communities began to emerge within it. The smaller of these two were the merchants, business owners, and professionals who mostly arrived before 1885. They stood increasingly at odds with the more recent and more numerous poor laborers and farmers who had fled Sicily for unknown prospects in Louisiana.

One of the key native industries developed by this merchant class in the 1890s was that of macaroni, better known today as dry semolina pasta. A protectionist tariff opened this growing market to profitable domestic production, and by 1910 the French Quarter boasted no fewer than eight major pasta manufacturers supplying most of the region. Three large purpose-built macaroni factories still stand in the Quarter today: Federico Macaroni, which today houses Irene's restaurant; Taormina Brothers Macaroni, home to Muriel's on Jackson Square; and Jacob Cusimano's factory, now the Le Richelieu Hotel. Other international food empires trace their roots to this time and place in New Orleans, most notably Progresso Foods, founded on Chartres Street by the Uddo and Taormina families.

ABOVE Louis Prima and his band posed around instruments (l to r): Irving Fazola (clarinet/sax), John Miller (piano), Bob Jeffers (bass), George Hartman (trumpet), Louis Prima (trumpet), Cliff LeBlanc (trombone), Leonart Albersted (banjo), Jacob Sciambra (clarient/sax), Burt Andrus (clarinet/sax), John Vivano (drums). Photo by Joseph H. Sciambra. Courtesy of the New Orleans Jazz Club Collections of the Louisiana State Museum.

A photograph taken of a St. Joseph's celebration at the ornate Royal Street residence of liquor distributor Andrew Patorno in 1904 depicted "Italian Colony Beauties" in costume, their suitors clad in white tie formal for the festive gala. The society page guest list was a who's who of the city's Italian elite. Attendees included Felix Tranchina, who along with business partner J. V. Olivieri not only belonged to the prestigious Southern Yacht Club but also sponsored trophies for their annual regatta. These were the aristocracy of Italian New Orleans, often unseen in our collective memory of the Sicilian immigrant experience.

Only thirteen years earlier, and just five days before the Feast of St. Joseph, a vigilante mob broke into the Orleans Parish Prison on Marais Street and murdered eleven defendants who had been acquitted or still awaited trial for a conspiracy to assassinate Chief of Police David Hennessey. Among the dead was the shipping magnate and White League veteran Joseph P. Macheca. Hennessey first came to fame in 1881 by apprehending the notorious Sicilian bandit Giuseppe Esposito in New Orleans. More recently, he had become entangled in a bloody feud between Sicilian clans competing for a monopoly of the city's fruit wharves. Sensationalistic news coverage of his October 1890 assassination stirred anti-Italian hysteria and implied that a sinister mafia organization plotted the murder and controlled much of the community.

The lynching of the Sicilian defendants remains a key touchstone of memory for Italian New Orleans and often characterized, despite thin evidence, of the American mafia's birth. Scholars have analyzed it in terms of race and xenophobia, given that Sicilians in this era were oftentimes not viewed as being "white." But one should consider that the lynch mob, represented heavily by old elites tied to the collapsing economies of sugar and cotton, attacked men associated with the rapidly rising fortunes of global produce. That the anti-Ring "Reformers" also dominated the lynch mob reveals political as well as economic motivations for their attack. It is possible they also resented the vigilante tactics used by Sicilians, a method of social and political control heretofore reserved in New Orleans for elite whites.

While it is doubtful that any true crime syndicate operated among New Orleans Sicilians before the 1920s, the "Italian Colony" centered in the lower French Quarter could be a violent place, marked by extortion schemes perpetrated by criminals claiming membership in the Black Hand racket. Such activity paralleled the petty banditry of Sicily and became more common as the Sicilian peasant class grew in New Orleans. Their chief targets were the wealthier Italians who had come to America to get away from just such activity. The most spectacular case of such crime outside of the fabled "Ax Man" murders came in 1908 with the abduction and murder of young Walter Lamana, the child of a St. Philip Street undertaker. The following year, the gunning-down of related bandits by a family of wealthy wine merchants signaled the limited toleration that the Italian elite bore for such extortion rackets. Indeed, the elite importers, wholesalers, and manufacturers of the Italian Colony formed a protective union in 1910 and were well on their way toward obliterating, through both legal and extralegal means, the sort of petty criminality brought from the old country. In stark contrast to 1891, their efforts received broad approbation in the mainstream press. In fact, had it not been for the advent of Prohibition in 1919, the elite may well have established an iron control over the Italian Colony.

Italian New Orleans Comes of Age, 1919–1945

Prohibition criminalized a crucial segment of the New Orleans economy at a time when white audiences began discovering jazz, and night clubs came into vogue. Italian businessmen, having long operated at the intersection of alcohol and music, navigated a fine line between profitability and criminality during Prohibition. Clubs like Masera's, at St. Louis and Bourbon Streets, had been in business since the 1880s and had evolved from a nineteenth-century oyster saloon to a cabaret to, ultimately, an Italian restaurant. After 1919, Masera's became a major site for both jazz and illegal booze. The 1920s also saw the humble riverfront spaghetti restaurant, a phenomenon that had become wildly popular with non-Italians across the nation in the 1910s, evolve from mom-and-pop eateries into nightclubs with tuxedoed waiters. Such was the path of Turci's, which opened on Decatur Street in 1917 but moved to Bourbon

> The collaboration between Italians and Afro-Creoles in particular helped to shape the character not only of music in New Orleans but also its cuisine.

Street in 1924, where it featured jazz music and illegal booze. Despite frequent trouble with Prohibition enforcement, numerous Italian-owned clubs began to appear on Bourbon Street, ushering in the start of its so-called "golden age" in the 1920s.

With the end of Prohibition, club owners who had managed to avoid jail were able to turn the profits from illegal booze sales into openly-run nightclubs along Bourbon Street. Survivors included Masera's and Turci's, which were joined by the famous Shim Sham Club in 1934 operated by New Orleans Sicilian musical sensation Louis Prima and his brother Leon. La Lune, the long-running Latin theme club, had been opened by Johnny Panzeca at the 800 Bourbon Street address of his parents' grocery. Panzeca, like many operators who gambled on bootleg liquor during Prohibition, turned his commercial activity toward legitimate nightclubs, banking, and real estate. Whether illicitly acquired or not, the gains earned during Prohibition helped finance the growth of the city's entertainment sector and nurtured growth in tourism, the city's top source of commerce today.

Yet while Prohibition made temporary "criminals" of most club owners, it also gave rise to more permanent and diversified crime syndicates like those run by Sylvestro Carollo and later Carlos Marcello. Though including associates from many ethnicities, the Italian leadership of organized crime in New Orleans tied it to larger syndicates in places like New York and Tampa. The well-known association between brothers Huey and Earl Long and New York mob boss Frank Costello filtered into many aspects of Louisiana's civic and economic life. Certainly from a political standpoint, Italians in New Orleans had never been so powerful as they were in the 1930s and '40s. In 1936, Huey Long ally and businessman Robert Maestri became mayor of the city with significant support of the Long machine. Organized crime enjoyed broad acquiescence from state and local officials well into the 1970s, though its very nature prevents an accurate accounting of its full extent.

This time period also saw the maturation of Italian societies such as the Carnival Krewe of Virgilians, whose legendarily lavish balls began in 1935 and ran until 1964, when fewer of the old-line krewes continued to exclude Italians. As the city expanded in the 1920s and '30s, the second generation of Sicilian immigrants also moved to the suburbs, most notably expanding up Esplanade Avenue and building homes in Gentilly.

Italian New Orleans Since 1945

By the end of World War II, Italians had become a fundamental part of New Orleans culture, having become fully integrated into the city's civic, political, and cultural life. Sicilian musicians like Nick LaRocca, Louis Prima, Sharkey Bonano, Santo Pecora, Wingy Manone, and many others had made an essential contribution to jazz. In the 1950s and '60s, the studio of Cosimo Matassa in the French Quarter recorded legendary names of R&B music, including Jean Knight, Little Richard, and Fats Domino. Indeed, the collaboration between Italians and Afro-Creoles in particular helped to shape the character not only of music in New Orleans but also its cuisine as symbolized by the fusion of ingredients and multigenerational partnerships, such as the one that flourished between the legendary Creole chef Nathaniel Burton and restaurateur Joseph Segreto at Segreto's (formerly Masera's) in 1945 and his son S. Joseph Segreto at Broussard's in 1973.

New Orleans, like many of the great cities in the North, had become by the 1960s and '70s a place where one might find Italian names in places of civic and economic importance. Examples include Pascal F. Calogero Jr., the son of a Ninth Ward police officer who became Chief Justice of the Louisiana Supreme court under Mayor Sidney Barthelemy, or Joseph C. Canizaro, who in the late 1960s built the Lykes Brothers Steamship Company building (today the Loews Hotel), the first high-rise structure to appear on the newly widened Poydras Street.

Expressions of Italian-American civic pride are most visible today at the Piazza d'Italia, built in the 1978 adjacent to the American Italian Cultural Center on South Peters Street, as well as the Monument to the Immigrant located on the New Orleans Riverwalk. Both bear the vision of the city's greatest champion of Italian culture, Joseph Maselli. And, as reductivist as it is to describe the muffuletta as an essential Italian contribution in present-day New Orleans, one must acknowledge the cultural significance of Central Grocery, the shop that sells the most famous version of the sandwich—not just as a culinary representation of Italian culture, but as the last outpost remaining from an earlier era of mercantile life on Decatur Street that had brought so many immigrants from the Mediterranean in the first place.

ABOVE *Procession, Feast of the Assumption of Mary, Versailles Community, New Orleans East, 1978*, by Mark J. Sindler, from The Vietnamese Documentary Project.

Carrying on Traditions

After the fall of Saigon in 1975, many of the South Vietnamese who fled to the United States landed in Louisiana, and not by accident. Our humid southern climate, fertile Gulf waters, and spicy cuisine offered an environment very similar to their own. In addition, many of the Vietnamese exiles were Catholic, so both local and national Catholic charity organizations worked to locate them in a welcoming religious environment as well. According to the Migration Policy Institute, in 2015, the New Orleans Vietnamese community ranked twenty-third in the nation and the largest in the state, numbering more than eleven thousand. Today the estimate is closer to fourteen thousand.

Many Vietnamese turned to fishing, some even moving down closer to the Gulf, but others stayed in the city working in restaurants, factories, and salons, later opening their own small businesses that today dot the city's landscape. Close-knit Vietnamese communities have grown and prospered in eastern New Orleans and on the West Bank, with their own churches, community centers, restaurants, bakeries, and groceries.

The Vietnamese community in the east, Versailles, flooded after Hurricane Katrina, yet they worked tirelessly and were one of the first neighborhoods rebuilt and open for business, offering inspiration to all New Orleanians. Since then, many Vietnamese-owned businesses have expanded in order to capitalize on the larger metropolitan market, the most notable being the restaurant industry.

Casual or high-end dining, New Orleans is a foodie town: good food is good food, and in the last few decades, that has included Vietnamese food. New Orleanians have embraced Vietnamese cuisine at some of the more popular restaurants like Nine Roses, Pho Tau Bay, Kim Son, and Dong Phuong, where dishes like pho, bun, and banh mi need no translation. But more recently, and inevitably, Vietnamese and New Orleans fusion cuisine has exploded, and Mopho, Café Minh, Namese, and Maypop offer some of the city's freshest and most exciting Asian–New Orleans fare.

Generations of Vietnamese Americans live and work in New Orleans, on both the East and West Banks, while honoring their cultural traditions. Today they are joined by people from all over the city for the Tet Festival celebrations that also take place in nearly every elementary school in New Orleans.

-Nancy Dixon, PhD

RIGHT Elsa Enamorado and Oscar Reyes dance the "Jarabe Lloreno," a Honduran folkloric dance, at the Independence Day Festival, ca. 2015. Photo by Cheryl Gerber.

"Little Honduras"

The Big Easy. The Crescent City. The City that Care Forgot. There are plenty of nicknames used to describe the city of New Orleans, but here's a sobriquet that might sound foreign to some: Little Honduras. Though better known to residents of the Central American country, it's an appropriate moniker, as New Orleans is now home to the largest group of Hondurans outside of the country.

Since the beginning of the twenty-first century, Central American immigrants have flocked to New Orleans for a number of reasons, and no other nationality in that group is represented in greater numbers than Hondurans.

"The current Honduran population is the result of at least three generations arriving since [the] beginning of the [twentieth] century with the commercial activities of companies like Standard Fruit & Steamship Company and United Fruit Company, both of which had headquarters in New Orleans," says Mayra E. Pineda, a native Honduran and the president and CEO of the Hispanic Chamber of Commerce of Louisiana. "Families started establishing themselves in the area and becoming part of the community and in turn attracting new immigrants. In the following decades, several waves of Honduran immigrants reached the city looking for the American Dream and better opportunities. The most recent waves of Hondurans arrived after Hurricane Katrina and were instrumental in the clean-up and reconstruction efforts of the city. However, we cannot ignore the many Hondurans that have also fled the country escaping insecurity, high living costs, and no opportunities."

A large portion of recent transplants from Honduras to New Orleans are children, many of whom are coming to reunite with family members and often fleeing dire economic situations and the threat of gang violence.

The impact of the rich cultural contribution the Honduran community has brought to the city cannot be underestimated, and nowhere is that more visible than in the city's booming restaurant scene, which has become a veritable olio of Latin American cuisines.

Food has always held a nostalgic, transportive power, often acting as a lifeline that helps us stay in touch with our roots. It's a tangible connection to home—one you can touch, see, smell, and—most importantly—taste. This culinary lifeline is often found in the informal social sector—in home kitchens, living rooms, barbeques, back alleys, and food trucks.

For chefs like Melissa Araujo, a Honduran-born chef who calls New Orleans home and runs the pop-up restaurant Alma, it's an opportunity to share the dishes of her homeland at weekly events and chef's dinners.

Though Hondurans may make up the majority of the Central American population in the city, the ties they have established since arriving here display a community that is anything but monolithic. Restaurants provide a good example of this fusion, where a variety of Central American cuisines are often offered and packaged as one, something indicative of the various backgrounds that makeup the restaurant's owners and staff.

At Fiesta Latina in Kenner, for example, owner Delmy Cruz is El Salvadoran, her husband hails from Mexico, and the kitchen staff is mostly from Honduras. What results is a vibrant and creative menu, full of traditional Latin American specialties respectful of the delicate nuances that exist in each.

New Orleans, with its rich multicultural background and history, is one of the best examples that the American story is, after all, an immigrant story. Who better to tell this story than the Honduran community in New Orleans, where yet another vibrant patch has been sewn onto the ever-changing American quilt.

-Helen Freund

Ancestral Suits

Patrina Peters, Big Wild Queen of the Red Hawk Hunters

by Maurice Carlos Ruffin

It's winter 2017. Patrina Peters sits at a high table. She's alone in her Ninth Ward home, no retainers or ladies-in-waiting. But make no mistake about it. Ms. Peters is a queen.

Along the far wall, beneath photos of family and a certificate of appreciation from the mayor of New Orleans, Mitch Landrieu, stand two figures, one electric blue and one dark pink. The figures are seemingly made of nothing more than sparkling beads and ethereal feathers, spirits made corporeal. These are her "suits" from those days when she reigned as Big Wild Queen of the Red Hawk Hunters, an example of New Orleans' unique Mardi Gras Indian culture, where African Americans wear colorful ceremonial clothes and take to the streets or "mask." The Mardi Gras Indians mask out of respect for the Native Americans that helped their ancestors. "If it had not been for the Indians, some of our ancestors would not have been freed," Peters says. "My uncle and them made sure we knew the reason why we put the suit on."

ABOVE Peters donning her suit. Photo by L. Kasimu Harris, 2017.

For many decades, New Orleans was one of America's most important ports of commerce. Among the most valuable cargo deposited along the banks of the Mississippi River were people. Once transferred from ship to land, these people were often held in slave pens and sold from auction blocks for roughly the price of a modern-day used car. Some were sold to nearby plantations. Others were forced to work in the tony townhouses of downtown New Orleans as slaves. Sometimes, these enslaved humans caught the disease that renowned physician Samuel Cartwright called "drapetomania." The only symptom of this disease was that it caused slaves to flee their captivity. Outside of the slave-holding empire, in the swamps, were the free lands of Native American tribes. Occasionally, sufferers of drapetomania made it to these territories, where they were protected by the tribes. This was an act of love.

Love lasts forever. The proof is on the streets of modern New Orleans, where during Mardi Gras one can find tribes of Mardi Gras Indians dancing and singing exuberantly. Like chess pieces, you will

> "This was a suit I knew I had to hit the streets in because it told my son's story."

recognize the members of a tribe by how they move. The Spy Boy, well ahead of the main body and on the lookout for a potential challenge from other tribes. The Wild Man, brandishing a symbolic staff and clearing the way for royalty. The King, monumental in his finery, singing the traditional song, "Indian Red."

For Big Wild Queen Peters, the tradition is also about family. Around 1970, her uncles and aunts, as members of the Flaming Arrows, formed the first tribe in the Ninth Ward, a large neighborhood that previously had no tribal representation. Peters explains that her aunts were trailblazers—and "they were also mothers, wives, working women." In addition to making her own suit and assisting in the creation of her husband's suits, Peters' aunt, Beatrice McFadden-Burnes, sang "Indian Red," a role from which women were usually excluded.

Peters' son would inherit the family's attraction to masking. "He lived for Mardi Gras," Peters says. When Damond was two years old, he walked for miles banging an oil bottle, surrounded by family. Years later, Damond would take on a more formal role. As Wild Man Dee, he performed not only on the streets, but also at the New Orleans Jazz and Heritage Festival. Peters says her son changed the image of the Wild Man. Instead of costuming himself in a simple or plain suit, she explains, "Damond brought pretty to the Wild Man. His suits were elegant. His suits were beautiful." But at age nineteen, Damond was murdered.

In her grief, Peters searched for a way to honor the memory of her son and keep his legacy alive. She decided to become the Big Wild Queen. But first, she needed a suit. Damond had already begun making a new suit prior to his death, but it was not finished.

Peters removes the clear covering protecting the pink suit. Every suit must tell a story, and this one is no different. The main panel depicts a Mardi Gras Indian on a bridge, his bow and arrow raised to signal his tribe. It parallels a true-life story of Damond warning his tribe of an approaching group and the possibility of a challenge.

Damond had completed most of the intricate beadwork. Peters had the pants shortened and made other adjustments. "In 2011, Mardi Gras morning, I hit the street." Peters smiles. "This was a suit I knew had to hit the streets in because it told my son's story. In telling his story, I told my story."

Peters also masked in 2012. But following a serious illness, her doctor forbade her from masking in her 2013 suit. Wearing such heavy garments and crossing the city as Big Wild Queen was too dangerous. But today, a younger generation, including Peters' granddaughter, continues the tradition of paying respect to those who showed compassion to their ancestors.

OPPOSITE Masking Mardi Gras Indian Queen, Patrina Peters, Wild Queen of the Red Hawk Hunters, at her home. Photo by L. Kasimu Harris, 2017.

Part II:

SPACE AND PLACE

Pythian Temple

The Pythian Temple, located at the corner of Loyola Avenue and Gravier Street, was completed in 1909. The seven-story building was constructed by The Grand Lodge, Colored Order of the Knights of Pythias of Louisiana, a club that was founded in 1880 and dedicated to "friendship, charity and benevolence." Built at a cost of two hundred thousand dollars, the Pythian was purported to be the "biggest business enterprise ever attempted by the colored race in the United States." Among the African-American–owned businesses occupying the offices and retail space was the Unity Industrial Life Insurance Company, led by C. C. Dejoie. Along with a former public school teacher named O. C. W. Taylor, Dejoie founded *The Louisiana Weekly newspaper*, which had its first office in the Pythian Temple.

The Pythian Garden, an open-air venue on the roof of the building, made a lasting impression during the early days of jazz. Trumpeter Manuel Perez led the Pythian Orchestra. Louis Armstrong said of Perez, "Emanuel couldn't speak so much English, but his horn would speak any language." A cigar maker like his father, Perez is said to have taken over as the city's most prominent trumpet player after the death of Buddy Bolden, influencing Armstrong, King Oliver, and Freddie Keppard. The club closed in 1927 and was later reopened by A. J. Piron, whose New Orleans Orchestra played a smoother style of jazz that allowed him entrée to the stages of the Southern Yacht Club and the New Orleans Country Club. Piron is thought to have founded the first African-American music publishing company.

The Pythian's owners fell on hard times during the Great Depression, and a lawsuit left the building in receivership in 1933. In 1936, the state used the Pythian as temporary quarters for black patients of the old Charity Hospital while the new "Big Charity" was being completed on Tulane Avenue.

In 1944, Colonel R. E. E. deMontluzin, the developer of the Gentilly Terrace neighborhood and owner of vast holdings in the then undeveloped eastern marshes of New Orleans, purchased the Pythian for eighty thousand dollars. The Pythian was renamed the Industries Building and became the employment offices for Higgins Industries, the company that famously supplied the federal government with the boats that landed at Normandy on D Day. There were two entrances for job seekers at the Industries Building: whites entered through the Saratoga Street (now Loyola Avenue) entrance; blacks were directed around the corner to a Gravier Street entrance.

ABOVE From *Architectural Art and Its Allies, Louisiana Architectural Association*, March 1908. Courtesy of New Orleans Public Library.

ABOVE Courtesy of the Charles L. Franck Studio Collection at The Historic New Orleans Collection.

"The Eighth Wonder of the world is not located in the Orient, in the Occident, nor at the North Pole, but right in the city of New Orleans, in the prosperous State of Louisiana. It is not a temple that is dedicated to the gods, but it is a mammoth, modern, up-to-date building, dedicated to the living and built by Negro brains and Negro capital. The name of this pretentious and magnificent structure is the Pythian Temple of New Orleans."

-Green P. Hamilton, *Beacon Lights of the Race*, 1911

The neighborhood surrounding the Pythian was redeveloped in the 1950s. Known as the Civic Center, the area became home to a new city hall, main library, post office, and rail terminal. DeMontluzin renamed his building the Civic Center building and had the façade covered with porcelain and aluminum to match the new city hall. In later years, the building fell into disrepair. By the time Hurricane Katrina struck in 2005, the former Pythian Temple was unoccupied.

In 2017, Green Coast Enterprises and its project partner Crescent City Community Land Trust completed the renovation of the Pythian Temple. Tenants began moving into the Pythian's sixty-nine apartments in March 2017. The building is part of the revitalization of the Central Business District, which now includes the Loyola Avenue streetcar, a booming restaurant scene, and several other redeveloped historic properties.

ABOVE Courtesy of General Interest Collection-Office Buildings, New Orleans Public Library.

ABOVE Photo by Romy Mariano, 2017.

DO NOT TOUCH
FLOWERS SHRUBS

1762 - 1803
CALLE DEL MAINE

“A Graceful Curve of the River”

Urbanism, architecture, and the emergence of a distinctive metropolitan character

by Richard Campanella

Nineteen years had passed since a teenaged Jean-Baptiste Le Moyne, Sieur de Bienville, first eyed the lower Mississippi. It was now spring 1718, and Commandant General Bienville returned to this flat and fluid environ to, according to Company of the West records, “establish, thirty leagues up the river, a burg which should be called New Orleans, where landing would be possible from either the river or Lake Pontchartrain.”

For his outpost, Bienville favored a particularly sharp meander roughly halfway between the river’s mouth (itself far too dynamic) and the bluffs by Baton Rouge (too distant from the sea). The site’s relatively elevated river banks would limit flooding; its commanding perch would help defend against enemy ships; and a backswamp ridge (Bayou Road) and inlet (Bayou St. John) would connect it to Lake Pontchartrain and the Gulf of Mexico, providing alternative ingress and egress to the shoal-prone river.

Topography and hydrology thus heavily informed the location and formation of New Orleans. But of course these inanimate phenomena had no agency in urban development; that came from human decisions. Much of the three-hundred-year history of New Orleans is a story of people *fighting* geography, by engineering rigidity upon a delta fundamentally defined by fluidity. That intercession enabled the emergence of a splendid built environment. It also occasioned the deterioration of the underlying natural environment, yielding an urban precarity unequaled on the North American continent.

While the founders were unaware of the consequences of hardening a soft delta, they did readily observe how water moved and where land lay higher and drier. When Assistant Engineer Adrien de Pauger laid out the streets of today’s French Quarter four years after Bienville selected the site, he pointedly positioned the grid to utilize fully the scarce high ground. So too the *arpenteurs* (surveyors) who laid out narrow French long-lot plantations on the natural levees, such that each of the *concessionaires* would have riverine access

OPPOSITE TOP LEFT The Luling Mansion, near the Fairgrounds, built in 1865 and originally surrounded with expansive manicured gardens, embodied the Italianate and Picturesque aesthetics en vogue from the 1850s through 1870s. Photo ca. 1900. Courtesy of the Library of Congress.

OPPOSITE TOP RIGHT This home at 1025 St. Louis Street, built in 1840 by and for prosperous free people of color, is a fine example of the Greek Revival style draped upon the townhouse typology. Photo by Pableaux Johnson, 2017.

OPPOSITE BOTTOM Madame John’s Legacy at 628 Dumaine is among the best surviving examples of West Indian-influenced French Creole architecture, and was literally upon the ashes of the 1788 Good Friday Fire, which destroyed most remaining French-era buildings. Photo by Pableaux Johnson, 2017.

RIGHT In the Fifth Ward, a long line of Late-Victorian shotgun doubles, the likes of which were built by the thousands throughout working-class neighborhoods in the 1870s through 1900s. New technologies, such as indoor plumbing, rendered the shotgun obsolete by the 1910s, when bungalows and later ranch houses became the standard New Orleans residential.Photo by Walker Evans, 1935. Courtesy of the Library of Congress.

ABOVE This splendid home on Prytania Street, featuring Queen Anne and Eastlake traits of Late Victorian design, reflects the architectural ebullience of the Guided Age. By the early twentieth century, excessive detailing came to be viewed as gaudy and ostentatious, and designers gravitated toward simplicity and rusticity, giving rise to the Arts and Crafts Movement, and later to Modernism, with its clean lines and open spaces. Photo by Romy Mariano, 2017.

and a slice of the arable upland. Years later, when Spanish authorities decided to expand the urban footprint after the 1788 Good Friday Fire, they also selected the high ground of today's Central Business District as the city's first *suburbio*, or faubourg (inner suburb). By the early 1800s, the river-hugging morphology of the expanding metropolis mimicked the deltaic plain's curvaceous ridges. "I have termed New-Orleans the crescent city," wrote visitor Joseph Holt Ingraham in 1835, "from its being built around the segment of a circle formed by a graceful curve of the river at this place." He could have just as well cited topography as the inspiration for the enduring nickname.

Equally graceful was New Orleans' distinctive built environment, informed not by England and northern Europe, as were Northern cities, but rather by the customs of the Caribbean and the "Creole Atlantic." To be sure, Pauger's rectangular street grid was pure French imperial urban planning, and the surrounding ramparts were right out of Sébastien Vauban's military engineering manuals. But the cityscape itself looked like few other spots on the North American continent, with its hundreds of West Indian-influenced structures, mostly set back from the street, with small gardens and chicken coops surrounded by picket fences. As an emergent tradition rather than an inscribed order, this first generation of "Creole" architecture reflected building customs from France and the Franco-Afro-Caribbean region and adapted locally through experimentation. Their signature traits included walls made of brick or mud mixed with moss (*bousillage*) set within a load-bearing timber frame; an oversized "Norman" roof, usually hipped and double-pitched; spacious wooden galleries supported with delicate colonnades and balustrades; staircases located outside on the gallery; centralized chimneys; French doors and shutters on all apertures; and an absence of hallways and closets. Wrote English Captain Philip Pittman during his 1765 visit, "most of the houses are . . . timber frames filled up with brick" and "one floor, raised about eight feet from the ground, with large galleries round them. . . . It is impossible to have any subterraneous buildings, as they would be constantly full of water."

Circumstances changed in the late 1700s, by which time Spain controlled the colony, and Creole architecture transformed as well. The aforementioned 1788 fire destroyed 856 of New Orleans' original housing stock, and a second blaze six years later destroyed another 212. Spanish administrators responded to the 1794 blaze with new building codes to prevent fires, mandating, according to Cabildo records, new houses to be "built of bricks and a flat roof or tile roof," while extant houses were to be strengthened "to stand a roof of fire-proof materials," their beams covered with stucco. "[All] citizens must comply with these rules," the dons decreed.

The fires and codes largely ended that first phase of bucolic abodes in New Orleans proper, though they would persist in rural areas for another generation. They would become even less suitable in the American era, when the city's population would double every fifteen years. Land values rose, housing density increased, and picket fences and vegetable gardens became a thing of the past.

But Creoles still predominated, and Creole builders continued to erect "creolized" structures now exhibiting Spanish and Anglo-American influences. Thus, in the early 1800s, a second and more urban phase of Creole architecture emerged. For smaller residences, this meant the transformation of the circa-1700s wooden galleried houses to the brick Creole cottages we have today. For larger residences, it meant brick common-wall townhouses and storehouses featuring arched openings, wrought-iron balconies, and a carriageway leading to a rear courtyard, all behind an elegantly Spartan stucco façade. What once felt like a West Indian village was now starting to look like a Mediterranean city. Wrote Scottish visitor Basil Hall in 1828, "What struck us most were the old and narrow streets, the high houses, ornamented with tasteful cornices, iron balconies, and many other circumstances peculiar to towns in France and Spain." Contrast Hall's quote to that of Pittman to visualize the difference between first-generation "country Creole" and second-generation "city Creole" architecture. While specimens of the former phase are rare today, more than 740 examples of the latter still stand in the French Quarter, mostly dating to the 1810s–1830s.

Creoles in this era increasingly found themselves competing with ever-growing populations of Anglo-Irish Americans, who settled disproportionately in the upper *banlieues* (outskirts). Like all migrants, the Americans brought their cultural baggage with them, and that included an architectural preference informed by the Enlightenment, which itself found inspiration in Classical antiquity. The style came to be called Neoclassicism, and one of its offshoots would be known as "Greek Revival." The intellectual rationale behind it—for order, rationality, dignity and decorum—soon crossed the Atlantic and found its way to New Orleans. By the 1820s, Ionic porticos started appearing on Canal Street; gabled roofs came to outnumber hipped roofs; squared doorways replaced arched openings; heavy granite lintels were installed above apertures; delicate colonnades disappeared for Classical columns; and dentils appeared along previously smooth entablatures. Interiors were affected too: staircases previously set outside on the gallery now came indoors, and hallways were designed into floor plans, reflecting the Anglo value placed on privacy.

By some accounts, Neoclassicism set the old Creole building customs on a trajectory of decline. "The Americanization of the Crescent City has long been completed, at least architecturally," wrote architectural historian James Marston Fitch, "and the whole nation is the poorer for it." An alternative interpretation holds that, rather than wiping them out, Americanization drove Creole and Afro-Caribbean designs

LEFT After World War II, with widespread municipal drainage and urban development increasing as subdivision-scale tract housing, ranch and other suburban styles for new homes were erected on grade-level concrete slabs—a bad idea in a deltaic environment, but highly popular throughout the 1950s and 1960s. Seen here is Pontchartrain Park, opened in 1955 as the first modern subdivision to welcome African-American homebuyers. Like most other twentieth-century neighborhoods on New Orleans' East Bank, it flooded deeply after Hurricane Katrina in 2005. Photo by Pableaux Johnson, 2017.

into further evolution. That stage entailed the dovetailing of one local innovation—the rotation of the traditional Creole cottage such that its roofline, typically parallel to the street, became perpendicular to it—with a related idea for elongated houses likely imported from Haiti. What resulted were long narrow houses, the type that would be later nicknamed "shotguns."

What once felt like a West Indian village was now starting to look like a Mediterranean city.

Folklorist John Michael Vlach defined the prototypical shotgun house as "a one-room wide, one-story high building with two or more rooms, oriented perpendicularly to the road," although all aspects vary widely. Researchers have proposed a number of hypotheses explaining the origin and distribution of this distinctive house type. One theory, popular with tour guides and amateur house-watchers, holds that shotgun houses were designed in New Orleans in response to a real estate tax based on frontage rather than square footage, motivating narrow structures. There's one critical problem with this theory: no one can seem to find that tax code.

Could the shotgun be an architectural response to slender urban lots? Indeed, narrow houses accommodate urban density; demolish one cottage and you've got space for two shotguns. While this may explain the explosion of shotgun construction in the late 1800s, it raises the question of why we see shotguns in open fields with no such spatial limitations. Could the shotgun have evolved from indigenous palmetto houses or Choctaw huts? Unlikely, given its appearance in the Caribbean and beyond. Could it have been professionally designed? Roberts & Company, a New Orleans sash and door fabricator, developed blueprints for long houses in the 1860s–1870s and even won awards for them. But then why do we see similar houses here a half-century earlier?

An alternative hypothesis holds that elongated houses diffused across the "Creole Atlantic." Vlach noted the abundance of such abodes in the West Indies and traced them to enslaved populations of Saint-Domingue (now Haiti) who had been removed from the western and central African regions of Guinea and Angola. His research identified a gable-roofed housing stock among the Yoruba peoples, which he linked to similar Ti-kay structures in modern Haiti. Vlach suggests that the 1809 exodus of Haitians to New Orleans after the 1791–1804 revolution brought this vernacular house type to the banks of the Mississippi. "Haitian émigrés had only to continue in Louisiana the same life they had known in St. Domingue," he wrote. "The shotgun house of Port-au-Prince became, quite directly, the shotgun house of New Orleans." Indeed, in the 1810s–1820s, long houses start to appear in the rear of the French Quarter and the Faubourg Tremé, where many émigrés settled alongside francophone Creoles.

Starting around 1850, a subtle change began to appear in New Orleans architecture: fading Creole, solemn Spanish, and austere Greek Revival designs began to give way to a more ornate and luxurious look. Behind it was the rise of the Romantic Movement, a reaction to the lofty ideals of the Enlightenment and the expanding domains of science and industry. Romanticism responded by celebrating nature, emotionality, and the specialness of the individual. Unlike Enlightenment thinkers who admired Classical antiquity, Romanticists fancied the glory of the Renaissance and the poignancy of medieval ruins, particularly in Italy. After the Napoleonic Wars, with pent-up demand for what architectural historian Joan Caldwell described as "sheer aesthetic enjoyment," Italianate designs gained popularity as the "aesthetic of luxury." Campaniles, loggia, bowed bays, arcades, bracketed eaves, decorative moldings, and segmented arches appeared throughout England. Pattern books made their reproduction efficient and inexpensive, and the style spread, inexorably, to New Orleans, which had plenty of nouveau riche eager to showcase their affluence. Among the Italianate style's local champions were architects William and James Freret, James Gallier Jr., Albert Diettel, and most of all, Henry Howard. Early local examples included the magnificent Robb Mansion (1854) on Washington Avenue, whose lavish landscaping helped inspire the sobriquet "Garden District," and the Luling Mansion (1865) near the Fairgrounds, it too originally surrounded by sprawling Tuscany-style gardens. These and a few other villas, however, were the exception. Most local architects applied Italianate detailing—segmented-arch apertures, heavy molding, fancy brackets—as an overlay to standard local house types. We have thousands such Victorian Italianate façades today, mostly dating to the 1850s–1900s and peaking in the 1890s.

By century's end, design exuberance had reached its zenith. Among the sundry panaches of this late-Victorian era were Stick, with its emphasis on wooden detailing ("stick work") and its variants, Queen

Anne, distinctive for its towers and turrets, and Eastlake, with its brackets, quoins, railings, spindles, and skin-like shingling. There was also Richardsonian Romanesque with its sturdy, stony countenance; francophile Second Empire and its mansard roofs; imposing Gothic with its elegant ogives; Tudor with its nostalgic rusticity; and a flamboyant expression of classical and Renaissance motifs known as Beaux-Arts. Architecture blossomed in this era, almost literally, with florid embellishments and cornucopias of fruit bandied all over exteriors and interiors. Motifs got mixed and matched ad nauseam, and home sizes grew ever larger, as if to say what's worth doing is worth overdoing.

Starting around 1909, California Bungalows would be built citywide by the thousands, in places such as Gentilly Terrace and Broadmoor, both of which would be explicitly billed as "Little California."

And that's what drove the counter-reaction. It came to be known as the Arts and Crafts movement, and it eschewed ostentatious excess and machine-made panache in favor of an earthier, hand-crafted look. It would take the form of the Craftsman cottage and the "bungalow," whose nationwide popularity, mainstreamed by Greene and Greene Architects and sold as kits through catalogs, would be paralleled by a revival in Spanish and Mediterranean styles for everything from homes to theaters to markets to automobile dealerships. The inspiration for these new styles came not from the Northeast or England, nor from medieval or ancient precedents, but from an entirely new source: California.

Golden State architecture found good terroir in New Orleans. The city had finally, in the 1890s, installed a modern municipal drainage system to drain the backswamp, and by the early 1910s, the groundwater level had lowered, the soils dried out, and land once deemed threatening and useless suddenly became valuable real estate. Developers, homebuilders, mortgage-lenders, and city officials all had vested interests in creating modern, auto-friendly subdivisions in the former wetlands, and middle-class New Orleanians could hardly wait to escape the cramped old riverfront precincts for new environs with names like Lakeview and Gentilly. Starting around 1909, California Bungalows would be built citywide by the thousands, in places such as Gentilly Terrace and Broadmoor, both of which would be explicitly billed as "Little California." Similar West Coast-inspired building styles would appear in Lakeview, Old Metairie, Arabi, and across the river.

There was, however, one grave unforeseen consequence. The removal of swampwater opened up air pockets in the soil body, which oxidized the organic matter, which in turn opened up more cavities. Fine particles of silt and clay settled into those spaces, and the soil consolidated below the level of the sea. The deltaic plain, whose topographic profile was originally gently inclined and entirely above sea level, now took the shape of a series of bowls straddling sea level. The very human engineering enacted to expel unwanted water from inside the city had the effect of juxtaposing outside water levels *above* the city. More and more, New Orleans would be dependent on levees and floodwalls to prevent that outside water from pouring in, and on pumps and drainage canals to expel inside water out. Yet so secure was local society in its confidence that engineering technology had neutralized the age-old problems of topography and hydrology that builders abandoned the centuries-old custom of pier-based construction in favor of concrete slabs poured directly at grade level. Worse yet, such ranch-house subdivisions were built in the very areas (Lakeview and Gentilly first, Metairie and New Orleans East later) that were lowest to begin with—and sinking the fastest and deepest below sea level: the worst architectural idea in the worst geographical place.

By this time, an intellectual challenge to Western cultural assumptions in everything from literature to religion had made headway in Europe, particularly after the First World War. Adherents were known as "Modernists," and the architects among them, working with new materials like steel frames and sheet glass, rejected Victorian ebullience in favor of openness, horizontality, minimalism, and function over form. In New Orleans, Modernism was at first fused with traditional styles: witness the modernized Gothic of the Pere Marquette Building on Common and Baronne (1925), the former Masonic Temple on St. Charles and Perdido (1926), and the modernized Neoclassicism of the Orleans Parish Criminal Courthouse (1929) at Tulane and Broad. Similarly amalgamated styles would become known as Moderne, Streamline Moderne, and most famously, Art Deco, of which New Orleans boasts many fine examples, among them Lakefront Airport Terminal (1934), the F. Edward Hebert Federal Building on Lafayette Square (1939), and the now-empty Charity Hospital (1939).

The catastrophe of World War II further vindicated Modernism. Art Deco and any hint of Neoclassicism came to look ominous for their association with fascism, whereas their antitheses—taut surfaces of aluminum and glass,

LEFT Craftsman-style California bungalows, an architectural style which swept the nation in the 1910s, became so popular in New Orleans that parts of Broadmoor and Gentilly Terrace were specifically marketed as "Little California." Seen here is Music Street in Gentilly, which boasts a particularly fine concentration of the Craftsman style. Photo by Pableaux Johnson, 2017.

ABOVE Despite the public perception of New Orleans as a city of historical architecture, local society enthusiastically embraced Modernism from the late 1940s through early 1970s. Seen here is a Curtis and Davis-designed Modernist home on Audubon Boulevard. Photo by Pableaux Johnson, 2017.

crisp edges and smooth curves, capacious sun-lit interiors—looked refreshing, even liberating of the past. The International Style, though it originated before the Second World War, became a premier Modernist idiom, and it found a receptive audience in postwar New Orleans. The city at the time strove to expand, with new bridges and highways, a new railroad station, buses replacing old streetcar lines, and an ambitious new Civic Center replete with International Modernism. Commercial interests were also gearing up for the future—this was the beginning of the oil boom—and they too wanted the latest look. During the 1950s and 1960s, wrote Tulane architecture professor John Klingman, "New Orleans was receiving national and even international attention for its then contemporary Modernist design."

Modernism in New Orleans had a variety of geographies. Its signature was the array of Central Business District skyscrapers erected starting in 1965, when a new technique enabled engineers to build higher by driving pilings deeper into the hard-clay suballuvial surface. Three prominent examples were the Plaza Tower (1965), designed by Leonard Spangenberg; the International Trade Mart (1965, now the World Trade Center), designed by Edward Durell Stone; and One Shell Square (1972), by Skidmore, Owings, and Merrill, still the city's tallest building at 697 feet. All were International in style, as were most other new office buildings, and together they gave the city a lofty new flat-topped skyline, save for the visually astounding Curtis and Davis–designed Louisiana Superdome (1975).

If there is one residential neighborhood where Midcentury Modern formed an integral cityscape, it's Lake Vista. Designed by the Orleans Levee District in 1936 upon manmade land, Lake Vista reflected "Garden City" concepts in its layout—diverse parcel shapes along long, curving superblocks, with centralized greenspace and amenities. After World War II, Lake Vista became an ideal place for new residential architecture, and dozens of horizontally massed, flat-roofed Modernist homes were built here, each exuding the future-leaning spirit that matched the mid-century zeitgeist of the city.

If there was one building that symbolized that spirit—and as well as its subsequent souring—it was the Rivergate Exhibition Hall. Designed by Curtis and Davis in the Expressionist brand of Modernism and situated dramatically where Canal and Poydras met the Mississippi, the great pavilion opened in 1968 in time for the city's 250th anniversary. At first, the Rivergate was a success: architects admired its dazzling freeform arches and vaulted ceilings, and the business community saw both the exhibition hall and the adjacent International Trade Mart as a sign of New Orleans reasserting itself on the world stage. By one estimate, a steady stream of bookings for floor shows, special events, and Carnival balls at the Rivergate generated $170 million during its first five years.

Yet only twenty-seven years after its celebrated opening, the Rivergate met the wrecking ball, to be replaced by a building whose design was the utter antithesis of Modernism: the retro-revival Harrah's New Orleans Casino. While architectural aficionados were outraged by the destruction of the Rivergate, many New Orleanians in the 1990s were indifferent if not glad to see it go. The local embrace of Modernism had unraveled, and in its stead came a revival of historicity and neotraditionalism.

What changed was the arc of the city's destiny. After well over a century as the largest city in the South, New Orleans saw its population begin to decline in the 1960s, as school integration triggered white flight to suburban parishes. The exodus intensified in the 1970s and '80s as the loss of the tax base and subsequent divestment exacerbated structural and social woes. Containerization, meanwhile, sapped most port jobs, and the oil bust thinned the ranks of petroleum employment. Crime soared, blight mounted, and civic spirit sank.

With a mediocre present and a bleak future, New Orleanians sensed their best days were behind them. So they turned their heads in that direction and found what they were looking for: a source of civic pride in the past, even if it needed some burnishing and selective amnesia. And what most convincingly evinced the past's power to inspire was the city's vast inventory of splendid old buildings. They told romantic stories, and their fanciful ornamentation emoted warmly of the familiar and the known. Modernism, on the other hand, seemed to do the exact opposite. In the minds of many folks, New Orleans architecture *was* historical architecture, and if a historical building was razed for a cutting-edge Modernist replacement, the loss was not mitigated; it was doubled.

Into this extraordinary turnaround arrived Postmodernism, which incorporated traditional motifs in otherwise contemporary structures and appealed to those who found Modernism to be icy and supercilious. Likewise, for residential construction, homebuyers increasingly opted for a retro-revival look, including Creole-style steep hipped roofs and Victorian turrets. Architects created pastiche designs for developers, who featured them in pattern books, making them convenient to select and efficient to build. The trend only intensified after Hurricane Katrina: a study conducted by this researcher of thousands of new homes erected after the 2005 deluge revealed that historical styles prevailed overwhelmingly, by a 14-to-1 ratio, over contemporary designs. For better or worse, a populist consensus seems to have emerged that the new New Orleans ought to look like Olde New Orleans—despite that the city had since its founding exhibited a completely different sensibility, importing new ideas, experimenting, and adapting for local use.

With that legacy in mind, and with the recent resurgence in civic confidence and outlook, it is hoped that the worldwide interest in sustainable contemporary design and urban water management—in which postdiluvian New Orleans has served as both impetus and laboratory—may once again make this city the paradigm of thoughtful urbanism displayed by French engineers when they first created "a burg...called New Orleans" three hundred years ago.

Capital of World Commerce

Cotton made New Orleans a major international port during the nineteenth century

by Robert L. Dupont, PhD

For almost a century after its founding, New Orleans languished, a sometimes-forgotten colony, an oft-resented burden on the treasury, and a difficult-to-govern amalgam of residents of questionable loyalties. At the time of the Louisiana Purchase the city had a population of approximately ten thousand and thus was ill-positioned to play a major role in the country's development. Yet within two decades of the Purchase, a confluence of factors raised the population, profile, and role of New Orleans to one of international significance. The marginal city became central to the world economy. This new status would eventually decline as new modes of international commerce took precedence, but for most of the nineteenth century and beyond, New Orleans enjoyed the spotlight as an international city—largely due to the influence of the port.

The city's path to prominence depended on the intersection of geography, politics, demography, technology, and commerce. Bienville's decision to locate New Orleans near the mouth of the Mississippi River began to pay dividends as the newly formed United States controlled the trans-Appalachian region.

OPPOSITE View of the Mississippi River levee at New Orleans, ca. 1860. *Souvenir of New Orleans.* Courtesy of The Historic New Orleans Collection.

RIGHT Plantations on the Mississippi River from Natchez to New Orleans, original by Marie Adrien Persac, 1858. A Mississippi River chart with plantations marked and four additional insets added by Joseph Aiena, 1931. Courtesy of The L. Kemper and Leila Moore Williams Founders Collection at The Historic New Orleans Collection.

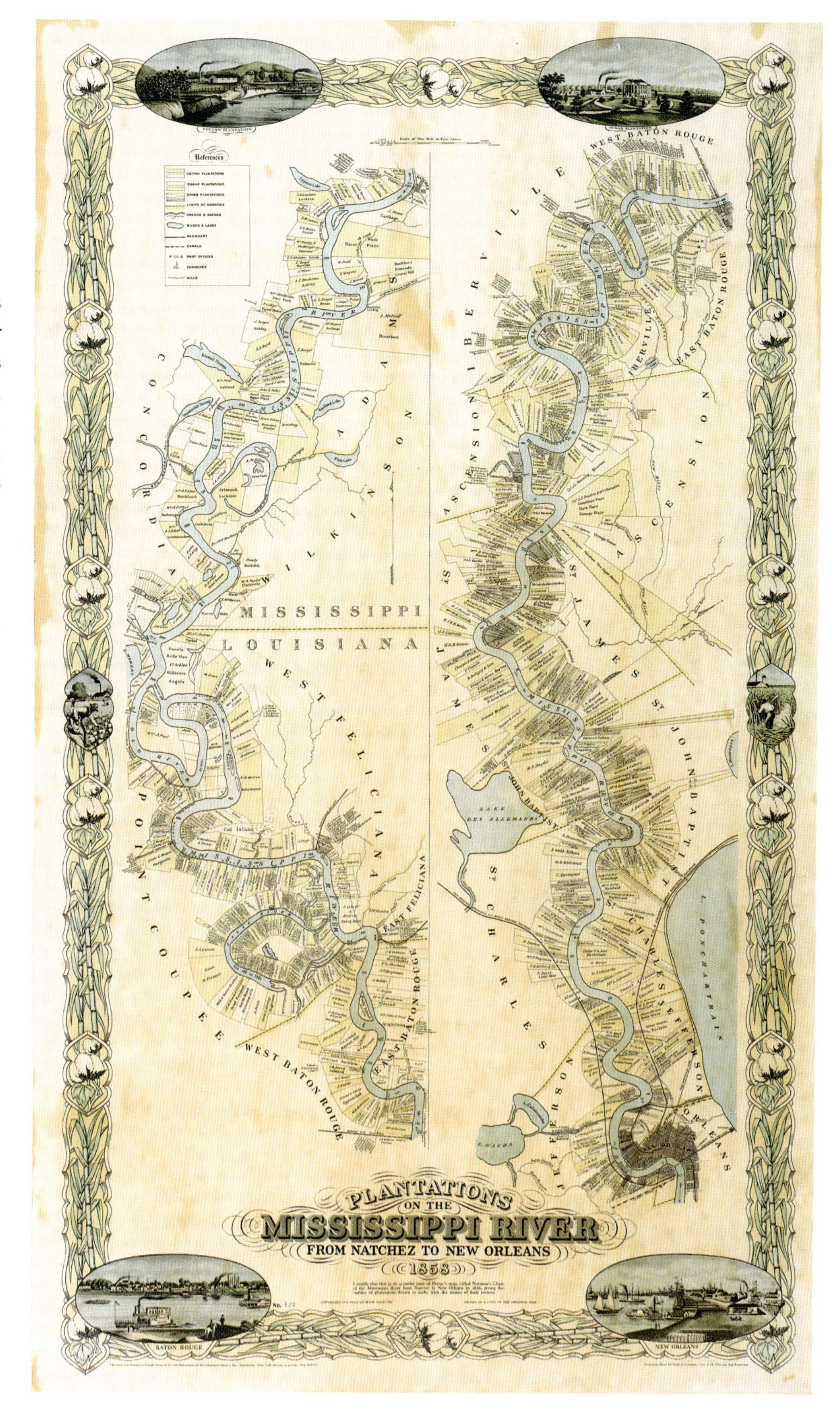

The new settlers found the trip back to the East arduous but appreciated the ease of river travel via the Ohio River into the Mississippi. In 1803, control of New Orleans passed to the Americans and provided the West with unfettered commercial opportunities. At the same time, unrest in the Caribbean contributed to a substantial influx of immigrants to the city and reinforced its multi-racial and (to the new Americans) exotic nature. For the United States, the Purchase meant an enormous expansion of U.S. lands and the acquisition of the commercial, transportational, financial, and strategic linchpin to the Mississippi Valley. The entry of New Orleans into the United States—however difficult the assimilation process—elevated the city to world status.

New Orleans was able to take advantage of its new circumstances as the result of technological changes that emerged at the start of the nineteenth century. The means to produce granulated sugar and the efficient processing of cotton boosted both local agriculture and the economy of the South. The increased traffic on the Mississippi River took advantage of steam power to combat the strong currents of the river, making the trip upstream a less difficult passage.

The portrait of the city that emerges by 1820 is complex—a polyglot, multiracial citizenry in a growing city blessed with a crucial location. The next forty years raised New Orleans from provincial to international status as one additional element is introduced—the development of the plantation economy across the southern United States. The commercial traffic to and from the Midwest was significant; the cotton shipments from the South were transformative.

During the first half of the nineteenth century, the locus of cotton production in the United States moved from the upper to the lower South even as it expanded in scope and productivity. The newer, more fertile lands in Georgia, Alabama, Mississippi, and Louisiana attracted large-scale plantations; the new plantations demanded more and more slaves. New Orleans became the ideal location for shipping cotton, but also for slave-trading, banking, financial exchanges, and insurance—in other words, both the support structure for the plantation system and the subsequent distribution of the raw material the system produced.

At the time of the Purchase, most trade to and from the port involved the U.S. Eastern Seaboard and totaled approximately $2 million. By the mid-1830s the majority of trade involved overseas ports with a product value of $54 million. Much of the increase mirrored the growth of the cotton trade. U.S. cotton production in 1800 totaled 36.5 million pounds. By 1840 that production grew to more than 670 million pounds, feeding the textile mills of the Industrial Revolution. The colonial exports of tobacco, rice, and indigo continued but were overtaken and eventually dwarfed by the sugar and cotton trades. Raw materials left the port directly to Europe or to be transshipped from the eastern United States; returning ships brought manufactured goods to the newly enriched city and hinterlands. The city's access to the Mississippi was crucial in this distribution of goods via steamboat, whose visits to New Orleans grew from twenty in 1814 to more than 1,200 in 1834. One source suggests that New Orleans was the world's fourth busiest port by the year 1840.

Throughout the 1840s, New Orleans' share of the cotton trade continued to grow. The productivity of the lower South overshadowed the Atlantic states, and shipping figures reflected the imbalance. Gulf of Mexico ports from 1845–1849 handled more than 70 percent of cotton exports. New Orleans dominated the Gulf ports with more than three-fifths of the trade. Only Mobile, Alabama, was a significant competitor but remained at only 40 percent of the New Orleans totals. Consider, also, that Europe in 1849 consumed approximately 2,500,000 bales by contemporary estimates. Thus the Gulf states filled more than 60 percent of European demand with the majority of the supply transshipped via New Orleans.

The decade of the 1850s reinforces the pattern set earlier. Domestic product of nearly 2,800,000 bales in 1850 increased to 4,300,000 ten years later. The proportion of the crop exported declined as U.S. manufacturing grew, but the mills of Europe—especially Great Britain with its estimated 21,000,000 spindles—depended on Southern plantations and New Orleans shipping. By the late 1850s, Britain received cotton from producers all over the world, but two-thirds came from the American South—and most of that came through New Orleans. At no other time in its history would the Crescent City play such a significant economic role in the world economy.

Governments from Europe and South America established consulates in New Orleans to represent their citizens and protect commercial interests. The new wealth generated by commerce attracted artists and performers as well as speculators and investors. Population grew rapidly. From a base of slightly more than 27,000 in 1820, the 1830 figures showed an increase of nearly 70 percent. The following decade's growth was even more dramatic—from 46,082 in 1830 to more than 102,000 in 1840, placing the city as the third largest in the United States. By the start of the Civil War, the New Orleans population ranked sixth in the country with a population of more than 168,000, nearly ten times the municipal population of 1810.

BELOW Workers push bales of cotton into high density compress at the Port of New Orleans, February 1917. Photo by Nancy Ewing Minor. Courtesy of The Charles L. Franck Studio Collection at The Historic New Orleans Collection.

A favorable location and trade from the neighboring Southern states were not sufficient to fulfill the most ambitious of the city's plans. The Eastern Seaboard cities, notably New York, contended for commercial supremacy by attracting the growing trade of the Midwest via the Great Lakes, rivers, canals—especially the Erie Canal—and, eventually, railroads. The population base of the lower Mississippi Valley was meager compared to the Northeast, and imports failed to reach the level necessary to sustain a profitable two-way trade with Europe. These potential weaknesses in the city's relative position did not become apparent until the latter part of the nineteenth century and the destruction wrought by the Civil War.

The portrait of the city that emerges by 1820 is complex—a polyglot, multiracial citizenry in a growing metropolis blessed with a crucial location.

The city's strategic location and affluence in the first half of the nineteenth century made New Orleans a key target in the Civil War. In April 1862, Union forces occupied New Orleans and deprived the Confederacy of the city's trade profits and international connections. In subsequent years, New Orleans recovered from the war, population growth resumed, and the port remained active. Federal investments in navigation, particularly the constructions of the Eads jetties at the mouth of the Mississippi River, contributed to the recovery, and tonnage eventually exceeded pre-Civil War levels. But the relative importance of the city in the world economy began a slow decline. Rates of growth did not match the rapidly industrializing parts of the United States, and immigration lagged. By 1890, New Orleans was no longer listed among the top ten cities in the United States by population.

The New Orleans port continued to depend heavily upon cotton shipments; however, the American South lost market share to new producers in Egypt, India, Turkey, and Australia. Population shifts in the United States diverted business from New Orleans, and the rapid development of the country's railroads favored other urban areas. New Orleans retained a significant commercial presence, and the port handled a portion of the bulk goods from the Midwest, such as grain and coal. Unfortunately, the commercial opportunities exceeded the capacity of the port's infrastructure. As commerce moved toward the twentieth century, the port of New Orleans remained firmly in the nineteenth.

Lack of progress along the river had roots in the political system. The New Orleans City Council exercised control over the docks but lacked the financial resources to initiate improvements. The Council contracted the port operations to private business, but in the 1880s and 1890s facilities continued to lag the competition. In 1896, the Louisiana Legislature, in cooperation with business and political interests in New Orleans, established a public board to oversee the docks and expanded the port's boundaries to include adjacent parishes. The legislation was consistent with the national progressive movement, which sought to de-politicize important governmental functions, while at the same time entrusting those functions to the public sphere. Business interests dominated such local boards, although strong political organizations could control operations through influence on the appointment process.

The new board faced a range of problems. Much of the port resembled what had been in place for decades; improvements had been haphazard and ad hoc. In addition, new modes of transportation demanded integration with incoming cargo. In spite of natural barriers, the railroad expansion came to New Orleans, and the various lines competed for space along the river. For decades, the city council controlled the allocation of port access and was reluctant to give up that power. The new governing entity, the Dock Board, found its agenda full, tasked with the allocation of wharf space, safety, cargo storage, railroad access, and marketing—in other words, the preservation of the port's market share.

ABOVE Workers offload bananas from a conveyor belt at the wharf, ca. 1930. Photo by Nancy Ewing Minor. Courtesy of The Charles L. Franck Studio Collection at The Historic New Orleans Collection.

In 1901, the last of the private contracts expired and port operations passed entirely into the hands of the Dock Board. Court cases clarified the Board's powers and reduced the role of the city council. Under the ambitious leadership of Hugh McCloskey, members pledged to modernize the port and its operations. Initial actions were mundane; the Board promulgated rules to prevent dumping of rubbish into the river and enforced fire safety regulations. Larger issues, though, could not be ignored. The Board began an ambitious construction program to provide permanent, covered spaces for cargo to replace temporary sheds. Solid wharves took the place of flimsy piers and posts. The Board purchased a tug to be converted into a fire-fighting vessel.

Port finances provided another challenge. The Board reduced port fees to attract business, improved collections, and invested the new revenue into improvement projects. With the Legislature's cooperation, the Board pledged revenue toward $2,000,000 in bonds (approximately $50,000,000 in 2015 dollars) for new construction. The Board responded to regional needs for export facilities that served cotton and lumber interests; import facilities received special attention which included coffee and bananas. As early as 1903, 70 percent of port tonnage utilized public wharves.

Dock Board actions alone could not solve the transportation conflicts. Private railroad interest clamored for access to the docks and competitive advantage. To bring order to the river front, the New Orleans City Council established the New Orleans Public Belt Railroad, a publicly owned and operated rail line that traversed the entirety of the port and assumed responsibility for moving freight without regard to any one railroad or other. The effect upon port business was immediate: cargo moved efficiently, reducing overhead and port charges. By 1915, Mayor Martin Behrman bragged to his counterparts across the nation of the city's success in improving the port and the movement of goods.

The Dock Board considered marketing an important function, and members attempted to enhance business through advertising, pamphlets, and organizing trade associations with upriver colleagues. One such effort reminded businesses of the port's proximity to the Panama Canal, which began construction in 1903. The city's commercial leadership hoped for a future in which Canal trade would be focused on New Orleans. As the nation anticipated completion of the Canal, the city's political leadership lobbied to become the site of an exposition that would mark the event. An advertising campaign named New Orleans the "logical point" for the celebration, but the Congress chose San Francisco instead. Several organizers of the New Orleans effort went on to found a shipping line to serve the South American market, but the line failed within six months. Only the Pan-American Life Insurance Group, founded in 1911, provides a glimpse into the energy expended trying to establish a more robust international presence for the city and its port facilities.

Underlying economic and demographic conditions prevented New Orleans from improving its share of national trade. Cities of the East and Midwest assimilated millions of immigrants, who provided labor for the post-Civil War industrial expansion. New Orleans had neither the industrial nor population base to compete. In addition, the city's river location on somewhat questionable alluvial land was not favorable to large-scale railroad and distribution infrastructures. Cotton production eventually declined, although new products such as petroleum boosted port business. At the beginning of the twenty-first century, the various ports of southern Louisiana handled hundreds of millions of tons of cargo; New Orleans alone accounted for more than sixty-eight million tons. These impressive statistics no longer establish the Crescent City among the world's most significant locations, but New Orleans retains its historical status as an international city due to the historical and ongoing connections to the world provided by the port.

World Expositions

ABOVE 1884 World's Industrial and Cotton Centennial Exposition. Illustration by Joseph Eppler. *Puck*, December 1884. Courtesy of The Historic New Orleans Collection.

1884 World's Industrial and Cotton Centennial Exposition

The completion of the Eads' jetties at the mouth of the Mississippi River in 1876 prompted an increase in the port's grain trade of more than 100 percent in just two years, levels of commerce not seen since before the Civil War. New Orleans was open for business and wanted the world to know it. So in December 1884, the World's Industrial and Cotton Centennial Exposition opened in the burgeoning Uptown area between the river and the grand mansions of St. Charles Avenue, then known as Upper City Park. Once the site of the Boré sugar plantation, the land was used in 1866 as the staging area for the Ninth Cavalry, the African-American "Buffalo Soldiers." Even though the expo was not completed on schedule, by all accounts it was impressive. The Main Building, designed by Gustav M. Torgerson, included towers reminiscent of the Louvre and a music hall in its center that seated eleven thousand. Nearly all the states and more than fifteen countries were represented, almost a third of them from Central and South America. Mexico's hall, the Alhambra Palace, seemed to outshine the rest. Unfortunately, due to mismanagement and budget woes, the exposition was an economic failure, and all that remains is an iron ore rock from the Alabama exhibit. In 1886 the grounds were renamed Audubon Park, and in 1894 the city turned to John Charles Olmsted, whose family's firm was responsible for New York's Central Park, to design what has become one of New Orleans' most popular public spaces, home to the Audubon Zoo, riding stables, a golf course, tennis courts, and a swimming pool.

ABOVE Poster from 1984 World's Fair Canal Street Gate, ca. 1983. Louisiana World Exposition. Courtesy of The Historic New Orleans Collection.

1984 Louisiana World Exposition

The crowds were smaller than expected, the national media panned it, and the whole thing ended in bankruptcy, but the impact of the 1984 World's Fair on New Orleans is indisputable. Indeed, few events have so definitively shaped the city's landscape. Organizers of the Fair, which opened in May 1984, promised an extravaganza that would attract visitors from around the globe, sending a powerful message that New Orleans was ready for the twenty-first century. Instead, due to competition from other expositions, tepid support from the federal government, and internal bickering, the nation largely ignored the festivities. But for New Orleanians, the World's Fair was an unforgettable party. In the striking amphitheater designed by Frank Gehry, they attended concerts by Willie Nelson and Julio Iglesias, heard Dick Cavett and Bob Hope tell jokes, and watched themselves broadcast live on the *David Letterman Show*. Water slides, a German beer hall, raucous nightclubs, and international pavilions delivered the world to the Crescent City. A gondola carried passengers across the river, and a monorail carried them around the fair grounds. And when it was over, the structures built for the various spectacles were converted into the Riverwalk Mall, the Ernest N. Morial Convention Center, and the apartment buildings that became cornerstones of the Warehouse District neighborhood. When the organizers announced that the Fair would close, New Orleanians rushed to buy souvenirs that still grace the shelves of offices and family homes, reminders of a spectacle that continues to reverberate in the city's memory.

Big-Time City

The transformation of Poydras Street marked a turning point for the city in the 1970s

by Jack Davis

Even at the beginning of 1970, Poydras Street was starting to launch. Running 1.2 miles from old riverfront warehouses to the still-new Interstate 10 over Claiborne Avenue, it was about to become the most arresting physical manifestation of one of the most dramatic decades in New Orleans history. The transformation would happen quickly and would stop abruptly not long after the decade's end. A booming oil industry would drive the construction, down Poydras, of more than a dozen Houston-class international-style corporate office towers—along with hotels and a new federal courthouse—before the bust came in the mid-1980s.

But the 1970s marked more than this building boom. The decade produced dramatic changes in nearly all aspects of New Orleans life. It locked in place the main features of an urban landscape that wouldn't remake itself again so thoroughly until after Hurricane Katrina. The changes jolted a second-tier city lagging behind the metro leaders of the New South into a more prominent role in the global economy and culture. A surprisingly vibrant economy supported the region's optimism that the city was regaining lost stature, that an active port and booming oilpatch would make big new things possible. State and local officials believed in ambitious economic-development plans. The physical landscape—new office buildings and hotels erected faster and higher than ever before, old neighborhoods and historic landmarks treated with a new reverence—created a geographic pattern that would remain until well into the twenty-first century.

Social and political worlds were also becoming startlingly different from the previous decade, triggering more changes in the decades to come. The most important driver, which ran through every architectural commission, brass-band parade, and menu, was the change in race relations, revolutionized in large part by a new mayor who came to City Hall in 1970 determined to integrate business, society, and culture. Mayor Moon Landrieu personally accelerated the trajectory of the local civil rights movement that would get New Orleans closer to social justice. Landrieu's election in turn had been propelled by the Voting Rights Act of 1965, which made black voters a powerful force in local government. Throughout the 1970s, New Orleans was a city successfully shaking off racial handicaps, nurturing a conviction that its economic future was big, taking pride in the character of its characters, and expressing an intense chauvinism about its food, music, and buildings. This in turn prompted confidence that tourism would become another major industry: if we like ourselves so much, then surely others will.

The year 1970 saw the first Jazz & Heritage Festival organized by producer George Wein. He had declined a 1962 invitation to stage a music festival because of the city's persistent segregation. The push toward integration now appealed to him. After two successful launch years at Congo Square, Wein's locally managed fest moved to the Fair Grounds racetrack infield, where it has been growing and cultivating local talent ever since.

Also in 1970, the city's first restaurant critic, University of New Orleans history professor Richard Collin, published his *Underground Gourmet* guidebook and began a provocative weekly column in *The States-Item*. His ten years in that role unlocked a vibrant community conversation about food, chefs, and cooking that continues in a city where food is ever more important and everyone is a critic.

Ole Miss quarterback Archie Manning was chosen most valuable player of the 1970 Sugar Bowl game in New Orleans and joined the Saints in 1971. He stayed with the team into the 1982 season, braving losing seasons and sacks with such grace and skill that he cemented the Saints as the unifying factor it would become in New Orleans social life, able to bring fans across racial lines. The 1970s were the Archie decade.

In 1971, the influential book series *New Orleans Architecture*, by the Friends of the Cabildo, began its galvanizing eight-volume inventory of endangered neighborhoods and buildings, with the first six books

OPPOSITE The Louisiana Superdome under construction. Photo by David M. Kleck. Courtesy of Curtis & Davis Office Records, Southeastern Architectural Archive, Special Collections Division, Tulane University Libraries.

published in nine years. Great scholarship and advocacy fortified the preservation movement. City Hall under Mayor Landrieu was often receptive to the preservationists and created historic districts and "growth management" policies that saved much of the city's physical character even as it welcomed developers.

The early 1970s showed another New Orleans asset—capable news media. There were two substantive daily papers, including the afternoon *States-Item*, which had just been liberated from the control of its bigger brother *The Times-Picayune* and demonstrated its independence right up until 1980, when the papers were merged. At least two TV stations competed with quality news, including political scoops and investigations. And alternative weekly newspapers—*The Vieux Carré Courier* and the 1972 arrival *Figaro*—kept the rest of the media challenged and under scrutiny.

In 1970, the view up Poydras from the top of the thirty-three-story International Trade Mart, opened three years earlier at the foot of the street, was remarkable. The narrow four-lane portion near the river, long a utilitarian home to port-service businesses, had been widened to match the newer stretch beyond as it approached the interstate highway

The changes jolted a second-tier city lagging behind the metro leaders of the New South into a more prominent role in the global economy and culture.

constructed in the late 1960s. The widening was conceived in the early twentieth century to help truck movement for the port. But that need seemed less pressing now. Poydras was seen after World War II as a key link to a Riverfront Expressway that would cross in front of the French Quarter as part of a region-wide network of big, fast highways. In the mid-1960s, under Mayor Victor Schiro, the street was expanded from 74 feet near the river end to 134 feet. But in 1969, the Riverfront Expressway was abruptly cancelled by the new Richard Nixon administration, which accepted preservationists' warnings that the project would harm the French Quarter. And Poydras received a new mission. Schiro came to see it as a corridor of new corporate construction: "The Park Avenue of the South." In the end, the street's uniform use and design—a double row of tall new buildings used mostly by oil companies—almost looked planned. But it was largely luck.

The view from the top of the International Trade Mart also revealed an abundance of neglected, century-old commercial buildings. With quality architecture and quality construction, these were the kind of historic streetscapes that would later be put into protected historic-preservation districts in other neighborhoods. But, in this view, they were seen as raw land where zoning allowed much taller structures. The blocks of nineteenth-century, two-to four-story buildings two or three streets removed from Poydras itself were prime for demolition to create surface parking—which ran rampant until Landrieu's worried City Hall staff put a moratorium on business-district demolitions, and then put preservation restrictions in place in the mid-1970s.

The widened and landscaped Poydras had made a step in the direction toward its future grandeur by serving as a more prestigious approach to the two key buildings where Poydras and Canal Streets came together near the riverfront—the 1967 International Trade Mart and its neighbor, the swooping 1968 Rivergate Exhibition Hall, with its dominant roof rising in an eye-catching curve. But the longer vista up Poydras at the beginning of 1970 featured no new construction. The only modern structure on the horizon, in fact, was off in the distance, on Loyola Avenue blocks up from Poydras, near the Pontchartrain Expressway and the approach to the Mississippi River Bridge that had been built in the 1950s. The forty-five-story Plaza Tower building had opened in 1968 on a bet that Loyola would become the boulevard of corporate architecture. But two forces not yet visible on the streets downtown would make Poydras happen.

First, the price of oil would increase over the decade, from $3.39 a barrel in 1970 to $37.42 or higher in 1980. That justified more exploration and production, much of it enabled by new technologies that facilitated wells in wetlands and in deep water offshore. Louisianans developed skills that served the big companies, and the big companies believed that New Orleans would be a convenient and entertaining regional headquarters.

Second, the Superdome would rise out of the ground. Already approved by Louisiana voters in a 1966 constitutional amendment that created a state-sponsored Superdome Commission, the massive but almost graceful Superdome would outsize rival Houston's Astrodome. Construction began in 1971 on the building that would become New Orleans' chief icon into the twenty-first century.

Long discussed in tandem with a desire for a professional football franchise for New Orleans, the idea of a covered stadium made a news splash in the last days of the 1965 Democratic primary for mayor, when Vic Schiro, seeking his second full term against a tough competitor, City Councilman James E. Fitzmorris Jr., announced a plan. He proposed an all-weather stadium big enough for two football fields and accommodating sixty thousand people, with parking for twenty thousand cars on a donated hundred-acre site in the Lake Forest section of eastern New Orleans. Construction would be contingent on landing a pro football team. While Schiro's narrow November victory may have been helped more by his steady performance during Hurricane Betsy two months earlier, he credited his stadium plan for part of his 3,319-vote margin over Fitzmorris.

The Superdome idea had many parents. Schiro and his careful biographer, Edward F. Haas, argued that this mayor originated it. And David Dixon, the effective and tireless promoter and catalyst behind both the Superdome and the football team, often regarded as the inventor of the stadium, said later that Schiro's campaign announcement was "where we got our start." It was a fast start, indeed. Governor John McKeithen endorsed the idea at the end of 1965 and pledged to build a great dome before he left office, perhaps counting on a second term that would carry him to 1972. He appointed finance and site-selection committees and pushed the statewide constitutional amendment vote that would bring state management and a hotel tax to pay for it.

On November 1, 1966, the National Football League awarded a New Orleans a franchise—with some effective leverage from the powerful Louisiana congressional delegation, which had helped the NFL obtain an exemption from antitrust regulation. The new Saints played their first regular season game in September 1967 at Tulane's capacious stadium, and bided the years until the opening of the Superdome.

A critical decision had been where to put it. Eastern New Orleans remained in consideration, and some advocated the lakefront or East

Jefferson. But support emerged quickly for a location in downtown New Orleans—supported by Governor McKeithen, Dave Dixon, the Chamber of Commerce, and, importantly, by City Councilman-At-Large Moon Landrieu. Landrieu was a champion of locating economic assets and investment in the core areas of the city. He believed strongly in having the stadium downtown and helped arrange for the specific location, on mostly abandoned railroad company property. For the good of the city, Landrieu said in a recent interview, "I was determined to put it downtown." As chairman of the Superdome Commission, he pushed the project along, and as mayor he strongly influenced the Dome's opening and management. Downtown stadiums, with their ability to stimulate nearby real estate development and to bring in people from the suburbs and other cities, are now regarded as good planning and the norm for most major sports teams.

This stadium, with a durable and singular design by architect Nathaniel C. Curtis, has performed those services over four decades and has constantly been refreshed, particularly in the year after Katrina. Its opening followed significant cost overruns—from $36 million in the early sales pitches to $163 million—as well construction delays. The NFL committed to playing the January 1975 Super Bowl IX there but had to move the game to Tulane, because the Dome wasn't ready. Opening day was August 3, 1975.

By then, Poydras Street high-rises had been sprouting. In 1972, Joseph C. Canizaro, a young independent Mississippi-born developer, opened the Lykes Center. And that year Shell Oil Company moved into what is still the city's tallest building, One Shell Square; it is almost identical to Shell's Houston headquarters, One Shell Plaza, which opened the previous year. (Bill Rushton, tough-minded architecture critic for the weekly *Courier*, sized up the new Poydras style by labeling the New Orleans building "One Square Shell.")

Local developers made space available for Texaco, Mobil, Amoco, Exxon, Gulf, Louisiana Land and Exploration, Freeport-McMoRan—most of which moved out of smaller, older quarters elsewhere in the Central Business District. Three of the Poydras Street towers went up directly across from the Dome. Two of the companies, Amoco and Mobil, were in the development that abutted the Dome, called Poydras Plaza, which also offered a Hyatt Regency Hotel and a headquarters for Entergy. At the river end of Poydras, the International Rivercenter proposed a Hilton Hotel and six other office and residential towers on twenty-three acres. Nearby, at the foot of Canal Street, was Canizaro's Canal Place project, an office tower married to a shopping mall and hotel.

And then it all stopped. The price of oil dropped after 1980, kept sliding, and crashed dramatically in 1986, when Saudi Arabia put new supplies of crude on the market. It was "the worst recession to hit the Pelican State in modern times," *The New Orleans Advocate* wrote in 2015. Businesses and banks closed, subdivisions were halted, Louisiana oil production virtually stopped, and the state's unemployment rate became the highest in the country. There were doubts about whether oil reserves in the Gulf were still worth going after. Oil companies started to consolidate and leave town, back to their headquarters cities elsewhere, including Houston.

The oil companies' loyalty to New Orleans was also undermined by the perception by some oil executives that New Orleans carnival organizations and country clubs didn't welcome them, the so-called "Boston Club mentality," and that Uptown was either too snooty or dangerous for their families. The last Poydras oil buildings in the developers' pipeline were completed in the mid-1980s. Canizaro was last, in 1986, with the expensively finished Louisiana Land and Exploration building, which featured two large heroic sculptures by Enrique Alferez flanking the doors.

The exuberance of the 1970s led to an unfortunate coda—a World's Fair in 1984. The Fair grew from civic confidence built during the oil surge, the sense that—with the Dome and the Saints and integration—New Orleans could compete on the world stage for tourism and big events. It was conceived as a venture in urban renewal of key, underpriced, and underutilized land, and ultimately the fair served that purpose. But many of the factors that led to the oil bust and the state recession overhung its planning and execution. With construction beginning in 1981 on an eighty-two-acre riverfront site between the International Rivercenter and the Mississippi River Bridge, the World's Fair opened late and incomplete. It proved to be underfinanced and underattended, with a 7.3-million-person gate against a projected 12 million, and filed for bankruptcy protection to stay open through its last day, November 11, 1984.

The Fair's theme, "World of Rivers: Fresh Water as a Source of Life," was in many ways an aesthetic success, thanks to Frank Gehry's riverfront amphitheater, postmodern architect Charles Moore's "Wonderwall" of fancy and surprise snaking through the site, and gondolas crossing high over the Mississippi River on a wire (and perhaps on a prayer: *The Times-Picayune* reported that Archbishop Philip Hannan's gondola got stuck over the water for fifteen minutes after he blessed it on its opening). There was a crush of people on the first day, with 83,000 through the gates, but on the second day, only 30,000 came. Locals were able to come back for the entertainment and food, building up the city's talents at putting on a show for themselves and visitors. But the out-of-towners needed for success stayed away. The overall effect was of a hot-season outdoors trade show, albeit one with a NASA space shuttle and Vatican paintings on view.

While it proved that the economic optimism of the 1970s was over, the fair did leave a legacy, in many ways positive. Its main exhibition hall was converted to be the New Orleans Convention Center, the first stage of the Ernest N. Morial Convention Center that allows the city to compete for large conferences. Many historic industrial and commercial buildings in the surrounding area, later known as the "Warehouse District," became converted to residences, art galleries, restaurants—a new and now vital neighborhood. It provided a template for rehabilitating old commercial buildings in such neighborhoods as Bywater and Marigny, and in the Central Business District itself after the banks closed down. At the same time, the success of the Convention Center undercut the mission of the existing exhibition hall; the 1968 Rivergate ultimately was demolished in 1995 to give its footprint to Harrah's New Orleans Casino, the state's only land-based casino and another major aspect of the new entertainment-tourism dominance.

This is where the Poydras boom left the city, with enough office space to last decades. Even now, Poydras corporate buildings are being occupied by hotels—Loews for Lykes, Hyatt House for Mobil—serving as evidence of the city's economic shift to heavier dependence on tourism and entertainment.

The 1970s made a physical New Orleans that would survive largely unchanged until 2005. The city would begin a recession and spiritual decline in the 1980s that would last through the century and beyond—until the shock of Hurricane Katrina re-energized its people, economy, and culture once more.

Part III:

CONFLICT AND FREEDOM

Jordan Noble

"At eight o'clock [p.m.] when the fog became particularly heavy, it was this boy's drum, rattling away in the thick of battle, 'in the hottest hell of fire,' that helped to serve as one of the guideposts for the fierce battling American troops."

Marcus Christian, *Negro Soldiers in the Battle of New Orleans.*

Jordan Noble was the first famous New Orleans drummer. As a fourteen-year-old boy, he joined the Seventh Regiment of the US Army under the command of General Andrew Jackson. When Jackson's troops defeated the invading British forces in the Battle of New Orleans on January 8, 1815, Jordan's drumbeat was more than just entertainment. And though the battle took place after the official ending of hostilities, the victory served as a rallying point for Americans, especially the residents of New Orleans, who had only joined the United States three years earlier.

Born into slavery in Georgia, Jordan was sold to Lieutenant John Noble of the Seventh Regiment on June 2, 1814, and joined Lieutenant Noble on the battlefield. Jackson's camp included two bands who entertained the troops. Drummers communicated orders for food and ammunition, awakened troops, and set the tempo and direction of marches. According to author Jerry Brock, "At times of engagement drummers would help rally the troops, push their adrenaline level, raise their spirits and focus their thoughts of purpose and reason as they prepared to kill or be killed. Then later they'd beat the somber, muted and profound death rattle of the funeral march when burying the dead. This was heavy lifting for anyone—much less a 14-year-old and perhaps more than a teenaged drummer boy could fully comprehend."

ABOVE Jordan Noble in 1887. Courtesy of The Historic New Orleans Collection.

Noble later served under Jackson in the Florida War in 1836 and was the drummer for the Washington Artillery during the Mexican War. He was among the contingent of free colored veterans who participated in the "Glorious 8th" ceremonies in 1851, the first time African Americans were invited to join the annual celebration of the Battle of New Orleans. Noble formed his own tradition—a New Year's salute by his band to the chief officers of the city, the military, and the press. According to historian Freddi Williams Evans, the popular performances of military marching cadence would influence the evolution of jazz.

In 1861 Noble helped form the Native Guards, a regiment of approximately fifteen hundred free colored soldiers, to help defend New Orleans against Union troops. Noble had attended several national conferences advocating for equal rights, and historians continue to debate the motivations of the Native Guards, who dissolved after federal troops took control of the city in April 1962. In July 1863, Noble organized a command of black soldiers to serve the Union.

Noble remained a prominent musician in the city, performing at the 1884 World's Industrial and Cotton Centennial Exposition in New Orleans, as well as in the funeral procession of President James Garfield. Noble died in 1890. He is buried in St. Louis Cemetery No. 2, Square 3.

WM. ROY, Commander. J. H. WRIGHT, Quartermaster. E. E. ADAMS, Adjutant.

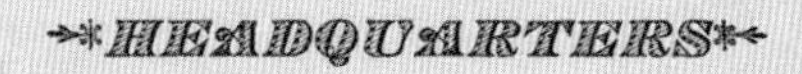

Jos. A. Mower Post No. 1,

G. A. R., DEPARTMENT OF LOUISIANA.

New Orleans, June 4th, 1880.

To all Old Soldiers and the Public generally:

THIS IS TO CERTIFY THAT THE BEARER,

JORDAN B. NOBLE,

is a veteran of 1812-15; 1836, Florida War; 1846, Mexican War, and was a Captain in the Seventh La. Vols., Union, raised for the defense of New Orleans in 1863. The "long-roll" beaten by him called the American soldiers to arms on the approach of the British in December, 1814, and amid the din of that memorable conflict on the plains of Chalmette, January 8, 1815, the rattle of his drum was heard. He followed the flag of his country through the everglades of Florida, in Gen. P. F. Smith's Brigade, and over the cactus-crowned hills of Mexico, in the ranks of the far-famed Washington Artillery, where the beating of his drum first awoke the echoes, where now rest in eternal bivouac fifteen thousand Union soldiers.

This aged veteran of many wars desires to support himself in his old age by giving "field music" entertainments in which his historic drum, which he has always retained, will be used. We ask the "boys" everywhere to be good to the old man, and help him along. He is an upright, worthy old gentleman, and will not attempt to BEAT *anything but his drum.*

Given by order of the Post this Fourth day of June, A. D. 1880.

WM. ROY, ***Post Commander.***

E. E. ADAMS, ***Post Adjutant.***

New Orleans, April 27, 1880.

We, the undersigned, recommend JORDAN B. NOBLE, Gen'l Jackson's Drummer, to all persons as a worthy, upright and honest man and one that has done good service in the Wars of 1812, ***Battle of New Orleans,*** 1815, ***Florida,*** 1836, ***and Mexico,*** 1846, ***as a Drummer.***

Ex-Governor LOUIS A, WILTZ,
General JNO. L. LEWIS,
Commodore WM. D. HUNTER,
J. N. LAVILLEBEUVRE,
Colonel A. W. HYATT,
Colonel J. B. WALTON
GEO. NICHOLSON,
THEO. A. JAMES,
W. L. McMILLAN,
Honorable ROBERT C. DAVEY,
L. ADAMS,
General A. S. BADGER,
Ex-Governor BENJ. F. FLANDERS,
GEN. THOS. C. ANDERSON.

ABOVE This certificate, dated June 4, 1880, from the Grand Army of the Republic, Department of Louisiana, Joseph A. Mower Post No. 1, proclaims Noble to be a "worthy, upright and honest man who has done good service." The post asks the "boys" to treat "this aged veteran" with kindness and to help him as he attempts to support himself by giving "field entertainments" using his historic drum. Courtesy of The Historic New Orleans Collection.

ABOVE
Official presidential portrait of Thomas Jefferson by Rembrandt Peale, 1800. Courtesy of White House Historical Association Digital Library.

Portrait of Napoleon Bonaparte. *Head of Emperor Napoleon* by Jacques Louis David. Courtesy of Muse Beaux.

Portrait of Le Général Toussaint L'Ouverture. Artist unknown. Courtesy of New York Public Library.

"Louisiana is Ours!"

An international crisis led to the Louisiana Purchase

by Jon Kukla, PhD

"Louisiana is ours!" Up and down the eastern seaboard in May 1804, orators raised a jubilee of rhetoric for the one-year anniversary of the Louisiana Purchase. Dr. David Ramsay's "Oration on the Cession of Louisiana" in Charleston, South Carolina, was typical. Except for independence and the Constitution, Ramsay proclaimed, "the acquisition of Louisiana [was] the greatest political blessing ever conferred on these states." One hundred fifty years later, historian Bernard DeVoto expanded Ramsay's comparison: "No event in all American history, not the Civil War, nor the Declaration of Independence, nor even the signing of the Constitution was more important."

The international crisis that culminated in the Louisiana Purchase of 1803 made New Orleans the focal point of geopolitical decisions that transformed the history of North America and shaped the contours of today's world. Napoleon Bonaparte, King Carlos IV of Spain, President Thomas Jefferson, and their diplomatic representatives were the most prominent of the fateful decision-makers. Less visible, perhaps, were thousands of ordinary American men and women who made the decision to move their families across the Appalachian Mountains into the valley of the Ohio River, the major eastern tributary of the

Mississippi. Patterns of frontier settlements created the stage upon which world leaders acted.

France founded the Louisiana Territory in 1682 and governed it from New Orleans until the 1760s, when Louis XV gave the colony to his Spanish Bourbon cousins as compensation for the loss of Florida and Caribbean islands to Great Britain in the French and Indian War. Carlos III of Spain valued Louisiana chiefly as a vast wilderness buffer that he could use to keep aggressive Anglo-Americans away from the gold and silver mines of Mexico, which comprised half the annual export trade of the entire Spanish empire. Seen from Madrid, settlement and population growth in Louisiana were secondary concerns—until after the American Revolution. In 1775, about 150 English settlers had followed Daniel Boone into Kentucky, but once the war ended, their numbers grew rapidly. Kentucky and Louisiana each had about 30,000 European residents in 1784. By 1800, Louisiana had 70,000 residents, compared to 326,000 in Kentucky and Tennessee alone. The docks, warehouses, and merchants of New Orleans played a vital role in the transportation of agricultural exports upon which the frontier economy depended.

At first, American settlers accepted Spanish control of New Orleans as a temporary annoyance. As their numbers grew, however, Patrick Henry of Virginia spoke for many frontier families when he said, in 1788, that he would "rather part with the confederation than relinquish the navigation of the Mississippi." Within a few years President Jefferson contended that "there is on the globe one single spot, the possessor of which is our natural and habitual enemy. It is New Orleans, through which the produce of three-eighths of our territory must pass to market."

Against a background of separatist intrigue in the Ohio Valley, Thomas Pinckney in 1795 negotiated a treaty with Spain assuring American access to the Mississippi and a "right of deposit" at or near New Orleans. The right of deposit enabled Americans to transfer cargo from river-going vessels, such as barges or bateaux, to ocean-going ships. No sooner was the ink dry on the treaty, however, than America and Spain were caught in the clash between Great Britain and France in the Napoleonic Wars.

Soon after becoming first consul in 1799, Napoleon pressed to regain Louisiana by a secret treaty with Spain. He planned to recapture the sugar island of Saint-Domingue (now Haiti) and supply it with provisions from Louisiana. While Napoleon's troops invaded Saint-Domingue, in New Orleans the Spanish intendant, Juan Ventura Morales, ignited a serious clash with the United States. In October 1802, he revoked the American right of deposit in violation of Pinckney's Treaty. It seemed too senseless to be true. Reasonable men assumed it was simply a blunder by the resident tax collector in New Orleans.

In fact, the fateful order to close the port of New Orleans to Americans came directly and secretly from the royal court. While Carlos IV spent his time hunting and tinkering with clocks, statecraft fell to his queen and her former lover, Manuel de Godoy. Annoyed that Spain had been pressured to return Louisiana to France, they thought that closing the port of New Orleans would tweak the Americans and embarrass Napoleon. Instead, thousands of Kentucky militiamen made ready to march on New Orleans while President Thomas Jefferson dispatched James Monroe to Paris with authorization to buy New Orleans.

Early in 1802, Napoleon had sent his brother-in-law, Charles Victor Emmanuel Leclerc, and 60,000 troops to recapture Saint-Domingue from rebel leader and former slave Toussaint L'Ouverture. The expedition was a dismal failure. By October—when Morales was closing the port of New Orleans—General Leclerc, 54,000 troops, and the French dream of a revived Caribbean empire were all dead. News reached Napoleon early in 1803, and he exploded: "Damn sugar! Damn coffee! Damn colonies!"

That April, Monroe joined Robert Livingston in Paris, and they approached Charles Maurice de Talleyrand about buying New Orleans. Jefferson had authorized them to offer as much as twelve million dollars for the city and its environs—the area on the east bank of the Mississippi then known as the Isle of Orleans. To their surprise, Talleyrand wondered aloud what they might pay for the entire territory of Louisiana. Negotiations ensued, and by early May the Americans had a treaty with Napoleon. The price for more than doubling the size of the United States was eighty million francs, or fifty million dollars, financed by Dutch bankers at six percent for twenty years, so that Napoleon could get his money immediately and resume his war with Great Britain and its allies.

The French still refer to the transaction as the Sale of Louisiana, but to Americans it was the Purchase, because no territorial acquisition before or since did more to set the course of American history. The Mississippi and its western tributaries alone drain one million square miles. International negotiations, completed in 1819, refined the boundary between American and Spanish territories, settled the area of the Louisiana Purchase at 883,072 square miles, and surrendered the Gulf Coast of Mississippi, Alabama, and Florida to the United States. When the Dutch loans were repaid, the nation's overall expenditures for the Louisiana Purchase totaled $23,527,872.57. Americans generally tally the cost at about four cents an acre. The inhabitants of Louisiana might have reckoned their price at eleven sous a head for every man, woman, and child in the territory.

While Jefferson regarded the purchase of Louisiana as "an act done for [the nation's] great good," he also felt it was "a thing beyond the Constitution." Accordingly, on July 16, 1803, Jefferson informed his cabinet that "they will be obliged to ask from the people an amendment to the Constitution." In the end, however, Treasury Secretary Albert Gallatin wrote a memorandum justifying the Louisiana Purchase by the implied powers "enjoyed by every nation." Jefferson then sent the treaty to the Senate. After two days of perfunctory debate, his party ratified it by a 24-to-7 vote on October 20 while saying "as little as possible on the constitutional difficulty."

Most Americans agreed that the Louisiana Purchase was a "great good"—except for a group of New England Federalists, led by Senator Timothy Pickering of Massachusetts, who organized the nation's first secession movement. Their goal was a separate confederation of the five New England states (Connecticut, Massachusetts, New Hampshire, Rhode Island, and Vermont) and New York. When Alexander Hamilton declined to run for governor and led New York away from this northern confederacy, Pickering and his friends set their hopes on Vice President Aaron Burr.

Burr lost the New York governor's race in a landslide, focused his rage on Hamilton, and challenged him to their famous duel. As Hamilton bled to death in New York City on July 12, 1804, Burr fled west. Within six weeks he was in Cincinnati, plotting with James Wilkinson to rob the banks at Natchez, Baton Rouge, or New Orleans and thereby finance a filibuster expedition against Mexico. This odd aftermath of the Louisiana Purchase, of the first New England secession movement, and of the murder of Alexander Hamilton is known to history as the Burr Conspiracy.

As this melodrama of secession, murder, and conspiracy took shape to the north, Napoleon's resident colonial prefect, Pierre Clément de Laussat, prepared for the transfers of sovereignty in New Orleans.

Accepting the territory from Spain on November 30 in ceremonies at the Cabildo, Laussat then conveyed the city and colony to US commissioners William Charles Cole Claiborne and General James Wilkinson on December 20,1803.

From Jamestown in 1607 and Plymouth Rock in 1620 until the Louisiana Purchase, Anglo-American civic life had been the domain of Protestant, agrarian, English-speaking white men. Whites were free, blacks were slaves, and Native Americans did not count. Now Claiborne and Wilkinson watched in shock from the balcony of the Cabildo as free black militia units helped lower the tricolor of revolutionary France and raise the stars and stripes. The "formidable aspect of the armed Blacks & Mulattoes, officered and organized, is painful and perplexing," Wilkinson reported in an urgent dispatch asking for more troops. Claiborne gave thanks that the militia had "universally mounted the Eagle in their Hats" instead of the tricolor cockade of the French Jacobins, but Louisiana's free people of color (who had few significant counterparts in the society of the Atlantic coast) posed a dilemma for the new American authorities, whose actions were being watched closely throughout the country.

The French still refer to the transaction as the Sale of Louisiana, but to Americans it was the Purchase, because no territorial acquisition before or since did more to set the course of American history.

The implications of the Louisiana Purchase were shaped by events and attitudes from the French and Haitian revolutions. "The People of Colour are all armed," Wilkinson wrote, "and it is my Opinion a single envious artful bold incendiary"—in short, a man like Toussaint L'Ouverture—"might produce those Horrible Scenes of Bloodshed & rapine, which have been so frequently noticed in St. Domingo." Louisiana in 1803 seemed different and threatening. Amid its "gabble of tongues" and array of complexions—ivory, café au lait, copper, and ebony—a nation that habitually saw people only as black or white began its encounter with ethnic and cultural diversity born of expansion and immigration.

Here, in a microcosm, the United States faced the human consequences of the Louisiana Purchase for the first time. For the moment, Jefferson instructed Claiborne to cloak the new regime's misgivings about the colored militia, confirm them in their posts, and treat them favorably "till a better settled state of things shall permit us to let them neglect themselves." Controversies over race, religion, law, language, and culture

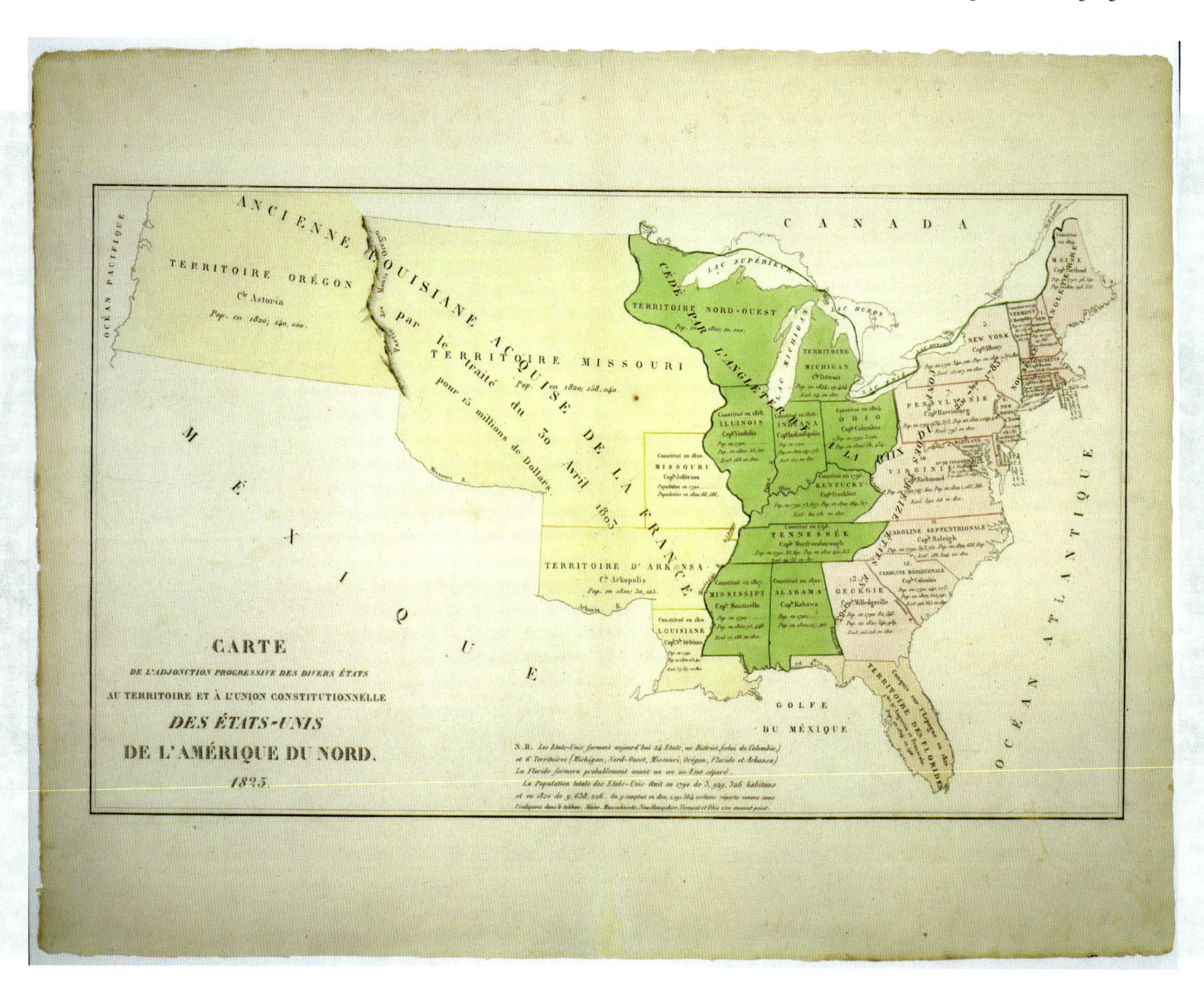

ABOVE *Des États-Unis de L'amerique du Nord, 1825,* by Jean Alexandre C. Buchon. Map of the contintental United States showing the Louisiana Purchase in yellow. From the French edition of Carey & Lea's American Atlas, published in Paris in 1825. Courtesy of The Historical New Orleans Collection.

not only delayed Louisiana's statehood until 1812, but rumbled like an earthquake along the vulnerable fault lines of nineteenth- and twentieth-century American society and government.

Starting at the Cabildo in New Orleans on December 20, 1803, five million Americans along the Atlantic Seaboard accelerated a long encounter with diversity sustained throughout subsequent centuries by geographic expansion and immigration. By arousing sectional jealousies and eroding fundamental compromises wrought by the Philadelphia convention of 1787, the Louisiana Purchase set America on a course toward the Civil War. After 1812, the land north of the current Louisiana-Arkansas border was renamed the Missouri Territory, to avoid confusion with the new state of Louisiana to the south. The nation's debate over slavery grew increasingly angry, while the consequences of the Louisiana Purchase scoured at the mortar of the Constitution, and the New Englanders' arguments for state rights and secession went South. In 1820, the Missouri Compromise, which admitted new states, in pairs, one slave and one free, to keep a balance of power in the Senate, was implemented. It held the nation together for another forty years. But "the Missouri Question," as the implications of the Louisiana Purchase were known, haunted the conscience of America until the cannon roared at Fort Sumter—and long beyond.

Travelers who actually visited New Orleans soon after the Louisiana Purchase witnessed this human dimension—and none described it more eloquently than the Jeffersonian polymath and engineer Benjamin Henry Latrobe. Born in England, Latrobe had immigrated to Philadelphia, then the nation's largest city, and designed several major buildings as well as the city's innovative water system. Commissioned to install a water system for the Crescent City, Latrobe arrived by ship early in 1819. Anchored off the French Quarter in a dense fog, Latrobe recorded his own encounter with the diversity of New Orleans: "So thick a fog enveloped the city that the ear alone could ascertain its existence," he wrote. Unlike the rumble of coaches and carriages that he remembered from London, or the "incessant clash of drays" of Philadelphia, he encountered "on arrival in New Orleans in the morning, a sound more strange than any that is heard anywhere else in the world. . . . It is a more incessant, loud, rapid, and various gabble of tongues of all tones than was ever heard at Babel"—a bustling urban place filled with Catholics, Creoles, French, Spanish, Africans, Native Americans, West Indians, Anglo-Americans, and free people of color—all engaged in a long and slow and too often tragic journey toward a world whose history bends toward eventual inclusion.

RIGHT The Louisiana Purchase consists of three separate agreements between the United States and France: a treaty of cession and two agreements providing for the exchange of monies in the transaction. The volume shown here is the French exchange copy of the convention providing for the settlement of an earlier debt owed by France to the United States. Courtesy of National Archives Building, Washington, D.C.

Auction Block

New Orleans was America's largest slave market

by Erin M. Greenwald, PhD

The manifest of the brig Ajax out of Norfolk, Virginia, on September 12, 1835, included the names of eleven children—Bill, Isaac, John, Monroe, Lewis, Washington, Robert, Phillis, Elisabeth, Mary, and Lovey—who stepped on board not as passengers but as cargo bound for antebellum America's largest slave market: New Orleans. Ripped from their families, their communities, and their homes, they were among the more than one million enslaved men, women, and children forcibly relocated from the Upper South (Maryland, Virginia, Washington, DC, and North Carolina) to the Lower South (Georgia, Alabama, Florida, Mississippi, Louisiana, and Texas) between the 1808 US ban on the international slave trade and the close of the Civil War. They were also among the more than two million people sold during the entirety of the antebellum domestic slave trade through the long-distance and regional trades as well as through court-ordered sales triggered by bankruptcies, estate auctions, and probate proceedings. In contrast to this internal trade, historians estimate that from the time the first dedicated slave ship arrived in Virginia in 1619 until the closure of the international slave trade nearly two hundred years later, approximately 450,000 African captives were carried to the United States and its colonial antecedents.

New Orleans, a city long known as the center of the antebellum cotton trade, was also the center of the domestic slave trade, a trade in people that operated within the confines of the United States and its territories. More men, women, and children were sold in the New Orleans slave markets in nineteenth-century America than anywhere else.

Its prominence as a hub for the buying and selling of what historian Walter Johnson has termed "people with a price" grew not only from its status as an active port city, but also from a complicated confluence of developments. Not least among them were three key factors. Eli Whitney's 1793 invention of the cotton gin turned a task previously considered too labor-intensive to be profitable—the removal of a short-staple cotton boll from its seeds—into an efficient procedure. Now, anyone with enough land and labor to plant, tend, and pick the crop could process it and make money doing so. The second factor was a significant increase in American territory. The Louisiana Purchase of 1803 more than doubled US territory and gave planters and would-be planters access to thousands of acres of prime agricultural land and a powerful waterway to bring their produce to market. Added to lands acquired in 1803 were broad swaths of country, stretching from Georgia to Texas, ceded by or stolen from American Indians in the early decades of the nineteenth century. By 1850, according to historian Sven Beckert, two-thirds of American cotton "grew on land that had not been part of the United States a half century earlier," and much of it flowed through the port of New Orleans. Finally, a widespread collapse of the tobacco economy that had sustained much of the Upper South, particularly in the Chesapeake region, in previous centuries meant that planters and farmers in Virginia and Maryland found themselves with a surplus of enslaved laborers at the exact moment of the international trade's closure. It was a perfect storm, one that brought far-reaching legislation, technological innovation, an economic collapse, and the pursuit of property to bear on the lives of millions of people subject to the United States of America's unique brand of racialized, hereditary slavery.

The eleven children who arrived in New Orleans in the fall of 1835 were among the nearly 71,000 documented people brought to the city by the coastal slave trade between 1819 (the first year with regular reporting) and 1860. When members of Congress passed the 1808 ban on the international trade, they sought to discourage the illegal introduction of captives by requiring all vessels carrying enslaved people from one US coastal port to another to keep meticulous records related to each shipment. These records, collected by the US Customs Service and now housed at the National Archives, include the names, sexes, ages, heights, and shipper-determined colors (black, brown, chestnut, yellow, etc.) of each vessel's human cargo. They provide a sense of the volume of people caught up in the New Orleans–bound trade, but they do not reveal the full story, as only coastal voyages were tracked.

Untold numbers of men, women, and children were forced to travel long distances along rivers, streams, and bayous, on foot, stage coaches, mule carts, and even railroad cars. Sometimes, as was the case with the sixty-three enslaved people who arrived in New Orleans aboard the Hibernia in 1831, their journey involved being placed first in a coffle that was marched through towns and countryside before being loaded onto a Mississippi River steamer to be sold downriver.

Whatever the path, the voyage to the New Orleans slave markets was one that could result in malnutrition, exhaustion, and even illness. Arriving slaves were often sick—heart sick at being separated from their families, but also physically sick from their travels. When Solomon Northup, a free black man kidnapped in Washington, DC, in 1841, arrived in New Orleans, he was sent first to one of two slave pens run by Theophilus Freeman, where Northup noted that he and his fellow captives "were required to wash thoroughly, and those with beards, to shave." They were then issued new clothing to replace those worn by travel. Men, Northup continued, received "hat, coat, shirt, pants, and shoes; the women frocks of calico and handkerchiefs to bind about their heads." Purveyors of plantation clothing, the articles of cheap, coarse cotton fabric and rough brogans destined to clothe and shoe the enslaved, flourished in New Orleans, as traders sought to spiff up their human wares and mask their frailties prior to sale.

For Northup and others, though, clothing could not long conceal illness contracted during the journey south. Within days of arriving in New Orleans, Northup and his shipmates, who had traveled with him from Virginia, began showing outward symptoms of the smallpox virus. Rather than allow the disease to spread, Freeman sent Northup, another man, and two women to Charity Hospital.

Charity Hospital was one of several health care facilities in antebellum New Orleans to accept and treat enslaved patients. Others included Circus Street Infirmary, the Hôtel Dieu, and Touro Infirmary. Touro, which opened its doors in a former mansion near the

OPPOSITE Interior view of a room with a rotunda ceiling during an auction of slaves, artwork, and goods in the Saint Louis Hotel. *Sale of Estates* by William Henry Brook, 1842. Courtesy of The Historic New Orleans Collection.

BELOW Slaves shackles used in the Middle Passage, late eighteenth to early nineteenth century. Courtesy of The Historic New Orleans Collection.

river (across the street from the present-day Ernest N. Morial Convention Center) in the mid-1850s, ministered to a range of mostly poor patients, but, as historian Stephen Kenney has shown, of those admitted in the five-year period before the Civil War, nearly 45 percent were unfree. Among these enslaved patients many were like Northup, brought to an infirmary following their journeys to New Orleans in the domestic slave trade. Traders such as Bernard Kendig appeared regularly in the column of Touro's patient register reserved for those paying the bills. The intent was simple: keep enslaved property alive and restore their health, so that traders could achieve maximum profitability through their sale.

The men, women, and children who survived their infirmary visits were returned to traders and readied for sale in one of the more than fifty sites across antebellum New Orleans, where people were bought and sold in large numbers. Some enslaved individuals, like Alfred, a skilled brickmaker, and Phoebe, who was listed in an 1856 advertisement as a "French and American cook and good washer and ironer," climbed atop elevated wooden platforms to be bid upon at public actions. Others, like Northup, were sold from storefronts, showrooms, or slave pens, with interested buyers examining, questioning, comparing, and selecting human property at their leisure.

More men, women, and children were sold in the New Orleans slave markets in nineteenth-century America than anywhere else.

Other than the levee along the Mississippi River, the site with the longest lineage of slave trading in New Orleans sits upon the ground where today's Omni Royal Orleans Hotel now stands. As early as the 1790s, the Chartres Street side of the block bounded by St. Louis, Royal, and Toulouse Streets was home to a number of coffeehouses, or tavern-like spaces, where men gathered to socialize, gossip, drink, gamble, and conduct business, including the buying and selling of real and chattel property. In the early decades of the nineteenth century, this stretch of French Quarter property was populated in turn by New Exchange Coffee House, Tremoulet's Exchange, Maspero's Exchange, Exchange Commercial Coffee House, Elkin's Exchange, Hewlett's Exchange, and finally the City Exchange. This last property, known more commonly as the St. Louis Hotel, opened in 1838, and supplanted the activities of its predecessors, which had been torn down to make room for the hotel's construction.

The St. Louis Hotel is perhaps the most notorious slave-trading locale in a city itself notorious for slave trading. The original structure stretched the length of St. Louis Street between Chartres and Royal and burned just two years after its completion. Quickly resurrected, its centerpiece was a domed rotunda in the classical style, where multiple times a week planters, hotel guests, tourists, and other spectators gathered in an opulent setting to watch and participate in the spectacle of humans being offered up for sale at auction on three separate blocks (one of which was reserved for sheriff's sales).

Interested buyers whose financial circumstances prevented them from purchasing enslaved laborers outright could finance their purchases directly through traders or brokers, but the more likely course of action was to seek a mortgage with one of New Orleans's many banks. Depending on the year, buyers might finance such mortgages through the Second Bank of the United States—the federally chartered bank, which in 1831–1832 had, according to historian Edward Baptist, extended 5 percent of all available commercial credit in the United States to the single slave trading firm of Franklin, Armfield, and Ballard—or they might approach one of several local and regional banks headquartered in New Orleans. Property banks (financial institutions whose assets were based on the value of real and moveable property), such as Citizens Bank, whose offices were conveniently located in the same block as the St. Louis Hotel, issued mortgages on enslaved people in much the same way that modern-day financial institutions issue mortgages on houses.

By the time the St. Louis Hotel opened its doors, the trade had spread across New Orleans. An 1829 ordinance that banned traders from housing (but not selling) enslaved people within the bounds of what is now the French Quarter prompted the emergence of two distinct slave-trading districts. The first, where traders' facilities were located within a one-block radius of the downriver intersection of Esplanade Avenue and Moreau (now Chartres) Street, lay just beyond the prohibited area. Here numerous traders, including Franklin, Armfield, and Ballard; S. F. Slatter (brother of Baltimore-based trader Hope Hull Slatter); Walter Campbell; Theophilus Freeman; F. M. Wilson; W. F. Talbott; John Hagan; Joseph Smith; and others imprisoned thousands of men, women, and children behind tall walls, designed to hide them from public view prior to their sale.

The second district was located upriver from the city's core near Factors' Row. This area, now known as the Central Business District, was where banks, slave depots, cotton and sugar factors, notaries, and planters' hotels were clustered together, allowing prospective out-of-town buyers—a group that made up the lion's share of those frequenting the New Orleans slave markets—the convenience of proximity. A Mississippi planter staying at the St. Charles Hotel on St. Charles Avenue between Gravier and Common Streets, for example, could step out of either of the hotel's side exits, walk away from the river, and within less than two blocks find himself surrounded by slave pens.

It is difficult to determine just how many individuals found themselves caught up in the trade and were sold in New Orleans's antebellum slave markets. Economist Laurence Kotlikoff estimates that between 1804 and 1862 New Orleans hosted sales of more than 135,000 enslaved men, women, and children. Given the volume of enslaved people who arrived just in the coastal trade, however, this figure seems low, especially when taking into account forced (bankruptcy and sheriff's sales) and voluntary sales of entire plantations and their laborers. A single one of these types of transactions could include a hundred or more people.

For the thousands who found themselves bought and sold in New Orleans each year, though, the volume of the trade is less relevant than the human suffering embodied in each of their sales. A single notarized transaction might include the sale of three people. Perhaps the three were a group, people who knew each other or were even related, but more often than not, those sold in the New Orleans market were sold without regard to family ties. Their sales, recorded in mortgage documents and bills of sale, shattered not only their own lives but the lives of those loved ones and community members left behind.

OPPOSITE Advertisement for February 23, 1856 slave auction at J. A. Beard & May auctioneers in New Orleans. Courtesy of The Historic New Orleans Collection.

UNLIMITED CREDIT SALE

OF A

Valuable Gang of Georgia and South Carolina

FIELD HANDS

AND A WASHER AND IRONER, AND DINING ROOM SERVANT.

BY J. A. BEARD & MAY,

J. A. BEARD, Auctioneer.

SATURDAY, FEBRUARY 23, 1856.

AT 12 O'CLOCK,

Will be sold at AUCTION, at Banks' Arcade, without limit,

The following described Slaves, to-wit:

1. MARY, aged 18 years, a field hand.
2. HARRIET, aged 21 years, do do
3. MAHALA, aged 28 years, do do and fair cook.
4. PRISCILLA, aged 33 y'rs, do do do do
5. LEWIS, aged 24 years, do do and wagoner.
6. EDMUND, aged 26 years, do do and hewer.
7. JOHN, aged 22 years, do do
8. JOHN WILKINSON, aged 28 years, No. 1 dining-room servant.
9. SAM, aged 30 years, field hand and wagoner.
10. ELIZABETH, aged 20 years, fine washer and ironer, and fair cook.
11. MARY JANE, aged 22 years, a good field hand.
12. LYDIA, aged 28 years, do do
13. BURREL, aged 23 years, No. 1 field hand.
14. WILLIS, aged 23 years, extra No. 1 field hand.
15. PHŒBE, aged 23 years, a No. 1 French and American cook and good washer and ironer, and her child MARY ANN, 3 years.
16. FRIDAY, aged 24 years, cotton field hand, slightly ruptured. All fully guaranteed against the vices and maladies prescribed by law.

TERMS:

Twelve months credit for approved city acceptances or endorsers, with interest of 7 per cent. per annum from date.

Acts of sale before Wm. Shannon, Notary Public, at the expense of the purchasers.

The Slaves can be seen by applying at the office of the Auctioneer.

BULLETIN PRINT, 37 GRAVIER ST.

INFAMOUS!

VIDE LORD PALMERSTON'S SPEECH.

HEAD-QUARTERS, DEP'T OF THE GULF,
NEW ORLEANS: *May* 15, 1862.

As the OFFICERS and SOLDIERS of the UNITED STATES have been subjected to REPEATED INSULTS from the WOMEN, calling themselves 'LADIES,' of NEW ORLEANS, in return for the most scrupulous NON-INTERFERENCE and COURTESY on our part, it is ordered that hereafter when any female shall by word, gesture, or movement, insult or show contempt for any OFFICER or PRIVATE of the UNITED STATES she shall be regarded and held liable to be TREATED as

A WOMAN OF THE TOWN

PLYING HER VOCATION.

By command of

Maj.-Gen. BUTLER

New Orleans and the Civil War

The conflict transformed the city from capital of the Cotton Kingdom to frontier of emancipation

by Lawrence N. Powell, PhD

During the first two years of the American Civil War, starting with the humiliating retreat at First Manassas and the bloody split decision at Shiloh nine months later, about the only major victory Union forces could point to was the capture of New Orleans. It was the South's largest city as well as the downriver anchor of the country's foremost commercial artery, and when it fell on April 29, 1862, four hundred miles of the river were flung open all the way to Vicksburg, setting the stage for dividing the Confederacy in two. News of the city's capture came as a shock to the high command in Richmond, not to mention the residents of New Orleans. Weeks earlier, upon learning that the largest invasion fleet in American history had assembled just beyond the mouth of the Mississippi River, it was easy for residents to take refuge in the myth of the city's impregnability against amphibious assault: large battleships would have trouble navigating the silted-up passes at the river's mouth, it was believed, and steaming against the Mississippi's formidable currents would not prove much easier. Then there were those formidable artillery placements at Forts Jackson and St. Philip, on opposite banks of a river that was running higher than anyone could remember. Passing those guns would not be easy.

Yet Union battleships commanded by Commodore David D. Porter, sailing in single file while exchanging fire with Confederate gunners, ran that gauntlet in the early morning hours of April 24, with little loss of life and minor physical damage. Four days later, after Confederate forces inside Fort Jackson mutinied, transports carrying eighteen thousand troops under the command of Major General Benjamin F. Butler arrived in New Orleans. The South's preeminent metropolis was now under Union control, lost to the Confederacy for good.

True, New Orleans was still in a war zone. From its bivouac grounds federal armies launched raids into nearby Confederate territory. The siege of Port Hudson and the ill-fated Red River campaign began here. But hereafter New Orleans' military significance was modest. The same can't be said of its political significance, though. In that regards, New Orleans was immensely consequential. The city became a staging area for emancipation—a world-changing event whose repercussions live on today. The dress rehearsal for Reconstruction also played out here in the waning years of the war.

The roots of these events reach back to New Orleans' antebellum past. The city had risen spectacularly on commerce floated to its levees by the river's current and the power of steam. As a port, New Orleans led the nation in the value of exports, the tonnage surpassing even that of New York. Its levees, heaped with commodities and forested with masts, steamboats stretching beyond number side-by-side halfway across the river, never ceased to marvel travelers. (The year of Lincoln's election, some 3,500 steamboats landed in the city.) By 1840, antebellum New Orleans had become a great banking center, famous for its innovativeness and links to great merchant banks in London, Amsterdam, Paris, and New York. In 1860, the Crescent City could count more millionaires per capita than any comparable American metropolis.

The pace of change was furious, the tempo swelling the net worth of everyone who had placed early bets on undeveloped land. November to May was the height of the commercial season, and people poured in from around the country to buy and sell. It was truly a continental influx, but much of the business community was northern-born. There were arrivals from Europe and Latin America, even from the Pacific Rim. By 1840, this erstwhile colonial backwater of largely French-speaking Latin Creoles and African-descended slaves had become the third most populous city in the nation, to say nothing of a cosmopolitan melting pot. New subdivisions, called faubourgs, sprouted from the weeds of ancient plantations. Above Canal Street

OPPOSITE On May 15, 1862, Maj. General Benjamin Butler issued the infamous "Woman's Order" in an attempt to stop discourteous treatment of Union soldiers by the women of New Orleans. Courtesy of The Historic New Orleans Collection.

a bustling business district loomed in the so-called American Sector. To service the burgeoning lake trade, the New Basin Canal was dug. To improve public health, a new waterworks went into service. New Orleans' first gaslight company (founded by a theater impresario-cum-banker) supplied many of its darkened streets with better lighting.

It was a city of excess, immoderate in everything it did. New Orleans boasted more dance halls than houses of worship (which sometimes doubled as ballrooms). Gambling was practically a way of life. And no city in America guzzled more alcohol per capita than this new Gomorrah near the Gulf. Harvest time was when the good times rolled in New Orleans. Boarding houses filled with bachelors and young fathers, the town pulsing with "the nervous activity of men who were only staying a little longer," wrote *Harper's Magazine* in 1853. The extended-stay sojourners included the northern criminal class, particularly pickpockets and con artists. Then summer approached and the city fell silent. July and August heralded the arrival of yellow fever. Some summers the scourge struck with concentrated fury, as happened in 1853, when an estimated nine thousand died in the epidemic, burnishing New Orleans' reputation as "the Necropolis of the South."

Yet at the start of the economic takeoff that vaulted New Orleans into the front ranks of American cities, it was hardly obvious it would storm ahead as a Southern metropolis. For decades to come trade receipts from the Ohio Valley marked it as a western town. Western produce—wheat, pork, tobacco, rye, whiskey, to sample a few of those receipts—was the accelerant that powered New Orleans' explosive growth following the War of 1812. New Orleans' first generation of wholesale grocers, forwarding agents, and commission merchants built their businesses around marketing those commodities. Yet by the 1830s it was becoming increasingly evident that sugar and cotton were overtaking western produce. Both staples had come on stream as early as 1795, sugar leading the way after the Haitian Revolution sidelined that island's cane industry. But it was cotton that stood next in line to inherit the throne, and by the 1840s cotton had become king. The American South had the ideal climate and soil for raising the short-staple variety. The textile mills of the English midlands, the cradle of first industrial revolution, couldn't get enough of it. But one spot in the South surpassed all others in per-acreage productivity: the inexhaustibly rich bottomlands of the lower Mississippi Valley, the vestibule to New Orleans' hinterland. And as those lands began to release their natural bounty, New Orleans mutated into a Southern town just at the moment that the transportation revolution reoriented the flows of western trade. Grains that once reached the East via New Orleans now reached the East by way of canals and rail lines. The grain trade didn't dry up—it actually increased in volume. It was New Orleans' market share that declined. Meanwhile, cotton surged into overwhelming dominance.

That transformation reshaped the character and ethos of the city's business and political establishments. Those earlier merchants were generalists. One day they might receive a cargo of wheat on consignment, the next day might find them swapping sugar for sorghum, and the day after that buying cotton on their own account. But around the late 1820s and early '30s, a new breed of specialist commission merchants started emerging—cotton factors. Their major customers were large cotton planters, to whom they provided full-service care. Instead of speculating on cotton, they received the ginned harvest from their rural clients on consignment, got the cotton insured, arranged for its storage, supervised its sale to foreign and domestic buyers, and saw that it was pressed into

ABOVE *Farragut's fleet passing the forts below New Orleans*, by Mauritz Frederik De Haas, 1863-1867. The painting shows flag officer David Farragut's fleet passing Fort Jackson and Fort St. Philip, downriver from New Orleans, in April 1862. Courtesy of The Historic New Orleans Collection.

ABOVE Signing of the Ordinance of Secession of Louisiana on January 26, 1861, by Enoch Wood Perry, Jr. Courtesy of Louisiana State Museum.

heavier bales for transshipment to cotton mills at home and abroad. Each transaction generated a modest commission. So did the supplies that the factor ordered for his planter clients in the countryside—brogans, cheap coats and pants, salted pork for their slaves, four-in-hand carriages and other luxuries for the "big house." Every item was paid for with credit advances against the yet-to-be harvested crop. To increase the supply of credit, the city's largest factors, who formed a small oligarchy, and a few grocers and wholesalers branched into banking. Antebellum New Orleans banks weren't savings institutions or banks of deposit. They bore a closer resemblance to investment banks. A few of them even functioned as conduits for huge inflows of international capital. It was these merchant-controlled banks that supplied much of the credit and capital that built the Cotton Kingdom.

In 1860, the Crescent City could count more millionaires per capita than any comparable American metropolis.

It could never have been built without the workings of the interstate slave trade. Between the adoption of the US Constitution and breakup of the Union, but especially after 1820, when slave sales began to track the international demand curve for cotton, a million or so enslaved people were ripped from Maryland and Virginia and relocated to the lower South. Professional slave traders were responsible for carrying an estimated two thirds of them to the old Southwest, with at least half that number, if not more, channeling through New Orleans. By 1830, New Orleans had become the slave mart of America. Planters from Texas, Arkansas, Louisiana, and Mississippi came to buy slaves on credit, much of it supplied by the city's merchant-dominated banks. Those financial institutions never blanched at the domestic slave trade. Slave mortgages comprised the most valuable assets in their portfolios. Slave property appreciated in value faster than land. The cultural and psychological impact of this trade on New Orleans' sense of itself can scarcely be minimized. It was another reason the Crescent City became a Southern city: the slave trade was everywhere, seeping into every pore of the city's being.

Whirlwind growth is usually disruptive, upending established hierarchies and threatening the mores and customs of ancient populations. Antebellum New Orleans was hardly spared the whiplash of rapid change. The Americanization of the cotton port, which turned up the heat on the already inflamed rivalry between the English-speaking and the Creole populations, occasioned the town's dismemberment between 1836 and 1852 into three quasi-autonomous municipalities. The flood of German and Irish immigration into New Orleans in the 1830s, '40s, and '50s triggered an outbreak of nativist violence. But, in the way of profound repercussions, nothing surpassed the Southernization of the city's economy. The escalating sectional conflict over slavery in the territories dragged New Orleans deeper into the fever swamp of pro-slavery Southern nationalism. It distorted the lens through which the world was seen. Old trading partners in the Ohio Valley came to look like a menacing picket line of Free State aggression. The rise of political abolitionism, culminating in the founding of the Republican Party, heightened the South's feeling of growing isolation. John Brown's 1859 raid on Harper's Ferry raised the specter of northern fanatics plotting slave revolts. All were sectionalizing shocks that knocked New Orleans loose from its psychological mooring to the Union.

Yet New Orleans was still a pro-Union city. It would remain so during Lincoln's election, casting at best a reluctant vote for secession. But at the same time the political and ideological leanings of the city's establishment had taken a decisive pro-slavery turn. In the 1850s, New Orleans became a springboard for feckless efforts to expand the empire of slavery by means of filibustering invasions of Cuba and Nicaragua. Meanwhile, because it had become the nerve center of the Deep South, the city attracted more and more "fire-eating" Southern nationalists. Even the region's foremost business journal, the New Orleans-based *DeBow's Review*, became a megaphone for pro-slavery viewpoints and scientific racism, beating the tocsin for reopening the Atlantic slave trade.

No segment of the population bore a heavier brunt of Southern radicalization than New Orleans' *gens de couleur libres*. They weren't the urban South's largest free black community, but they were the most prosperous, cohesive, sophisticated, and self-confident. Their numbers more than doubled when a heavy influx of Saint-Domingue exiles arrived in 1809 and '10 from Cuba. New Orleans' free people of color formed the backbone of the urban middle class. Many were skilled artisans. Others ran retail businesses. Several free women of color operated boarding houses. Thanks to early investments in undeveloped town lots, their net worth improved. That relative prosperity made possible a rich associational life, fostered through schools, a poetry journal, a philharmonic society, and self-help and fraternal societies. They could even point to a proud tradition of military service in defense of home and hearth, epitomized by valor during the 1815 Battle of New Orleans.

But as the sectional conflict simmered to a boil, New Orleans *gens de couleur libres* fell under the gaze of an increasing surveillance state. They were ordered to register as if they were resident aliens. They were forbidden to return home if they left the state. Soon, their private organizations and fraternal societies were dissolved, and they were ordered not to hold meetings without white auditors present. The final insult was the outlawing of private acts of manumission, followed by a legislative invitation that city's *gens de couleur libres* (not a few of whom were slaveholders themselves) choose a master. Only one free man of color is on record as having accepted the offer. The more common response was to emigrate or go underground.

After its capture New Orleans became the headquarters of the military Department of the Gulf. The Union occupation that followed is popularly remembered for General Benjamin F. "Beast" Butler's alleged corruption and overreach. That broad-brush depiction gets at many of the essentials. A wartime commission exposed quite a bit

of ethically challenged activity. Butler's brother was a war profiteer—as were a good many locals, for that matter. Butler himself could be implacable, bringing an unruly mob to heel by hanging a gambler who had hauled down a US flag and then cut it into pieces for distribution as souvenirs. The walleyed general expelled Confederate sympathizers who refused to sign a loyalty oath. He censured and seized pro-Confederate newspapers, silenced pro-Confederate pulpits. He jailed the pro-Confederate mayor, John T. Monroe. It was Butler who ordered that the epigraph "The Union Must Be Preserved" be etched on the plinth of Andrew Jackson's equestrian statue in the square that bears his name. Two acts got Butler into hot water, provoking an international outcry that resulted in his recall: his notorious "woman's order," announcing that any woman found insulting the Union military would be treated as a woman of the town "plying her avocation"; and his seizure of bullion in the possession of foreign consuls.

Yet the occupation's most far-reaching significance was political and racial. There were, for example, the food and jobs that Butler made available to New Orleans' famished working class, plus the sanitation campaign he swiftly launched. The pro-Confederate mayor and city council had deliberately let New Orleans become filthier than ever, hoping that yellow fever might accomplish what undermanned Confederate troops never did: decimate Union ranks. But Butler paid the white working class to scrape a decade of offal from the streets of the French Market, then enlisted many of these often foreign-born workers in the Union army.

And then there were the upheavals of emancipation. The truth is, Abraham Lincoln's initial war aim was not emancipation. It was the preservation of the Union, and it was only the exigencies of the Civil War that caused him to elevate the conflict into a crusade for freedom. Much of the credit for swaying Lincoln, along with a host of skeptical Union generals,

TOP LEFT Drummer Jackson, about ten to twelve years old, in a tattered shirt and pants, 1865. Courtesy of The Historic New Orleans Collection.

BOTTOM LEFT Jackson in a Union service uniform, 1865. Courtesy of The Historic New Orleans Collection.

belongs to the slaves themselves. They literally freed themselves by running away, forcing the question of their future status onto the national agenda. This happened everywhere Union lines became within reach. But nowhere was this self-emancipating energy more active and historically consequential than in the Union-occupied Department of the Gulf, headquartered in New Orleans. Young men were the first to abscond. But soon whole slave families, even entire plantation communities decamped. It happened whenever Union armies arrived in the neighborhood. An 1863 military expedition into Bayou Teche, for example, returned to New Orleans unexpectedly trailing a five-mile caravan of four hundred carts and eight thousand slaves. The vast majority was settled at Camp Parapet on River Road, in neighboring Jefferson Parish. But as more refugees crowded in, and sanitation conditions worsened, the Union high command was forced to improvise policies—a wage system, for one; enlistment in the Union army, for another—that eventually blossomed into a full-blown program of emancipation. It is a complex story, all the more vital for having unfolded in what had recently been the central slave mart of the Northern Hemisphere.

ABOVE *Blackbeard of New Orleans,* by Samuel T. Blessing, ca. 1864 - 1872. Print caricature showing General Benjamin Franklin Butler dressed as a pirate carrying a bloody sword and holding a woman by the hair. At upper right is a man waving his arms in a window; below him is the phrase *John Bull.* Courtesy of The Historic New Orleans Collection.

The city became a staging area for emancipation—a world-changing event whose repercussions live on today.

Other unintended consequences stemmed from wartime occupation. One of the most important was the dress rehearsal for Reconstruction that saw the city's free people of color take center stage. In the spring of 1861, fifteen hundred free men of color had offered to fight for the Confederacy. Although the governor incorporated them into the state militia as the Native Guards, the local Confederate commander declined their services. After the occupation they made the same offer to Butler and eventually he accepted. In September 1862 they were mustered into the US Army as the Native Guard. Thereafter, the march toward equal citizenship rights, without regard to race or previous condition, gathered momentum, with free men of color in the lead; their sophisticated advocacy, as well as their martial sacrifices, nudged Lincoln and the North toward widening the door of citizenship to black people more broadly.

As for the fate of one of antebellum America's most powerful communities of merchant capitalists: it collapsed into a puddle. Defeat derailed the city's banks and deranged its credit and marketing networks. Emancipation upended old ways of marketing cotton and sugar and supplying the new sharecropper class. Meanwhile, rail lines allowed Memphis, Mobile, and even Charleston to haul away more and more of New Orleans' share of the cotton market. Even the Texas cattle trade was diverted. New Orleans would spend the better part of half a century trying to regain its economic footing.

Freedom Train

Activism by New Orleans' free people of color led to the Plessy v. Ferguson case

by Keith Weldon Medley

Plessy v. Ferguson is arguably Louisiana's most famous civil rights Supreme Court case. It involved eighteen prominent Louisiana citizens who challenged a law that separated blacks and whites on railroad trains. This group of writers, businessmen, educators, lawyers, ex-Union soldiers and a newspaper publisher constructed a well-planned legal and civil-disobedience campaign to overturn the law in the courts and in the land of public opinion. Their mission was to construct a legal, social, and civil disobedience campaign against racial segregation. They called themselves "The Citizens Committee For The Annulment of Act No. 111, Commonly Known As The Separate Car Law."

Homer Patris Plessy

Homer Plessy was born Homere Patris Plessy in New Orleans on St. Patrick's Day, March 17, 1863. In later documents, he was listed as Homer Adolph Plessy. His birth certificate lists his parents as Adolphe Plessy and Rosalie Debergue, both designated as "colored" residents of the city. Adolphe Plessy was a carpenter; Rosalie was a seamstress. Homer's grandfather was Germain Plessy, a white native of France who arrived in New Orleans from Haiti in the early 1800s. He produced a number of children, including Homer's father, through a union with a free woman of color named Agnes Mathieu.

Homer Plessy was born two months after the Emancipation Proclamation became effective in Louisiana. His early life brought the promise of Reconstruction in Louisiana and the expansion of citizenship rights for people of African descent. He grew up with the right to vote, run for office, and board any train he wished. Interracial marriages were legalized and the Louisiana Constitution of 1868 integrated the school system. In 1888, he married Louise Bordenave. Homer wasn't as well-known or prosperous as others on the Citizens Committee, formed in 1891, but he had been active in an education reform movement in New Orleans. When the committee asked for volunteers, Homer Plessy stepped forward.

John Howard Ferguson

John Howard Ferguson was born in 1838. A native of Martha's Vineyard, he studied law in Boston. After the Civil War, he journeyed to New Orleans and settled in the uptown section of the city. He practiced civil law and became a member of the Louisiana Legislature in 1877. In 1892, Governor Murphy Foster appointed him to be the lead judge in Section A of the Orleans Parish Criminal Court, a month before Plessy stood before him. The court then met at Lafayette Square.

At the time Ferguson arrived in New Orleans, Homer Plessy was but a toddler. Confederate sympathizers looked upon men such as Ferguson as carpetbaggers. John Ferguson married into the family of an outspoken Unionist named Thomas J. Earhart, who strongly denounced slavery and the Confederacy during the Civil War. In October of 1865, a newspaper index listed Earhart as one of the city's first attorneys to swear an oath of allegiance to the Union.

The Fourteenth Amendment

On June 25, 1868, Louisiana rejoined the Union and approved the Fourteenth Amendment two days later. The following month, the Fourteenth Amendment granted equal protection of the law to citizens regardless of color. This Amendment in effect nullified the Supreme Court's infamous 1857 Dred Scott decision that proclaimed blacks have no "rights which the white man was bound to respect."

In 1890, with the ending of Reconstruction, the Louisiana State Legislature passed a mean-spirited law that segregated people on railroad trains. In the case of interracial couples, the law physically separated husbands, wives, and children. Additionally, it mandated that railroad companies provide an additional coach even if only few black passengers purchased tickets. For the Louisiana legislators of African heritage (there were eighteen black members of the legislature), the law prohibited them from traveling with their fellow government officials or many of their constituents.

OPPOSITE A ticket for the East Louisiana Railroad company. Courtesy of The Historic New Orleans Collection.

In 1891, to stem the tide of race baiting and the rolling back of civil rights in the south, members of the Citizens Committee reported to the Exchange Alley offices of the recently founded *Crusader*, a newspaper primarily for people of color, where they planned their strategy. Many in the group belonged to the free people of color caste that existed in Louisiana before the Civil War. The person who used his influence to call the Citizens Committee together was Alexandre Aristide Mary. Mary was a member of the Radical Republicans during Reconstruction, a wealthy philanthropist, a co-founder of the Unification movement in 1873, and a leader of protests against segregated schools in 1877. Mary assessed the passing of the Separate Car Act as a way to return to the caste system that existed before the Civil War.

Plessy in Tremé

Homer Plessy's home at the time he caught the train was located at 1108 North Claiborne Avenue in the Faubourg Tremé. In the 1890s in Tremé, "grand dancing festivals" were given by benevolent and social organizations such as the Big Three Social Club, or a "committee of gentlemen" who raised money to benefit widows or improve libraries. Social and benevolent clubs met monthly at Economy Hall, Hope Hall, and Congregation Hall where the Citizens Committee held protests and fund-raising rallies.

One of Homer Plessy's qualifications as the test case was that he looked white enough to obtain a ticket and enter the train, but under Louisiana law he was black enough to be arrested for doing so.

Outside of Homer and Louise's front door, every four minutes, mule-powered streetcars of the Canal and Claiborne line clopped by on route to open-air fruit and vegetable markets in downtown New Orleans. Outside of their bedroom window, Congregation Hall hosted Saturday night "grand dancing festivals" where New Orleanians swayed to the sounds of Professor Joseph A. Moret's String Band.

Plessy's Moment

In preparation for his sojourn, the Citizens Committee enlisted Homer Plessy to board a white-only train car and be arrested. The goal was to create a test case that would not only overturn the Louisiana law but also strike down all the other segregation laws that sprouted throughout the South after the end of Reconstruction. One of Homer Plessy's qualifications as the test case was that he looked white enough to obtain a ticket and enter the train, but under Louisiana law he was black enough to be arrested for doing so.

Plessy had four tasks: Get the ticket. Get on the train. Get arrested. Get booked. On June 7, 1892, Homer Plessy traveled the nearly two miles from his residence in the Tremé to the train station at the Press Street railroad about two miles away. He purchased a first-class ticket on the East Louisiana Railroad Number 8 train that was scheduled to depart at 4:15 p.m. for a two-hour run to Covington, Louisiana. As boarding time neared, Homer walked toward the first-class coach, past the cars with "Colored Only" designations and the prominently posted "Separate Car

Act," and took a seat in the first-class accommodation. The whistle blew, the doors shut, the steam blasted from the engine, and the East Louisiana train's wheels creaked forward. As the train inched away, conductor J. J. Dowling collected tickets. He paused when he got to Plessy and asked him: "Are you a colored man?"

"Yes," said Homer Plessy.

"Then you will have to retire to the colored car," Dowling responded.

Plessy asserted that he was an American citizen who paid for his ticket and intended to ride to Covington. Dowling then signaled the engineer to bring the Number 8 train to a dead stop. Detective Cain took over, cautioning Plessy, "If you are colored you should go into the car set apart for your race. The law is plain and must be obeyed."

Again Plessy refused to budge and said he would rather go to jail than abandon the coach.

At 4:35 p.m., twenty minutes after the train's scheduled departure, Detective Cain and "volunteers" on the train forcibly dragged Plessy from the "White Only" coach and executed the arrest near Royal and Press Streets

At the Fifth Precinct station on Elysian Fields Avenue, Plessy submitted to the same booking procedure applied to the array of drunks, petty larcenists, and foul-mouthed New Orleanians arrested that day on the city's streets. But his charge of "Violating the Separate Car Act" was anything but a typical Tuesday-evening New Orleans petty crime. Members of the Committee converged at the Fifth Precinct station and had Plessy released on bond. Homer still held his first-class ticket as he and his compatriots made their way across Elysian Fields and back toward Tremé. They had just purposefully, intentionally, and openly defied Governor Murphy Foster, Supreme Court Chief Justice Francis Nicholls, and the 1890 Louisiana Legislature. Homer wasn't thirty years old. Yet, the future of civil rights rode on his day in court. Judge John Howard Ferguson had been on the bench only a few months when the Plessy case arrived on his docket, and he upheld the segregation law stating that Plessy was not deprived of equal accommodations.

"We as freemen still believe that we were right and our cause is sacred. In defending the cause of liberty, we met with defeat, but not with ignominy."

—Citizens Committee statement following *Plessy v. Ferguson* decision

Despite their best efforts, on May 19, 1896, in a seven-to-one vote, the United States Supreme Court agreed with Ferguson and issued a ruling granting states the authority to forcibly segregate people of differing races. Writing for the majority, Benjamin Harrison–appointee Justice Henry Billings Brown dismissed Plessy's Fourteenth Amendment claims and pointed to separate schools and bans on interracial marriages as precedents. As far as determining race, this too was left to the discretion of Louisiana and other states. The lone dissent came from Justice John Marshall Harlan whose opinion became a beacon for later advances in civil rights court cases:

> The destinies of the two races in this country are indissolubly linked together, and the interest of both requires that the common government of all shall not permit the seeds of race hate to be planted under the sanctions of law. The thin disguise of equal accommodations for passenger in a railroad car will not mislead anyone, nor atone for the wrong this day done.

The Supreme Court remanded the decision to the Louisiana Supreme Court. Upon receiving the news, the Citizens Committee issued a final statement before disbanding: "We as freemen still believe that we were right and our cause is sacred. In defending the cause of liberty, we met with defeat, but not with ignominy."

BELOW The Citizens Community. From *The Crusader*, 1891. Courtesy of the Plessy and Ferguson Foundation.

"Liberty has always had a hard road to travel, whenever prejudice was the consulted oracle. The United States will not be an exception to the rule, as long as race antipathy will be allowed to overshadow every other within our territory. But the obligation of the people is resistance to oppression."

The Crusader, August 1891

Antoine

Shortly thereafter, *The Crusader* ceased publication. And in January of 1897, his constitutional claims dismissed, Homer Plessy returned to Section A, presided over by Judge Joshua Baker. Accompanied by Citizens Committee treasurer Paul Bonseigneur, Plessy changed his plea to guilty, paid a $25.00 fine, and walked into the brave new world of American apartheid. It wasn't until 1954 when the Supreme Court reversed itself in Brown v. Board of Education.

When Plessy Met Ferguson Again

In 1996, I met a twentieth-century Plessy relative, Keith Plessy, at an event commemorating the hundredth anniversary of the United States Supreme Court of the Plessy v. Ferguson decision.

It wasn't until 2004 that filmmaker Phoebe Ferguson became aware of her ties as a descendant of John Howard Ferguson, the judge who ruled against Plessy. The revelation about her great, great grandfather precipitated her moving back to Louisiana from New York.

She and Keith Plessy subsequently met at the Preservation Resource Center, where Keith Plessy told her that the story of their families would no longer be about Plessy versus Ferguson, but would now be the story of Plessy and Ferguson. The two have since formed a friendship and a foundation in New Orleans for the promotion of education and preservation of civil rights sites.

Their efforts symbolically raise the question: If Plessy and Ferguson can reconcile after a century of being two names that stood for strict racial separation of citizens, then perhaps we all can move beyond centuries of bitterness and rancor. Using their history in New Orleans' tricentennial year, Keith and Phoebe seek to guide their histories past the America in conflict, and forward to America in resolution and reconciliation.

NOTICE

New Orleans Public Service Inc. has been advised by its attorneys that the U. S. District Court has denied motions of the Company, and the Mayor and Superintendent of Police of the City of New Orleans for a stay of the effective date of that Court's injunction against these defendants in the case declaring unconstitutional the Louisiana laws requiring segregated seating on transit vehicles. The Company's attorneys further advise that the Court by order issued May 30, 1958, fixed the effective time of the injunction at 12:01 A. M., Saturday, May 31, 1958. The injunction reads:

"IT IS FURTHER ORDERED, ADJUDGED and DECREED that the defendants, their successors in office, assigns, agents, servants, employees and persons acting on their behalf, be and they are hereby permanently enjoined and restrained (1) from enforcing the aforesaid statutes requiring plaintiffs and other Negroes similarly situated to submit to segregation in the use of the buses, street cars, street railways and trolley buses, and (2) from doing any acts or taking any action which would require any public transportation facility, or its drivers, to segregate white and Negro passengers in the operation of buses, street cars, street railways, or trolley buses in the State of Louisiana."

The Company's operations have been changed to conform to the injunction of the Federal Court.

NEW ORLEANS PUBLIC SERVICE INC.

ABOVE The fight for integration lasted for decades after *Plessy v. Ferguson*. This public service announcement was issued by New Orleans Public Service, Inc., giving notice that company had lost its legal challenge against the federal court order to desegregate all seating on city buses and streetcars. Courtesy of The Historic New Orleans Collection.

"Oh, Lord, how long!"

New Orleans was a battleground for the woman suffrage movement

by Pamela Tyler, PhD

The decades-long national movement for woman suffrage provoked a protracted and complex struggle in the Crescent City. Not all men in New Orleans opposed votes for women, nor did all local women favor suffrage for themselves and their sex. Among the women who supported suffrage, there was intense disagreement over the best path to follow toward their goal. Indeed, divisions among women in the New Orleans suffrage movement were deeply and bitterly etched, with consequences that stretched beyond the city itself.

A movement for women's rights had flowered in the northern states well before the Civil War, but the ingredients that spawned it—urbanization, growth of a middle class, women's education, women's organizations—were scarce in the antebellum South. Because the early campaign for woman suffrage had links to the movement to abolish slavery, most white southerners viewed it with suspicion and distaste, with the result that public opinion in the South tended to dismiss woman suffrage as an alien idea touted by Yankee abolitionists and "strong-minded women."

Yet pro-suffrage sentiment flickered in parts of the South, nowhere more strongly than in New Orleans. Caroline Merrick began advocating votes for women after a sudden and unpleasant epiphany regarding women's legal disabilities. Merrick, wife of a State Supreme Court justice, served on the board of St. Anna's Asylum, a refuge in New Orleans for poor women. In dismay, she learned that the will she had witnessed in 1879, made by a German woman on her deathbed who intended to leave her savings to St. Anna's, was not valid because Merrick and the other female board members had no legal standing to serve as witnesses. Wrote Merrick, "The bequest went to the state, and the women went to thinking and agitating." Later that year, Merrick and Elizabeth Lyle Saxon gathered four hundred signatures for a petition appealing, unsuccessfully, for women's enfranchisement. Both women spoke on the subject before the Louisiana Constitutional Convention, by invitation.

The 1884 World's Industrial and Cotton Centennial Exposition, a world's fair held in New Orleans to promote trade and reconciliation between North and South, sparked a slight warming toward the concept of votes for women. A woman's department showcased the work and creativity of women, instilling pride in their sex among local women. Distinguished women lectured under the auspices of the Exposition. Trenchant remarks from strong, confident outsiders like Frances Willard and Julia Ward Howe about progressive issues such as education, jobs, temperance, and women's rights proved transformative for some women, while even the sight of females on a platform, commanding a room, likely impressed others powerfully. Nationally renowned suffragist Susan B. Anthony addressed not only a crowd at the centennial, but also local high school girls, a group of working women, and an audience of New Orleans schoolteachers. Everywhere, she wooed locals to give suffrage a fair hearing.

Caroline Merrick concluded that, after these experiences, New Orleans women became "club-able." Merrick herself founded the Portia Club in 1892, the first suffrage club in Louisiana. Beginning with nine "strong, progressive, intellectual women," the growing group soon sponsored a variety of discussions, including "Would municipal suffrage for women be a benefit to New Orleans?" and "Disabilities of women in Louisiana." Portia members, southern women of the comfortable classes, held a memorial service upon the death of pioneer suffragist Lucy Stone, fêted Susan B. Anthony on her birthday, and entertained Carrie Chapman Catt, thus honoring three "strong-minded" northerners. Clearly, cross-pollination was occurring, with "Yankee" ideas about women's rights beginning to flower in New Orleans.

In 1895, nine younger Portia members hived off to form the ERA (Equal Rights for All) Club, an organization that, according to Merrick, "soon outgrew its mother." Portia and ERA cooperated on the voting rights issue with the National American Woman Suffrage Association (NAWSA) under the aegis of the Louisiana State Suffrage Association, of which Merrick was president. ERA members soon numbered in the hundreds, and while they worked for numerous progressive causes, woman suffrage was always the chief focus.

In 1898, Louisiana men met in New Orleans to rewrite their state's constitution once again, this time intent on disfranchising black voters by means that could technically avoid violating the Fifteenth Amendment. When women presented a petition to the convention's suffrage committee urging them to extend the vote to women, delegates called a special evening session and invited nineteen Portia and ERA members to occupy the rostrum in crowded Tulane Hall. *The Times-Picayune* reported a large attendance of members, packed galleries, and frequent applause for the three women who addressed the gathering. Portia member Florence Huberwald noted that governments derive their just powers from the people's consent, then pointed out: "We are people, we are the governed, we may be taxed, imprisoned, and hung, but we cannot vote." NAWSA's Carrie Chapman Catt, who had traveled to the city expressly for the occasion, spoke for over an hour and held the crowd's attention "for every minute of it." Seventy-eight-year-old Caroline Merrick, who had appealed for suffrage at the previous constitutional convention in 1879 and did not expect to live to attend a third such meeting, literally fell to her knees to entreat the men in power to grant suffrage to women.

Delegates responded patronizingly to these intelligent, heartfelt appeals by thanking the women politely for their "interesting addresses." Caroline Merrick's weary frustration found an outlet in a letter to Mississippi suffragist Belle Kearney: "I am so dead tired and heart-sore I almost wish I were lying quiet in my grave . . . The Convention has apparently forgotten the women. They discuss the needs of every man . . . Oh, Lord, how long!" Yet, in the end, what Merrick called "a mere crumb" fell from the convention's table: the new constitution included a provision allowing tax-paying women to vote on issues of taxation.

New Orleans women seized this seemingly insignificant change in their political status and wielded it masterfully to demonstrate their political clout. ERA Club member Kate Gordon promptly organized the Women's League for Sewerage and Drainage in order to build support for creation of a modern sewerage and water board in New Orleans. The low-lying city, long plagued by epidemics and street flooding caused by primitive sewerage disposal and totally inadequate drainage, had a chance to pass a two-mill property tax with which to bring its infrastructure into the twentieth century, and for the first time, female votes could be cast. Gordon and her allies methodically compiled a list of ten thousand property-owning women and targeted them in an education campaign. Canvassing door to door and holding sixty-three parlor meetings, the women tirelessly stressed the plan's merits and the importance of women

OPPOSITE *The Awakening*, by Henry Mayer. The torch-bearing female symbolizes the awakening of the nation's women to the desire for suffrage, striding across the western states, where women already had the right to vote, toward the east where women are reaching out to her. Printed below the cartoon is a poem by Alice Duer Miller. Courtesy of the Library of Congress.

ABOVE Caroline Elizabeth Merrick, 1901. Courtesy of the Internet Archive.

exercising their right to vote. Because the constitution had provided that timid women might cast their ballots by proxy rather than dare the masculine environs of polling places, Gordon's group spent the entire election day voting hundreds of proxies, which by law had to be cast in the appropriate precincts. The measure passed, a victory for neophyte women voters and a personal triumph for Gordon, who received accolades in the press and a gold-handled umbrella from the mayor.

This demonstration of suffrage strength in the South led to Kate Gordon's elevation to a post of national prominence in 1901. NAWSA's president, hoping to make inroads among southern states, rewarded Gordon for her political success by naming her correspondence secretary for the group. Gordon moved temporarily to New York to immerse herself in the national suffrage campaign. She soon engineered the selection of New Orleans as the site of the 1903 NAWSA annual convention.

Meanwhile, coverage in the local press gave strong evidence of women's civic activism. The ERA Club pursued a wide array of civic betterment projects, including a child labor law, a juvenile court in New Orleans, a curfew for minors, teacher pay raises, elected school boards, admission of women to Tulane's School of Medicine, creation of a state tuberculosis hospital, and appointment of factory inspectors. A core group of New Orleans women were following a trajectory described by historian Anne Firor Scott, who identified the process by which southern women frequently progressed toward suffragism. First came work in church groups; from this, some women went on to voluntary associations that undertook to reform urban-industrial society's problems. From the realization that their much-touted womanly "influence" was insufficient to correct these problems, some women then progressed to the stage of embracing woman suffrage as the most essential reform of all, the change that would replace women's indirect influence with genuine electoral power.

Jean Gordon, Kate's younger sister, articulated this continuum succinctly. Realizing ruefully that ERA Club members had complained, to no avail, to city government of various ills plaguing New Orleans, she commented, "No woman who has ever tried to take a hand in public matters did not see that the question of woman suffrage is at the basis of absolutely all reform. Every woman's club is, and should be, a kindergarten school for woman suffrage." After testifying at the legislature for a child labor bill in 1908, where she took a "hammering" from representatives of the state's mill owners and saw lawmakers persuaded to vote against children's welfare, she again lamented the inadequacy of women's "influence" and concluded, "If I had never been a suffragist before my recent experience, I would immediately become one."

By the second decade of the twentieth century, both the national suffrage movement and the suffrage movement in New Orleans were steadily gaining strength. Progressivism, a reform movement then reaching its height, saw women as natural allies, and progressives worked for women's enfranchisement. Just as the national momentum began to surge, however, the local movement experienced a schism from which it never recovered.

Two paths led to votes for women: individual amendments to the various state constitutions, or one amendment to the US Constitution. By the state path, some women might never vote because, conceivably, some conservative states would never amend their constitutions. By the federal path, all the nation's women would be enfranchised in one swoop, once the necessary three-fourths of states ratified an amendment passed by both houses of Congress. Beyond the South, by 1914 nine states had enfranchised their female citizens fully by amending their constitutions, and in other states, women enjoyed partial suffrage in certain types of elections. Each success had come at enormous human and financial expense; many failing state campaigns were waged as well. NAWSA leaders began to pin their hopes on a federal amendment, reasoning that congressional delegations from suffrage states would certainly support a federal amendment (for fear of offending the female vote) and that delegations from areas where the progressive sentiment was strong were also pro-suffrage. Momentum for a federal amendment swelled.

ABOVE Program from the Thirty-fifth Annual Convention of the National American Woman Suffrage Association, held in New Orleans, March 19-25, 1903. Edited by Harriet Taylor Upton. Courtesy of The Historic New Orleans Collection.

Many white southerners, however, feared a federal suffrage amendment. These individuals believed that by bringing federal intrusion into state electoral matters, such a measure would bring a resurgence of the black vote. Southern lawmakers, asserting that easily swayed or bought black voters were a corrupt element in politics, professed to see black disfranchisement as a progressive reform. State by state, they had recently eliminated the bulk of the black vote, by instituting poll taxes, literacy tests, and other subterfuges, sabotaging the Fifteenth Amendment but justifying their actions as "reasonable safeguards" protecting the integrity of the ballot. Federal control over the electoral process might end these subterfuges and weaken the Democratic Party, the enforcer of white supremacy in the South. By this reasoning, a federal woman suffrage amendment posed a dire threat to what had come to be called "the southern way of life."

For southerners motivated primarily by considerations of race, woman suffrage by state amendment was the only acceptable approach; a federal amendment was anathema. Kate Gordon fell into this group. She wanted the ballot for "the intelligent, educated white women of the South" but hoped that "the negro as a disturbing element in politics [would] disappear." Her rhetoric on the subject of white supremacy was more extreme and blatantly racist than that of any other southern suffragist. However, within the ERA Club, many women felt that, in order to obtain the vote for themselves, they could countenance seeing black women vote as well.

Disenchanted with NAWSA strategy, which increasingly directed its energies toward a federal solution, Gordon in 1913 formed the Southern States Woman Suffrage Conference (SSWSC), dedicated to pursuit of state amendments only. She had hoped to lead a coalition of suffragists in the southern states, but their support of SSWSC was lukewarm. Gordon certainly expected the membership of the New Orleans ERA Club to follow her lead, but in this she was disappointed. A quiet revolt ensued because most members were not as ideology-driven and race-obsessed as Gordon. Many ERA members joined with Lydia Wickliffe Holmes of Baton Rouge to form the Woman Suffrage Party (WSP), which affiliated with NAWSA and began an energetic campaign for passage of the federal amendment. The ERA Club, at Gordon's behest, responded by expelling anyone who affiliated with WSP rather than Gordon's SSWSC.

"We are people, we are the governed, we may be taxed, imprisoned, and hung, but we cannot vote."

—Florence Huberwald

Suffragists who supported a federal amendment both disagreed with Gordon's racist ideology and resented her heavy-handed ways, commenting on her "jealousy and dominant authority," labeling her "selfish [and] arrogant." By all accounts, Kate Gordon was a gifted public speaker, a dedicated reformer, and a highly intelligent woman, but also an inflexible leader who generated tensions. Prone to pettiness, she viewed the rival suffrage group as a personal betrayal. Gordon's group and the maverick Woman Suffrage Party never managed to work cooperatively together.

New Orleans, which had boasted one of the strongest suffrage movements in the South, was, ironically, the force that blocked woman suffrage in Louisiana. In 1916, a state suffrage amendment came up for a vote in the legislature and lost 59–50. The machine-controlled New Orleans delegation had opposed it, 24–4. Hoping for a better outcome in 1918, WSP members went in person to an ERA meeting, offering to cooperate with Gordon's faction to achieve passage of the state amendment in the 1918 session, but were told that no cooperation would be possible unless their group repudiated its prior support for the federal amendment. Thus ERA and WSP worked separately, and, as it happened, successfully, for passage of the state amendment, which led to a referendum. New Orleans boss Martin Behrman, who wanted no reform-minded female voters in his electorate, ordered his seventeen ward leaders to deliver their votes against it. Despite Governor Ruffin Pleasant's strong backing of the amendment and despite its success in nearly every parish in the state, the patronage-rich Behrman machine, doling out favors and jobs, crushed the divided New Orleans suffragists, who wielded nothing more than petitions, ads, and speeches. The city vote was 5,411 for and 14,492 against, and it tipped the scales against woman suffrage.

Both WSP and ERA leadership specifically blamed Mayor Behrman for the amendment's defeat, comparing him to the Kaiser and referring to his "autocratic" ways. Coming only days before the Armistice, these comments rankled and Behrman struck back, alluding to Gordon's contentious personality. "Miss Gordon's support of suffrage had as much to do with its defeat as my opposition," he observed, probably correctly. Gordon histrionically announced plans for a highly symbolic rally at the Liberty Monument, the marble shaft at the foot of Canal Street that commemorated the 1874 "Battle of Liberty Place." In this battle, irate unreconstructed southern whites temporarily seized control of New Orleans from the Reconstruction state government, until federal troops arrived and ended their insurrection; the monument thus served to celebrate white supremacy. Gordon planned to drape the Liberty Monument in black, "in mourning for the repudiation of state's rights principles." WSP members pointedly declined to participate.

In 1920, New Orleans men and women again addressed the issue of woman suffrage. The Nineteenth Amendment passed both houses of Congress and, by summer, had won approval in thirty-five states, needing but one more for ratification. Louisiana lawmakers introduced both the federal and a state suffrage amendment, and a titanic struggle began. Three factions emerged: ratificationists (pro–federal amendment), states' righters (pro–state amendment), and antis (no suffrage for women under any conditions). Victory in this three-cornered fight would go to the group that could ally with one of the others. Each suffrage faction wanted the other to have a vote on its amendment first, the assumption being whichever measure went first would be defeated and the one remaining might be passed with a coalition of pro-suffrage support.

When the legislature debated the relative merits of the two amendments, galleries were packed and feelings ran high. A mid-June session turned into an uproar with all sides shouting; the Speaker of the House broke two gavels trying to keep order and the press reported "tumult," "wrangling," and "terrific noise." The sergeant-at-arms repeatedly attempted to clear the floor of visitors, without success, and parliamentary maneuvers continued as each faction struggled to force the other into a vote on its measure. After a fraught six weeks, the contentious issue finally died in Louisiana; the house killed the federal amendment and the state amendment failed in the senate.

In a sad irony, Kate Gordon, who had worked for woman suffrage for over twenty years, traveled to Nashville in August 1920 to lobby against the federal suffrage amendment, but Tennessee lawmakers, by a one-vote margin, approved the measure. Though favoring votes for women, she inveighed against the federal measure not for the effect it would have on women, but for the effect she maintained it would have on southern blacks. Although New Orleans suffragists never agreed on the appropriate vehicle for achieving the cherished right to vote, the federal machinery of the Nineteenth Amendment at last enfranchised all women. In November 1920, New Orleans women proudly voted in their first presidential election.

"The Man Who Won the War For Us"

Andrew Higgins and the pivotal role of New Orleans during WWII

by Jerry Strahan

In September 1943, as the U.S. Task Force attacked Marcus Island in the Pacific and General Douglas MacArthur's forces captured Salamaua in New Guinea the American Navy totaled 14,072 vessels. 12,964 of these boats, representing 92 percent of all Navy craft, were designed by Higgins Industries, Incorporated of New Orleans. 8,865 were actually built at Higgins' New Orleans plants.

Founder and president of this remarkable company was Andrew Jackson Higgins, an outspoken, rough-cut, hot-tempered Irishman with an incredible imagination and the ability to turn wild ideas into reality. He hated bureaucratic red tape, loved good bourbon, and was the sort that tended to knock down anything that got in his way.

To the Navy's Bureau of Ships, which favored the large Eastern Seaboard shipyards, Higgins was nothing more than an arrogant small boat builder from the South—a thorn in its side. To the Marine Corps, however, which was desperately searching for an effective landing craft, he was a savior.

He hated bureaucratic red tape, loved good bourbon, and was the sort that tended to knock down anything that got in his way.

Higgins rose to international prominence during World War II for his design and mass production of naval combat motorboats—boats that forever changed the strategy of modern warfare. The Allies no longer had to batter coastal forts into submission, sweep harbors of mines, and take over enemy-held ports before they could land an assault force. The "Higgins boats," as they were called, gave them the ability to transport thousands of men and hundreds of tons of equipment swiftly through the surf to less-fortified beaches, thus eliminating the need for established harbors.

The New Orleans company actually designed and produced two basic classes of military craft. The first class consisted of high-speed PT boats, which carried anti-aircraft machine guns, smoke-screen devices, depth charges, and Higgins-designed torpedo tubes. Also in this class were the anti-submarine boats, dispatch boats, 170-foot freight supply vessels, and other specialized patrol craft for the Army, Navy, and the Maritime Commission.

The second class of craft designed and built by Higgins in New Orleans consisted of various types of landing craft such as: LCPs (Landing Craft Personnel), LCPLs (Landing Craft Personnel, Large), LCVPs (Landing craft Vehicle Personnel), and LCMs (Landing Craft Mechanized). These were constructed of wood or steel and were used to transport fully armed troops, light tanks, field artillery, and other mechanized equipment and supplies essential to amphibious operations. These are the boats that made the landings at Guadalcanal, Normandy, Iwo Jima, and thousands of other assaults possible. Without Higgins' uniquely designed craft there could not have been mass landing of troops and materiel on European shores—or the beaches of the Pacific islands, at least not without a tremendously higher rate of Allied casualties.

Higgins was born in 1886 in Columbus, Nebraska. In 1906 he moved to Mobile County, Alabama and later to New Orleans. In New Orleans he found permanent work with a lumber importer and exporter.

By 1916—at age thirty—Higgins had enough capital to start his own business, the A.J. Higgins Lumber and Export Company, located in the Hibernia Bank building in New Orleans' Central Business District.

It was because of his lumber business that Higgins became involved in boat building. He needed specialized boats and barges that could haul logs out of the south Louisiana swamps. Unable to find such craft he decided to design and build them himself.

OPPOSITE Born in Nebraska, Andrew Higgins started his own business, located in the Hibernia Bank building in the Central Business District, in New Orleans in 1916. Courtesy of the collection of Jerry Strahan at the National WWII Museum.

A rugged, shallow-draft craft was required, capable of running up on river banks and sandbars, then retracting itself without damage to the hull or propeller. By trial and error, Higgins developed the spoonbill-bow Eureka, the direct ancestor of the military's personnel landing craft. Soon, others took notice and wanted these unique boats for their own businesses.

Higgins was proud of his boat. It had speed, durability, and maneuverability. There were times potential customers doubted these qualities. On those occasions Higgins took skeptics through a trial course on Lake Pontchartrain. He would steer the Eureka over floating logs, turn it at breakneck speed in its own length, and finish by running the craft up the lake's concrete sea-wall. By the end of the test most passengers believed in both the boat and God.

In 1934, Higgins contacted the Navy's Equipment Board to see if it had an interest in his shallow draft Eureka. It didn't. He approached the Board again in 1936 and received the same reply. Finally, in 1937 the Secretary of the Navy officially recognized the need for landing craft and created the "Continuing Board for the Development of Landing Boats." This new Board authorized Higgins to build a 30-foot boat for testing. Higgins recommended a 36-foot or even a 39-foot model, either of which would be capable of carrying more men and equipment.

The Board was adamant—the boat had to be 30-foot. They wanted a craft that would fit the already existing davits on their ships.

Higgins got so exasperated, that without an order—and at his own expense, he built a 36-foot boat in his downtown St. Charles Avenue plant, and shipped it to Norfolk, demanding that it be tested.

As a result of the test, the Marine Corps felt that the Eureka had proven that it was the most effective personnel landing boat available. Still, the Navy stubbornly continued pushing boats designed by its own Small Boat Division. Competitive sea trials held in 1940 forced the Navy to concede the inferiority of its designs and adopt the 36-foot Eureka as the military's standardized personnel landing boat. Higgins had won the first battle, but his war with the Navy's Bureau of Ships was far from over.

While Higgins had been developing personnel landing craft and motor torpedo boats, he had yet to design tank landing craft or tank lighters as they were often called. For almost four decades the Navy had been trying to develop a suitable craft capable of transporting artillery from ships at sea to the shores of enemy held beaches. Several designs had been tried, but all had failed.

In March 1941, it appeared that the United States might have to seize the island of Martinque to halt its use as a German submarine base. Such an operation would require an amphibious assault. Marine Corps General Holland Smith had absolutely no faith in the Bureau's ability to design and produce the craft that the Marines would need. He turned to the one person he believed could accomplish it—Andrew Higgins.

Smith sent Marine Corps Lt. Victor Krulak to New Orleans in September 1937, to show Higgins a photograph of a very unique craft. Krulak, an assistant intelligence officer, had gotten permission from the Marines, the Navy, and the Japanese, to "observe a Japanese amphibious assault on Chinese positions at the mouth of the Yangtze River." During this 1937 assault Krulak photographed a ramped Japanese landing barge. Smith wanted to know if Higgins could replace the Eureka's rounded bow with a ramp similar to the one on the Japanese craft. If possible, the advantages would be enormous.

Higgins enthusiastically accepted the challenge and offered to build a prototype at his own expense. Immediately, he had his men begin modifying a Eureka at his St. Charles Avenue plant. On May 26th Navy

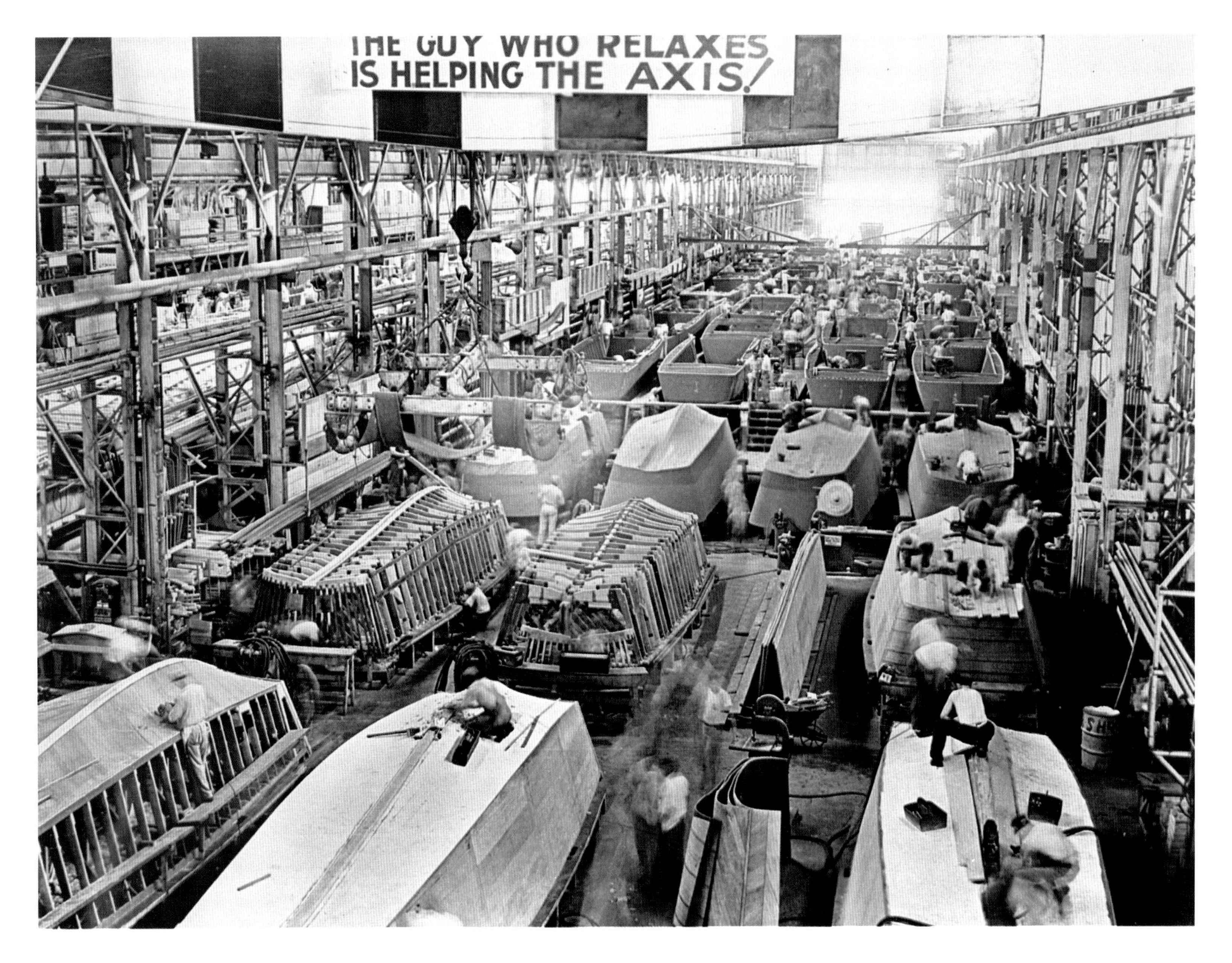

OPPOSITE By the end of the war, Higgins Industries had produced more than 20,000 boats. Finished boats were shipped by rail from the Higgins plant near City Park to Bayou St. John, in Mid-City, where they were tested. Courtesy of the collection of Jerry Strahan at the National WWII Museum.

ABOVE The Higgins boat assembly line at Higgins' City Park Plant, New Orleans, 1940. Courtesy of the collection of Jerry Strahan at the National WWII Museum.

Commander Ross B. Daggett, representing the Bureau, came to New Orleans and witnessed the first trial run of the ramped Eureka. As a result of the tests, the next day Higgins received a call from the members of the Bureau's Continuing Board for the Development of Landing Boats. They informed him that a special committee would be sent to New Orleans in three days to officially test his newly designed ramped craft. Additionally, they requested that he have sketches of a 45-foot tank landing craft ready for their review. Higgins informed them that instead of drawings he would have a tank lighter built and in the water when they arrived.

"It can't be done," the Board member replied.

"The hell it can't," Higgins responded, "just be here in three days."

When the Marine Corps and Navy officials arrived in the Crescent City they found not only a 36-foot ramped Eureka, but also a completed tank lighter. The boat had been designed, built, and put in the water in 61 hours. Higgins and his crew had accomplished in less than three days what the Navy's Bureau of Ships had not been able to accomplish in almost three decades.

After successful trials, the Bureau immediately ordered 49 additional 45-foot tank lighters and instructed Higgins that "every means practicable be taken to expedite completion and delivery of ten of these craft." They had to arrive in Norfolk, no later than June 15th. This gave Higgins approximately two weeks to build and deliver ten tank lighters. He now had two major problems—space and material.

His St. Charles Avenue plant was already at capacity and his City Park facility, located next to Delgado Trades School, though not complete, was in full production building boats for the British. And even though he was building another larger shipyard on the Industrial Canal, it would be at least a month before that facility would be usable.

To solve the problem he closed off an entire block of Polymnia Street, which bordered one side of his downtown St. Charles Avenue plant and transformed it into a temporary warehouse and fabrication yard. The actual assembling of the craft took place in an old stable located on the block, which Higgins had recently purchased. The ceiling in the stable was so low that cranes couldn't be used. The steel, sometimes weighing as much as a ton, had to be carried in on men's shoulders.

Because of the drastic measures taken by Higgins, the residents of Polymnia Street could not drive their automobiles to their homes, trucks could not make deliveries to the houses or businesses on the closed-off block, and garbage vehicles could not pass through for their collections.

Few people complained. This was the least sacrifice they could make for the war effort, though a brothel owner whose business was located on the closed-off block argued that the "racket destroyed romance" and threatened to take the matter up with the proper officials.

After the problem of locating a construction site was solved, steel had to be acquired. Higgins' normal suppliers could not guarantee such a large shipment on such short notice. Therefore, he took matters into his own hands. After all, the government had instructed him to use "every means practicable."

The industrialist discovered that a barge load of the type of steel needed was anchored up river near Baton Rouge. He sent a fleet of trucks and his armed plant guards to persuade the consignee to release the metal—still more steel was needed. He had a Birmingham steelmaker called off a golf course on a Sunday afternoon and convinced him to allocate the additional material. Then, he had the Navy pressure Southern Railway to attach the flatcars of steel to the rear of a passenger train headed to New Orleans.

Detroit could not immediately ship the 100 engines needed so Higgins sent trucks across the South to purchase engines from dozens of retail outlets. That left him missing only one key ingredient; the heavy bronze rods needed for the propeller shafts. When he couldn't find a mill to supply the shafting on such a short notice, he looked to oil field supply companies in Louisiana and Texas. Shafting was located in Texas, but the owner refused to sell. There was no time to have the Navy expropriate the material.

So, Higgins sent a company truck, a few of his workers, and a pair of heavy duty wire cutters on a midnight raid to the Texas depot. With Texas Rangers in hot pursuit, his company truck crossed the state line and back into the friendly jurisdiction of the Louisiana State police. Arrangements had already been made for prompt payment to the benevolent Texas corporation.

Higgins' men worked around the clock. As a result of their efforts nine landing craft arrived in Norfolk by special train twelve days after the verbal order was given. The deadline was met even though several boats had to be painted while en route by rail to Virginia.

World War II offered Higgins opportunity. Had the Japanese not bombed Pearl Harbor, he probably would have remained a successful, but small, Southern boat builder. Because of the war, he rapidly became an international figure and New Orleans became the epicenter of landing craft design and production.

Higgins' company encompassed seven plants and employed over 20,000 workers. His facilities occupied more than 100 million square feet, of which 5 million were under roof. In those facilities more than 64 different products were produced, including some parts destined for the Manhattan Project and the production of the first atomic bombs.

Higgins' part in the Manhattan Project has not yet been fully declassified. However, it is known that those working on the Project at Higgins' Michoud facility in eastern New Orleans were considered part of the company's "carbon division."

Higgins Industries output for the war effort was massive. During one fifteen month period 25,779 freight cars delivered over 910,000 tons of material to the company's three main New Orleans boat plants. Using that material and more, the workers at Higgins Industries produced an incredible 20,094 boats for

LEFT Color page advertisement showing American infantry troops storming a beach from one landing craft while a light tank rolls off another. Courtesy of The Historic New Orleans Collection.

the war effort. At its production peak the Higgins plants turned out a combined total of 700 boats in a single month.

Higgins did more than just produce the boats, though. He offered classes in their use. In the summer of 1941, the industrialist established the Higgins Boat Operators and Marine Engine Maintenance School. He understood that in order for his uniquely designed new landing craft to achieve maximum effectiveness, "his instructors" would have to teach the future operators, or coxswain as they were called, proper beaching techniques.

Classes were first held at Higgins' St. Charles Avenue plant. Later, as the military increased the number of trainees, instruction was moved to the lobby of the City Park plant, then to the company's West End facility on Lake Pontchartrain.

It was on Lake Pontchartrain that Higgins trained thousands of coxswain. Those same coxswain were at the helm of Higgins boats when they hit the enemy held beaches of Normandy and the numerous islands of the Pacific. The Navy took a page from Higgins' school and established similar training facilities under the instruction of their personnel. Many of the Navy's instructors received their initial training at Higgins New Orleans school.

Marine Corps General Holland Smith on December 6, 1941 wrote to the industrialist "Often I ponder the question, 'Where the Hell would the Amphibious Force have been without you and your boats?'"

The Higgins boats produced in New Orleans were used in every major amphibious assault during World War II. They were also heavily relied upon after the soldiers hit the beaches.

New Orleans became the epicenter of landing craft design and production.

In the 1990s, Krulak (at the time a retired Lt. General) explained to me that the Higgins boats were basically "the pickup trucks of the Pacific." Once a beachhead had been taken, the ramped LCVPs and LCMs would switch from carrying troops to transporting supplies, armament, ammunition, and vehicles. He believed that Higgins' greatest accomplishment was that he gave the Allies the one thing that they desperately needed, "a bridge to the beach."

Lest there be lingering doubts concerning Higgins' impact on amphibious warfare and the outcome of WWII, a statement made by Supreme Allied Commander Dwight Eisenhower should lay them at rest. Eisenhower once described Higgins to historian Stephen Ambrose as, "the man who won the war for us."

The boats produced in Higgins' New Orleans plants, the landing craft training that took place on Lake Pontchartrain bordering New Orleans, and the parts milled by his company's "carbon division" were all critical pieces of the Allied victory. The contributions of the men and women of Higgins to the war effort cannot be overstated.

THE NATIONAL WWII MUSEUM

For nearly ten years, Gordon H. "Nick" Mueller and historian Stephen Ambrose worked together to create a museum commemorating the Second World War, and on June 6, 2000, the 56th anniversary of D-Day, the National D-Day Museum opened in New Orleans, dedicated to the Battle of Normandy and other landings as well as the liberation of France.

A 4,000,000-dollar capital expansion begun in 2004 has allowed the museum to grow from one to five pavilions on an expansive six-acre campus. The museum's focus has also greatly expanded to include the European Theater, Pacific Rim, Home Front and Beyond, and in 2003 it was designated by Congress as the country's National WWII Museum. In 2009, the Solomon Victory Theater, Stage Door Canteen, and American Sector Restaurant and bar opened to serve, entertain, and educate museum visitors. Other highlights include the John E. Kushner Restoration Pavilion, dedicated to preserving and restoring relics of the War; The US Freedom Pavilion: The Boeing Center, the largest building in the museum, primarily showcasing air power; and more recently, the exhibits, the *Road to Berlin: European Theater Galleries*, *Road to Tokyo: Pacific Theater Galleries* and *The Arsenal of Democracy: The Herman and George Brown Salute to the Home Front*. An exciting new exhibit, *PT-305: The Ride of a Lifetime*, attracts visitors to its floating exhibit on Lake Pontchartrain by offering tours and rides on the restored Higgins-built boat.

The state of the art multimedia National WWII Museum is the most visited museum in the city and one of the most popular in the nation. Nick Mueller was honored for his vision and dedication by being awarded the French Legion of Honor Medal in 2016 alongside Tom Hanks and Tom Brokaw, longtime champions of The National WWII Museum in New Orleans.

ABOVE Courtesy of the National WWII Museum.

Engine of Equality

New Orleans was a frontier for legal battles and protests that fueled the Civil Rights movement

by Kara Tucina Olidge, PhD

By the turn of the century, Jim Crow was embedded in the consciousness of America with the seminal film *Birth of a Nation* (1915). The film fueled the fears of white Americans by criminalizing African Americans. Despite the terror and brutality during this period, African Americans still challenged the injustices taking place in the United States, like the "separate but equal" precedent, by documenting acts of violence in black communities, presenting cases in courthouses, organizing peaceful protests, and staging sit-ins. Slowly the fissures began to spread throughout Jim Crow, resulting in several mid-century landmark events that would redirect the course of this nation. First, the US Supreme

Court declared the segregation of public schools unconstitutional in Brown vs. Board of Education (1954). Ten years later, President Lyndon B. Johnson signed the Civil Rights Act of 1964, followed by the Voting Rights Act of 1965.

People worldwide read about these landmark decisions and saw black-and-white images of the marches, sit-ins, and other nonviolent protests that would be identified as the Civil Rights Movement in the United States. These iconic pictures of the Movement—Mrs. Brown and her daughter on the steps of the State Supreme Court in Topeka, Kansas; police using water hoses and attack dogs on African Americans in Selma, Alabama; and the bus boycott in Montgomery, Alabama—would shape how we understand these historic events. With the exception of *Plessy vs. Ferguson*, many are not aware of civil rights activism in New Orleans and its relationship to a movement that broke down the walls of segregation by exposing the brutality and injustices of Jim Crow in the United States. In the annals of history, New Orleans is often forgotten during this period; however, the "city that care forgot" played a pivotal role in the movement that changed this nation.

Desegregating New Orleans: Education as a Battleground

During the 1930s, African Americans in the United States joined organizations across the nation to fight for their constitutional rights as citizens. It was during this time that the National Association for the Advancement of Colored People (NAACP) created the Legal Defense Fund (LDF) to challenge segregation in the Unites States. The inequities in public education became a primary battleground as school facilities and educational resources intended for African American students, as well as African American teachers whose salaries, were substandard at best. The NAACP also began to build its case against the Orleans Parish School Board (OPSB). LDF's director, Thurgood Marshall, who later became the first African American justice on the United States Supreme Court, encouraged a New Orleans lawyer, A. P. Tureaud, to join LDF; Tureaud eventually served as counsel for the NAACP New Orleans chapter. Working closely with Marshall, Tureaud filed a case in New Orleans that set a precedent of equal pay for African American teachers across the state. In McKelpin vs. Orleans Parish School Board (1941) Tureaud argued that inequity in salaries based on race and color was unconstitutional. While OPSB filed a motion to dismiss the case because federal courts lacked jurisdiction over a state-controlled matter, Marshall and Tureaud recognized its importance. Despite OPSB's attempts to delay the case, Tureaud received a favorable ruling in June 1942 from the Louisiana Supreme Court, establishing the "complete equalization of salaries of Negro teachers with that of the white teachers in the schools of New Orleans."

LDF lawyers also argued that the substandard facilities and educational resources African American students were forced to use violated their constitutional rights. Tureaud advocated for a consolidation and conversion program that would provide better facilities for those students. His efforts were met with resistance, since many of the schools identified for conversion were in white neighborhoods. In *A More Noble Cause: A. P. Tureaud and the Struggle for Civil Rights in Louisiana*, biographers Rachel Emanuel and A. P. Tureaud Jr. note that Rosana Aubert vs. Orleans Parish School Board (1948) was "one of the longest-running school desegregation cases, changing names twice, spanning a quarter of a century, and having more than 35 hearings"; it became Tureaud's "most publicized case." He would go on to file five cases in neighboring parishes arguing that African American students were being denied equal protection under the Fourteenth Amendment of the US Constitution to be educated in safe and sanitary schools. By the 1950s, many schools were converted without obstruction even though, as Tureaud noted, "school desegregation was one of the things that most white officials did not want." Marshall, Tureaud, and LDF staff realized that to dismantle segregation in public schools meant changing the system entirely through integration. This also meant overturning Plessy vs. Ferguson, which Tureaud believed could finally be accomplished in view of recent victories in federal court.

Given LDF's change in strategy, Tureaud, along with Marshall and Robert Carter, filed Bush vs. Orleans Parish School Board on September 4, 1952. Tureaud argued for African American students' rights under the Equal Protection Clause of the Fourteenth Amendment, this time directly challenging the "separate but equal" precedent. LDF filed four cases—in South Carolina, Kansas, the District of Columbia, and Virginia—to test the constitutionality of segregated schools. While these cases were moving through their respective court systems, the Supreme Court handed down the Brown vs. Board of Education ruling in 1954, overturning *Plessy vs. Ferguson*. After Brown, Tureaud resumed the Bush case in 1955 in New Orleans, since southern states were refusing to comply with the US Supreme Court ruling. The OPSB was one of the staunchest opponents of the Brown decision. Despite the US District Court for the Eastern District mandating that New Orleans schools desegregate in 1956, it would take four more years for OPSB to comply.

On November 14, 1960, four elementary-aged African American girls were escorted by federal agents into all-white public schools in New Orleans. Ruby Bridges would be the lone student to integrate William Frantz Elementary School, while Gail Etienne, Tessie Prevost, and Leona Tate would integrate McDonogh No. 19 Elementary School, facing hatred and daily threats of violence. Not only were these young girls subjected to overt acts of racism, they also were often isolated during the school day because of the visceral community reaction to school desegregation. In her PBS interview, *Ruby Bridges: A Class of One*, Bridges discusses how her teacher, who had relocated from Boston to teach at Frantz Elementary, had no idea that the school was being integrated. Despite racial tensions just steps away from the school's entrance, her teacher would greet her and teach her daily, even though she was the only child in the classroom. After their enrollment, Etienne, Prevost and Tate, known as the McDonogh Three, were not only taught in a separate class but soon were the only three students in the entire school. In the 2004 oral history *We Were Born to Do This*, conducted by Brenda Square for the Amistad Research Center, Tate remarks, "We tried to be sociable. It was like the white children wanted to talk to you but they couldn't. . . I do remember the white parents removing their children from school and I think by the end of that [first] day they were totally gone."

Boycotts, Sit-ins, and Freedom Rides

As OPSB began the long journey to desegregate schools in New Orleans, the Civil Rights Movement was experiencing a second surge of energy from college-aged students who began organizing and creating nonviolent strategies to challenge discrimination in commercial sectors. Inspired by the Student Nonviolent Coordinating Committee's sit-ins in Atlanta and Nashville, students from Xavier, Southern, Dillard, and Tulane Universities joined the Consumers League of Greater New

OPPOSITE Protesters on Canal Street, 1961. Photo by Constance Harse. Courtesy of the Amistad Research Center, the Constance Harse Papers, Tulane University.

Orleans (CLGNO) in 1959 to organize a protest against discrimination in businesses on Dryades Street. Founded by Reverend Avery Alexander and Dr. Henry Mitchell, CLGNO sought to end racially biased employment practices in African American neighborhoods and major shopping districts. CLGNO initiated a series of negotiations with Dryades Street business owners but failed to make any gains in securing employment opportunities. This led to the 1960–1961 boycotts in major shopping districts, including Dryades Street, Claiborne Avenue, and Canal Street. The first boycott was held on Dryades Street, a predominantly Jewish merchant district heavily frequented by African Americans. In his highly acclaimed book, *Race and Democracy: The Civil Rights Struggle in Louisiana, 1915—1972*, British historian Adam Fairclough names Rudy Lombard (a student at Xavier University), Oretha Castle (a student at Southern University at New Orleans), and Hugh Murray (a white graduate student at Tulane University) among the student boycotters. Lolis Elie, a young black lawyer, as well as Xavier University Professor Dr. Raymond B. Floyd, who was head of CLGNO were on hand to address any challenges the students faced. The boycott proved to be successful.

By 1960, college students from local colleges and universities formed a local chapter of the Congress of Racial Equality (CORE) to continue nonviolent protests in New Orleans. The organization was founded in 1942 and became one of the leading activist organizations in the Civil Rights Movement. In *Our Minds on Freedom: Women and the Struggle for Black Equality in Louisiana, 1924-1967*, Shannon Frystak points out that CORE's New Orleans chapter was dominated by women: Oretha Castle, Julia Aaron, Doretha Smith, Joyce Taylor, Ruthie Wells, Katrina Jackson, Sandra Nixon, and sisters Shirley, Jean, and Alice Thompson were among the initial members. Along with other CORE members, they picketed stores on Canal and Dryades Streets, conducted sit-ins, and protested local segregated eateries, entertainment venues, and hotels. Often the peaceful protests required the assistance of other civil rights organizations because they resulted in CORE members being arrested after Mayor deLesseps ("Chep") Morrison issued orders to suppress civil disobedience in New Orleans. On September 9, 1960, seven members of the New Orleans chapter of CORE were arrested and charged with criminal mischief for staging a sit in at the Woolworth store on Canal Street. The very next day youth members from the NAACP Youth Council, led by Raphael Cassimere, followed suit and picketed Woolworth in protest of segregation and the arrest of CORE members. By September 17, 1960, CORE field secretary Jim McCain, Reverend Avery Alexander, CLGNO members, Sydney Goldfinch, and students Oretha Castle, Rudy Lombard, Cecil Carter were arrested for civil rights activities in major shopping districts. Despite the continuous arrests by the New Orleans police and harassment by white mobs, their strategies impacted business establishments. One year later, members of the New Orleans Chamber of Commerce and other local economic leaders formed a coalition to negotiate a settlement to end protests in New Orleans commercial districts.

On November 14, 1960, four elementary-aged African American girls were escorted by federal agents into all-white public schools in New Orleans.

By May of 1961, CORE organized the Freedom Rides, a series of interracial bus rides from Washington DC to New Orleans that tested the Supreme Court's decision to ban discriminatory practices on interstate buses and bus terminals. Fairclough suggests that "Freedom Rides also gave CORE a new sense of identity and cohesion, an esprit de corps fueled by shared danger and common purpose." He argues that New Orleans was pivotal because it was the final destination for the Freedom Riders: "The Crescent City Chapter played an especially important part in the project, providing food and shelter throughout the summer of 1961." New Orleanians Jerome Smith, Jean Thomson, Doris Jean Castle, Dave Dennis, and Julia Aaron participated; Smith was brutally beaten in McComb, Mississippi, and Thomson and Aaron were jailed for sixty days in the Mississippi State Penitentiary. As acts of violence increased against the Freedom Riders in Alabama and Mississippi, New Orleans became a safe space for those involved. Civil Rights activist Matt Suarez affirms in Kim Lacy Roger's *Righteous Lives: Narratives of the New Orleans Civil Rights Movement* that the debt owed to families who housed and fed protestors is too high to be repaid: "There will be no repaying [Oretha Castle's] family . . . because that's a one-, two-, three- . . . five-room house and one bath and there were times when sixty were sleeping there her mother cooked and fed all of them three meals a day . . . without getting money from anybody." Xavier University, at the urging of then dean of men Norman C. Francis, would also house Freedom Riders when they were flown to New Orleans by federal marshals after having been attacked in Anniston, Birmingham, and Montgomery, Alabama.

LEFT Tessie Prevost entering McDonogh No. 19 Elementary School, November 14, 1960. Courtesy of the Amistad Research Center, the New Orleans School Integration Photographs, Tulane University.

The New Orleans sit-ins, pickets, boycotts, and arrests continued for years, culminating in the massive Freedom March in September of 1963. These activities in New Orleans and across the South influenced the passage of the Civil Rights Act of 1964, which overturned all segregation laws in the United States. New Orleans was becoming a desegregated city. With the collective activism of the NAACP, the CLGNO, CORE and other organizations and advocates, African Americans were gaining access to the vote, supported by the efforts of leaders such as Albert Dent, Virginia Collins, C. C. DeJoie, and Llewelln Soniat, Reverends Avery Alexander and A. L. Davis, and then lawyers Revis Ortique, Ernest "Dutch" Morial, and Lolis Elie. Their activism was in turn supported by white community members who believed in a desegregated nation including then city councilman Moon Landrieu, and all recognized the inevitable change the South was facing after Brown v. Board. They saw the strength of demonstrations and protests that took the battle for equality out of the courtrooms and into the streets and understood the tenacity of the black vote as a mobilizing force. They were on the right side of justice. Not only would this movement impact the passing of the Civil Rights Acts of 1965, it also resulted in Morial becoming Louisiana's first black US Attorney, where he worked in the Department of Justice Civil Rights Division. He would go on to be the first black mayor of New Orleans, serving two terms, from 1978—1986.

Past is Prologue

The legacy of New Orleans as a significant center of protest during the Movement, and its role in toppling Jim Crow across the South, has been slighted by many historians, but its role is undeniable. The advancements of African Americans in civic and political leaderships are evident throughout our city and the nation. Their strategies of collective activism are being tapped by the present generation to continue to fight against injustices in education, housing, poverty, and the inequality of mass incarceration. Because of their brilliance and commitment to justice, we rise.

ABOVE CORE protesters singing after a rally at a skating rink in Jonesboro, La., 1965. Second from left is Jerome Smith, CORE field secretary. Courtesy of the Amistad Research Center, the Ronnie Moore Papers, Tulane University.

Part IV: SPIRITS AND SIN

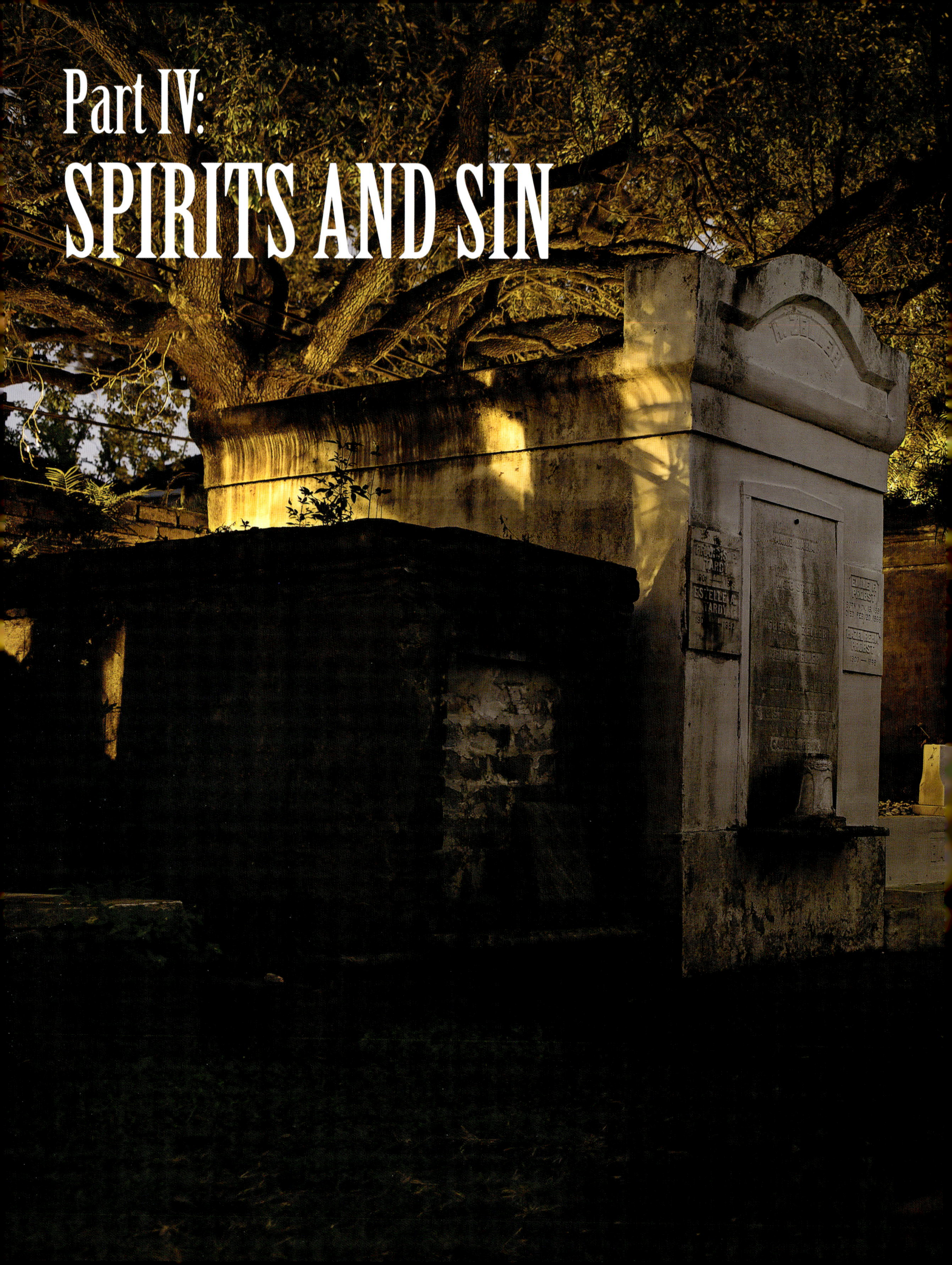

Zeller, by Frank Relle, 2013. Taken at Lafayette Cemetery No 1. From the series *Nightshade*.

Models of Piety

The Ursuline nuns and the roots of New Orleans Catholicism

by Emily Clark, PhD

There was nothing extraordinary about the weather in New Orleans in the summer of 1734. It was hot, and for three days in the middle of July the rain poured down in such torrents that the streets turned to mud. It was not a good time to have a parade, but the city's little band of Ursuline nuns and their students were determined to treat New Orleans to a grand spectacle. As soon as the sky cleared that afternoon, twenty little girls dressed as angels lined up in front of a classmate splendidly attired as St. Ursula, a sparkling vision in a silver gown and crown of faux pearls and diamonds. Eleven girls dressed in white and holding palms cut from the swamp fell in line behind her, representing the eleven thousand virgins who accompanied St. Ursula on her daring, all-female fifth-century missionary campaign. The nine nuns pulled their thick black veils over their faces, took their places behind a monstrance bearing the reserved sacrament, and set off with dozens of the rest of their students, lighted tapers in hand, for a march across the city to their new convent.

This was the grand entrance the Ursulines had imagined for themselves when they left France for Louisiana, and it made up for the undignified circumstances that marked their arrival in 1727, when they scrambled from wobbly pirogues onto the banks of the Mississippi and walked unnoticed through empty streets in the predawn light. The sisters of 1734 would be profoundly disappointed to know that their glittering procession has since been all but forgotten. The image of them that endures in the popular imagination is a nineteenth-century painting that shows them standing meekly on the riverbank with a Capuchin friar indicating what the nuns were expected to do by pointing at a group of presumably unconverted indigenous people. In fact, the impressive procession comes much closer to representing the historical reality of the Ursulines: what they did in New Orleans they did on their own terms, in ways that underscored how essential women were to the success of both church and state in the colony.

The twelve Ursuline nuns who arrived in New Orleans in the summer of 1727 already knew exactly what work the men of the colony wanted them to do, and it was not the conversion of the indigenous population. The Company of the Indies had made a contract with the nuns to administer the colonial capital's struggling military hospital. If the women wanted to apply themselves to the work of Indian conversion, they could, as long as it did not interfere with putting the hospital to rights. The Ursulines were not nursing sisters, but they agreed to take on the hospital because they were passionately intent on securing the future of Catholicism in French Louisiana by educating the colony's women and girls in the tenets and practices of the true faith. Native American women and girls were at the top of their list.

Like their patron saint and her eleven thousand virgin companions, the Ursulines were intrepid, determined missionaries who did not conform to what early modern Europeans expected of women, especially vowed religious women. Before the Ursulines were recognized as a religious order, nuns were uniformly cloistered contemplatives, walled off from the world that they sought to save through prayer alone. The Protestant Reformation of the sixteenth century opened up a space for another kind of religious woman, one who sought to serve God through action in the world. The first Ursulines made the case that the future of Catholicism depended on the perpetuation of the true faith by the mothers who were every child's first teacher. Protestantism spread on the wings of literacy, so in order to do their jobs properly, Catholic mothers had to know not only how to recite their catechism but how to read and write it as well. By the end of the seventeenth century, there were ten thousand Ursuline nuns throughout France, educating girls in order to secure the future of Catholicism. They were, in effect, France's great internal missionary order.

In 1639, the order added international missionary activity to their portfolio when Marie Guyart, known as Marie de l'Incarnation, an Ursuline sister from Tours, France, established an Ursuline convent in Québec and embarked on a campaign of indigenous conversion. Her work inspired hundreds of women in France to enter the Ursuline order in hopes of joining the mission to the Native Americans. One of them was Marie Tranchepain, the nun charged with establishing an Ursuline convent in New Orleans. She was not enthusiastic about agreeing to manage the colonial hospital, but if it got her and her sisters in religion to New Orleans, she believed that they would find a way to do the missionary work to which they were committed. She was right, though the sisters' conversion campaign did not unfold among the Native Americans as they imagined it would, but instead among the thousands of enslaved laborers they encountered in French colonial Louisiana.

Mother Superior Marie Tranchepain dreamed of converting Native Americans for twenty-eight years before she set sail for Louisiana. The young novice, Marie-Madeleine Hachard, probably shared her vision, but within a few months of her arrival in New Orleans, she artlessly revealed the precipitous evaporation of Marie Tranchpain's dream. "The blacks are also easy to instruct once they learn to speak French," she wrote to her father in the spring of 1728. By contrast, she deemed the Native Americans who were supposed to be the objects of the nuns' evangelism poor candidates for conversion. They were baptized with "trembling because of the tendency they have to sin," she lamented.

The Ursulines never seem to have thought twice about extending their conversion campaign to the enslaved inhabitants of New Orleans. By the summer of 1727 there were roughly one thousand enslaved women and girls in and around New Orleans, and the nuns offered catechism classes to them every afternoon for an hour and a half. In 1730, a group of laywomen formed a religious association under the auspices of the nuns and dedicated themselves, among other things, to catechizing the enslaved and sponsoring them for baptism. The Ladies' Children of Mary numbered more than eighty members and included women of all social ranks. Three of its members were either enslaved or free women of African descent. Together with the Ursulines, the Ladies' Children of Mary achieved remarkable success: hundreds of enslaved people were baptized into Catholicism in the fifteen years after they began their work, a disproportionate number of them women. This initial wave of evangelization and conversion was to have significant and lasting consequences for the New Orleans Catholic community.

They educated hundreds of free and enslaved girls, built a social services infrastructure, administered the colony's first hospital, and mounted a massive conversion campaign among the enslaved.

The Ursuline sisters were fervent about their conversion project, but they were equally dedicated to the order's original purpose, female catechesis and education. Their model was unusual for its time because it made provision not only for girls whose families could afford the boarding school fees that were customary for a convent education, but also for young women of no means. Like their sisters in France, the New Orleans Ursulines ran an elite division that charged for tuition and board alongside a day school open free of charge to any girl who wanted to attend. Both divisions accepted girls of all racial backgrounds throughout the colonial period. Though the student body was relatively small for the first few decades after the Ursulines' arrival, by the end of the eighteenth century there were upwards of a hundred girls passing daily through the convent gates and into its classrooms. The Ursulines' sweeping educational project ensured a large Catholic community well versed in religious doctrine and duty, but it had an equally significant impact in the secular realm as well. By the middle of the eighteenth century, women were actually slightly more likely than men to be literate, a phenomenon unmatched in neighboring British colonial America.

OPPOSITE Mother Superior Marie Tranchepain led Ursuline nuns from France to New Orleans in 1727, inspiring the somewhat misleading painting *Landing of the Ursulines* by Paul Poincy, 1892. Courtesy of the Ursuline Convent.

ABOVE Created by Sergio Papucci in 1997, this mosaic depicts the Battle of New Orleans and the nuns praying to Our Lady of Prompt Succor. The mosaic is located in the Old Ursuline Convent herb garden. Photo by Romy Mariano, 2017.

ABOVE *Ursuline Convent*, April 2, 1899. Photo by Marie Louise Morgan. Courtesy of The Historic New Orleans Collection.

The Ursulines were intrepid, determined missionaries who did not conform to what early modern Europeans expected of women.

The devastating attack by the Natchez on Fort Rosalie in late 1729 was a turning point for New Orleans. An estimated 235 French men, women, and children were killed and dozens more left wounded or orphaned. Many inhabitants were terrified by the very real possibility that the capital city would soon fall to the same fate and made plans to leave Louisiana. The Company of the Indies gave up on the colony, and in 1732 turned it over to the French crown. Those who stayed sought ways to assuage their fear and redoubled their efforts to turn New Orleans into a place of civility and prosperity. The formation of the Children of Mary was part of that response, as inhabitants turned to their faith and to the nuns who propagated it for both solace and practical strategies for survival and stability. The sisters did more than inspire and instruct, however. They were propelled by the Natchez attack into an unlikely expansion of the services they provided the city when they agreed to take in some thirty girls orphaned by the violence. Virtually overnight, they established the city's first orphanage. It was a major innovation for both the city and the nuns.

In early modern France, orphans were not necessarily bereft of parents. Frequently they were the children of single parents who did not have the resources to care for them. In small settlements like New Orleans, the civil authorities paid families to care for those classified as orphans in a system that resembled modern foster care. Convents sometimes took in an orphan or two as well. Only big cities in France had separate institutions that cared for large numbers of such children, the kinds of establishments that today would be recognizable as orphanages. Various orders of religious women, such as the Sisters of Saint Joseph, supplied the management and labor for such places, but never Ursulines. When the New Orleans sisters agreed to take responsibility for dozens of orphan girls in the wake of the Natchez attack, they broke with tradition and broadened the spectrum of their service well beyond anything they would have done in France. The Ursulines ran the city's only orphanage for more than one hundred years, from 1730 until the city transferred this responsibility to the Poydras Orphan Asylum in 1834 (Now the Poydras Home, that provides senior care).

In France, there was a broad spectrum of vowed religious life comprising priests, friars, brothers, canons, nuns, canonesses, and sisters. All priests were religious men, but not all religious men were priests. There were orders of brothers and canons who took solemn vows but were not ordained, who, like certain orders of nuns, canonesses, and sisters, specialized in running hospitals and residential institutions that provided social services for the poor, disabled, abused, abandoned, and delinquent. In New Orleans, all the religious men were ordained, either Capuchin friars or Jesuit priests. Although both orders considered themselves missionaries, in New Orleans their activities were generally limited to saying Mass and performing the sacraments of the Church, especially baptism, marriage, and the last rites. The only other religious order in town, the Ursulines, performed the heavy lifting when it came to the missionary work of conversion while also sustaining their customary work of female education. They also stepped into the breach to undertake the kind of responsibilities that other religious orders, male and female, would have shouldered in France. In addition to the unaccustomed work of running the hospital and an orphanage, the New Orleans sisters took in battered women.

Young Marie-Madeleine Hachard reported proudly to her father in 1728 that she and her fellow nuns were "going to follow, all at the same time, the functions of four different communities, that of the Ursulines, our first and principal Order, that of the Hospitalieres, that of the Saint Josephs and that of the Refuge." With respect to this unaccustomed workload, she assured her father that "all our community is so happy that it cannot be expressed." The attrition in the ranks of the New Orleans community suggests that not all shared Hachard's enthusiasm and stamina. Only four of the original twelve who arrived in 1727 were still at the convent six years later. Nonetheless, by the mid-1730s New Orleans boasted a full spectrum of social services, thanks to the nuns who were willing to move beyond their initial job descriptions.

The history of early New Orleans Catholicism, like the history of religion, is more than the history of the institutional Church and the men who ran it. There was no religion—indeed there was no Church—without the people in the pews and the religious observances, codes, and moral conduct that they practiced not only in the sanctuary on Sunday, but also in their homes and the public spaces they traversed every day. The New Orleans Ursulines' influence over this capacious religious realm was substantial and lasting. They were not the first Catholic missionaries to set foot in the capital city being carved from the virgin forest on the banks of the Mississippi; Jesuit priests and Capuchin friars preceded them by a few years. The nuns were, however, arguably the most successful of them all. They educated hundreds of free and enslaved girls, built a social services infrastructure, administered the colony's first hospital, and mounted a massive conversion campaign among the enslaved. This last achievement was perhaps their greatest and most enduring. The Catholicism so closely identified with New Orleans would have withered without the black majority who shaped it and supported it. A northern journalist visiting New Orleans in 1805 informed his readers that, no matter when you visited the churches of New Orleans, "the chief audience is formed of mulatresses and negresses." These women were models of exactly the kind of maternal piety the Ursulines hoped to foster in colonial New Orleans: "Mothers bring their infants: some cry and occasion other disturbances," yet meanwhile the women could be "seen counting their beads with much attention and remain long on their knees." A few years after Watson visited New Orleans, Henriette DeLille was born to a free woman of color whose African-born great-grandmother learned her catechism in the household of a member of the Ladies' Children of Mary. DeLille grew up to found the Sisters of the Holy Family, an order of nuns made up of free women of color established in the 1830s. As New Orleans marks its tricentennial, Henriette DeLille's case for canonization is in its final stages at the Vatican. The Ursulines who arrived in 1727 surely hoped that New Orleans would someday produce a saint, but almost certainly never imagined playing a part in making that a reality.

ABOVE Touro Synagogue, located at the corner of St. Charles Avenue and Gen. Pershing Street, was designed by architect Emile Weil and dedicated in 1909. Photo by Nancy Morgan Minor. Courtesy of The Charles L. Franck Studio Collection at The Historic New Orleans Collection.

Shalom, New Orleans

Jewish roots date back to city's founding

The first Jewish settlers arrived in New Orleans in the early 1700s, Spanish and Portuguese Sephardic Jews who had fled the Iberian Peninsula, settled in the Caribbean, and later moved to the Gulf Coast. In New Orleans, they were subject to the *Code Noir*, decreed by the French and maintained by the Spanish, which called for their expulsion. The French did not strictly impose the law, but the Jewish settlers had more difficulty under Spanish rule. After the Louisiana Purchase and with the larger influx of European immigrants in the nineteenth century, the Jewish population of New Orleans grew. But not until 1828 was a synagogue established in the city.

The majority of the newcomers were merchants, including Maurice Barnett, who with his son, Maurice Jr., ran one of the largest and most active slave markets in the city at the St. Louis Hotel on Royal Street. He also fought to defend the city alongside perhaps the most prominent Jewish New Orleanian, Judah Touro, in the 1815 Battle of New Orleans.

Touro initially made his way as a broker consigning goods from ship cargo in the port of New Orleans and later invested his money in real estate, amassing a fortune, one that he would bestow on New Orleans and cities throughout the United States. In New Orleans, he established a free public library, donated to the development of two synagogues, and established a hospital during a yellow fever outbreak; today we have both Touro Synagogue and Touro Infirmary.

In 1840, Leon Godchaux, a Jewish peddler from Lorraine, arrived in New Orleans and transformed the sugar industry upriver; he also established a commercial shopping district on Canal Street by opening the doors to "Leon Godchaux, French and American Clothier," later The Leon Godchaux Clothing Company—the largest clothier in the city for more than thirty years. Later that century, Isidore Newman would open nearby Maison Blanche department store; both stores were household names for New Orleans shoppers for more than a century.

In 1906, Newman founded Isidore Newman Manual Training School, now Isidore Newman School. The Mannings, New Orleans' first family of football, sent all three of their children—Peyton, Eli, and Cooper—to Isidore Newman School.

Jewish philanthropists have a long history of generosity to New Orleans schools, such as Samuel Zemurray, a fruit peddler who founded Cuyamel and United Fruit Companies. Zemurray bequeathed his home, upon his death in 1961, to Tulane University, to be used as the Tulane University president's residence; he also funded the nation's first school of public health and tropical medicine at the university and in 1924 endowed Tulane's Department of Middle American Research, later the Roger Thayer Stone Center for Latin American Studies, named after his son-in-law.

Sugar mogul Isaac Delgado founded Delgado Central Trades School in 1921, now Delgado Community College, as well as the Isaac Delgado Museum, currently the New Orleans Museum of Art, the state's premier art museum.

Anti-Semitism in Europe during World Wars I and II brought orthodox Jews to the American South, many of whom were unwilling to assimilate, unlike the city's reform Jews. Jim Crow ushered in an era of white supremacy and a growth in the Ku Klux Klan; crosses were burned in the yards of Jewish and African-American families alike. Not surprisingly, the Jewish congregations in New Orleans supported civil rights and racial equality at a time when many white New Orleanians didn't.

The Jewish community was often socially isolated as well. Even though in 1872 the first King of Rex, Lewis Solomon, was Jewish, there has not been a Jewish king of Carnival since. Today traditional krewes are much more inclusive, and in 1996 L.J. Goldstein started the first Jewish Carnival krewe, Krewe du Jieux, replete with hand-painted bagels and a reigning King of the Jieuxs with his Jieuxish-American Princess consort. In 2009 that honor went to writer Rodger Kamenetz and his wife, writer Moira Crone. Kamenetz stated that the parade is "both artistic and a fun way to hang out, melding Jewish humor with the activities of Carnival."

In New Orleans today, there is an active Jewish community in the city and in the suburbs, but Kamenetz described "a growing Jewish scene in the Marigny/Bywater, where there is no synagogue: Kol HaLev, a younger crowd that meets monthly for chanting and meditation, a more informal celebration of Jewish faith." Such celebration is representative of the longstanding and profound faith of the city's Jewish community and embodies the tenacity of earliest New Orleans Jews before the city's first synagogues were built.

-Nancy Dixon, PhD

Rosh Hashanah Katrina

We crept out of Baton Rouge dark a convoy of two
slipped past the Guard at Jefferson and followed the river to Oak
still dark on Pine the street lined with drying tinder
one spark and a wind and our world would blaze

We were at the edge of a New Year raw and scattered
the magnolias dying ,the oaks still standing
the new moon like an empty socket in the sky
that God's spies looked for from the hills of Jerusalem
the end of one year, beginning of another
while our roofers climbed to patch missing slates with felt.

On our way to Touro after the light
smoke rose from Audubon then fire:
an old house burned in a furious silence

Touro 's chapel packed with Feds from out of town
we sat outside the doors, and talked
brothers and friends, sisters and friends
What we'd lost. How we got by.
Faint streams of Hebrew,
the rabbi's voice then the shofar's cry.
I closed my eyes and remembered
the sun rising over Pine
pink dawn and the empty moon
High above three white heron sailed
one by one like an off hand blessing

-Rodger Kamenetz

MINERVA
BENEVOLENT ASSOCIATION

Cities of the Dead

New Orleans' iconic cemeteries evolved from necessity and diversity

by Sally Asher

For more than two centuries, New Orleans' cemeteries have represented the city's geography and diverse cultural and religious traditions from colonial times to modern day. No other American city's cemeteries have their aesthetics and emotion. They are outdoor museums with constantly evolving art, thanks to time and the elements. They are gathering places for reflection and celebration that frequently pulse with the rhythms of jazz funerals and the festive solemnity of All Saints' Day. The tombs, which resemble miniature houses, are laid out in rows like city blocks, reflecting the architectural styles of New Orleans from the eighteenth century on. Visitors can find elegant tombs with stained glass and marble columns much like the ornate mansions on St. Charles Avenue, or simple stepped-top tombs like some of the modest homes spread around the city. These tombs, mausoleums, cenotaphs, and sarcophagi are frequently watched over by mournful angels, curious sphinxes, stalwart soldiers, regal Greek and Roman Gods, and even crying dogs and protective elks. They are more than resting places for the deceased but are denotative of the city's habitude of continually transposing its quagmires into culture.

When Jean-Baptiste Le Moyne, Sieur de Bienville, saw the site of the city he would found on the east bank of the Mississippi, he wrote, "[O]n the banks of the river is a place very favorable for the establishment of a post with one of the finest crescents on the river." A fine crescent it might have been, but the surrounding area was predominantly swamp. In 1725, the city established St. Peter Street Cemetery, its first official cemetery, located in the modern French Quarter. Earlier burials took place alongside the Mississippi. Burials at St. Peter were entirely below ground and workers dug ditches around it, using soil to build up the land. They could not, however, surmount the sodden earth. It was common after a heavy rain to find the deceased floating down city streets. While most were horrified, merchant John Pintard took a pragmatic approach in a letter to his wife in 1801:

> It is of little consequence whether one carcass is given a prey to crayfish on land—or the catfish of the Mississippi—I believe in either case of burial—a body is speedily devoured & transmigrated in crayfish or catfish—dressed by a French cook & feasted upon by a greasy Monk—a fair lady—a petit maître or savage who in their turn supply some future banquet—Heavens what luxury! Mon Dieu, quell sort! Give my bones terra firma I pray.

The city sought to solve the problem in 1789, closing St. Peter Street Cemetery and opening St. Louis Cemetery No. 1 (425 Basin St.), with wall vaults, above-ground tombs, and grand society tombs.

From 1789 until 1823, St. Louis No. 1 was the city's principal burying ground. It was divided into sections for Catholics, non-Catholics, and African Americans—in this case, slaves, as free people of color were buried with their respective religions. Early burials were done in a haphazard manner, which explains the cemetery's maze-like paths. Over time, St. Louis No. 1 decreased in size to make way for the widening of Basin Street and the extension of Tremé Street. Still, it did not lose its character. First, there were the above-ground tombs, initially built for practicality, but their later funerary design was influenced by contemporary Parisian cemeteries, particularly Père Lachaise, established in 1804. Second, there were the wall vaults sometimes described as being like ovens or cells of a honeycomb. The wall vaults serve two purposes and are true to their name—they function as walls and as vaults. They are the least expensive option for multiple burials. When it is time for someone to be interred in a wall vault, the marble plaque is removed and the layer of brick and plaster behind it is broken down. If there is a casket inside, it is taken out and the remains are moved to the side to make room for the newest resident. Third, there were the society tombs. In the nineteenth century, benevolent associations were formed to help people pay medical bills but also to guarantee them a respectable burial place in consecrated ground. Society tombs varied from the elaborate Italian Benevolent

OPPOSITE Minerva Benevolent Association tomb in Metairie Cemetery, ca. 1970. Photo by Ninette Maumus. Courtesy of The Historic New Orleans Collection.

ABOVE View of women placing flower wreaths on tombs in St. Roch Cemetery, 1935. Courtesy of The Historic New Orleans Collection.

Society tomb, made of marble, to the Dieu Nous Protège Society tomb for African Americans, made of brick and plaster.

In the nineteenth century, benevolent associations were formed to help people pay medical bills but also to guarantee them a respectable burial place in consecrated ground.

Varieties of these tombs can be found in almost all New Orleans cemeteries, but St. Louis No. 1 remains the city's most frequently visited, despite the Roman Catholic Archdiocese of New Orleans' change to visitation rules. Since March 2015, entry is only permitted with a licensed tour guide registered with the archdiocese or through special permission. This policy was sparked when the archdiocese sought to end vandalism, particularly to the grave of Marie Laveau, the cemetery's most popular resident. For decades, visitors marked her grave with countless red x's with the hope that they would curry the Voodoo Queen's favor and have their wishes granted. The significance of marking three x's on Laveau's tomb is a mystery. Some claim they were crosses that got turned on their sides over time; others believe they represent "the father, the son, and the holy ghost," or "the gods, the spirits, and the deceased souls." But regardless of their origins, some unscrupulous tour guides perpetuated these myths and encouraged people to mark up Laveau's tomb. In the early twentieth-century it was commonly done with coal or brick dust that washed off with each rain, but it unfortunately evolved into permanent markers, lipstick, and even nail polish. Many believed this act paid homage to Laveau, but they didn't realize that they were also disturbing her close neighbors. Very close. Scholar Carolyn Morrow Long recently discovered that eighty-four people reside in Laveau's tomb: family members, friends, and neighbors, of all ages (including newborns), races, and genders. Long explained that aside from being a voodoo priestess, Laveau was a healer and devout Catholic, and she frequently offered her tomb as a final resting place to those in need.

St. Louis Cemetery No. 2 (300 N. Claiborne Ave.) was established decades later to keep the city's growing population safe. It was a common belief that certain diseases such a cholera and yellow fever were caused by miasmas—poisonous vapors that arose from cemeteries. The new cemetery was located 1,800 feet beyond the city limits, which at the time comprised the boundaries of the French Quarter. It was one continuous parcel running from Canal to St. Louis Streets; the division into three squares, as it stands today, was done when new streets were cut through. Furthermore, its surrounding landscape was drastically changed in 1968, when the Claiborne Expressway was built along North and South Claiborne Avenue. The rows of serene live oaks, which shaded many a grave, were replaced by concrete and road noise. By the 1970s, St. Louis No. 2 had fallen into despair, with crumbling wall vaults and a high crime rate, earning it the nickname "Slums of the Dead," a moniker the cemetery is still trying to shake. In 1974, the archdiocese proposed to demolish its wall vaults and, almost immediately, concerned citizens formed Save Our Cemeteries (SOC). They saved the wall vaults, and the non-profit's focus has since grown and expanded to the preservation, education, and restoration of New Orleans cemeteries. Amanda Walker, Executive Director of SOC, says that since the 1970s the organization has completed many restoration projects, hundreds of clean-ups, and several tomb restoration and maintenance workshops in which they have taught the proper techniques and tools required to restore New Orleans' iconic above-ground tombs. SOC has been a vital champion for the cemeteries, preserving and strengthening their richness for all.

Originally founded in 1832, Lafayette No. 1 (1416–1498 Washington Ave.) is the second-most visited cemetery in New Orleans and the most represented in popular culture. *Easy Rider*, a 1969 film featuring actors Peter Fonda and Dennis Hooper as bikers who picked up prostitutes for an LSD-induced, sex-filled romp in the cemetery, was shot without permission in St. Louis No. 1; subsequently the archdiocese banned filmmakers from its cemeteries except for approved educational and documentary films. Lafayette No. 1, which is city-operated, remains available to filmmakers and thus is generally the archetypical New Orleans cemetery in film and television. Its most sought-out tomb – the tomb of the Mayfair witches, characters in Anne Rice's novel The Witching Hour – doesn't exist. Rice made up the tomb, drawing inspiration from the Lafayette and Jefferson Fireman's tombs.

Beyond these more celebrated cemeteries, New Orleans has many others spread throughout the city—so many that there is even a streetcar line called "Canal Streetcar–Cemeteries," which starts at the foot of Canal Street and ends at a cluster of cemeteries on City Park Avenue. Here you'll find Cypress Grove (120 City Park Ave.) and Greenwood (5200 Canal St.), established by the Fireman's Charitable and Benevolent Society in 1840 and 1852, respectively. Greenwood's most recognizable landmarks are a granite structure forty-six feet tall, featuring a mustached fireman with a hose at the ready, and the Benevolent Protective Order of Elks society tomb, which is topped by a large bronze statue of an elk. Nearby are St. Patrick Nos. 1, 2, and 3 (5000 block of Canal St. and 100 block of City Park Ave.), established in the mid-nineteenth century to accommodate the influx of Irish immigrants. Gates of Prayer No. 1 (4824 Canal St.), founded in 1858, was originally the Tememe Derech Cemetery but was later absorbed in 1939 by the Congregation Gates of Prayer. Charity Hospital Cemetery (5050 Canal St.) is home to thousands of indigent dead. It also houses the Hurricane Katrina Memorial, dedicated three years after the disaster, which serves as the final resting place of more than eighty bodies that remained unidentified or unclaimed after the storm.

BELOW Fireman and Elks tombs at the entrance to Greenwood Cemetery. Photo by Nam Vu, 2010.

If you walk northeast about five blocks you will find Holt Cemetery (635 City Park Ave.), which was originally an early burial ground for the city's indigent population and was re-established by Dr. Joseph Holt in 1879. Holt Cemetery requires that family and friends of the deceased pay the cost of digging the respective graves and keep them well-tended. Holt is unusual for New Orleans because it has below-ground graves and many handcrafted markers made from wood, Styrofoam, and even spray-painted street signs. A short drive west brings you to Metairie Cemetery (5100 Pontchartrain Blvd.), which, despite its name, is located in New Orleans. A former racetrack with broad roads, lagoons, and landscaped grounds, it has earned a place on the National Register of Historic Places. It has some of the most beautiful examples of funerary architecture in the city. At the other end of City Park Avenue is St. Louis No. 3 (3421 Esplanade Ave.), founded in 1854 and commonly referred to as the "angel cemetery" for the large numbers of angels resting on tops of its tombs. Venture into the 8th Ward for St. Roch Nos. 1 and 2 (1725 St. Roch Ave.), established in 1876 by Father Peter Leonard Thevis, fulfilling a vow to build it if his congregation was spared from the yellow fever epidemic of 1868. A notable feature is its ex-voto room, containing an altar with offerings left by people thankful for their prayers being answered: leg braces, crutches, false teeth, artificial limbs, and glass eyeballs.

In total, New Orleans has forty-two cemeteries. Aside from their beauty, what makes them truly special are the incredible stories and diversity of their residents, reflecting every era of the city's colorful history. In St. Louis No. 1 you can find chess champion Paul Morphy; the "father of architecture," Benjamin Latrobe, Creole gentleman Bernard de Marigny; and Homer Plessy of the landmark case *Plessy v. Ferguson*. Musicians Ernie K-Doe, Earl King, Paul Barbarin, Danny and Blue Lu Barker, and George Guesnon make their home in St. Louis No. 2. So do pirate Dominique You; Claude Tremé, namesake of Faubourg Tremé; the "Drummer Boy of Chalmette," Jordan Noble; the first black lieutenant governor, Oscar Dunn; the venerable Henriette DeLille; "Chief of Chiefs" of the Mardi Gras Indians, Allison "Tootie" Montana; and the first black warrior hero of the Civil War, André Cailloux. St. Louis No. 3 has jazz pianist Emma Barrett, Storyville photographer Ernest J. Bellocq, restaurateur Jean Galatoire, celebrated architects James Gallier Sr. and Jr., Big Chief Donald Harrison Sr. of the Guardians of the Flame, and civil rights leader A.P. Tureaud. Lafayette No. 1 houses Confederate General Harry T. Hays and Judge John Howard Ferguson. Greenwood Cemetery is home to New Orleans character Ruth "Ruthie the Duck Girl" Moulon and Confederacy of Dunces writer John Kennedy Toole. Musicians Buddy Bolden, Babe Stovall, and singer Jessie Hill are in Holt Cemetery. Metairie Cemetery has the remains of numerous mayors, governors, and military leaders as well as Popeye's founder Al Copeland, Storyville madam Josie Arlington, trumpeters Al Hirt and Louis Prima, and Ruth Fertel of Ruth's Chris Steak House. Many of these individuals were mourned and celebrated with two of New Orleans' unique traditions—jazz funerals and second lines.

Some scholars date jazz funerals back to music at military funerals in the late nineteenth century, and others point to roots further back, in West African traditions where the deceased were honored through music. Today's jazz funeral is an evolution of both. This tradition continues to evolve and be redefined, and welcome or not, cemeteries are undergoing a slow evolution as well, among the ways being that cremation is becoming more common.

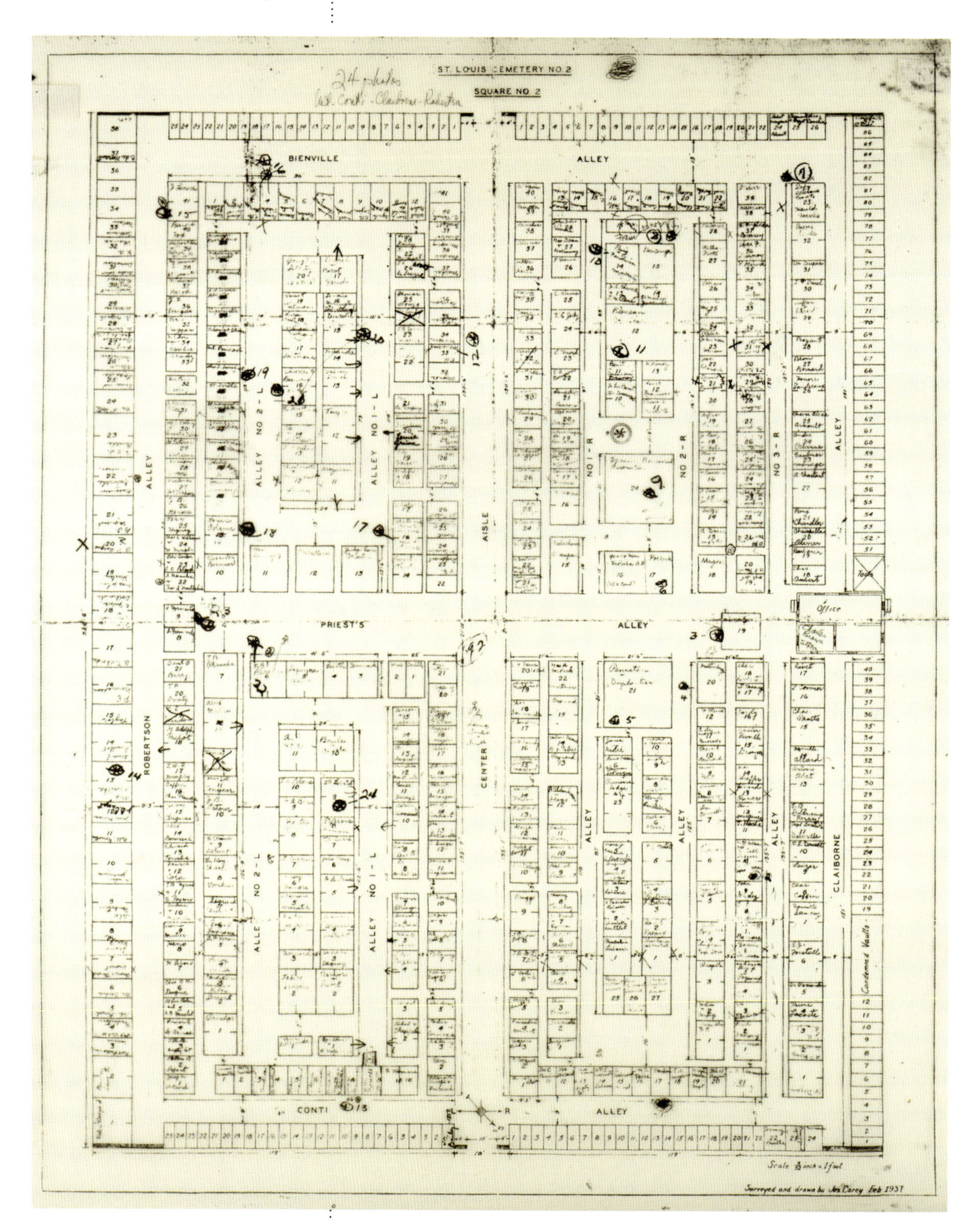

BELOW St. Louis No. 2, Square No. 2 by Joseph S. Carey Surveyor, February 1937. Courtesy of The Historic New Orleans Collection.

Surprisingly, in the 1880s, New Orleans was one of the few major cities to have a cremation society. Their main argument for cremation were sanitary concerns, contending that above-ground burial was a "dangerous and filthy practice." Among the society's proposed policies was that any indigent individual or person dying of smallpox should be cremated. The society gained such strength that in 1884 it purchased land on Canal Street just a few blocks from the streetcar station and the following year issued stock for the erection of a crematory. They proposed that to help New Orleanians get more comfortable with the controversial practice, they would start by burning garbage in their crematory before they did people. In 1886, the Vatican prohibited Catholics from joining cremation societies—a ban which held until the 1960s—and the New Orleans Cremation Society dissolved soon after, citing the "prejudice existing in religious minds." They donated their surplus funds to the homeless—the very people they had hoped to one day cremate. Over time, cremation has become less controversial, and will perhaps be responsible for a change in cemeteries' geography and significance. Gerard L. Schoen, III, the Community Outreach Director and Funeral Director of Lake Lawn Metairie Funeral Home and Cemeteries, predicts that three out of four Americans will be cremated by 2035. This is why he sees Save Our Cemeteries' mission as so vital. "As we head into the next generation," Schoen says, "cremation will change the landscape of permanent memorialization to smaller ones, which means our New Orleans cemeteries as we know them today will become more treasured as outdoor museums." All the more reason to protect and venerate them.

It was a common belief that certain diseases such a cholera and yellow fever were caused by miasmas—poisonous vapors that arose from cemeteries.

Throughout its existence, New Orleans has grappled with the tension between popularity and authenticity. Citizens are in a constant balancing act, welcoming visitors to share and participate in its traditions while at the same time trying to protect and preserve them. Each year hundreds of thousands of visitors walk through New Orleans' cemeteries, and it comes as no surprise that New Orleans' most popular tomb is the most illustrative of this particular struggle. Marie Laveau's tomb, like the city itself, is steeped in mythology, magic, religion, and history that is not only misunderstood but often grossly misinterpreted. The tomb is simultaneously vandalized and memorialized, and it epitomizes the city at its worst—slavery and segregation—and at its best—unity and healing. It is difficult to predict the evolution—or dissolution—of specific traditions or landmarks in the years to come. But like New Orleans itself, at the core of the cemeteries are the people: a diversity of races, religions, and ages, thrown together by choice and by fate, for now and eternity.

HALLOWED GROUND

Just a few of the famous New Orleanians buried in the city's cemeteries.

ST. LOUIS NO. 1

Location 425 Basin Street

- Voodoo queen Marie Laveau
- Chess champion Paul Morphy
- Architect Benjamin Latrobe
- Creole gentleman Bernard de Marigny
- Homer Plessy of the landmark case *Plessy v. Ferguson*

ST. LOUIS NO. 2

Location: 300 N. Claiborne Avenue

- Singer Ernie K-Doe
- Guitarist, songwriter, and singer Earl King
- Drummer Paul Barbarin
- Banjoist Danny Barker and wife and vocalist Blue Lu Barker
- Pirate Dominique You
- Claude Tremé, namesake of Faubourg Tremé
- "Drummer Boy of Chalmette," Jordan Noble
- Louisiana's first black lieutenant governor, Oscar Dunn
- The venerable Henriette DeLille
- "Chief of Chiefs" of the Mardi Gras Indians, Allison "Tootie" Montana
- André Cailloux, the first black warrior hero of the Civil War

ST. LOUIS NO. 3

Location: 3421 Esplanade Avenue

- Jazz pianist Emma Barrett
- Storyville photographer Ernest J. Bellocq
- Restaurateur Jean Galatoire,
- Celebrated architects James Gallier Sr. and Jr.
- Big Chief Donald Harrison Sr. of the Guardians of the Flame
- Civil rights leader A.P. Tureaud.

LAFAYETTE NO. 1

Location: 1416-1498 Washington Avenue

- Confederate General Harry T. Hays
- Judge John Howard Ferguson.

GREENWOOD CEMETERY

Location: 5200 Canal Boulevard

- Famed French Quarter character Ruth "Ruthie the Duck Girl" Moulon
- *Confederacy of Dunces* writer John Kennedy Toole.

HOLT CEMETERY

Location: 527 City Park Avenue

- Trumpeter Buddy Bolden
- Singer and guitarist Babe Stovall
- Singer Jessie Hill

METAIRIE CEMETERY

Location: Junction of I-10 and Metairie Road

- Popeye's Chicken founder Al Copeland
- Storyville madam Josie Arlington
- Trumpeter and bandleader Al Hirt
- Trumpeter and singer Louis Prima
- Ruth Fertel of Ruth's Chris Steak House

Conjurers

Voodoo in New Orleans evolved from its African roots

by Rev. Dwight Webster, PhD

Voodoo, Vodou, Vaudou, and *Vodun* are terms for an African-derived spiritual discipline that exists in New Orleans and several other parts of the African diaspora, particularly in the Caribbean. Its origin in the United States is a result of the trans-Atlantic slave trade, which for centuries took millions of enslaved Africans from their homelands to the United States on a journey known as the Middle Passage or *Maafa* (meaning great tragedy/disaster in Kiswahili). In this essay, I will use the term "Vodun" when referring to the African-originated religious system that developed, and the term "Voodoo" when referring to generic or commercial practices. When referring to the religious discipline in Haïti, I will use the term "Vodou" in keeping with Creole nomenclature and the research of historian Albert J. Raboteau and anthropologist Michel S. Laguerre.

Included among the more generic practices are those some refer to as Hoodoo. Voodoo and Hoodoo are often referred to as conjure, root work, magic, and witchcraft as well. Hoodoo developed as a departure from the African Vodun, in which there was the worship of a High God and lesser deities, forces, powers, ancestors, and elders by adherents whose communities shared a world-view and values. The practices and beliefs of Voodoo in New Orleans incorporated Native American herbology and European superstition and focused on the use of items, fluids and forces to provide paying clients with a wide range of cures and curses, protection and punishment, in New Orleans often known as gris gris.

Vodou etymologically comes from the term *Vodun*, used by the Ewe/Fon peoples of West Africa to mean great spirit, deity, something apart or separate, creator, God. The neighboring, and later European-dominated, Yorùbá people also had an effect on the development of Vodou since they were carried primarily to Brazil and Haiti, and those in Haiti, after the Revolution, voluntarily or involuntarily migrated to New Orleans. With the onset of chattel slavery in the fifteenth century and its steady increase, the enslaved captives embraced spirit-beings or deities identified as lwas/loas or *mystères*, *orishas*, and *vodun* from the western and west-central regions of Africa. The religion is often characterized by the classification that John S. Mbiti popularized, African Traditional Religion. After studying beliefs and practices of hundreds of African faith communities, he discovered that their structural and ontological features evidenced an essentially monotheistic but diffuse spiritual hierarchy. They believed in a supreme being and venerated lesser spirit-beings, much like the monotheistic spiritual hierarchy found in Catholicism and Islam. In fact, Vodou is linked to them but is an African-derived, Black spirituality, which helped the Black community resist the enslavement, European oppression, and white supremacy imposed upon them.

Changes over Time and Territory

New Orleans Vodou is on a continuum that extends from the ancient Kingdom of Dahomey (now Benin), Ghana, Togo, Nigeria, and the Angola–Congo region, across the Atlantic to the Caribbean, then to New Orleans, and points beyond. The religion moved with and through many peoples—including Euro-Americans, who added their own twists to and departures from its African practice. It is clear, though, that Africans and, later, African Americans embraced practices of those who could both heal and harm, or *Obeah*, a term derived from the Ashanti Obaye, whom European imperialists in Africa labeled witch doctors. Much later, Europeans and Americans brought to Vodou their own brand of witchcraft, one that we consider Hoodoo and sometimes Voodoo today, replete with pin-riddled dolls mixed with forms of Freemasonry, notably top hats, aprons, and other vestments instead of the power-tapped African ritual figures. Writers in Hollywood and elsewhere, with an affinity for the exotic and the erotic, have all but bankrupted the original term Vodou, leaving us with today's Voodoo and Hoodoo.

Sainte-Domingue (today Haiti), originally colonized by both the Spanish and French, became the home of Vodou in the Western Hemisphere starting in the early eighteenth century. Vodou in Haïti was eclectic. In addition to African regional sub-divisions, there were three main spirit families or lwa: *Rada*,

OPPOSITE *Marie Laveau*, by Frank Schneider. Courtesy of the Louisiana State Museum.

Petro and *Ghede*. *Rada* originated in Africa and was concerned with peace, harmony, family and advancement, by far the larger division of the religious practices transferred by enslaved Africans to New Orleans. Petro, on the other hand, originated in Haiti and has roots in violence, as a necessary response to slavery. Finally Ghede is associated with death and the souls of the dead.

The story of New Orleans Vodou is a tale of deviations in the practice. As a religion or religious system, it is consistent with the descriptions of African Traditional Religion. Variations emerged as Vodou moved from Africa to the Americas and from the communal to a more personalized practice. Eventually, the ravages of slavery, the destruction of institutional support, the loss of communal memory, and also the individualistic and corporate pursuit of the more commercialized Voodoo contributed to this deviation.

The Impact of Voodoo on New Orleans Culture

Vodou as a religion in New Orleans did retain some features of its African origins and roots. There remained a belief and worship in a supreme being, *Gran Met-la* (from *le Grande Maître* or Grand Master) or *Bondye* (from *Bon Dieu* or Good God), the supreme creator, administrator and judge, but he was not involved in the day-to-day affairs of humankind, and other African deities who survived by name through Haïti to New Orleans often became the focus of activity and interest. *Li Grande Zombi*, also known as *Damballah Wedo*, or the serpent deity, remains a major component of religious practices in New Orleans in several locales. Contrary to their Western identification as evil, in the African cosmology, snakes or serpents were regarded as representatives of wisdom and knowledge by Vodous, or worshippers. The New Orleans practice and ritual are less literal than the Haitian counterpart and hence are subject to personal interpretation. Women were and continue to be more dominant in New Orleans, while men were more dominant in Haitian Vodou. Manbo is the term for high priestess, the role of female leadership in both Haïti and New Orleans, and there are several high priestesses practicing in the city today. Their male counterparts are known as houngans and sometimes doctors. Ironically, the imposition of Roman Catholicism on slaves in New Orleans, often as a result of the eighteenth-century *Code Noir*, intended to manage and control them, instead gave cover to the fusion and practice of Vodou as well as its derivatives. Similarities still exist between the two today in part because many New Orleans Vodou leaders visit Haiti for initiation and training.

From the end of the eighteenth century through the nineteenth century, the presence and practice of Vodou in New Orleans became a mélange. Accounts of ceremonies, rituals, and practices are often racist and biased, depicting these activities as more of a circus sideshow than aspects of a practiced religious belief system. As Freddi Williams Evans, author of the seminal text, *Congo Square: African Roots in New Orleans* writes:

> By the mid 1880s, the mythology of Voudou had become institutionalized. . . . Some [white] writers on the subject sensationalized this belief system and way of life . . . Voudou grew in adherents and transcended economic, social, and racial lines at the same time the ritual practice itself was becoming commercialized. A national firm manufactured, advertised, and sold charms along with powders, and some ceremonies themselves had become a spectacle with announcements published in local papers . . . that referred to Congo Square, "Voodoo and Orgies Held Sway Here."

The sensationalized commercialization of Vodou includes amulets, talismans, ju-ju, gris-gris, and mojo paraphernalia still associated with Voodoo today, but even more with its secondary and divergent trajectory, Hoodoo. Scholars agree that whatever Voodoo is or has become in the United States in general and New Orleans in particular, it is far different from what adherents originally embraced as a balanced Vodou religious system in Africa and the Caribbean.

Leaders of the spiritual practices—houngans, manbos, and others—often studied the effective use of charms and medicine as apprentices. They found that their use opened up not only protective and punitive pathways but also business opportunities fed by superstitious fear and attraction to the exotic and the erotic. In popular New Orleans culture today, the twentieth-century New Orleans musician Dr. John (Malcolm John "Mac" Rebennack) selected his stage name as an homage to the nineteenth-century Doctor Jean Montanée, a celebrated Vodou priest, or doctor, as they were often called. Researcher Denise M. Alvarado maintains that the latter was the "loa of drummers and root doctors, and patron to male Voudou practitioners and female root women," a fitting name for Rebennack to honor. Also called Bayou John, or Prince John, Montanée, reportedly born in Senegal, was possibly of eighteenth-century Bambara royalty. His culinary, clairvoyant, and cultic skills gained him considerable power and a large following. Today Dr. John, who sings of Voodoo and Hoodoo, claims that a nineteenth-century relative of his was arrested with the Voodoo King, Dr. Jean, for practicing Voodoo and prostitution.

The religion moved with and through many peoples—including Euro-Americans, who added their own twists to and departures from its African practice.

Born at the turn of the nineteenth century, Marie Laveau is widely recognized as the New Orleans Voodoo Queen. She reigned supreme for just over half a century, from 1830-1881, and at least one of her two daughters, both named Marie–Marie Helöise Euchariste Glapion and Marie Philomène Glapion–continued her work, and although never achieving Laveau's prominence, created the appearance of immortality. Before her death in 1881, Marie Laveau was able to amass considerable influence and wealth, aided by her intelligence network of informants. As both a hairdresser and *femme de couleur libre*, or free woman of color, she had access to wealthy white households. Her power and influence spanned race, gender, and class. Laveau made secret visits to clients seeking her succor in their private homes. But she also made her presence known and felt publicly. Raboteau notes:

> Each account [of Laveau] mentions the presence of a snake representing the god Li Grand Zombi; drumming, singing, dancing; possession, which usually begins when the priestess comes into contact with the snake god; oracular statements by the possessed priestess and priest; possession of the devotees; the pouring of rum or other liquors as a libation to the god; the spewing of liquor from the mouth of the priest as a form of blessing; Catholic syncretistic elements such as candles, an altar, prayers to the Virgin.

Raboteau termed such practices "Haitian Afro-Catholic synthesis." These displays were disquieting and disturbing to the general public but contributed to Laveau's popularity and infamy. The commercial aspects of the practice, as well as an overall public hostility toward and fear of the unknown and the occult, all contributed New Orleans Vodou's plateau, and after her death, no other practitioner emerged to match, much less exceed, the impact she had on the New Orleans Voodoo scene. She is buried in St. Louis Cemetery No. 1 at St. Louis and Basin Streets; however, recently the cemetery has restricted access to her tomb, the second most popular in the nation after Elvis Presley's. Many who visit (and sometimes vandalize, recently painting it pink) the tomb, leave offerings motivated by the belief that she still wields power and grants petitions.

Louisiana State University professor Kodi A. Roberts offered a somewhat different take on the popularization of Voodoo in his recent book *Voodoo and Power: The Politics of Religion in New Orleans, 1881–1940.* As Voodoo continued its transformation into a divergent Hoodoo, it continued to attract followers of diverse racial, gender, spiritual, ethical, and economic backgrounds. He argues:

> [I]t was *the search for power* that led practitioners, male and female, Black and white, rich and poor, to seek out Voodoo. Workers exploited these perceived dichotomies, incorporating the social and economic advantages of whiteness and wealth by association with affluent interracial clientele. Racialized perceptions of power and spirituality led an interracial population of practitioners to a set of spiritual practices demonized by popular association with Africa and with Blackness.

Roberts was clear that Voodoo had a staying power through post-Reconstruction, the Jim Crow era, and beyond because of the power it imparted to believers by developing an effective alternate economic system that benefitted marginalized people. However, such alternate economies are often abused, and many were not strict Voodoo practitioners but in it simply for financial gain. That was not, however, an aspect of the Vodou initially brought to New Orleans.

Part of Voodoo's survival, and to an extent economic success, was realized through Black Spiritual churches, which had gained acceptance as legitimate establishments. They achieved this by formally organizing and gaining recognition as legally constituted religious institutions or churches—unlike the Voodoo temples that preceded them. The nineteenth-century movement termed Spiritualism had both Black and white devotees in its early days. They believed that the living could communicate with the dead, or spirits, and interact with them through mediums and spirit guides. Black people had long suffered racism in the Christian church, and Spiritualist churches were no different, so by the first quarter of the twentieth century, Black Spiritualist churches began popping up in New Orleans. Some practitioners in the North made their way to the South in search of more fertile fields in order to expand as a form of evangelism. In New Orleans this religious expression took root and was fed by the streams of Protestantism, Catholicism, Pentecostalism, Native American religions, and Voodoo. It became identified as the Spiritual Church Movement or the Black Spiritual Movement.

Mother Leafy Anderson moved to New Orleans in 1920 to establish the Amelia Street Church of Eternal Life, the first Black Spiritualist church in the city. According to Anderson scholar Lisa K. Clark, "The confluence of demographics, social politics and the historical significance of oppression within the Voodoo community provided a fertile theater for her church to grow in New Orleans." Ironically, Anderson capitalized on that fertile environment yet publicly claimed no connection between her brand of Spiritualism and the practice of Voodoo. Nonetheless, many agreed that magic and sorcery played a significant role in the Black Spiritualist church including anthropologist and student of Vodou, Zora Neale Hurston, who upon observing Black Spiritual churches, noted that they had "a strong aroma of Hoodoo." In other words, by the twentieth century there began a convergence of Voodoo and Hoodoo that remains today.

In New Orleans, Voodoo is still being practiced by people of diverse racial and economic backgrounds. In the city there is a Voodoo Society, along with temples, shops, museums, and botanicas where ritual items are sold. Ava K. Jones is a practicing Yoruba Manbo in the city, and in 2000, the New Orleans Saints hired her to lift a longstanding curse on the football team. Manbo Sallie Ann Glassman, who apprenticed in Haïti, has an established Peristyle, Achade Meadows in the Bywater area, and she also runs a nearby botanica in the New Orleans Healing Center. Formally established in 1990, the New Orleans Voodoo Spiritual Temple on Rampart Street, founded by Oswan and Manbo Miriam Chamani, serves as another visible outpost for New Orleans Voodoo. Both Glassman's and Chamani's practices and systems are consistent with the African–Haitian Vodou continuum in cosmology, spiritual hierarchy, ritual, and belief, but not surprisingly, some commerce associated with the trappings of tourism, support both temples. The more popularized legacy of Voodoo is seen in businesses, such as Voodoo BBQ & Grill; the New Orleans VooDoo Arena Football Team (defunct as of 2015); the annual Halloween Voodoo Music and Arts Experience; Voodoo Vodka; and gris-gris and Voodoo geegaws sold in tourist shops throughout the French Quarter and beyond.

If New Orleans is indeed one of the most African cities in the United States, as some scholars argue, part of the credit goes to the ongoing presence and practice, in one form or another, of the African-derived spiritual discipline known as Vodou/Voodoo/Hoodoo. Perhaps it was this African flavor that influenced the Supreme Chief of the Grand Council of the Vodoun Religion of Benin, West Africa, Daagbo Hounon Houna, to visit New Orleans and the Afro-sensitive Christian Unity Baptist Church in the mid-1990s. During his brief visit he assured those of us gathered there that his mission was one of peace. We received him, in our house of prayer, in that spirit. When, as Christian Unity's pastor, I invited him to pray, he did so. He shared a translation afterwards that helped those who were present to reconnect a circle that had been broken by oppression, time, and space.

Howard French wrote about Daagbo Hounon Houna's 1996 visit from Ouidah to the United States and to New Orleans in particular in his *New York Times* article, "At African Heart of Voodoo, Pride over Heritage," stating that his aim was "to make clear . . . that among its boundless mysteries Vodoun has nothing to do with the common Western perception of sticking pins in dolls to persecute real or imagined enemies." Daagbo Hounon Houna went on to explain that "There are women who cannot conceive children, men who cannot find work and elders who cannot find peace . . . Vodoun restores hope. It protects our land and brings the cool breeze." In part, the Supreme Chief's aim was to strengthen the religious ties with the City of New Orleans and his African home, the home of Vodou.

THANKS
TO ST. ROCH
THANKS
TO
St LUCY
THANKS
THANKS
THANKS
THANKS
THANKS
THANKS
THANKS

The Saffron Scourge

Yellow fever took the lives of thousands in nineteenth century New Orleans

by C. W. Cannon, PhD

OPPOSITE During the yellow fever outbreak of 1868, Father Peter Leonard Thevis promised to build a shrine and cemetery if his parishioners were spared. The St. Roch Cemetery was established in 1876. Photo by Alexey Sergeev.

From the first major outbreak in 1796 to the last one in 1905, yellow fever was a terrifying reality for residents of New Orleans. Though other cities also suffered from periodic visitations of the "saffron scourge," no city suffered more than New Orleans, and no city became as closely identified with the disease as the Crescent City.

Today, more than a century since the last outbreak, the memory of the horror of yellow fever has seeped into the consciousness of the city, and into how people perceive New Orleans, in ways that are not always evident on the surface. There's a broad sense in the national imagination that New Orleans is a place of terrible danger. After Katrina, that cultural hunch came to light in national news coverage. *The Washington Post* reported from the city in stark, grim tones as another hurricane season approached: "The first day of June looms like the Sword of Damocles over New Orleans. It's a doomsday date that preys on the city's psyche." Such diction is not new in representations of New Orleans. Because of storms? Crime? Sin? Sure, all of the above, but nothing played a greater role in establishing New Orleans as the grim reaper's American headquarters than the spectacles of death that played out every few summers over the course of the nineteenth century—when both New Orleans and the United States came of age.

Yellow fever killed tens of thousands of Americans in the century before the cause of transmission was finally identified—the *aedes aegypti* mosquito. But it also traumatized those whose lives it spared. Losing loved ones was part of the horror, but the gruesome spectacle of the disease's symptoms also proved difficult to forget. In his later years, Unitarian minister Theodore Clapp recalled tending to fever victims in New Orleans as a young man: "Scarcely a night passes now, in which my dreams are not haunted . . . by the distorted faces, the shrieks, convulsions, the groans, the struggles, and the horrors which I experienced thirty-five years ago."

The name "yellow fever," like "saffron scourge," is an indication of one of the signs of the disease in light-skinned people, a yellowing of the skin due to the virus's attack on the liver. It is a hemorrhagic fever, which causes internal and external bleeding through the nose, ears, even eyes. Delirium could set in, especially in the final stages. Internal bleeding in the stomach also led to a particularly frightful symptom, the regurgitation of partially digested blood, which was said to resemble old coffee grounds. This symptom was a sign that the disease was well advanced, and it gave the illness its Spanish name: *vomito negro* (black vomit).

The mortality rate varied from outbreak to outbreak but all in all, most patients did survive, earning lifelong immunity. For this reason, an erroneous distinction began to be drawn between the susceptibility of native New Orleanians and "outsiders." After the first major outbreak, in 1796, the Baron de Pontalba, Joseph X. Delfau, confided in letters to his wife that it appeared that strangers, especially English and American, were more likely to be taken by the disease than the Creole natives. Indeed, it came to be known as the "stranger's disease," as, in successive epidemics, newcomers perished at higher rates than established natives.

The first US territorial governor of Louisiana, William C. C. Claiborne, had the misfortune to encounter the dreaded "stranger's disease" during his first year in the city. He fell ill, along with his wife and daughter. Only he survived. Yellow fever would also take his second wife five years later, in 1809.

George Washington Cable, in his epic 1880 masterpiece of old New Orleans, *The Grandisimmes*, also depicts the "stranger's disease" at its deadly work. The novel's protagonist, Joseph Frowenfeld, comes to New Orleans from Philadelphia as the eldest son of a large family—all of whom but himself die in the first pages of the novel, days after their arrival.

The conviction, not totally accurate, that natives were less likely to contract and die from yellow fever led to some dark designs during the US Army's occupation of New Orleans during the Civil War. Many Confederates openly hoped for "Yellow Jack" to visit the city during that time, though he stayed away until the war was over. A man by the name of R. R. Barrow of Terrebonne Parish actually devised a biological warfare scheme to attack Northern soldiers. He proposed smuggling in the corpse of a fever victim wrapped in blankets and then distributing the infected blankets around the city. The plan was not acted on and wouldn't have worked anyway, but it's instructive for showing the suicidal mania of Confederate true believers, and for illustrating the period's misunderstandings about the disease's transmission.

There were competing theories about what caused the disease and its rapid spread during epidemics. One theory focused on the environment, and another on the constitutions and lifestyles of infected patients. Barrow's reasoning was a common and sensible intuition, that the disease was transmitted by germs—called "fomites"—clinging to items that a victim had been in close contact with. This theory led to many wise prevention measures, like fumigation of ships coming from outbreak areas, that were beneficial for general public health even if based on a misunderstanding. The routine fumigation of quarantined vessels in the late nineteenth century was designed to kill germs that spread yellow fever, but it also happened to kill the real culprits, the mosquitoes.

Another theory was that "filth" was at the root of the disease's spread. The perception that New Orleans is an especially dirty place is one of the most undying features of the city's long notoriety. The first Union military governor at New Orleans during the Civil War, Major General Benjamin Butler, was convinced that the city's poor sanitation was a danger to his troops and to the civilian public, so he instituted a clean-up campaign. Canals and streets were cleared of waste, including the many animal carcasses that littered the city, and first floor exteriors of buildings were whitewashed with a lime disinfectant. It appeared to be effective, since the city experienced no outbreaks until 1867 (which is also when greater trade resumed after the war, bringing more ships—bearing mosquitoes—from Caribbean ports).

The 1867 outbreak also called the "filth" theory into question, since it began in the Garden District, one of the cleaner areas of the city, rather than in poorer, more densely populated, and therefore "dirtier" districts downtown.

The "filth" theory easily degenerated into blaming the lifestyles of disreputable members of society, including immigrants. In terms of total dead, the 1853 epidemic was the worst to strike the city. It took with it nine thousand souls, including many newly arrived Irish and

BELOW "The Great Yellow Fever Scourge, Incidents of Horrors in the most fatal districts of the Southern States: The Decimation of Canal Street,the Broadway of New Orleans." *Frank Leslie's Illustrated Newspaper*, September 28, 1878. Courtesy of The Historic New Orleans Collection.

German immigrants. Some critics identified the lifestyle choices of the immigrants as part of the problem, alleging that they drank too much, caroused in the dangerous night air, and lived in unsanitary conditions by choice or by national predisposition. A substance believed to waft from still swamp waters, called "miasma," was thought to carry the infection through the air, particularly at night. Thus what we call "night life" today was thought by many to pose a fatal danger. Interestingly, laboring in the sun was also considered to be an unhealthy lifestyle practice. Seamen were thought to be particularly susceptible—and contemptible, for exposing others—because of the same set of factors associated with the immigrants of the 1850s: drinking, staying out late, and putting in long hours during the day building the city and greasing the wheels of its trade empire.

ABOVE St. Louis Cemetery. From *Frank Leslie's Illustrated Newspaper*, September 28, 1878. Courtesy of The Historic New Orleans Collection.

But the theory that the keys to prevention were clean living, staying indoors at night, and avoidance of hard labor was contradicted by the group that visibly suffered the least from the fever, who got it less and were less likely to die if they did contract it: people of African descent. They, too, worked long hours in the hot sun, and they also engaged in social activities at night, the only free time for most enslaved people in the antebellum era. The experience of Afro-New Orleanians offers an interesting contrast to other historic examples of oppressed people in the midst of public health disasters. The Jews of medieval Europe, for example, faced genocidal reprisals when their Christian neighbors noticed that Jews got the black plague less and concluded that they therefore must be causing it. On the contrary, the desperate need for black New Orleanians to tend the sick, bury the dead, and keep the city on its feet during epidemics led to an increase in mythical stature, if not legal status (indeed, the first fifty years of American rule saw a consistent and focused erosion of the rights of free blacks as well as legal paths to freedom for slaves). This was especially the case for the nurses of African descent, free and enslaved, who tended the sick. The mythical status today of Marie Laveau, for example, owes a great deal to her work as a fever nurse. Upon her death in 1881, Lafcadio Hearn penned a glowing obituary, praising her medical abilities in particular: "Her medicines were almost infallible . . . In the great epidemic of 1853, a committee of citizens was appointed to wait upon her, and beg her to lend her aid to the fever-smitten, numbers of whom she saved." The dire crisis brought about by "Bronze John" (another one of the disease's many colorful appellations) led to a recognition of the need not only for black labor but also for black talent. The *Louisiana Courier* wrote in 1839 of Afro-Creole nurses "who unite skill with experience in treating yellow fever. We are convinced that the recovery of the sick depends more on their attention and discrimination than on the skill of the physician." These nurses, acting in most cases without the guidance of a self-described physician, applied an effective pharmacopeia that drew on African as well as Native American precedents, and the white population could not but acknowledge the efficacy of this Afro-Creole knowledge base.

Indeed, the various treatment methods offered up by what passed for licensed physicians in the early nineteenth century is a horror show in itself. It included bleeding, cupping, leeches, and mercury-based poisons like calomel, none of which bore any curative effects, though they certainly did contribute to the suffering of the patient.

Some enslaved people also saw the epidemics as a window of opportunity in which to resist. During the epidemics of 1804, 1837, and 1853, fear of revolt became palpable enough among whites to suggest that at least some slaves may have actually been working toward that aim. During the 1853 outbreak, Governor Paul Octave Hébert called out the state militia to protect against the possibility.

The outbreak of 1853 may be the most iconic of the summer scourges, for the scope of its devastation and for the way details of the disaster have been woven into literary representations. The apocalyptic mode is quite common in depictions of New Orleans. There must be historical reasons for this. It's hard to imagine a more apocalyptic scene than New Orleans in the summer and fall of 1853. In the words of one witness, whose account was gathered by Benjamin Trask in *Fearful Ravages: Yellow Fever in New Orleans 1796-1905*, "Coffin rumbled after coffin; the funeral columns defiled almost constantly for months from every street." Add to the thousands of corpses the creak of hearse wagons over cobblestone, the acrid smoke from burning barrels of tar, cannon blasts to disperse the non-existent "miasma," and bonfires fueled by victims' belongings in every street. And free-flowing liquor to man up the burial squads—because, besides medical and funeral services, bars also thrived, while almost all other commerce screeched to a halt. The otherwise bustling waterfront came to an eerie standstill, with no traffic in or out of the quarantined city. As in hurricanes in our time, people of means, especially women and children, left at the earliest sign of the

It's hard to imagine a more apocalyptic scene than New Orleans in the summer and fall of 1853.

fever's spread. Left behind were people of limited means and not a few human vultures, preying on the desperation of people in crisis. In the words of Ludwig von Reizenstein, who witnessed the 1853 epidemic, "Those who could flee had already fled, and those who remained behind either lacked the means to travel or were held there by some sort of responsibility. Perhaps there were also those for whom ambition and filthy greed dictated that they risk their little lives despite all arguments to the contrary."

That old New Orleans trope of denial is true of the yellow fever era, too. In the early stages of outbreaks, government, commercial interests, and press were often uniform in playing down the impending crisis. The advice of the *Daily Picayune* in July 1837 was typical: "It is very much doubted whether the yellow fever does really exist in this city. Only a few cases of aggravated bilious attacks. Don't be alarmed—keep cool and don't fight. You are as safe in this city as any other place, with temperance and prudence in diet."

However, just as with natural disasters today, the silver lining to catastrophe could be found in the selfless actions of dedicated public servants and volunteers. Before there was the Red Cross, the Howard Association of New Orleans, formed in 1837, brought together a brave cadre of volunteers devoted to helping others in times of dire need. Sometimes simply called the Howards, the group took its name from John Howard, a British humanitarian and prison reformer who contracted and died of typhus in Russia in 1790. The association called for volunteers in the early stages of each outbreak. A request in the newspapers for Howard Association volunteers was often the sign to wary citizens with the wherewithal that it was time to leave town. Then the average men and women who answered the call put themselves in harm's way for as long as they were able, tending the sick, checking on their neighbors, and seeking homes for orphans. The New Orleans Howards became especially good at this work and sent representatives to other cities in the grip of the fever to lend aid, such as Norfolk, Virginia, in 1855. The willingness of New Orleanians to aid other communities in crisis was reciprocated in many ways by the rest of the country. Charity drives to help fever victims at New Orleans were common in all major American cities. Indeed, the eagerness of Northerners to help their fellow Americans in the Deep South was even held up as a sign that sectional strife could be overcome in the years before the Civil War.

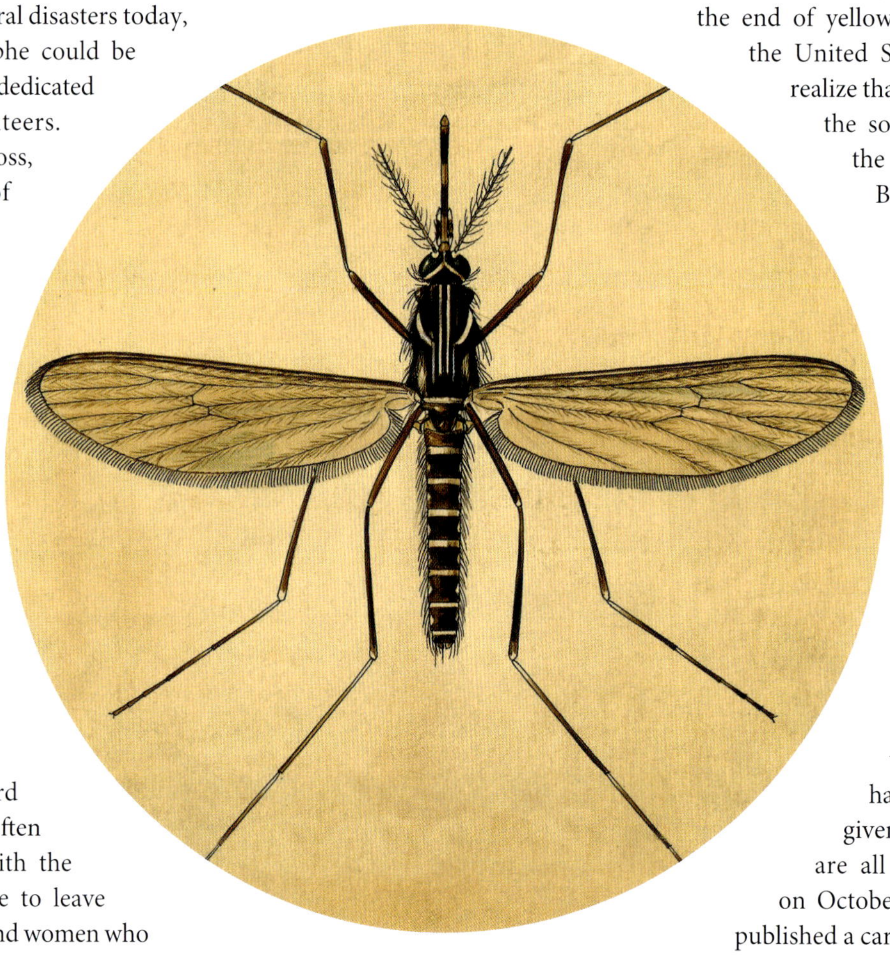

New Orleans medical professionals also contributed much to the worldwide effort to understand and combat yellow fever. Dr. Jean Charles Faget noted in 1858 how the yellow fever patient's pulse slows in proportion to the rising fever, a symptom that became known as "Faget's sign." Cuban doctor Carlos Juan Finley was the first to figure out that the virus was transmitted by a particular species of mosquito, but the first to translate his work into English was New Orleans doctor Rudolph Matas, in 1882, in the *New Orleans Medical and Surgical Journal*.

Though the severity of the 1853 epidemic prompted Louisiana to establish the country's first state Board of Health, in 1855, charges of government inaction were common. As early as 1799, during the Spanish period, James Pitot had averred that "[a]n active government, benevolent and enlightened, would have soon eliminated" the fever's recurrence. During the 1867 outbreak, the president of the New Orleans Board of Health, S. A. Smith, complained in a letter to his counterpart in New York, "The Board of Health of this State, unlike yours, has no means provided by which it could act with any effect in meeting the exigencies of an epidemic."

Eventually forceful government action did lead to the end of yellow fever in New Orleans and in the United States. It was necessary first to realize that the *aedes aegypti* mosquito was the source of transmission. By 1902, the chairman of the New Orleans Board of Health, Dr. Quitman Kohnke, was convinced. When the next—and last—epidemic struck in 1905, Kohnke put out the word: "Yellow fever never was conveyed by filth, and never depended on dirt; it always depends on the conveyance of the germ by the particular mosquito." Teams were sent throughout the city to screen the homes of patients and to get people to cover their rainwater cisterns (all seventy-five thousand of them) with screens, or with cheesecloth handed out by the city. People were given lapel pins reading "My cisterns are all right—How are yours?" And on October 13, 1905, the *Daily Picayune* published a cartoon of a giant mosquito named Madame Stegomyia (another name for the *aedes aegypti*), bags packed, departing the city. The caption read, "Farewell Forever."

The effects of our long relationship with yellow fever on the imagination and mythology of New Orleans are equally as interesting as the factual history of the disease and its treatment. William Wyler's 1938 film *Jezebel*, set in 1853, is one of the few cinematic depictions of yellow fever in New Orleans. Josh Russell's 1999 novel, *Yellow Jack*, is also about that year's fever. But a man who lived through it brought to the page one of the most imaginative stories built around yellow fever. Baron Ludwig von Reizenstein had immigrated to New Orleans from Bavaria, with a wave of other political refugees, in 1848. The 1853 epidemic affected him deeply and informed his dark portrayal of New Orleans society in the era. In his novel *The Mysteries of New Orleans*, published serially in the radical German language newspaper *Louisiana Staats-Zeitung* in 1856, Reizenstein frames the fever as a curse for the city's role in promoting slavery, and as a means toward the violent overthrow of the society slavery created.

The fever as curse idea is also developed by George Washington Cable, who lost his own son to the fever in 1878, the worst outbreak since 1853. Cable promotes the notion of yellow fever as a "stranger's disease" at the beginning of *The Grandisimmes*. This choice is at least at little strange, since the fever of 1878 dispelled the myth of native invincibility by taking a high number of natives, including little George Cable and 2,300 other children. However, like Reizenstein, Cable also links fever epidemics to the crime of slavery. Embedded in *The Grandisimmes* is the "Story of Bras Coupé." It tells the tale of an enslaved African who places a voodoo curse on the plantation of his captivity, destroying the crops and bringing on a fever which takes many, including his master.

Charity drives to help fever victims at New Orleans were common in all major American cities.

Folk culture also recorded the memory of yellow fever's horror in interesting ways. The larger-than-life stature of Marie Laveau has a lot to do with her conduct during the 1853 epidemic, but there was also faith in the intercession of Saint Roch during the 1867 outbreak. Saint Roch had ministered to victims of the black plague in fourteenth-century Europe, eventually succumbing to the disease himself. In 1867 New Orleans, Father Peter Leonard Thevis had good cause to fear that "Bronze John" would lay waste to his largely immigrant laborer parish in the Third District. So he promised Saint Roch that he would erect a shrine to him if yellow fever passed over his parishioners. Not a one of them died, Father Thevis kept his promise, downtown's Washington Avenue was re-named St. Roch, and now the neighborhood also bears the name of the patron saint of "miraculous cures."

The hero of 1905, Dr. Quitman Kohnke, underlined an important cultural point about yellow fever in New Orleans when he observed that "[t]yphoid fever can exist all over the country, and nobody seems to care very much about it, though it kills a great many people. Yellow fever cannot exist anywhere in the southern country without the whole world, apparently, knowing about it . . . out of all proportion to the seriousness of the disease and the danger of its conveyance."

The hyperbolic impulse Doctor Kohnke describes might have less to do with the disease than with the place in which it occurs. In our time, we have had cause to wonder why a hurricane in New Orleans is perceived differently than a hurricane somewhere else. It is not just the good times that get blown out of proportion in New Orleans. Our challenges and crises, too, are magnified to mythical dimensions. Thus yellow fever in New Orleans attains the symbolic force of a plague on the nation, where we can explore sin, redemption, human fallibility, and heroism on a monumental scale.

OPPOSITE *Aedes Agypti*, by Amedeo John Engel Terzi. Courtesy of Wellcome Images, Wellcome Library, London.

CHARITY HOSPITAL

"My debts having been paid and the above provisions having been executed, a sale shall be made of all that remains, which, together with my small lot, I bequeath to serve in perpetuity to the founding of a hospital for the sick of the City of New Orleans."

These words, included in the will of a French sailor named Jean Louis, began one of New Orleans' greatest innovations in public health—Charity Hospital. In his last official act as colonial governor, Bienville founded the first hospital for the poor using the funds left behind by Jean Louis. The hospital, located on Rampart Street, between St. Louis and Toulouse Streets, opened in 1736. By 1933, the fifth incarnation of Charity Hospital stood dilapidated and overcrowded on Tulane Avenue. Hospital administrators requested funds from the President Franklin Roosevelt's New Deal agency, the Public Works Administration. Although a hospital for the poor seemed a perfect fit for the New Deal, the pathway to its replacement was lined with political squabbling.

The disagreements centered on costs, but there were also accusations of patients staying too long and, worse, taking advantage of the free services when they could afford treatment elsewhere. According to historian Robert D. Leighninger Jr., the Orleans Parish Medical Society, which opposed the new hospital, provided a list of recent well-to-do patients that included the governor and his son, state legislators, police officers, and the niece of Huey Long. Long, by then a US senator, was at war with FDR and the political establishment in New Orleans. He stormed into the hospital dispute, effectively halting negotiations with the federal government, which refused to allow Long to control the funds. Talks resumed following Long's assassination in 1935 and construction began in 1936. The twenty-story Art Deco building was the tallest in the city when it opened in 1940, despite sinking eighteen inches into the soft soil over the course of three years.

Big Charity became a hive of health services and a teaching facility that gave invaluable experience to generations of doctors and nurses. Historian John Salvaggio described it as "a model for health care for indigents years before modern federal health-care programs were put into effect."

Control of Big Charity passed between several state agencies, with Louisiana State University taking control in 1997. Following Hurricane Katrina, the facility was ruled unsalvageable by state officials, despite a thorough clean up job conducted by doctors and military personnel. A state-owned, privately run replacement, LSU Health Sciences Center, opened on Canal Street in 2015. Big Charity still stands empty on Tulane Avenue.

GUNGA DEN
ON TAILORS
ALTLRATION
HILE YOU W
AUNDRY
GUNGA
APPEARING
Beth Collins
IT'S
TERRIFIC!
IN OUR
11 YEAR

A Wicked City?

From Storyville to Bourbon Street, New Orleans' lurid reputation attracts curious visitors and would-be reformers

by Alecia P. Long, PhD

Three hundred years is a long time to suffer a bad reputation. In fact, the sheer longevity of the idea that New Orleans is somehow a bad girl among her sister cities makes it all but impossible to successfully challenge the idea. Take, for example, a story that appeared in *Vanity Fair* magazine in November 1934, titled "New Orleans is a Wicked City." The author, Marquis W. Childs, promised his readers "an excursion into the glamorous past, and an examination of the sordid present." For Childs, the most damning aspect of the city's toleration for wickedness was embodied in a still-thriving prostitution district, to which he provided very good directions, perhaps inadvertently, to readers who should wish to find it for themselves.

The particulars of the city's allegedly sordid present had been brought to light two months earlier, when Senator Huey P. Long roared into town, surrounded by armed bodyguards, accompanied by hundreds of the state's National Guard troops, and animated by politically motivated outrage about allegedly widespread vice in New Orleans. Long ensconced himself in the Canal Bank Building, where he summoned and questioned numerous witnesses about the city's toleration of, if not outright support for, many kinds of vice, especially prostitution and gambling. Though Long refused to admit journalists, or the lawyers of those he questioned, into his hearings, he did have the proceedings broadcast on radio stations under his sway. In *Kingfish: The Reign of Huey P. Long*, Richard White describes how Long began each radio broadcast by promising to clean up gambling, to end graft paid to city officials, and to "stamp out prostitution," noting that "the red light district has expanded to the point of national disgrace."

In the end, everyone, including Childs, conceded that the scandal-mongering hearings were a sideshow, nothing more than an attempt on Huey's part to swing voters toward his purportedly more upright slate of candidates just days before an election. "What was really remarkable," Childs wrote, "was that anyone should, at this late date, even professedly for the purposes of making political capital, become aroused over the wickedness of the city at the end of the river. For New Orleans has been wicked for a long time."

Childs was certainly not the first journalist to offer a breathless exposé of the city's robust underworld. Fourteen years earlier, journalist Lyle Saxon authored a five-part series for *The Times-Picayune* titled "New Orleans Nights: Little Adventures in Devilment." The series began its run only days after Prohibition had taken effect nationwide and, despite this new inconvenience, the author promised to "set forth the many and devious ways one may see New Orleans in its new, officially sober iteration." Throughout the series a fictionalized couple goes out on the town night after night in pursuit of pleasure and excitement. On their first foray into devilment, they easily locate plentiful alcohol, gambling, and the option of sex for sale. And, as Childs had done, Saxon helpfully provided interested readers a map of how to find the same locations for themselves. Saxon's "New Orleans Nights" series anticipated the practice of using vivid descriptions of the city's establishments to not only titillate but also inform and perhaps convince readers that reform was long overdue. And, as had been the case in 1934, these kinds of newspaper stories—or anti-vice campaigns—often arose in close proximity to elections in which one candidate positioned himself as a reformer and his opponent as a protector of the city's politically powerful vice interests.

The city's reputation as a laissez-faire home for vice crystallized, at least in the twentieth century, in the segregated district that came to be known as Storyville. New Orleans had been attempting to corral prostitution into more manageable spaces since at least 1857. But in 1897, a newly optimistic reform administration, in power for all of one term, passed the ordinances that created the city's last but most notorious vice

OPPOSITE Two sailors talk to a barker outside the Gunga Den cocktail lounge at 325 Bourbon Street, ca. 1961. Photo by Norman Thomas. Courtesy of The Historic New Orleans Collection.

district. Brothel prostitution was still quite common in the nation's cities at the beginning of the twentieth century; what set New Orleans apart was the frank and direct way city officials chose to deal with it. Instead of ignoring brothels, protecting brothels through graft, or allowing prostitution to exist in informally recognized districts, New Orleans officials acknowledged their belief that sins of the flesh were inevitable. In response, they looked Satan in the eye, cut a deal, and gave him his own address.

That "address" encompassed all or part of nineteen city squares located just behind the French Quarter, home to more than 360 structures. Over the next decade that number actually increased as prosperous bar and brothel owners built flashy new establishments, especially on Basin Street, the district's gaudy main thoroughfare. Brothels were the main attraction, but barrooms, gambling dens, and all manner of entertainment outlets rose and fell in the seasonal economy that developed inside Storyville. Many out-of-town visitors came to the city during the winter racing season, which began in November and ended in early spring, after Mardi Gras. Some Storyville prostitutes simply stood in the doorway of their modest single-room cribs, calling to potential patrons and passersby. Other establishments sought to draw customers inside with such gimmicks as floor-to-ceiling photos of nude women, prize-fighting portraits and memorabilia, or draft beer to go, a nickel a bucket. Other saloons sought to impress customers with ornate finishes and decorative

ABOVE *Storyville Girl,* by Ernest J. Bellocq. Bellocq gained posthumous fame for his portraits of prostitutes made in Storyville. Courtesy of The Historic New Orleans Collection.

Brothels were the main attraction, but barrooms, gambling dens, and all manner of entertainment outlets rose and fell in the seasonal economy that developed inside Storyville.

details. In this category none exceeded Tom Anderson's Basin Street saloon, which opened in 1901. Besides being a well-known figure in the district, Anderson was also politically influential. Journalists sometimes referred to him as The Mayor of Storyville. In point of fact, he served as an elected representative to the Louisiana State Legislature, where he and like-minded New Orleans officials defended the district to its bitter end.

That end came in 1917, not because local reformers were successful or city officials agreed with the decision, but because federal officials ordered the closure of brothels and vice districts within five- to ten-mile zones around the training camps being set up to prepare soldiers for US entry into World War I. Despite vigorous efforts to defend segregated vice, New Orleans Mayor Martin Behrman received orders from Secretary of the Navy Josephus Daniels to close the district. Finally defeated, Behrman introduced an ordinance, and Storyville was officially closed on November 12, 1917.

ABOVE Orleans Parish District Attorney Jim Garrison, seen in his office in 1965, launched anti-vice campaigns in the French Quarter before making national headlines for his investigation into the assassination of President John F. Kennedy. Photo by Leon Price. Courtesy of The Historic New Orleans Collection.

Still, as Lyle Saxon and Marquis Childs remind us, vice and the city's reputation for it endured throughout the 1920s and 1930s. By the time the United States entered World War II, New Orleans had, once again, become an important hub of military activity. This time around, however, officials took a different approach than they had in the lead-up to World War I. In this instance, military officials largely chose to ignore the fact that soldiers and sailors routinely frequented brothels, gambling halls, and the flashy nightclubs and strip joints that had become a staple of the city's newly minted vice center on Bourbon Street. *In Bourbon Street: A History* Richard Campanella describes how "New Orleans exhorted a nearly gravitational pull on young males away from home for the first time, and military authorities did little to fight it," at least while the war was on. However, by 1949 military officials took steps to declare several morally questionable establishments off limits. In March 1949, for instance, the Navy declared twenty-eight bars, rooming houses, and brothels off limits to Navy and Marine Corps personnel.

For their part, local officials did what they had done for decades. They found ways to accommodate vice interests while occasionally siding with the most vocal reformers, at least around election time. In fact, the city's first post-WWII mayor, DeLesseps "Chep" Morrison Sr., rode to office on a wave of reform sentiment. But, just as so many of the city's leaders had done before him, behind the scenes Morrison found ways to accommodate those intermittently problematic but always profitable enterprises that fell outside the letter of the law.

By 1962, newly elected Orleans Parish District Attorney Jim Garrison threatened to upend the sinful status quo yet again, this time by declaring a war on vice in the French Quarter, especially on Bourbon Street. That so-called "war" did result in the closure of some nightclubs, most of which had reputations for criminality or obscenity, but it certainly did not deal Bourbon Street or the city's wicked reputation a deathblow. Mostly, Garrison's campaign generated publicity for him and forced vice operators to, once again, adjust their business models to reflect new realities. After 1962 there was less B-drinking and scamming of customers, and a little less skin exposed by the dancers in the strip joints, but, otherwise, Bourbon Street continued on in its slightly tawdry fashion.

Anyone who walked down Bourbon Street mid-1963 knew that Garrison was wrong when he predicted that all of the city's strip clubs would be closed by the spring of that year. In fact, a slightly surreptitious New Orleans brothel and the barely contained Carnival-season chaos on Bourbon Street were key features of the 1969 cult-film classic *Easy Rider*. As the film's New Orleans-shot scenes made clear, no matter how hard or how often reformers or publicity-seeking politicians sought to reform the city's "wicked" image, they mostly failed to disabuse the public of its ardent belief that the city was a place noted much more for laissez-faire morality with a low tolerance for people telling other people how to behave.

Yet there is another way to judge New Orleans in light of its blasé reaction to perceived deviancy. Let me suggest that, rather than being wicked, the city is simply realistic about human failings and foibles—and that this understanding, and tolerance, is perhaps the result of a great deal of travail, requiring New Orleans to adjust its social mores many times over, in its three centuries of existence. While still not much more than a village in size, the French colonial city of New Orleans became a critical link in Atlantic world trade networks. By the turn of the nineteenth-century it had become, under Spanish domination, a robust center of trade and commerce. By the time the United States purchased Louisiana in 1803, largely to get its hands on New Orleans, the city and its critical port facilities were on the verge of becoming one of the continent's and hemisphere's most important centers of commerce. For any city to succeed as an *entrepôt*, it has to, by definition, be open, not just to facilitating the exchange of foreign goods, but also to accepting migrants, immigrants, and refugees. This also requires confronting and absorbing unfamiliar ideas and cultural practices on a regular basis. Perhaps most importantly, New Orleanians learned to show tolerance for, and exercise a bemused patience with, the practices that welcoming strangers and maintaining a center of trade and commerce required.

As tourism rose in importance, especially during the twentieth century, that same approach and set of practices, initially borne of economic realities, prevailed. And while the city's reputation for wickedness has receded in prominence, it still winks at the visitor who wishes to behave in ways he or she might not even consider at home in Toledo, Tupelo, or Turin. For many people, an encounter with New Orleans has provided a bracing contrast with the more restrained environments from which they hailed. Tennessee Williams was just one of the many creative people drawn to the city in roughly the same era Childs deemed New Orleans wicked. Discussing the role the city played in inspiring his literary achievements, the Mississippi native reflected that in New Orleans, "I found the kind of freedom I had always needed

Anyone who walked down Bourbon Street mid-1963 knew that Garrison was wrong when he predicted that all of the city's strip clubs would be closed by the spring of that year.

BELOW 1950s postcard featuring Lilly "Cat Girl" Christine at the 500 Club on Bourbon Street. Collection of the Louisiana Endowment for the Humanities.

and the shock of it—against the Puritanism of my nature—has given me a subject, a theme, which I have never ceased exploiting."

I have lived in New Orleans for the last two decades, but as a native of Knoxville, Tennessee, and the daughter of a minister, I understand the relative freedom one feels on arrival in New Orleans. That sense of having room to explore, indulge, and push the boundaries one had been previously understood to be inviolable can be confused with wickedness, if one is steeped in a world view delimited by good and evil. And this freedom to explore and indulge has long been fostered by the city's openhearted embrace of the outsider, even as New Orleans insists upon retaining its own traditions. What makes New Orleans a world city, in fact, is that so many other people not only recognize and celebrate its appealing distinctiveness and unique cultural forms, but that they are compelled to come imbibe some of that magical elixir for themselves. As New Orleans begins its fourth century, something tells me that the bracing effervescence of its occasional naughtiness—real and imagined—will be part of what keeps the city afloat, not only as an absolutely must-visit tourist destination, but also an appealing place to live, work, be amused and, occasionally, really overdo it.

So, returning to the question with which this essay begins, is New Orleans a wicked city? I propose the only answer to that question can come from the people who attempt to explore and explain the city as they experience it in the myriad ways they are given the freedom to pursue. Marquis Childs passed away in 1990, but the city—and its slightly tarnished reputation—survived Childs and many others who shared his view. As they have done throughout the city's history, disapproving reformers will occasionally attempt to battle that reputation. But most New Orleanians continue to embrace their city's allure. As the saints come marching in to the city, year after year after year, they will always be accompanied by wicked sinners and curious spectators from around the globe. The beauty of New Orleans is that the city is willing and able to welcome and accommodate them all.

BELOW Bourbon Street in 2010. Photo by Cheryl Gerber.

Part V:
CUISINE AND CULTURE

French Market and Red Store, by Louis Dominique Gandjean Develle, ca. 1881-1884. Courtesy of L. Kemper and Leila Moore Williams Founders Collection at The Historic New Orleans Collection.

Ndar to New Orleans

The African roots of Louisiana's Creole cuisine

by Zella Palmer

The story of New Orleans Creole cooking begins at Saint-Louis, Senegal, a French colonial capital city founded in 1659. Saint-Louis, or Ndar, as it is called in the indigenous Wolof language, is where the Royal Concession of Senegal, later to be re-named the French Company of West Indies, was founded. The French Company of West Indies held the monopoly on slave trade and goods in French colonized territories in Africa and America from 1664 until 1674 and from 1719 to 1742.

At first glance, the French traders would have seen a thriving coastal city, an established cosmopolitan trade hub for gold, beautiful textiles, ivory, Arabic gum, peanuts, and palm oil; a chieftain class dominating politics, religion, and trade; master builders and artisans; an abundance of seafood caught daily in the Senegal River and Atlantic Ocean by Wolof men; the cultivation of millet crops in northern Senegambia and rice in southern Senegambia; and women, queens of the market, agriculture, and Senegambian cookery.

French-administered West African port cities grew along the West Coast from Saint-Louis, Gorée, and Ouidah. At these port cities, out of necessity, French traders tasted coastal West African cuisine for the first time—ancient cuisines rooted in cultural memory of the old Wolof, Xwéda, and Dahomey Empires. Dishes like *jollof rice*, *cheebu jën*, and *ceŋle* would have been completely foreign to their palate.

Creolization began early with Portuguese traders in the fifteenth century but it was the French who would become the premier colonial power in Senegal. From the onset, European traders interacted with Senegambian women on a daily basis for centuries. In many instances, Senegambian women became their arbiters, the providers of many of their meals and their common-law wives. The institution of mariage à la mode du pays, a system of common-law marriages between European men and African women, became the norm in Saint-Louis, creating an elite class of Euro-African women called the *signares*. "The signares kept European-style households and developed a fusion cuisine. The dishes they created for entertaining were designed to impress their French patrons and European guests," Jessica B. Harris explains in her 2011 book *High on the Hog: A Culinary Journey from Africa to America*. These *signares* were raised in the culture of *teranga*, a learned tradition that taught all Senegambians to treat their guests with the utmost respect and always to offer the best dishes of the house. Senegambian cuisine and etiquette would become the mother of Louisiana Creole cuisine and hospitality.

By 1719, French ships sailed from these port cities loaded with enslaved Africans headed towards Louisiana. Nearly six thousand enslaved Africans were sent to Louisiana during the French colonial period. From the outset, African and Native American labor became vital to building the city and surrounding region Almost immediately, enslaved Africans learned from Native Americans how to use local medicinal plants and crops to survive the harsh swamplands, and these enslaved Africans' transferable skills were put to use to clear the land and cultivate the first crops, indigo and rice. Ned Sublette points out in *The World That Made New Orleans: From Spanish Silver to Congo Square* that "[r]ice became, and remains, a staple of the Louisiana diet. In other words, Africans brought not only necessary manual labor, but also came with the knowledge, skills, and foods that were crucial to keeping the white settlers in Louisiana from starving." As in West Africa, the enslaved Africans in New Orleans cultivated and prepared the necessary foods for French settlers to survive in their new environment.

As the population increased under the French and Spanish colonial rule, so did the colonists' appetites and desire to entertain lavishly. Newspaper advertisements, records of sale, New Orleans census, and runaway notices reveal how valuable enslaved cooks and bakers were to the French and Spanish Creole class. "Excellent cooks" were sold at premium prices, while "plain" or "tolerable" cooks sold for less. Indeed, the enslaved cooks, domestics, bakers, marchandes (vendors), field hands, and fishermen were fundamental to growing New Orleans' economy and developing its signature cuisine. Equally important was the constant influx of Africans from West and Central Africa, Haiti, Cuba, and other southern slave states in New Orleans during the eighteenth and nineteenth centuries. Generations of Africans and those from the diaspora became the backbone of New Orleans kitchens. The culinary poetry they infused was a paean to their cultural memories and would ultimately create a world-famous cuisine that continues to be celebrated and revered three centuries later.

OPPOSITE Gumbo is a signature New Orleans dish with roots in Africa. Photo by Chris Granger.

Like Saint-Louis, Senegal, New Orleans was a major port city, and there was an economic need for viand-peddlers to sell food to sailors and businessmen. The *marchandes* and viand-peddlers, reminiscent of those in West African markets, sold produce and treats throughout the French Quarter and on the levees on behalf of their owners, and those with permission from their owners sold food as a way to supplement their own income. Some enslaved viand-peddlers were able to purchase freedom for themselves and for family members. Rose Nicaud, the most famous New Orleans *marchande*, bought her freedom in the early 1800s, after saving the money she earned selling her popular coffee brew. Nicaud sold café noir and café au lait from her pushcart throughout the streets of New Orleans until she was able to rent a permanent coffee stand with seats in the market. Nicaud's coffee became so beloved that her customers referred to it as "the benediction that follows the vespers." In honor of Rose Nicaud, the Frenchman Street coffee shop bears her name.

The number of viand-peddlers and *marchandes* increased by the time Lafcadio Hearn, nineteenth-century food writer, cookbook author, and illustrator documented recipes, Creole proverbs, and vendor call-and-response songs. Hearn gave a first-hand account of the New Orleans food economy produced by black labor: "There have never been so many fruit-peddlers and viand-peddlers of all sorts as at the present time—an encouraging sign of prosperity and the active circulation of money." The descendants of New Orleans *marchandes* and viand-peddlers can still be seen at second line parades and in front of businesses frequented by African Americans, selling pecan candy called prarines (pralines). Although the number of viand-peddlers are dwindling, one can still hear the melodious songs of New Orleans icon Mr. Okra as he plies his fruits and vegetables from his truck, much like his father before him and as African American street vendors have been doing for centuries.

The *Gens de Couleur Libres:* Butchers and Grocers

Like the former French-administered African port cities, New Orleans from its inception had both enslaved and *gens de couleur libres* (free people of color). The newly freed and *gens de couleur libres* were able to build a distinctive property- and business-owning class that would greatly contribute to New Orleans economy. Several operated and owned taverns, boarding houses, small grocery stores, food stalls, meat markets, and rental properties. Others rented carts from the mayor's office for their goods and hired labor to manage and sell from their stalls in the markets and on the levees.

Among these vendors, the most affluent were free women of color. The New Orleans Census of 1795 counted seventeen free black female household heads as *revendeuses* (second-hand dealers) and eleven *marchandes*. One of the most successful property and business owners was a free woman of color named Rosette Rochon. Born enslaved in Mobile, Alabama, in 1760 to a French planter and an enslaved African mother, Rochon opened numerous businesses in New Orleans, including grocery stores, butcher shops, and a cattle ranch; she owned real estate; and she even bought and sold slaves.

Free men of color in the butcher and grocery trade were able to build family businesses that would be passed down for generations. Before many were able to purchase physical locations, they leased stalls in the St. Bernard and French Markets in the mid-nineteenth century. Herbert Gabriel, a fruit stand owner in the St. Bernard Market, was able to buy out competing vendors and open Circle Food Store, a store still in operation today. Another nineteenth-century grocer of color was New Orleans

ABOVE *Cutting Scallions* by Gustave Blache III, 2012.. In celebration of Leah Chase's 90th birthday in 2012, the New Orleans Museum of Art presented an exhibition of Blache's paintings of Chase. Courtesy Gustave Blache III.

Voodoo Queen Marie Laveau's brother-in-law, François Auguste, who was listed as a butcher and victualer (cooked food vendor). Auguste's trade and business would be passed down to future generations, laying the foundation for pre-Katrina family-owned businesses like the Seventh Ward meat markets Bachemin's and Vaucresson's.

For decades, these meat markets, produce stalls, and groceries supplied food for many families and caterers in New Orleans African-American communities. The *gens de couleur libres* were tremendous assets to the New Orleans economy and their own communities. Their collective wealth allowed for entrepreneurial opportunities, a means of advancement for African-Americans without financial resources of their own, and the establishment of strong businesses, schools, clubs, communities, and benevolent associations.

Old Creole Cuisinières

When the Civil War ended, newly freed men and women from rural Louisiana flooded into New Orleans from nearby plantations, many desperately looking for food, shelter, and work. The domestic cooks brought with them the knowledge of old Creole *cuisinières* and *tantes* from the plantations, adding more nuance to New Orleans signature Creole cuisine. The 1929 edition of *The Picayune Creole Cookbook* notes, "Much of the cookery was invented at New Orleans, the metropolis of the Louisiana . . . but also a large part . . . was the product of cooks on the vast plantations that were almost like self-governing principalities scattered along the lakes, rivers, and bayous of fair Louisianne."

One of the plantation cooks to migrate to New Orleans during this period was Louisiana Governor Paul Octave Hébert's formerly enslaved family cook, Nellie Murray. Murray was a matrilineal descendent of Creole plantation cooks; she, her mother, and her grandmother were owned by Governor Hébert's family and lived on his plantation in Bayou Goula, Louisiana. Murray's haute culinary repertoire from her experience cooking and serving the governor and his guests promoted her into an elite class of caterers after the Civil War, and her aristocratic persona and exclusive clientele set her apart, making her a celebrity. By 1895, Murray had amassed a fortune. Her culinary talents and joie de vivre were celebrated in society circles in Paris, New York, and Chicago. Murray's most celebrated achievement was being named Chef de Cuisine at the Louisiana Mansion Club in 1894 for the Chicago World's Fair, where she singlehandedly introduced New Orleans' famed Creole cuisine on the world stage.

In post-Civil War New Orleans, wealthy Creole families that could afford to hire help still required the best to stay au courant in society. They hired highly skilled caterers and domestic cooks, preferably bilingual and with experience in Louisiana Creole haute cuisine. Women of African descent dominated the catering and domestic cook industry. French and Spanish Creoles longed for their tante's cooking. Poorer whites and newly arriving European immigrants lacked the culinary skills and local traditions that descendants of old Creole cooks had.

White women who were widowed or had suffered severe financial losses during the war found it difficult to maintain their high social status. Former mistresses lacked the knowledge to set "a dainty and appetizing table" and skills to prepare "fine old dishes" on their own. *The Picayune Creole Cookbook*, first published in 1901, would provide the solution. The cookbook promised "to show the earnest housekeeper how the best food may be prepared at the least cost" and "to preserve for future generations the many excellent and matchless recipes of our New Orleans cuisine, to gather these up from the lips of the old Creole cooks and grand old housekeepers who still survive."

White Creole males who previously worked in the food industry before the war fared better and maintained their executive positions as restaurateurs and executive chefs. As more European immigrants arrived from Germany, Sicily, and Ireland, opportunities in the restaurant and grocery industry grew. However, lower-class black males maintained low-wage positions as hotel and restaurant cooks, laborers, and servers, while middle-class black families in generational food businesses continued to serve the African-American community.

Revelations: "The Black Hand in the Pot"

By the mid-twentieth century, New Orleans had become a beloved food destination thanks to the Creole cuisine and culture. However, black New Orleanians continued to battle discriminatory Jim Crow laws, which disenfranchised African-Americans in the city. Although many restaurant kitchens in the French Quarter were run by an elite group of black chefs, such as Louis Bluestein at the Roosevelt and Louis Evans at the Pontchartrain Hotel, restaurant workers were only allowed to work in the French Quarter but were not allowed to dine there. However, Lena Richard would defy the odds. Richard was a caterer for more than thirty years, a chef, a restaurateur, a cookbook author, a frozen-food entrepreneur, a cooking-school proprietor, and the first and only black cook of the time featured on a New Orleans television show.

Another anomaly of the Jim Crow era was the celebrity of Edgar "Dooky" Chase Jr. and Leah Chase, proprietors of Dooky Chase Restaurant, located in the historic Tremé neighborhood near the once-thriving black business thoroughfare of Claiborne Avenue. Dooky Chase offered a place for both black and white Civil Rights activists to meet, organize, and eat Mrs. Leah's famous gumbo. Not only did it become a dining place for activism, but it also introduced fine dining to the black community. Before, black New Orleanians dined at home or in bars, sandwich shops, society functions, club meetings, church events, or at Dillard and Xavier University dinners. Both Edgar "Dooky" Chase Jr. and Leah Chase are recognized globally as being courageous restaurateurs during the Civil Rights Movement. Leah Chase was crowned as the Queen of New Orleans Creole cuisine in the late twentieth century. The story and culture of Dooky Chase Restaurant epitomizes New Orleans Creole cuisine and culture.

One of the Civil Rights activists that frequented Dooky Chase Restaurant during the Civil Rights era was a young and brave Rudy Joseph Lombard. In 1962, Lombard and friends challenged New Orleans' Jim Crow segregation laws when they sat at McCrory's five-and-dime white-only lunch counter on Canal Street. Their arrest launched the historic Lombard v. Louisiana case that would be fought and won in the US Supreme Court.

By the 1970s, restaurants like Chez Helene, Buster Holmes Restaurant, and Vaucresson Café Creole would be frequented by both blacks and whites. Mainstream food writers began to recognize black chefs' talents and culinary expertise in their publications. In 1978, Nathaniel Burton and Rudy Joseph Lombard published *Creole Feast: 15 Master Chefs of New Orleans Reveal Their Secrets*, the first publication to finally give proper credit to the contributions made by African-Americans to New Orleans' signature cuisine.

In 2005, Hurricane Katrina hit New Orleans with a vengeance, destroying many mom-and-pop restaurants in the New Orleans black communities and displacing thousands of black restaurant workers. Sublette describes the loss of "the collective knowledge of black New Orleans . . . scattered to the four winds . . . like tearing up an encyclopedia in front of an electric fan." Among the city's losses was one of its greatest chefs, Austin Leslie. Former chef and proprietor of Chez Helene and the father of "Creole-Soul," Leslie spent two days stuck in his attic during Katrina and died of a heart attack in Atlanta a month after being rescued. His death was commemorated in the first post-Katrina second line. Fortunately, some African-American–owned restaurants were able to rebuild, including Dooky Chase, Praline Connection, Willie Mae's Scotch House, and Lil Dizzy's Café.

Since Katrina, the restaurant industry has seen a 70 percent increase, welcoming and celebrating new restaurateurs and chefs from other cities. In spite of many challenges, black New Orleans communities opened new restaurants, such as Neyow's Creole Café, Dook's Place, Munch Factory, Heard Dat Kitchen, Café Dauphine, and others. In light of New Orleans' tradition of celebrating black women in the food industry, Leah Chase continues to be the Queen of Creole Cuisine, and Miss Linda Green, who won Food Network's *Chopped*, is the Queen of Yakamein. Both chefs embody a long history of matrilineal black cooks that represents the diversity of contemporary New Orleans cuisine with the "black hand in the pot."

Both Edgar "Dooky" Chase Jr. and Leah Chase are recognized globally as being courageous restaurateurs during the Civil Rights Movement.

In the history of New Orleans, African-Americans have made the greatest contribution to developing the city's signature Creole cuisine with their expertise and labor. They were the invisible cooks, butchers, bakers, servers, victualers, *marchandes* and viand-peddlers that built the culinary capital of the United States. Visit Saint-Louis, Senegal, and try *soupou kandja* or any other West African city that serves okra stew and there is no denying that Louisiana gumbo and many other signature New Orleans Creole dishes originated from that region. The culinary contributions of Africa and the African diaspora are too often left unmentioned, yet is truly a testament to their immense gifts, hard work, and ingenuity that African-Americans, through their pain and lack of recognition, were able to create one of the finest cuisines in the world. Celebrating the New Orleans Tricentennial offers a time to acknowledge the impact African-Americans have made on the New Orleans tourism economy and the making of its signature cuisine.

Making Groceries

Public markets were culinary incubators in nineteenth century New Orleans

by Sally K. Reeves

"Making groceries" is an old New Orleans expression that residents have long used to mean shopping for food. The expression derives from the French *faire son marché*—*faire* meaning "do" or "make," and *marché* meaning "market." Many New Orleanians remember doing just that at the old French Market, visiting daily or seasonally to purchase white "cooking" pumpkins or plaited twists of garlic. They walked from the vegetable building to the meat building amid the sounds and odors of squawking hens and fat, gobbling turkeys in cages. In earlier days, ducks and songbirds hung in these places before the state put an end to professional market hunting. The French called this hanging laisser le gibier se faisander, which meant suspending pheasant, duck, or snipe until it acquired a decidedly rotten taste, a curious delicacy.

One of the most conspicuous components of the old French Market was the gabled, turreted Bazaar

Market building. Its ubiquitous image on French Market Coffee bags and canisters, postcards, and coffee cups has made it an icon of local market history. Ironically, it was the sole location in the market where fresh food was never, and could not ever, be sold. Built in 1869 as an emporium for dry goods and dried or preserved foodstuffs, it was demolished during the Great Depression, lasting only 70 years. Yet if its familiar image stands as a symbol of the market, it does so despite its having been counter to nearly everything the public market system stood for.

Born in 1769 when Spanish Governor Alejandro O'Reilly established the first contract to supply meat for the public, the New Orleans market system functioned to control both prices and selling conditions for perishables. From colonial times until about 1890, it operated as a city monopoly. Beginning in the 1770s, regulations strictly limited the sale of butcher meat, seafood, fowl, fruit, and vegetables to market buildings within certain hours. Fishermen, hunters, and vendors, who for decades had peddled their wares along the levees, accepted the regulations when given a covered, well designed, centralized open-air market hall in which to display their merchandise. Concurrently, "groceries," understood to mean dried goods, beans, peas, flour, corn, coffee, salt, sugar, bacon, ham, and other longer-lived comestibles, could be sold only at "private markets" (corner stores) or at stands in public squares. These items were forbidden to vendors in the public markets—the 1869 Bazaar Market a glaring, politically driven exception.

There was something in the system for everyone "making groceries"—cattlemen, shippers, butchers, market gardeners, fruit and vegetable vendors, shoppers—and not least, municipal governments. The Spanish Cabildo realized thousands of *pesetas* from its market system, opening the way for city revenues to drive decisions about public markets in New Orleans. Still, market importance grew far beyond controlling the sale of perishables. A product and reflection of the distinctive range of New Orleans cultures, the city's public markets became social and political centers, economic engines, and tourist attractions, the focus of innumerable postcards, paintings, prints, and memorabilia. Citizens flocked to the markets on Sunday mornings to shop for the week's most important meal while enjoying the social occasion. The market was John James Audubon's first stop in New Orleans: "passing through the stalls," he wrote in his 1821 journal, "we were surrounded by Negroes, mulattos, and quadroons, some talking French, others a patois of Spanish and French, others a mixture of French and English." "The greatest market day is Sunday," wrote Benjamin Norman in 1840. "At break of day the gathering commences—youth and age, beauty and the not-so-beautiful—all colors, nations and tongues are commingled in one heterogeneous mass of delightful confusion." A century later *The New Yorker* was still describing the market in New Orleans, taking note of the "Sicilian" flavor of the stalls where a "huge fat man daintily tied up" aromatic vegetables for soup bunched amid cascades of fruit and herbs, garlic and vegetables.

From small beginnings in the Spanish period, the market system after 1800 had begun to grow. Five years after the Louisiana Purchase, the *Conseil de Ville* commissioned French-born architect Arsène Lacarrière Latour to plan a prestigious new market house. A palazzo-like monument completed in the fall of 1811 after three years of construction delays and contract disputes, the building was nearing its first anniversary when a monstrous hurricane in August, 1812 demolished it. The following year the council designed its replacement in-house, the first of a century of captivating City Surveyor designs of New Orleans market halls. That post-hurricane market of 1813, although repeatedly expanded and repaired, and altered by the Public Works Authority (PWA) in 1938, still stands, a veritable symbol of New Orleans history.

Throughout the nineteenth and well into the twentieth century, the French Market grew. Among its principal components were the Meat Market, site of Café du Monde; the Vegetable Market, added in 1822 and enlarged twice; three privately owned Red Stores built in 1832 and demolished during the Great Depression; and next to them the picturesque Bazaar Market, built in a struggle with the Reconstruction state legislature, which had temporarily broken the city's fresh food monopoly. At the lower end of the market near the Old Mint are the steel-framed Farmers' Market sheds, built by the PWA during the Great Depression. The PWA also built a replica of the meat market extending from Dumaine to St. Philip Streets, or "PWA No. 2," to distinguish it from the real Meat Market. It curves around a bend of Decatur Street, whether viewed from inside or outside. A modern addition is the complex of new Red Stores, built by the French Market Corporation during the 1970s across North Peters Street from the Vegetable Market.

There was something in the system for everyone—cattlemen, shippers, butchers, market gardeners, fruit and vegetable vendors, and shoppers.

As the city grew outward, other markets appeared. In the American Sector, City Surveyor Joseph Pilié in 1822 designed the St. Mary Market, the first market site outside the Quarter. In a nod to the Creoles, the city also added Pilié's vegetable market to the French Market complex that year. Suburbs and faubourgs, incorporated or not, were quick to introduce these essential elements to their infrastructure, as the City of Lafayette built a market on Jackson Avenue, and the Third Municipality built the Washington Market, both in 1837. The Tremé Market on Orleans Street appeared two years later. Within a century the New Orleans area had built a total of thirty-four public markets, continuing to add them to the system well into the twentieth century.

By 1884 the major markets included the French meat, fruit, and vegetable buildings, along with the St. Mary, Poydras, Tremé, Dryades, Magazine, Lafayette, Ninth Street, Soraparu, Claiborne, Burton, Delamore, Guillotte, Pilié, and Carrollton Markets, and, in Algiers, the St. John. These well-dispersed centers of food and society played an essential role in the city's cultural, economic, and political life. They generated their share of crime, graft, and disputes over rules and contracts, but also the satisfaction of shopping among crowds constricted into breezy, narrow thoroughfares. More importantly, market employment served as a professional stepping stone for young people, immigrants, and free people of color, and a commercial outlet for Native Americans. The market was a bastion of preservation for languages, culinary traditions, social occasions, and the drinking of

OPPOSITE The French Market, 1890. Photo by Georges Mugnier. Courtesy of the Clarence John Laughlin Archive at The Historic New Orleans Collection.

coffee. City ordinances made no distinctions in class, gender, or race among vendors or shoppers. It left management—and frequently construction costs—to the general lessors or "farmers," usually tough characters good at responding to free market forces.

New Orleans followed the old European system known as "farmer-of-the-market," in which bidders competed at auction to become the "farmer" or principal contractor. They leased the entire facility, and furnished a surety, paying the city on a monthly basis. The farmer then subleased the stalls to the butchers, fish mongers, and fruit or vegetable dealers, basing his bid on the costs and risks of stall rentals, fee collections, and the daily cleanup.

By the middle of the nineteenth century, the market complex was big business for both the public treasury and the private economy. The city had added the St. Mary, Poydras, Tremé, Washington, Port, Magazine, Lebreton, and Dryades markets to the system. It had also enlarged the French, St. Mary, and Poydras markets with halls for vegetables. Deftly, it had financed construction of some of the buildings by having the farmer build the market in return for full stall revenues for up to eight years. From 1815 to the 1850s, the city's take had grown from some $20,000 a year for the meat market alone to some $150,000 for the eight additional markets. By then a thousand people worked as butchers or members of the meat trades, and thousands more produced or sold fruit and vegetables. In the 1880s when the market leases were consolidated, the city's revenue was approaching $200,000 a year.

For a century, the aproned butchers standing beside their hanging sides of meat imparted an Old World sense to the market scene.

As the system expanded, the council's market ordinances grew in size and complexity. The ordinance of 1869 contained fifty-three articles, each with multiple sections. It regulated everything from stall fees, scales, and hours, to signs and the storage of boxes. Meat could not be brought into the market before 2:00 or after 5:00 a.m. The market had to shut down by noon—10:00 a.m. in summer. No sales could be made outside of the covered areas; no fires were allowed except for the heating of coffee and beverages. No spirituous liquors; no unwholesome meat; no sales of underage calves, lambs, or piglets; no iceboxes. No oyster sales—this came under another heading, the city's lucrative "oyster privilege" adjudicated to yet another "farmer." The ordinances, however, declined to interfere with the rights to stalls, except to restrict to two the number that a person could operate. Internal market relationships thus functioned with a sort of free market rhythm.

Rights to a butcher stall in a major market were lucrative. Stall No. 1 of the Poydras, situated right at the entrance, sold just after mid-century, along with a horse and cart, for $1400, the stall itself being worth some fourteen times that of the other items. The value derived both from the location and from the stand's strong "custom," or patronage. It was a given among vendors that once customers became familiar with a butcher and liked the quality of his meat, they made it a habit of returning. Stall rights were thus a tradable commodity, even though the city owned the property and the "farmer" held the lease.

Some butchers handled only certain kinds of products, selected mainly at the Jefferson City Stock Landing or *Marché aux Bestiaux*. The stock landing handled steer, pigs, sheep, milk cows, and calves, graded as either high quality or choice from Texas, or more generically third quality from "the West." The French-born butcher Bernard Tujague and his son Sylvain, both of whom had stalls in the Magazine Market, sold nothing but veal over the course of a combined thirty-three years there. When someone like Jean Galatoire made veal demi-glace, he would visit not just the French Market, but his customary veal dealer in the meat market.

Until after the Civil War, the French Market's Meat Market was the only legal source of fresh meat in the French Quarter. It was one block long, from St. Ann Street to Dumaine Street. People called it the Beef Market, or *Halle des Boucheries*. Not until the 1850s, three decades after other public markets appeared around town, did it become known generally as the "French Market," primarily because although founded by the Spanish, it was the market in the French part of town. Many of the butchers were French, mainly foreign-born, although there were Germans and Creoles as well. For a century, the aproned butchers standing beside their hanging sides of meat imparted an Old World sense to the market scene.

Butchering was a fraternal occupation—skilled and eventually unionized in response to procurement issues and regulations on slaughtering hours and conditions. Added to family and professional loyalty was the camaraderie of the immigrant experience. The so-called "Foreign French" immigrants came in the wake of the French Revolution, Waterloo, the July Monarchy, and the 1848 Revolution. Once arrived, they promoted their culture through the French Benevolent Society, the *Société Quatorze Juillet*, and the *Hôpital français*, led by the influential Gascogne butcher Octave Garsaud. The Butchers' Benevolent Association, composed primarily of French butchers, formed in 1867 to counter the power of the meat wholesalers and rose to national prominence, with 400 members, as the leader of the butchers' struggle against the famous Slaughterhouse Act of 1869, which mandated a single slaughterhouse in a location set within a political environment. The immigrant chain was still in effect at the turn of the twentieth century, the Galatoire and Touzet families being prominent examples.

Many of the old French restaurants of New Orleans were intimately connected to the French-born butchers and their families. One might speculate that the limited hours and exclusivity of the meat markets had a social and economic effect as butchers found natural outlets for their procurement contacts and the need to utilize unsold product that had to be removed from the market before morning's end. They probably drew on the culinary traditions of their native land in southwestern France, which lent them to the business of professional cookery. Toward the late nineteenth century there was also the issue of competition from beef brought in from Texas, not on the hoof, as before, but dressed, leaving for the market butcher a smaller role in the meat economy.

Jean Tujague was the first of more than forty French-born Tujagues who, over the course of the nineteenth century, moved to New Orleans from southwestern France. By 1886, Tujague family butchers worked markets from the French to the Magazine. Guillaume Tujague, arriving in 1850, married Marie Abadie, a butcher's daughter from a clan of over twenty French-born butchers. By 1856 he had opened a saloon on Decatur Street that would later become Tujague's Restaurant, working at the same time as a butcher at stall 49 of the French Market. His partner Roman Dazet came from a clan of Gascony butchers with stalls at the Poydras, Tremé, Dryades, Magazine, French, and St. Mary Markets.

Begué's Restaurant was another prominent French Quarter establishment founded by an immigrant butcher. Both of famed *cuisinier* Madame Begué's husbands, Louis Dutrey and Hypolyte Begué, got their starts in French Market meat stalls. When Elizabeth Kettering Begué predeceased Hypolyte in 1906, he remarried the widow of another French Market butcher. Begué himself was from a family that sent butchers to the Tremé and Poydras Markets as early as the 1850s. In the same decade another French Market butcher, Jean Marie Saux, founded the Chêne Vert Restaurant across from the nascent City Park in a building that at this writing serves as Ralph's on the Park. Irenée Dours, a member of a family of French Market butchers, succeeded Saux there, as did Fernand Alciatore, a private meat dealer. Fernand was from the family of Antoine Alciatore, who, although a French immigrant, was an exception to the pattern of the butchers. He came as a professionally trained chef. Antoine's Restaurant was not a saloon in its early stages like the others.

But William Maylie's was. Born in 1837 in the Haute-Garonne region of southwestern France, Maylie had settled in New Orleans by the 1860s, where he was instrumental in organizing the Butcher's Benevolent Association. By 1870 he had opened a saloon on Poydras Street at Rampart, across from the Poydras Market. His younger brother Jean Bernard, arriving in 1867, landed a butcher's stall at the St. Mary Market and worked part time as a bartender at the Maylie establishment. After William's death in 1880, Bernard and partner Hypolyte Esparbe, with their wives, the sisters Anna and Marie Buisson, expanded their business. Their landmark table d'hote restaurant flourished under Madame Esparbe, under Bernard's son William, and under the recently departed William III with his wife Anna May. Above the restaurant, the butchers and dairymen held their association meetings.

Not long after the Civil War, two unstoppable forces began to erode the power and profitability of the markets and the butchers—technology and state government. As early as 1864, the availability of locally manufactured ice began to undermine the case for the city's monopoly on the sale of perishables. Ice and then electricity came quickly into common use during the late nineteenth century, making it possible for corner store owners to offer wholesome goods without relying on cool

BELOW French Market butchers, 1895. Photo by Georges Francois Mugnier. Courtesy of The Historic New Orleans Collection.

ABOVE View of shoppers at French Market stalls. Photo by Georges Francois Mugnier. Courtesy of The Historic New Orleans Collection.

morning hours and breezy covered spaces or needing to discard unsold product and regularly clean the premises. It soon became untenable for the city to restrict the sale of perishables in the name of health and safety. The trend coincided with the decline of the French Quarter and the breakup of the butchers' virtual control of the meat supply in the wake of Louisiana's 1869 Slaughterhouse Act.

With the exception of the French Market, every public market in the city eventually closed. Corner stores multiplied, run by butchers familiar with their customers' preferences. Refrigeration, densely occupied neighborhoods, sizeable families, personal relationships, and relatively safe streets brought the butcher-driven corner store into its economic heyday for half a century.

During the 1930s, the French Market underwent a business-led modernization that took care to protect the wholesale food suppliers and vendors, giving it forty more years of authenticity. But in the 1970s it suffered a functional revision that resulted for the first time ever in the meat market's not offering meat and the vegetable market's not offering vegetables. Tourist's stock replaced comestibles in the principal buildings, with predictable and not strictly culturally positive results that have led to today's French Market flea market. Luckily, the French Market buildings have been continually preserved and offer sellers and buyers a clean and relatively safe retail environment. With some five thousand square feet at Decatur and St. Ann Streets, Café du Monde continues to operate as the market's oldest business and one of the city's most popular attractions. Supplemented by income from its control of nearby parking lots, the French Market Corporation has remitted more than two million dollars to the city's general fund in recent years. In the end, today's legacy is both the obvious culinary inheritance, but also the less visible fact that the city revenues shaped the history of public markets and continue to do so.

ABOVE A hand colored engraving by John James Audubom from *Birds of America*, 1835. Courtesy of Louisiana State Museum.

AUDUBON GOES TO THE MARKET

John James Audubon liked to tell people he was from Louisiana. A ruse to mask his illegitimate birth in Haiti, the story was made all the more believable by the impact of Louisiana's landscape on his career. According to historian Danny Heitman, Audubon began at least 167 of the 435 images in his classic, *The Birds of America*, while living in Louisiana. Among his travels around the state, his visits to the French Market made an indelible impression.

Audubon was bankrupt in 1820 when he set sail down the Mississippi River aboard a New Orleans-bound flatboat, but he had a plan: complete and publish his collection of life-sized paintings of the birds of North America. Crossing into Louisiana just a few days before Christmas, Audubon arrived in New Orleans at daybreak on January 7, 1821. The next morning, he made a beeline for the French Market, where he found rich source material. "...Went to the market having received information that Much and great variety of game was brought to it," he wrote in his journal. He found "Vast Many Malards, some teals, some American widgeons, Canada Geese Snow Geese, Mergansers, Robins; Blue Birds; Red wing Starlings—Tell Tale Godwits—everything selling extremely high." Looking for birds he could purchase and draw, Audubon was shocked at the price for a pair of ducks—$1.25—and disgusted by the unsanitary conditions, declaring the market "the Dirtiest place in all the Cities of the United States." An incident that evening may have colored his mood: his wallet was stolen during the festivities marking the sixth anniversary of the Battle of New Orleans. "I think the Knave who took it is now good deal disappointed and probably wishes I had it."

During his stay, Audubon earned money by painting portraits in a rented studio on Barracks Street, and kept his eyes on the sky, noting great flocks of bank swallows and purple martins. He was hired by the mistress of Oakley Plantation, located upriver in St. Francisville, to tutor her daughter. Audubon spent four valuable months at Oakley creating works that would appear in *Birds of America*, eventually relocated his family to the region. "The state of Louisiana," he wrote, "has always been my favorite portion of the Union, although Kentucky and some other states have divided my affections."

Published from 1827 to 1838 as a series of four volumes, each three and a half feet tall, *Birds of America* was a huge success, with subscribers paying as much as $1,000 for one full set. Approximately ninety survive to this day. In 2012 Christie's auction house sold a rare first edition for $7.9 million.

-Brian W. Boyles

Star Chefs

These culinary icons shaped the world's appreciation of New Orleans-style cuisine

LEFT Massachusetts-born **Emeril Lagasse** succeeded Paul Prudhomme as executive chef at the legendary Commander's Palace, then opened his acclaimed Emeril's restaurant in 1990 in the Warehouse District. His popular television shows, including *Emeril Live!* and *Eat the World with Emeril Lagasse*, emphasize the rich Cajun and Creole traditions of New Orleans. Photo by Cheryl Gerber.

RIGHT Popeyes Chicken & Biscuits founder **Al Copeland** started with one restaurant in Arabi and eventually went toe-to-toe with the biggest fast food companies in the world. His larger than life persona made him a civic institution in the city for more than thirty years. Courtesy of Kit Wohl.

ABOVE Raised in Opelousas, Louisiana, **Paul Prudhomme** opened K-Paul's Louisiana Kitchen with his wife, K, in 1979. From that French Quarter hotspot, he went on to make blackened redfish world famous, and became the first American to receive the *Merité Agricole* of the French Republic. Photo by Cheryl Gerber.

LEFT Born in Meridian, Mississippi, and raised in south Louisiana, **John Besh** has spearheaded a renewed appreciation of the culinary legacy of the state in the farm-to-table era. His acclaimed cookbooks and charitable initiatives continue to bring global attention to Louisiana's bounty, and attract visitors to his collection of restaurants in New Orleans, including August, Domenica, and Willa Jean. Photo by Cheryl Gerber.

"Wettest City on Earth"

New Orleans' love affair with the cocktail

by Allison Alsup

My relationship with this city of cocktails began years before I could legally imbibe, indeed even before I was aware of what a cocktail was or why I would possibly want to drink one. As a child living two thousand miles away in Oakland, California, I came across a drinking glass in the drawer my mother reserved for her keepsakes. It was wrapped in tissue paper like an expensive Christmas ornament. The glass was tall and alluringly curvy. In green, old-fashioned script, it proclaimed, Pat O'Brien's.

I asked why the glass wasn't with the rest in the kitchen. No doubt I was already sizing it up for milk.

"It's special, a souvenir," my mother said.

"Of what?" I asked.

"One night in New Orleans," she said. Her face had a far-off, dreamy look. Then she added the phrase guaranteed to forever sear an event in a child's brain. "You're too young to understand."

Fast forward some twenty years. I'm sitting with my fiancé in the courtyard at Pat O'Brien's. It's August, sweltering even at 10:00 p.m. I'm sure we're not the only ones who'd like to dive into the cascading fountain. We're considering moving to New Orleans after finding a charming wreck of a cottage for cheap. It's a familiar story.

We order Hurricanes. After all, I've never forgotten the glass in my mother's drawer. During that first round, the gravity of the venture remains. We don't know a soul here. The property lacks electricity, plumbing. It contains a dead cat. There's also the small fact that we don't really know how to fix a house.

Then, at some point during our second Hurricane, our hesitation evaporates. Moving to New Orleans becomes the best idea ever. We put in an offer the next day. Seventeen years later, we're still here. It's a familiar story.

If a cocktail (or two) can so sway those not yet living in New Orleans, consider the influence three hundred years of them have had on its residents.

In New Orleans a cocktail is more than a drink, a diversion, or vice—even more than a commodity. Rather, the cocktail is a cultural institution, one that has both shaped and been shaped by the city. The term "cocktail" may not have been coined in New Orleans (that honor goes to a Hudson, New York, newspaper in 1806), but it should have been. As Elizabeth M. Williams and Chris McMillan write in their cocktail history of the city, *Lift Your Spirits*, "historical accuracy doesn't stop many New Orleanians from asserting that claim. The city's history and culture make it both plausible and believable. Where else could the cocktail have been created, if not New Orleans?"

After all, how many cities can boast of having their own official cocktail? New Orleans is home not only to the Sazerac but also the Ramos Gin Fizz, the Crusta, Brandy Milk Punch, the Vieux Carré, Herbsaint, and for better or worse, the Hurricane. It's where a nineteenth-century apothecary named Antoine Peychaud manufactured the world's first commercial bitters on Royal Street. Today New Orleans is home to the Museum of the American Cocktail, and each July the city plays host to one of the nation's premier spirits event, Tales of the Cocktail. "I'm not sure that there's another city in the world where cocktails are more ingrained in the culture than they are in New Orleans," says Tales founder Ann Tuennerman.

And while in much of the country it remains taboo to speak openly of one's love of drink, New Orleans has never been very good at hiding its affections. With bars that never close and "go-cups," it doesn't take visitors long to realize that attitudes and laws here are often at odds with the rest of the country. "The go-cup culture allows us to take our drinks from one bar to the next. Or out for a walk with the dog. Or out to the park," explains Tuennerman. "It's just a part of the sense of celebration and freedom you feel all over the city."

New Orleans and cocktails have enjoyed such a close association that asking how the two became so inextricably muddled may seem like asking how fish came to live in water. For drinks historian Elizabeth Pearce, the answer lies in a mix of economic and cultural factors. The owner of Drink and Learn, Pearce gives tours and classes that tell the history of New Orleans through iconic cocktails. While the South's emphasis on hospitality plays a critical role in the city's enduring love of cocktails, Pearce notes New Orleans' spirited attitude began with its settlement, which, unlike other parts of the United States, wasn't undertaken by pious Puritans but by the sensual French.

"New Orleans was founded by people who believed in celebrating pleasure," she explains. "The city was built on the French social foundation of conviviality and bonhomie. It's a belief that your food and drink should be done well and are in fact, grounded in your identity." Case in point: in 1763, when France ceded control of New Orleans to Spain, the new governor sought to reign in the free-spirited French colonists, instituting laws that banned French wine and cognac. According to Pearce, some four hundred irate locals—most of whom had been drinking—gathered in *Place d'Armes* (now Jackson Square), shouting, "Give us back our Bordeaux! Take back your Catalonia!"

While the outcry may sound like little more than tipsy bravado, it cost the rebellion's leaders their necks. Pearce says New Orleanians learned an important lesson: don't protest alcohol restrictions publicly, just smuggle. It's an approach residents continued to take through Prohibition, when top federal agent Izzy Einstein dubbed New Orleans the "wettest city on earth."

OPPOSITE Ladies storming the Sazerac Bar at the Roosevelt Hotel ca. 1949. Courtesy of the Roosevelt Hotel.
RIGHT The Sazerac cocktail originated in New Orleans. Photo by Edsel Little.

Pearce also points to two other key historical factors that whetted New Orleans' taste for cocktails: money and tourism, both enabled by its position as a port city. With the invention of the steamboat, New Orleans became the gateway for key cargo like sugar, cotton, and coffee to move up the Mississippi River. Booming trade brought visitors, and New Orleans seized the opportunity to sell itself as a tourist destination.

Although alcohol was then ubiquitous across America, Pearce notes that cocktails required more than a bottle and a sawdust floor. "The gilded era of the cocktail is born from ornate rooms and the great temples of drinking. They thrived in cities where people had money to burn," she says. For example, in the early nineteenth century, if you wanted to order a glass of champagne, not a bottle, Pearce asserts, there were only two cities where this was possible: New York and New Orleans. Only in these two spots was the expensive bubbly ordered consistently enough that a bar could be confident of selling the rest of an open bottle.

Sumptuous hotels like the St. Louis or the St. Charles catered to those looking to wet their whistles, moneyed travelers and locals alike. Decades later, smaller but still glamorous establishments like the Sazerac Bar in the Roosevelt Hotel and the Carousel Bar in the Hotel Monteleone would take up the tradition of the upscale hotel bar—and maintain the tradition to this day. Indeed, step into any of the boutique hotels that have recently sprouted up in New Orleans, and chances are a chic cocktail bar will be occupying a place of privilege in the floor plan.

"Here in New Orleans, we think life is meant to be lived. We have this to offer the world," says Ti Martin, restaurateur and daughter of New Orleans food icon Ella Brennan. "On any given night it begins with a cocktail." As a child, Martin recalls she was expected to mix drinks during the numerous parties that took place in her parents' grand Garden District home. "We had an entire room devoted to a bar," Martin says.

And while some might balk at the idea of an eight-year-old serving up an Old Fashioned, Martin claims that the approach taught her to drink responsibly. "It was never about getting blotto—more like how European children are taught to drink wine at the family table," she explains. "By the time I was in college I knew how to handle myself. It was the kids from Omaha who came here to visit who were in trouble. Those were the ones you had to pick up from the bushes."

As an adult, Martin came to understand just how critical cocktails were to the business of food in the city. When she first expressed an interest in working in the family restaurants, her mother responded by handing over a copy of Stanley Clisby Arthur's *Famous New Orleans Drinks and How to Mix 'Em*. "You need to understand that a cocktail is a very important part of the meal," Martin remembers.

Indeed, decades before opening Commander's Palace or Brennan's, a seventeen-year-old Ella Brennan's first working stint was on Bourbon

BELOW The world famous Hurricane (left) and the Ramos Gin Fizz, another cocktail born in New Orleans. Photos by Nola Skip and Infrogmation.

ABOVE *Café Lafitte on Bourbon Street, New Orleans,* painting by Colette Pope Heldner, ca. 1935. Collection of Dr. Glen Parker. Courtesy of Jean Bragg Gallery.

Street, tallying the receipts at the Old Absinthe House, then owned by her brother Owen. In her autobiography, *Miss Ella of Commander's Palace*, co authored by Martin, Brennan describes the after-hours she spent sipping with her brother at the landmark Café Lafitte (now Lafitte's Blacksmith Shop) down the street as "the most informative of my career." Every echelon of society walked through the door of Lafitte's, Brennan explains; a cocktail in hand offered the shy young woman the social lubricant needed to mingle. "Some girls went to finishing school," she writes, "but I went to Café Lafitte." For Brennan, even the afterlife, which she dubs the "Saloon in the Sky," comes with cocktails.

In New Orleans the cocktail is a cultural institution, one that has both shaped and been shaped by the city.

As for Martin, cocktails continue to hold a place of importance at the tables she now helps to oversee. At Commander's Palace, the tradition of the twenty-five-cent lunch martini endures, and at sleek, modern SoBou ("South of Bourbon") in the French Quarter, food is in response to the cocktail menu, not the other way around. "We wanted to offer street fare–inspired plates that could match the flavor of cocktails," she explains. Bottles line the walls in an ode to the nearby New Orleans Pharmacy Museum, home to America's first licensed apothecary, where the line between a cocktail and medicine was often blurred.

About two months ago, my husband and I were leaving a food and cocktail event at the Ace Hotel when we passed a well-heeled family trio on the sidewalk.

"We can't do this where we live," the man said, raising a white plastic go-cup in our direction. He wore a button-down shirt, khakis, spectacles. If I had to guess, I'd say he was in insurance or accounting—certainly not the type to normally call out to strangers. Somehow the moment struck me as resonant. I thought of my mother's Hurricane glass, how I'd come full circle. Now I was the New Orleanian, one with the good fortune to sometimes write about cocktails.

"Yes," I replied. "It's wonderful when adults are allowed to be adults."

"Do this where I'm from and you get arrested," he said. He took a sip, revealing the one-sided grin of someone who's just gotten away with something naughty. It's a look we see quite a bit here.

"I'm very sorry to hear that," I said and raised my own go-cup. "But it's not too late to join us."

Royal
Bourbon
Dauphine

Carnival Time

Mardi Gras celebrations in New Orleans date back to eighteenth century

by Brian J. Costello

In the streets of New Orleans each year we mark one of the greatest celebrations on the globe: the pre-Lenten Carnival and its culmination of Mardi Gras, or Shrove Tuesday. For generations, this unique celebration of fantasy, pomp, and madcap antics has drawn hundreds of thousands of revelers each year to the City of New Orleans proper and its suburbs in the adjacent parishes of Jefferson, St. Bernard, and St. Tammany, as well as to other Louisiana cities and towns.

The Carnival season, and its one-day climax of Mardi Gras, traces its roots from the Bacchanalia and Saturnalia ritual promiscuity of Roman times. With the spread of Christianity, similar revelry occurred during the period of Carnival (Latin for "farewell to the flesh"), that extended from Twelfth Night, January 6, or the feast of the Epiphany of Christ, to Shrove Tuesday, the last day before Ash Wednesday and the forty-day penitential season of Lent. In France, Shrove Tuesday came to be known as Mardi Gras or "Fat Tuesday" in recognition of the daylong feasting before the Lenten fast.

The date of Mardi Gras depends on the date of Easter; the latter feast may fall as early as March 22 or as late as April 25. Lent, in turn, numbers forty days; the six Sundays occurring during the season are considered exceptional days and are not counted among the days of Lent. Mardi Gras, the final day of the Carnival season, therefore, may occur as early as February 3 or as late as March 9.

As early as 1743, elegant Carnival balls are recorded as being staged in the capital of the French colony, the emerging Creole city of *la Nouvelle Orleans*. When Louisiana passed from French to Spanish control, the new government in 1762 decreed that public masking was prohibited. After the brief return to French rule in 1800 and the ultimate transfer to American rule in 1803, the public observance of Carnival began to resume in Louisiana.

New Orleans' pre-Lenten balls increased in number, and in 1825 came mention of a procession of carriages bearing young men who had just returned home from their studies in Paris. The year 1835 was marked by the first newspaper description of widespread masking in the streets of New Orleans, as well as James R. Creecy's observation of the first known float, a "moving prison of the devil" drawn by horses disguised as dragons. Documentation of parading by organized groups per se began with the press coverage of Mardi Gras in 1837. Meanwhile, "American" or Protestant, Anglo-Saxon Southerners were beginning their own traditions of parading. Mardi Gras celebrations had been held by the Creole French of Mobile, Alabama since the days of French colonial rule, but it was not until the later antebellum period that the custom of parading in the streets gained hold. Elaborate New Year's Eve parades were held in Mobile beginning in 1830, and in 1840 allegorical, animal-drawn "cars" or "floats" were added to the lineup. The first-known of Mobile's parading groups was the Cowbellion de Rakin Society, the first of the many "mystic societies" to parade in that city's history.

The debate continues into the twenty-first century as to whether New Orleans or the Mobile stages the "oldest" Carnival celebration or which of the two was the "original" home of Mardi Gras. Both cities raise valid points in their respective cases, but the fact that Shrove Tuesday festivities were observed with parades of floats in New Orleans first suggests that this city, the undisputed "Carnival City," has a longer Carnival parading tradition.

In 1857, six former Cowbellions of Mobile and thirteen Anglo-Saxons of New Orleans presented the first "krewe" (an Old English rendition of "crew") parade in the Crescent City, that of Comus. Following the Civil War and the return to a sense of normalcy, other parading krewes were founded in New Orleans: the Twelfth Night Revelers in 1870, the Knights of Momus in 1872, and the Krewe of Proteus in 1882. The Rex Organization, founded in 1872, has been led each year by a succession of community leaders who bear the title "King of Carnival."

These five pioneer krewes entertained New Orleanians and visitors alike with parades of magnificent, papier-mâché floats built according to fantastic themes and bearing masked, costumed riders. Unlike

OPPOSITE Krewe of Rex Parade, 2011. Photo by Cheryl Gerber.

Z
TRAMPS

ABOVE Zulu Parade, 2015. Photo by Ray Laskowitz.

Carnival parades of the twenty-first centuries, these processions were quite intellectual in subject material and featured little tossing of trinkets or "throws" to the spectators. Those viewing the parades dressed in their best and sedately lined the routes to silently take in the splendor of the floats, maskers, and accompanying brass bands.

All of New Orleans' nineteenth-century parading krewes—save one, Rex—rolled at night. Each float of the night parades was circled by shrouded and dancing flambeaux bearers and led by a masked king who bore the name of the krewe and whose true identity remained forever secret to the public. This sense of mystery, coupled with the elegance of the invitation-only masked balls held by parading as well as non-parading krewes, added to the aristocratic traditions of this remarkable American holiday.

As early as 1743, elegant Carnival balls are recorded as being staged in the capital of the French colony, the emerging Creole city of la Nouvelle Orleans.

Personal memoirs and each year's *Picayune* and national press reports rapturously described the scenes that unrolled before New Orleans' Carnival crowds. Lyle Saxon, "Mr. Mardi Gras," describes the Rex parade in 1928 in his book, *Fabulous New Orleans*:

> Rex on his swaying throne was drawn slowly down the street. I could hear the cheers which greeted him and they grew fainter in the distance, drowned in the blare of the bands. One by one the gorgeously decorated floats passed before us, each telling some mythological story. There were satyrs, fawns, mermaids, centaurs, the like of which I had never seen before. Here the whole of fairyland had become a reality before my eyes. I counted the glittering cars [i.e., floats] as they passed. There were twenty in all and almost as many bands of music. And always that strange, unreal quality, that gaudy, blatant thing which I could not define then and which I cannot define now, except that it gave me the feeling of seeing a thousand circuses rolled into one.

Even in years marked by inclement weather, the krewes, local residents, and visitors braved the elements to celebrate before the onset of Lent. The Ash Wednesday edition of the *Daily Picayune* told of Comus' experience on Mardi Gras night 1909:

> ...when the pageant was in St. Charles Street, near Canal, the sheets of water borne on the breath of a strong wind, deluged men and cars floats alike. But all the while the dripping maskers danced and sported on their cars, Comus waved his goblet to the throngs under the sheds and the soaked musicians kept step to the suggestive strains of "It Looks to Me Like a Big Night To-Night."

In keeping with Comus' high artistic standards, one float-rider who dared to open an umbrella in an attempt to protect himself in that memorable tempest was fined $100 by the krewe Captain who thought the masker's action spoiled the beauty of the procession.

In 1899, snow on Lundi Gras spurred the Krewe of Proteus to postpone their parade to the First Friday of Lent, and in 1990 the Westbank Krewe of Alla rolled on St. Patrick's Day. These are the two known occasions in Greater New Orleans when carnival parades were staged after the season.

The twentieth and early twenty-first centuries saw the rise and fall of scores of parading krewes in New Orleans. Though all of the krewes maintained varying degrees of membership requirements, those formed during these latter two centuries were less discriminating than the aristocratic, white, male krewes founded during the nineteenth century.

Zulu, the first African-American parading krewe, was founded in 1909, and Venus, the first krewe of parading women, in 1941. The progenitors of the "super krewes"—parades having a large number of large floats carrying hundreds or thousands of riders and tossing tons of souvenir "throws"—began with Hermes in 1937 and Babylon in 1940. They were succeeded in the latter twentieth and early twenty-first centuries by even larger krewes such as Bacchus, Endymion, and Orpheus.

Meanwhile, the growth in the number of balls and parades in New Orleans proper spilled over into the adjacent suburban parishes of St. Bernard, Jefferson, and St. Tammany during this period. Accordingly, the number of parades in metro New Orleans peaked at an all-time high of sixty-four in 1990.

The controversial passage of anti-discriminatory laws spearheaded by New Orleans City Councilwoman Dorothy Mae Taylor in 1991 required parading krewes—most of which consisted of white men—to open their membership to minorities. The ancient krewes of Comus and Momus cancelled their 1992 parades and have yet to return to the streets, limiting their celebrations to balls only. In a similar vein, Proteus did not parade during 1992–1999, though it returned to the streets to great acclaim in the year 2000.

Despite modernization in parade design and transportation, many elements of nineteenth-century Carnival continue to the present time, including anonymous monarchs and krewe members, equestrian Captains and Lieutenants, and flambeaux born by robed and strutting bearers. Individual New Orleans parades have intensely loyal followings. Tucks is a favorite for its comic elements, including a float bearing a large toilet bowl into which spectators can toss beads and other throws caught from previous floats. Early in the season, the Krewe du Vieux leads small, horse-drawn floats with satirical, often risqué themes through the venerable streets of the French Quarter. Chaos and Le Krewe d'Etat are also satirical parades, offering jabs at current political personages and situations. In the week preceding Mardi Gras, the ladies of Muses painstakingly decorate high-heeled shoes for distribution to the masses. Hermes combines the old and the new, with nineteenth-century inspired float designs, equestrian lieutenants, flambeaux, and masses of souvenir throws. Mid-City has long charmed onlookers with its floats decorated in bright colored foil. Thoth is the beloved "krewe of the shut-ins" as its parade passes medical facilities whose patients and caregivers would otherwise not have an opportunity to view Carnival parades. Proteus, second oldest krewe of Carnival and oldest night parade, dazzles the masses with floats of nineteenth-century artistic excellence built upon period chassis.

On Mardi Gras itself, the mighty Zulu lures early risers for his spectacular parade of jungle-inspired motifs and highly coveted throws in the form of decorated coconuts. Rex, King of the Carnival, holds high Carnival at the head of his parade, followed by popular floats such as the Boeuf Gras (fatted bull, symbol of the feast before the Lenten fast) and Royal Calliope.

Throughout the day, organized walking clubs and hundreds of maskers make merry on the principal parade routes, as well as in the French Quarter and in other city neighborhoods. Among the most popular groups are the Skull and Bones Gang, the many tribes of Mardi Gras Indians, and the Baby Dolls, all traditions of the city's African-American population; the Jefferson City Buzzards and the late musician Pete Fountain's Half Fast Walking Club; the Society of St. Anne; and numerous other organizations who expend great time and expense in preparation and execution of each year's presentation.

Though individual and group maskers are not as numerous as in the earliest years of Mardi Gras, many may still be seen each year throughout the city. Some of the most exuberant are featured in the French Quarter costume contests sponsored by the city's significant gay community, including one on Bourbon Street in front of the bar Cafe Lafitte in Exile.

Many mainstream Americans, particularly young adults, make an annual pilgrimage to experience Carnival in New Orleans, sometimes hoping to behave as they would not normally in their hometowns. The city's mainline krewes, governmental and law enforcement officials, and other concerned citizens have long denounced such bawdy acts as revelers imbibing to excess and baring flesh in order to receive trinkets.

Despite modernization in parade design and transportation, many elements of nineteenth-century Carnival continue to the present time.

The City of New Orleans continues its mission to "clean up Carnival" and retain its time-honored traditions in a setting that families can enjoy.

Many thousands who visit New Orleans during Carnival never see a float, let alone a parade, but spend their entire stay in the French Quarter, taking in the sights and celebrating before the solemnity and abstinence of Lent. At midnight on Shrove Tuesday, mounted city police officers parade down Bourbon Street in order to clear the street of revelers. Behind the police follows a fleet of motorized street cleaners, signifying the end of another New Orleans Carnival and a return to "normalcy" in the City That Care Forgot, the Carnival City of the world: New Orleans, Louisiana.

BELOW Float design from Mistick Krewe of Comus 1956 parade, whose theme was "Our Early Contemporaries." Courtesy of Louisiana Research Collection, Howard Tilton Memorial Library, Tulane University.

Golden Crown

Tootie Montana revolutionized the art of Mardi Gras Indian suits

"You see, everybody can't be a chief," Tootie Montana once told writer Kalamu ya Salaam. "A person who masks under you, they have to look at you as superior in order for them to give you the respect and for you to be their leader. They've got to have that feeling."

Generations of Mardi Gras Indians looked to Allison "Tootie" Montana as a leader. Born on December 16, 1922, Montana was a gifted craftsman, a distinctive singer, and big chief of the Yellow Pocahontas Mardi Gras Indian tribe for more than fifty years. He achieved international recognition for the beadwork displayed in his suits each Mardi Gras Day.

The Mardi Gras Indian tradition arose during the 1880s just as the implementation of Jim Crow laws institutionalized a new era of repression for African Americans. The temporary (but by no means guaranteed) freedom of Mardi Gras opened up space for black cultural expression. The earliest tribes were influenced by the long history of exchanges between Native Americans and enslaved blacks in the region, the two groups in search of trade, comradeship, and sanctuary from whites. The practice of "masking" reaches back to sub-Saharan Africa, and scholars point to African roots reflected in the Indians moving from neighborhood to neighborhood, crossing social borders in elaborate, handcrafted artwork. According to Salaam, "the tradition is 'masked' as a Mardi Gras parade that is both acceptable to the dominant society and within the means of the African American community."

Indians hold specific positions within their tribe, defined by their position in the procession. The spy boy walks three blocks ahead of the group, on the lookout for approaching rivals. He signals back two blocks to a flag boy, who communicates any threats. The wild man stays close to the big chief, protecting his leader with a menace that makes clear that, for these participants and the neighbors and families who support them, masking is a religion, not a game.

Montana began masking in 1947. His great uncle, Becate Batiste, was the founding big chief of the Creole Wild West Mardi Gras Indian tribe, still recognized as the longest-running tribe in the city. Montana's father joined the Creole Wild West, then splintered off to become big chief of the Yellow Pocahontas. "My daddy was great in his way," Montana told filmmaker Lisa Katzman in the documentary *Tootie's Last Suit*, "but he never made the stuff I made."

Montana's distinctive style emerged in the three-dimensional figures that began to grace his suits, both as abstract designs and as representations of historical figures and Native American icons. "Everybody was flat," he told Salaam. "I was flat until I wanted to be different and then I just started doing it. I started raising my pieces up." Montana was a lather by trade, creating wooden frames for plasterers. These skills translated to innovations in his suits. His emphasis on beauty and his insistence on the craftsmanship as part of masking also worked to deescalate the violence that regularly erupted between tribes on Mardi Gras Day. Though she never masked, his wife Joyce was a constant partner in sewing and beading.

BELOW Big Chief Tootie Montana on his final Mardi Gras Day, 2005. Photo by Eric Waters.

Police harassment during the Indians' traditional St. Joseph Night parade sent Montana to the City Council chambers on June 27, 2005. As he described to council members the decades of rough treatment he'd experienced, Montana suffered a heart attack. The assembled representatives from the Mardi Gras Indian community instantly began singing "Indian Red." At his funeral at St. Augustine Catholic Church, hundreds of masking Mardi Gras Indians mourned the big chief, chanting, "Golden crown, golden crown—Big Chief Tootie's got a golden crown."

In 2009 the City Council issued a proclamation designating the first day of every Carnival season as Allison "Big Chief Tootie" Montana Day in New Orleans.

-Brian W. Boyles

ABOVE Muses shoe, the coveted throw from the popular women's carnival krewe. Photo by Bill Lavender, 2017.

Throw Me Something, Sister!

Women and Mardi Gras

Women have long participated in New Orleans Carnival, but until the twentieth century, they remained royal consorts to the all-male krewes. Iris, the longest-running female krewe, held its first Carnival ball in 1922, even though they did not parade until 1959. In 1941 the Krewe of Venus was the first to roll, and according to Arthur Hardy, not to a very favorable crowd; in fact they were pummeled with rotten tomatoes and eggs. But after the WWII Carnival hiatus, Venus persisted, hitting the streets again in 1946.

Although Venus and Iris were the only all-female krewes in New Orleans for decades, several others popped up in the metro area: Pandora in Gentilly, Diana and Helios in Metairie, and Cleopatra on the West Bank. In 2001 women made a colossal splash on the Carnival scene when the Krewe of Muses rolled on the traditional Uptown route, a neighborhood peppered with streets honoring Zeus's daughters, the nine muses.

Never before had the city seen an all-female superkrewe, but Muses was determined to make its mark—with a seventeen-foot fiber-optic stiletto heel, accompanied by a troupe of dancing fiber-optic butterflies. Muses looked to Zulu's signature coconut as a model for their coveted Muses show; few Carnival throws are more popular today. The krewe currently has a membership topping one thousand and a waiting list so long they had to shut it down.

Naturally, a shoe needs a suitable handbag: enter the Krewe of Nyx, the goddess of night, in 2012. Their decorated handbags are also a much coveted Carnival throw. The city's second all-female superkrewe, they even created their own dance team, the Nyxettes.

Female dance teams have marched in parades for decades but were usually affiliated with local schools. Now there are almost too many to name: the Pussyfooters, NOLA Cherry Bombs, Black Storyville Baby Dolls, Muff-A-Lottas, Camel Toe Lady Steppers—all crowd-pleasers during Carnival season and beyond.

-Nancy Dixon, PhD

The Olympic Bubble Burst.

A Great Kick on Noel, Sporl and Williams.

The Sporting Life

Boxing, baseball, and horse racing thrived during New Orleans' gilded age

by S. Derby Gisclair

Perhaps because New Orleans has defied the odds by being situated in such an improbable and, at times, inaccessible location, the city seems to have had an affinity for risk-takers, gamblers, and aficionados of the sporting life who enjoyed participating in or wagering on all manner of games and amusing diversions.

At the turn of the nineteenth century, there was a wave of immigration following the Haitian Revolution in 1791 and the Louisiana Purchase in 1803, resulting in nearly 90 percent of these new immigrants settling in New Orleans by 1809. In 1830 New Orleans absorbed another wave of immigrants, this time an influx of German and Irish settlers that caused the city's population to double. The city's diverse makeup produced an even broader selection of diversions and entertainment found nowhere else throughout the antebellum South. With everything from opera to cockfights, residents and travelers alike could find some source of entertainment at almost any hour of the day, even on Sundays. While other parts of the country observed the Sabbath seriously, Catholic Creoles, because of the French and Spanish influence in the city's development, felt unconstrained by the Puritan inhibitions found in New England. And New Orleanians would bet on anything and everything, from cockfighting to riverboat races.

The game of craps was introduced to America in New Orleans by the Baron Xavier Philippe de Marigny de Mandeville following a trip to London in 1801, where he learned the game hazard. It was modified by rivermen and became known as *crapaud* meaning "toad," referring to the way players crouched like toads when playing. The city's oldest and most prestigious social organization, the Boston Club, was established in 1841 to provide a venue for its members to play a card game similar to whist and bridge called Boston, said to have been devised by French military officers during the Revolutionary War.

Animal fighting appeared in New Orleans as early as 1817. Cockfighting, dog fights, and bearbaiting were among the more popular blood sports available around the city. Of these, cockfighting proved to be the most prevalent and the longest lasting. In his 1883 memoir *Life on the Mississippi*, Mark Twain immortalized cockfighting in New Orleans with a vivid account of a match he attended. While humane societies and other civic groups eventually managed to suppress most animal fights during the latter half of the nineteenth century, cockfighting survived in the shadowy underbelly of society until Louisiana became the last state to outlaw the practice in 2008—125 years after Twain's published description.

On June 30, 1870, the "Great Race of the Age" between the steamboats Robert E. Lee and Natchez began in New Orleans. Over the next three days, newspapers from coast to coast chronicled the progress of the two vessels as they steamed toward St. Louis to considerable fanfare and excitement along the banks of the Mississippi. The Robert E. Lee covered the 1,154 miles in 3 days, 18 hours, and 14 minutes, reaching St. Louis 3 hours and 44 minutes ahead of the Natchez. The race would be immortalized in songs, prints, and paintings, all but erasing the nation's memory of the paltry 36-mile race up the Hudson River in 1847 between the Vanderbilt and the Oregon.

However, among the myriad amusements, diversions, and entertainment available in New Orleans, there were three sports in particular where New Orleans garnered national and international attention during the 19th century – horse racing, boxing, and baseball.

OPPOSITE The front page of *The Mascot* newspaper on October 1, 1892, featured a story on problems at the Olympic Club following a series of high-profile boxing matches at the club. Wikicommons.

Horse Racing

During his visit to New Orleans in 1861, one of Europe's most noted bankers and personalities, Baron Salomon de Rothschild, observed, "The chief feature of the social make-up of the country is the horse races."

In a letter home dated April 20, 1861, he further noted, "The season lasts a week, but there is only one race a day. Yet the race track is the meeting place for all the ladies in the city . . . Since the race track belongs to a private society, like our Jockey Club in Paris, the members don't admit anyone but 'gentlemen.'" The Sport of Kings was clearly the domain of the elite in New Orleans.

The first known racetrack in Louisiana was established on General Wade Hampton's Houmas House Plantation between 1814 and 1815. The first racetrack in the New Orleans area was laid out for informal races in 1820 by Francois Livaudais on his plantation in the Faubourg Annunciation, near present day St. Charles and Washington Avenues. Just a few miles downriver in Chalmette, the Jackson Course opened in 1825, and in 1834 the Belle Point Course graced the city of Carrollton on the western edge of present-day Audubon Park. It was renamed the Eclipse Course in 1837. The following year the Metairie Course was established on the Orleans–Jefferson Parish line on the site of what is now Metairie Cemetery.

By 1840 New Orleans was the third largest metropolis in the country and by 1847 was the epicenter of horse racing in the country, boasting four active and competitive racetracks—the Bingaman Course in Algiers on the West Bank, along with the Eclipse, the Union, and the Metairie Courses on the East Bank. The Metairie Course attracted a panoply of the country's finest race horses that contended before the social elite of America and Europe, making it into the preeminent racetrack in America in the decade before the Civil War.

By 1840 New Orleans was the third largest metropolis in the country and by 1847 was the epicenter of horse racing in the country, boasting four active and competitive racetracks.

In 1854 the Metairie Course was the site of a series of legendary races between the Kentucky-bred Lexington and the Louisiana-bred Lecomte in the Great Post Stakes, set to be the best-two-out-of-three heats, each heat covering a four-mile distance on dirt. Before a capacity crowd of more than twenty thousand, which included former President Millard Fillmore, Lexington outran the field in the first heat on a muddy track, with Lecomte in second place by three lengths. The second heat was a repeat of the first, with Lexington beating Lecomte by four lengths. Hundreds of thousands of dollars, whole boatloads of cotton, and a fair number of mules changed hands on the results. The horses raced again on April 8, with Lecomte winning the match. Their third and final meeting on April 14, 1855, was won by Lexington, whose skeleton is preserved in the Smithsonian, while Lecomte is buried just south of Alexandria, Louisiana, in the town named in his honor.

Following the Civil War, racing in New Orleans resumed at the Metairie Course on December 22, 1866, but by 1872 financial troubles and setbacks forced the closure of the facility. The grounds were redeveloped into the Metairie Cemetery, and if you stroll the grounds you will notice that the plots are arranged around an elongated oval that follows the layout of the former racetrack. The Union Course fared much better during Reconstruction. Opened in 1852, the Union Course was the third-oldest thoroughbred racetrack in the country behind Saratoga and Pimlico. The four-hundred-acre complex at the junction of Bayou and Gentilly Roads became the Creole Course in 1859 and featured many notable horses such as Flora Temple, also known as the "Bobtail Nag" in Stephen Foster's "Camptown Races." The Union Course reorganized and reopened in 1866 and reorganized again in 1871 as the Louisiana Jockey Club. On April 13, 1872, the inaugural day of racing of the Louisiana Jockey Club at the renamed Fair Grounds featured the Grand Inaugural Post Stakes won by Monarchist, a son of the great Lexington. The Fair Grounds has hosted stable owners from General George Armstrong Custer to Sheriff Pat Garrett, whose racehorses ran before presidents and foreign royalty.

Boxing

The popularity of boxing in New Orleans dates to the early 1830s, when waves of Irish immigrants provided an enthusiastic audience. The Irish became masters of prize fighting in the nineteenth century as a way to earn money and gain social recognition. Prize fighting was illegal in New Orleans, as it was in most American cities. Early fights were held in rural settings, anywhere wooden posts and ropes could be hastily erected to define the ring and where paying crowds could be accommodated. They came to see bare-knuckle bouts carried out under London Prize Rules, a mixture of boxing and wrestling. Rounds would last as long as both fighters were standing, whether it was for ten minutes or ten seconds. If a fighter went down for any reason, the round was over.

ABOVE In 1854 the thoroughbred Lexington defeated Lecomte in a series of legendary races at the Metaire racetrack. Painting by Edward Troye. Wikicommons, Gooreen Collection.

In 1870, British champion Jem Mace chose New Orleans as the site for his title bout against American champion Tom Allen for a $2,500 purse and the world heavyweight championship. The two camps set out on May 10 for Kenner, just outside New Orleans. Mace defeated Allen in ten rounds over forty-four minutes before several thousand fans, including General Philip A. Sheridan. This match is believed to be the very first world championship prizefight; a bronze statue in Kenner's Rivertown area commemorates the event.

In January of 1890, the New Orleans City Council revised city ordinances to categorize prizefights sponsored under Marquess of Queensberry Rules, which required, among other things, that fighters cover their fists with padded gloves. These bouts could only qualify as "permissible exhibitions" if they were held within the rooms of regularly chartered athletic clubs. The most famous of these new athletic clubs was the Olympic Club, chartered in 1883 and located on Royal Street between Montegut and Clouet Streets. It boasted a ten-thousand-seat arena with a retractable roof, electric lights, and telegraph stations to accommodate newspapermen from around the world who came to cover boxing's elite.

The highpoint of New Orleans boxing came in September of 1892 with the Fistic Carnival of Champions, featuring three world championship bouts over three successive days at the Olympic Club. In the first match, between Jack McAuliffe and Billy Myer, McAuliffe won with a fifteenth-round knockout, retaining his world lightweight title and a $9,000 purse. The second match, between featherweights George "Little Chocolate" Dixon and Jack Skelly, admitted blacks to the Olympic Club for the first time, albeit in a segregated section. Dixon maintained his world featherweight title, pounding Skelly for eight rounds and causing such an uproar that it ended up being Dixon's first and last fight in the South. The third and final match was billed as the Second Battle of New Orleans and saw challenger James Corbett outmaneuver, outfight, and outlast champion John L. Sullivan, whom he knocked out in the twenty-first round to win the world heavyweight title and a $25,000 purse.

These fights marked the start of the modern era in boxing—the

RIGHT 1909 baseball card of Charles Fritz, Pelicans outfielder. (left) Baseball card depicting Pelicans infielder Ed Reagan, ca. 1906-1908. Courtesy of Derby Gisclair Collection.

BELOW 1910 photograph of the New Orleans Pelicans. "Shoeless" Joe Jackson is No. 12. Courtesy of Derby Gisclair Collection.

transition from quasi-legal bare-knuckle fights held outdoors during the day to gloved matches held indoors in the comfort of an electrically illuminated arena.

In 1893, the Olympic Club arranged a contest between local favorite Andy Bowen and Jack Burke of Galveston, Texas, for the lightweight championship of the South. The bout took place on April 6 and would become part of boxing history after the two fighters battled for 110 rounds over seven hours and nineteen minutes. Bowen was a scrapper who charged like an alley cat fighting for his ninth life. Burke broke both wrists and nearly every bone in his hands, and the bout mercifully ended in a draw, becoming the longest prizefight in American history.

ABOVE 1870 illustration of famed boxing match between Jem Mace and Tom Allen. Courtesty of Derby Gisclair Collection.

BELOW George "Little Chocolate" Dixon was the first African American boxer to fight at the Olympic Club in New Orleans. His eight-round pounding of Jack Skelly, who was white, led to the end of Dixon's boxing career in the South. Image found in *The Life and Battles of Jack Johnson* by Richard Kyle Fox, 1909.

Baseball

Baseball during the nineteenth century was still a work in progress. In many instances the game differed from city to city and state to state, based on the local variants of the predecessor games it replaced—rounders, town ball, and others. For that reason an umpire became a necessary part of the game, not to call balls and strikes, but to interpret the rules. Baseball is the first game in America that was learned from a book, and the umpire helped players to understand the "ground rules." New Orleans embraced baseball earlier than most Southern cities, building on a popular base of cricket teams on playing fields at the Delachaise estate near present day Touro Infirmary. Teams and leagues began forming in 1859 with the establishment of the Louisiana Base Ball Association, which operated until 1873.

During the Civil War, players from a New Orleans team called the Southerners were among more than fifty officers from the Louisiana Seventh Infantry captured following the battle at Rappahannock Station, Virginia, in November 1863. They were transported to Johnson's Island prison camp on the banks of Lake Erie near Sandusky, Ohio, where they taught their fellow prisoners and the Union guards how to play baseball in the narrow area between the rows of prison blocks. Among the prisoners were Lieutenants Michael McNamara and Charles Pierce, who organized a "championship" game between the Southern Club and the Confederate Club, won 19–11 by the Southern Club before a crowd of three thousand prisoners, soldiers, and civilians. Detailed accounts in prisoners' diaries and more obscurely in the local press dispel the common belief that baseball was codified in New York in 1845 as the Knickerbocker Rules and spread by Northern soldiers during the Civil War. Before the war New Orleans already had a thriving baseball culture, with nine teams competing in the Louisiana Base Ball Association.

In 1870, the Chicago White Stockings traveled to New Orleans to challenge the touring Cincinnati Red Stockings, who had played in the city for several weeks before moving on. Learning of the departure of the Red Stockings, the Chicago club decided to remain, and thus baseball's first spring training camp was established in New Orleans. From 1870 well into the mid-twentieth century, the city would host numerous major league teams for spring training, from the Boston Beaneaters to the New York Yankees.

The eyes of the world were on New Orleans for the 1884 World's Industrial and Cotton Centennial Exposition, which opened in December to much fanfare and provided, among other exhibits, a baseball field and schedule of games. Under the leadership of local businessman Toby Hart, the diamond was constructed on the far edge of the 249-acre site that is now home to Audubon Park. Hart was so taken with the game that he led the city's bid to secure a franchise for the newly formed Southern League, bringing the New Orleans Pelicans into the Southern League for the 1887 season alongside teams from seven other Southern cities and capturing the first of three league championships. Player-manager Abner Powell would innovate the game, instituting the practice of covering the infield with a waxed canvas tarp on rainy days. He would also introduce the practice of a regular Ladies' Day on the schedule in 1887 and would later introduce the rain check in 1889. The Pelicans played their games at Sportsman's Park, located at the foot of Canal Street across from present day Greenwood Cemetery.

New Orleans in the Gilded Age

Nineteenth-century New Orleans, along with the rest of urban America, underwent a cultural shift wherein people bought their food instead of growing it, purchased clothes instead of making them, and rented or bought homes instead of building them. The frenetic pace of the transition from a rural agrarian society to an urban industrial society, which afforded even middle-class workers more leisure time to enjoy sports, found

New Orleanians taking full advantage of the opportunities available to them. The proximity to Lake Pontchartrain spawned water sports, from swimming at the bath houses in West End, Milneburg, and Spanish Fort to yachting along the lakeshore and into the Gulf of Mexico. The founding of the 1,300-acre City Park in 1853 provided additional space for cricket, badminton, and other "picnic" games such as canoeing, rowing, and horseshoes. Hunting, fishing, golf, roller skating, billiards, fencing, wrestling, and track-and-field sports – the list goes on and on.

The May 10, 1870, match between British champion Jem Mace and American champion Tom Allen is believed to be the very first world championship prizefight.

Along the way, recreation turned into organized sports and became a viable commercial pastime for New Orleanians of all stations. In the great gumbo that was New Orleans during the nineteenth century, Irish, Italian, German, French, Spanish, and British immigrants all became Americans standing shoulder to shoulder at sporting events. Their appetite for entertainment was satisfied along with their growing pride that their country could produce athletes of such strength, courage, and stamina. Organized sports had begun to alter society. Without radio or television, the city's dozen or so newspapers chronicled the evolution of sports. Initially tucked away between the crime reports and ads of all stripes were stories about sporting events. There was no dedicated sports section, but by the latter part of the century sports coverage often overshadowed national events and even presidential elections on the front page.

In traditionally Catholic New Orleans, the Holy Trinity is irreverently referred to as garlic, onion, and celery. During the Gilded Age in New Orleans, however, it was horseracing, boxing, and baseball. An explosion of interest in athletic pursuits that one could both participate in and enjoy as a spectator provided the citizens of New Orleans and visitors to the city with ample opportunities to enjoy their newly acquired leisure time. America was feeling its way to a better life, and nowhere was this more evident than in New Orleans.

FISTICUFFS AND FIRSTS: A Timeline of Boxing in New Orleans

by Ricardo Coleman

MAY 10, 1870

The first world title match took place in present day Kenner between the British bare-knuckle champion **"Gypsy Jem" Mace** and **Tom Allen**. Mace stopped Allen in the 10th round.

SEPTEMBER 7, 1892

In the first heavyweight championship fight held under the "Marquis of Queensbury" rules, **James "Gentleman Jim" Corbett** knocked out **John L. Sullivan** in the 21st round to win the title at the Olympic Club.

APRIL 6, 1893

Jack Burke and **Andy Bowen** faced off in the longest prizefight in the history of boxing. The two engaged in a titanic struggle that lasted 110 rounds, and seven hours, nineteen minutes. When they answered the bell in the 111th round, the refereee mercifully declared the bout a draw. Afterwards it was discovered that Burke had broken all the bones in both hands.

DECEMBER 15, 1894

Andy Bowen died as result of injuries sustained during a prizefight with **George "Kid" Levigne**. The ensuing crackdown on boxing in New Orleans would last many years.

JANUARY 9, 1917

New Orleans-born **Pete Herman** won the World Bantamweight title from **Kid Williams** when referee Bill Rocan awarded Herman the decision in the 20-round bout.

FEBRUARY 10, 1928

Tony Canzoneri of Slidell defeated **Benny Bass** in a 15-round decision to win the World Featherweight title, the first of his three world titles in three divisions.

AUGUST 24, 1956

New Orleans' adopted son **Joe "Old Bones" Brown** captured the World Lightweight title from **Wallace "Bud" Smith** with a 15-round split-decision at Municipal Auditorium.

APRIL 29, 1963

Ralph Dupas won the World Super Welterweight title at the Municipal Auditorium from **Denny Moyer** in a 15 -round split decision.

APRIL 10, 1964

Willie Pastrano stopped **Gregorio Peralta** with a TKO in the 5th round to defend the WBA and WBC Light Heavyweight titles in front of a hometown crowd at the Municipal Auditorium.

SEPTEMBER 15, 1978

Muhammad Ali won the World Heavyweight title for the third and final time with a 15-round unanimous decision over **Leon Spinks** in the Superdome in New Orleans.

NOVEMBER 25, 1980

Sugar Ray Leonard defeated **Roberto Duran** in the infamous "No Mas" fight in the Superdome. After Leonard began to take command of the fight in round 8, at the 2:44 mark, Duran turned away from Leonard and uttered to referee Octavio Meyran, "no mas" which translates to "no more." With this victory, Leonard had avenged an earlier loss to Duran in Montreal.

DECEMBER 3, 1982

Don King's "Carnival of Champions" in the Superdome, featured two title fights and attracted attention from around the world. **Wilfredo Gómez** defended his WBC World Featherweight title against the WBC Super Bantamweight champion **Lupe Pintor**. The second main-event pitted the WBC Super Welterweight champion **Wilfred Benitez** against the former WBA World Welterweight champion, **Tommy" Hitman" Hearns**. Gómez defeated Pintor with a dramatic 14th round knockout to retain his title. Hearns defeated Benitez with a 15th round majority decision.

MARCH 18, 1991

New Orleans-born **John "Super D" Duplessis** lost by 4th round knockout to World Super Lightweight Champion **Julio Cesar Chavez, Sr.** Duplessis won various national, and regional boxing titles in a 40-3 career.

SEPTEMBER 9, 2000

WBC, WBA, and IBF Light Heavyweight Champion **Roy Jones Jr.** successfully defended his title against **Eric Harding** in the New Orleans Arena, scoring a technical knockout in the 10th round and winning the IBO Light Heavyweight title.

FEBRUARY 22, 2003

Lafayette native **Clifford Etienne** lost to **Mike Tyson** by KO in the 1st round.

Bohemian Revival

Artists and writers led the French Quarter renaissance of the 1920s

by John Shelton Reed, PhD

In the 1920s a bohemian scene emerged in the French Quarter of New Orleans that *The Double Dealer* magazine hailed in 1922 as "the Renaissance of the Vieux Carré." Some of the writers, artists, poseurs, and hangers-on involved were consciously trying to replicate the better-known bohemias of Paris and New York City, and in many respects they succeeded. With the support of local patrons, they created a number of cultural institutions, some short-lived but others more enduring, and contributed to the historic preservation and commercial revitalization that turned the French Quarter from a slum into a tourist destination and a center for nightlife, with housing for the upper-middle class. Ironically, this transformation drove out many of the working artists and writers who had helped to bring it about.

Origins

Anthropologist and novelist Oliver La Farge described the French Quarter of the 1920s as "a decaying monument and a slum as rich as jambalaya or gumbo." Most of its once elegant buildings had been divided into tenements rented to the poor, notably to the first- and second-generation Sicilian immigrants who by one estimate made up 80 percent of the French Quarter's resident population in 1910. In the years during and just after World War I, artists and writers began to move into the area immediately around Jackson Square, attracted by the cheap rents, faded charm, and colorful street life.

Although a few of the Quarter's new residents were native New Orleanians, most came from elsewhere. Several wrote for the city's daily newspapers and encouraged the developing scene by reporting on it. Lyle Saxon, for example, one of the first to adapt a historic building in the Quarter for his own use, used his platform at the *Times-Picayune* to encourage artists and writers to do likewise. Natalie Scott, a society columnist for *The States*, chronicled and promoted the bohemian goings-on in the Quarter, bought and restored several buildings, rented apartments to artists and writers, and lived in one herself.

Another source of aspiring bohemians was Tulane University. Its architecture students had for some time made measured drawings of the Quarter's old buildings, and art students from H. Sophie Newcomb Memorial College, the university's college for women, had been painting and drawing the picturesque ones. Graduates and faculty members from both programs established studios in the Quarter, showed their work in its galleries, and even moved there to live and to socialize. Other Tulane scholars and professors did so as well: Frans Blom and Oliver La Farge from the university's Middle American Research Institute, for instance, helped to establish a continuing Mexican connection that brought Mexican artists and writers to town and sent New Orleanians south for summer visits.

Business interests have often been cast as the villains in the story of the Quarter's revival, and it is true that some shortsighted developers were eager to raze it and replace it with clean, modern buildings. But it should be noted that many businesspeople saw the unique neighborhood's commercial potential. In fact, the first practical proposal for large-scale renovation came from the president of the New Orleans Association of Commerce, who suggested in 1919 that the old Pontalba buildings should be converted to studios and living space for artists. Looking back, photographer William "Cicero" Odiorne observed that "the revival of the old Quarter was a sort of civic project." Uptown New Orleanians were interested in "French Quarter Bohemianism," he said, because artists like him were "useful."

Personalities and Social Life

One of the Quarter's best-known figures at this time was William Spratling, a young artist on the architecture faculty at Tulane. In 1926 he and his apartment-mate William Faulkner (not yet a famous writer) self-published a slim book entitled *Sherwood Anderson and Other Famous Creoles*, described later by Spratling as "a sort of mirror of our scene in New Orleans." Comprising simply Spratling's drawings of their friends, with an introduction by Faulkner, the book gives an idea of the sort of creative figures involved

OPPOSITE Caroline Durieux, a lithographer, ca. 1925. Courtesy of The Historic New Orleans Collection, gift of Mrs. Edmund B. Richardson, gift of Joseph G. Bernard.

in the Quarter's renaissance. It included painter and teacher Ellsworth Woodward, lithographer Caroline Wogan Durieux, photographer "Pops" Whitesell, architects N. C. Curtis and Moise Goldstein, Mardi Gras designer Louis Andrews Fischer, pianist and composer Genevieve Pitot, activist and preservationist Elizebeth Werlein, and Tulane cheerleader Marian Draper. The best-known of the "Famous Creoles" today, however, are undoubtedly some of the dozen or so writers, including the young Faulkner, the even younger Hamilton Basso, and, of course, Sherwood Anderson.

Anderson first visited New Orleans in 1922, found it "surely the most civilized spot in America," and returned to take up residence in 1924 with his new (third) wife, Elizabeth. Already a celebrated writer, Anderson quickly became, in Spratling's judgment, "the Grand Old Man of the literati in New Orleans." The Andersons were at the center of the Quarter's busy social life in the mid-1920s, their apartment in the upper Pontalba building the scene of almost nightly gatherings and their Saturday dinner parties occasions for introducing locals to visitors like writers Carl Carmer, Anita Loos, Edmund Wilson, Edna St. Vincent Millay, and John Dos Passos, as well as publishers B. W. Huebsch and Horace Liveright.

ABOVE *The Double Dealer*, Volume III, No.17, May 1922. Courtesy of The Historic New Orleans Collection.

Contemporary accounts and memoirs make it clear that most of the Quarter's new residents enjoyed what Elizabeth Anderson recalled as "a social and congenial time." Even impecunious young bohemians (all of them white, in Jim Crow Louisiana) could usually afford (African-American) "help"—Faulkner, Spratling, and La Farge, for example, shared the services of a cook, who washed and cleaned as well—which made the frequent dinner parties and other entertaining possible. The Quarter also offered cafés for mid-day coffee and conversation, inexpensive Creole and Italian restaurants, and an abundance of speakeasies (at one point Elizebeth Werlein counted seventy-four in a nine-block radius). The ordinary social round was punctuated by special events like the racy, more-or-less annual "Bal des Artistes" to benefit the Arts and Crafts Club, or an ill-starred cruise on Lake Pontchartrain that Sherwood Anderson organized (immortalized, after a fashion, in Faulkner's novel *Mosquitoes*), all of it fueled by a flood of illegal alcohol. Elizabeth Anderson recalled, "We all seemed to feel that Prohibition was a personal affront and that we had a moral duty to undermine it." Certainly bootleg liquor was as easy to find and as emblematic of the scene as marijuana would be for a later generation of rebellious young people.

New Institutions

Several new institutions contributed to this flourishing of cultural activity, and benefited from it. All were largely bankrolled by business people and philanthropists who were not themselves "bohemian," but who valued the presence and enjoyed the company of those who were.

The Double Dealer was a literary magazine founded in 1921 by Julius Weiss Friend and Albert Goldstein, two young men from prominent New Orleans Jewish families, along with John McClure and Basil Thompson. For its five years of existence, it provided a gathering place and rallying point for the literary component of the French Quarter renaissance. Although its office was actually across Canal Street from the French Quarter, its staff, contributors, and hangers-on were very much a part of the Quarter scene, gathering most afternoons at the Pelican Bookshop on Royal Street for salami sandwiches and wine. Sherwood Anderson dropped by the office shortly after he arrived in New Orleans, and stayed on to become a mentor and frequent contributor.

The Arts and Crafts Club was for artists what *The Double Dealer* was for writers. Its lectures, classes, exhibits, and salesroom were open to the public, and its activities received extensive coverage in the local newspapers. The club was largely bankrolled by Sarah Henderson, a sugar-refinery heiress, and its activities appealed to a mix of working artists, serious amateurs, and the merely "artsy."

Le Petit Theatre du Vieux Carré began in 1916 as the local chapter of the Drama League of America, but a year later a group of twenty or so members started the Drawing Room Players Uptown. In 1919 they moved to the Quarter and in 1922 into the building it still occupies today at 616 St. Peter Street. The theatre provided a setting in which high-society mingled with bohemia. Many of the Quarter's artists, writers, and musicians were involved in the theater's production and design; the theater's founders, its management, and most of its audience were drawn from more privileged circles; and both groups participated as actors.

Uptown society people also experienced the Quarter's romance and squalor firsthand when organizations like the Daughters of 1776–1812, the Quartier Club, and Le Petit Salon renovated historic properties to use as clubhouses. Though by no means bohemians themselves, members of these elite women's groups invited the more presentable artists and writers to be speakers and guests, and they allied themselves with the Quarter's artistic element in the nascent historic preservation movement.

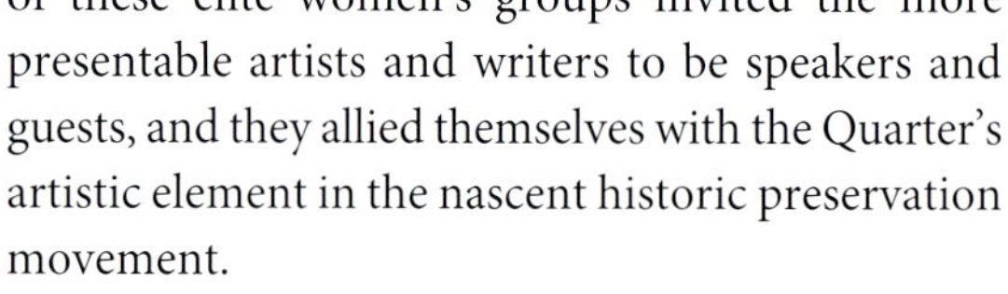

ABOVE Lyle Saxon in front of his cabin at Melrose Plantation in 1925. Courtesy of the Photography Collection at the State Library of Louisiana.

Transformation and Decline

Once a critical mass of artists and writers was reached, related businesses began to appear. As early as 1922, a walking tour recommended in *The Double Dealer* pointed out the Quarter's "restaurants, auction marts, antique shops, and book stalls," including such bohemian hangouts as John and Grace McClure's Olde Book Shoppe and the Arts and Crafts Club's galleries. That same year, a *New York Times* article headlined "Greenwich Village on Royal Street" observed that the Quarter offered "the usual teashops and antique shops and bookshops" one might find in the Village. The new cultural and commercial activity meant that Uptown New Orleanians who might never previously have set foot in the Quarter began to venture into it for lunches and shopping, for exhibits and classes at the Arts and Crafts Club, and for plays at Le Petit Theatre. Visits to the French Market for coffee became a common post-party activity.

The Quarter offered cafés for mid-day coffee and conversation, inexpensive Creole and Italian restaurants, and an abundance of speakeasies.

Some Uptown visitors liked what they saw so much that they purchased houses as rental property or for pieds-à-terre. Some of the more adventurous even moved into the Quarter themselves, many of them what would later be called "fauxhemians," like the fashionable young couple whose "impromptu studio party" led a society reporter to gush, "That's one of the advantages of being an artist . . . you can give such wonderful parties!" This sort of thing led more than one real artist to grouse that the Quarter was filling up with the kind of people "who rent an ordinary furnished room and call it 'my studio.'" *The New York Times* observed that "the French Quarter has suffered the fate of such quarters. It has become a fad. It has become, in a way, fashionable."

Inevitably, the Quarter's new appeal was soon reflected in rising rents and real estate prices. When Natalie Scott sold a St. Peter Street house she had owned for only sixteen months, she tripled her investment, and the value of Le Petit Salon's clubhouse almost quadrupled in six years. The days when Lyle Saxon could rent a sixteen-room house on Royal Street for sixteen dollars a month would not come again.

The Quarter was also "discovered" by visitors. In 1924 Saxon published a walking tour of the Quarter in his newspaper column, but he was dismayed by how many people took his advice to come have a look. He wrote later that the place had become a "mad house," with "a horde of tourists everywhere, and people riding around with horses and buggies, sight-seeing."

Increasing rents meant that fewer working artists and writers could afford to live in the Quarter, and the influx of tourists and of businesses catering to them meant that fewer wanted to live there anyway. By the 1930s most of those depicted in *Sherwood Anderson and Other Famous Creoles* had decamped. Faulkner went home to Mississippi, and Sherwood Anderson left for the mountains of Virginia; others went to New York, or Paris. Some went to Taxco, Mexico, and Santa Fe, New Mexico—where they got to see the same process repeat itself. Although some vestiges of bohemia, and even a few actual bohemians, remained in the Quarter, its bohemian moment had passed.

BELOW *Royal Street Bookstore 1920s,* by Alberta Kinsey. Courtesy of Jean Bragg Gallery.

Literary Lights

New Orleans, and the French Quarter in particular, created a welcoming and inexpensive environment for many writers.

ABOVE Alice Dunbar Nelson Alice Dunbar Nelson (1875-1935), a graduate of Straight University, now Dillard University, captures Creole life in her short story collection, *The Goodness of Saint Rocque*. Courtesy of the Schomburg Center for Research in Black Culture, Manuscripts, Archives and Rare Books Division, New York Public Library.

ABOVE Truman Capote (1924-1984), a New Orleans native, spent so much of his early childhood in the French Quarter that he claimed to have been born in the Monteleone Hotel, and called the city his "secret place." Photo by Carl Van Vechten, 1948. Library of Congress Prints and Photographs Division.

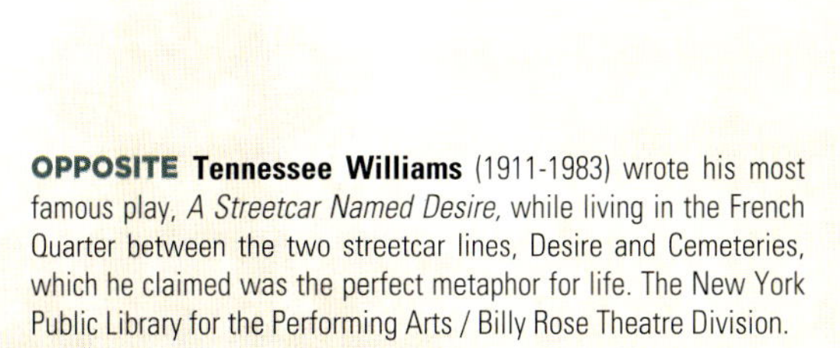

OPPOSITE Tennessee Williams (1911-1983) wrote his most famous play, *A Streetcar Named Desire,* while living in the French Quarter between the two streetcar lines, Desire and Cemeteries, which he claimed was the perfect metaphor for life. The New York Public Library for the Performing Arts / Billy Rose Theatre Division.

THEATER
TIME
DATE
PLACE
FS

BLKARTSOUTH
of the
Free Southern Theater

NKOMBO PUBLICATIONS
magazines & books of blk writing

FREEDOM HAIR PLAYERS
blk theater

BLK MIND JOCKEYS
soulful poets

Available For Performances Now

1716 No. Miro St. - New Orleans, La. 70150
Phone 947-1106 or 947-1107

PEACE & LIBERATION

Abundant Talent

Tom Dent was integral in BLKARTSOUTH movement

New Orleans poet, journalist, and activist Tom Dent created the Umbra Writers' Workshop along with Amiri Baraka in New York in 1962. Three years later, he returned to New Orleans to help support the Free Southern Theater and later co-found BLKARTSOUTH, a community writing and acting workshop for emerging black poets and playwrights. Members of BLKARTSOUTH performed poetry and short plays throughout the South. According to Dent:

BLKARTSOUTH is a New Orleans acting-writing workshop of the Free Southern Theater, which is developing some bad young blk writers from the South who are going to be heard from in the future. The workshop began with the objective of providing new theatrical material for the FST touring ensemble, but quickly expanded to include a quarterly devoted primarily to poetry: NKOMBO, five individual poetry collections by writers in the group, readings by the group in New Orleans and at several colleges in the South, plus the production of three scripts written in the workshop by themselves and the use of two of the scripts by the touring ensemble during the 1969 season.

These activities have given the Free Southern Theater a new creative depth, and go a long way toward proving that there is abundant new talent in the South, which is going to have a lot to say about the directions of blk writing. New Orleans itself, long a home of creole illusions, is developing a blk consciousness, what with the emergence of Nat Turner Theater and REVOLT magazine, Dashiki Theater, THE PLAIN TRUTH newspaper and the other hard-hitting projects in the last year or so.

Dent's 1967 profound play *Ritual Murder* has become a dramatic staple in New Orleans and continues to be taught in schools and performed in theaters throughout the city. Dent died in New Orleans in 1998 at the age of sixty-six.

-Nancy Dixon, PhD

ABOVE Courtesy of the Tom Dent Papers, Amistad Research Center at Tulane University.

OPPOSITE Tom Dent with Free Southern Theater poster. Courtesy of the Tom Dent Papers, Amistad Research Center at Tulane University.

Part VI: SOUNDS

Considered the "Holy Grail" of jazz, Louis Armtrong's first cornet, a Champion Silver Piston distributed by Lyons and Healy Chicago, was given to Armstong at the Municipal Waifs' Home in New Orleans in 1913. Courtesy of the New Orleans Jazz Club Collections of the Louisiana State Museum.

World on a String

When Louis Armstrong, Kid Ory, and Jelly Roll Morton left home, they made jazz a global phenomenon

by Bruce Boyd Raeburn, PhD

When Louis Armstrong boarded the riverboat *St. Paul* in April 1919 for his first extended excursion away from New Orleans with Fate Marable's orchestra, he was full of uncertainty. Would the world embrace or reject him? In retrospect, the answer is clear. During the next four decades the trumpeter became the nation's foremost jazz ambassador, capable of transforming lives on an international scale. Of course, as is always the case with heroic narratives, he had some help along the way.

Because the form is inherently improvisational and requires great skill, jazz is often described as complex, but in New Orleans it follows a simple formula: a beautiful melody rendered in surprising ways, with a big beat for dancing. Louis Armstrong, the pianist Jelly Roll Morton, and trombonist Edward "Kid" Ory, the three most significant contributors to the early development and explanation of New Orleans jazz, routinely made a point of reminding audiences that jazz is meant to be fun. They left the city in search of fame and fortune—particularly in Chicago, Los Angeles, and New York, before going international through recordings and touring—because of their desire for adventure and to avoid the social restrictions and competition that confronted them at home. But their music continued to celebrate the place and its lifestyle, because New Orleans jazz is played "from the heart," where memory and identity commingled for them.

Ferd Morton (born 1890) and Edward Ory (born 1886) were raised as Afro-French Creoles, an identity rooted in a colonial francophone past that did little to prepare them for life in the wake of the *Plessy v. Ferguson* decision (1896), which validated racial segregation. Jelly Roll (born Ferdinand Joseph LaMothe, his step-father's surname Mouton anglicized to Morton) jettisoned his Creole heritage, adopting a persona that fit his career ambitions and reflected his time in the Storyville red-light district and in black vaudeville. He resurrected it for interviews with Alan Lomax at the Library of Congress in 1938, where he expounded his views on jazz origins and his philosophy of how the music should be played, claiming that he descended from a long line of "Frenchmen." Conversely, Kid Ory nurtured his *Creolité* by speaking the language and recording songs such as "Blanche Touquatoux," "Eh! La-bas!," "Creole Bo Bo," and "C'est L'Autre Can Can" in the mid-1940s. Although Ory is recognized as the first leader of a "black" New Orleans jazz band to record, his lineage included only one African-American grandparent, interspersed with French, Spanish, and Native American ancestors. In contrast, Louis Armstrong (born 1901) was African American and grew up in the Back o' Town section of New Orleans, a rough Uptown neighborhood near Black Storyville, where the brothels and cabarets were indistinguishable. His experiences singing on the streets, the kindness of Jewish neighbors (the Karnofskys), and the training he received in reform school at the hands of Peter Davis in 1913–1914 combined to instill in him a discipline and musical imagination that was unparalleled. Armstrong was the last of the three to leave town but the first to achieve international celebrity.

For the musicians who migrated in the years 1900–1925, when jazz was achieving its initial idiomatic coherence and spreading across the globe, all roads led to Chicago, serving as a prelude to the massive Great Migration that brought hundreds of thousands of southern blacks to northern cities during and after World War I. The South Side of Chicago was a thriving black metropolis with cabarets, dance halls, restaurants, and theaters, and the proximity to companies such as Gennett, Columbia, Paramount, and OKeh provided opportunities to make records, which was the key to a musician's successful marketing. From 1915–1917, New Orleans musicians flocked to Chicago in increasing numbers. Bands such as the Original Creole Orchestra, Tom Brown's Band from Dixieland, and the Original Dixieland Jazz Band exposed Chicago audiences to an exciting new music that was still under construction, and scholars argue about the role

OPPOSITE Studio portrait of Louis Armstrong (left) and King Oliver, ca. 1919. Courtesy of the New Orleans Jazz Club Collections at the Louisiana State Museum.

ABOVE Kid Ory's Original Creole Jazz Band. Courtesy of the Hogan Jazz Archive, Tulane University.

Chicago played in reshaping it, particularly regarding a rhythmic shift from 2/4 to 4/4 that became the dominant paradigm. The basic formula of "collective improvisation," in which cornet, clarinet, and trombone (the "front line") backed by guitar, bass, and drums (the "rhythm section") engage in a polyphonic conversation, originated in New Orleans, but the first application of the word "jazz" to New Orleans music occurred when Brown's band played at Lamb's Café in Chicago. Because the term was loosely associated with vice districts, local musicians who resented the interlopers' popularity used it to castigate them, but the scheme backfired and the word helped to promote the band instead. On February 26, 1917, in New York, the Original Dixieland Jazz Band made the first jazz recording—a readily accessible product with sales surpassing a million units—the connection between New Orleans music and the term became irrevocable, attracting young people in search of musical thrills everywhere.

Jelly Roll Morton began traveling in 1907 and had been in Chicago as early as 1914 (he published his "Jelly Roll Blues" there in 1915), but in 1917 he relocated to Los Angeles, anticipating a fresh market with less competition. After a business deal gone awry in New Orleans, Kid Ory joined him there in 1919. Prior to his departure, Ory had developed what came to be known as "tailgate" trombone style (combining pitch bending, staccato accents, harmonic "popping," and a liberal use of *glissando*), and he was widely regarded as the top jazz band leader in the Crescent City after the demise of cornetist Buddy Bolden in 1906, employing cornetists Joe "King" Oliver and Louis Armstrong, clarinetists Johnny Dodds, Jimmie Noone, and Sidney Bechet, and the drummer Warren "Baby" Dodds (Johnny's younger brother). When Oliver left for Chicago in the summer of 1918 to join the remnants of the Original Creole Orchestra, Armstrong succeeded him and quickly attracted major attention. His popularity led to strife between Ory and Pete Lala, a Sicilian gangster and Ory's business partner, who was chummy with the police. When Ory broke his contract with Lala to showcase Armstrong on his own at Economy Hall in Tremé, the police began to harass customers waiting to get in, and crowds dwindled. Ory fled to Oakland and then to Los Angeles, "for health reasons." The move enabled him to release his first recordings, for the obscure Nordskog label in Santa Monica, as Ory's Sunshine Orchestra in May 1922, but lack of distribution minimized their impact.

Armstrong began working with Fate Marable's orchestra on the Streckfus riverboats in 1918—it became a safe way to explore other locations, with a guaranteed ticket home—but when Oliver asked him to join his Creole Jazz Band in Chicago in the summer of 1922, he decided to take a chance and move to the South Side, where the popularity of New Orleans jazz was gaining momentum. In 1923 Oliver's Creole Jazz Band recorded for Gennett, Paramount, Columbia, and OKeh, producing a series of classic recordings in a seven-month period that elevated jazz to a new level, thanks especially to Armstrong's emergence as a soloist.

Reacting to the buzz emanating from Chicago due to Armstrong and Oliver, Morton returned to the Windy City and recorded his "Milenberg Joys" in July 1923 for Gennett with a white New Orleans band, the New Orleans Rhythm Kings. Gennett was headquartered nearby in Richmond, Indiana, where the state legislature was dominated by the Ku Klux Klan—Gennett even made promotional records for them. When Morton was challenged on the racial issue, the trombonist George Brunies stepped in, asserting that Morton was a Cuban and not black, and pointing to a diamond inlay in the pianist's front tooth, which was accepted as proof of the claim. Despite segregation, New Orleans jazz provided an incentive to cross racial boundaries, based in a common love of improvised music, and musicians were willing to incur risks for the sake of collaboration. For jazz musicians, associating with the best players available was always the objective, despite social conventions that inhibited such connections.

The success of Armstrong's recordings with King Oliver's Creole Jazz Band actually led to the band's demise, after Oliver was accused of pocketing an undue share of the royalties. Armstrong and his second wife, the pianist Lil Hardin, along with the Dodds brothers, abandoned Oliver late in 1923 to pursue other options. Armstrong's rapid ascendancy as a dazzling instrumental soloist had worried Oliver, who felt overshadowed by the younger trumpeter, a situation that Lil Hardin exploited to set Armstrong up as a leader in his own right. After a year in New York as a star soloist with Fletcher Henderson's orchestra in 1924, Armstrong returned to Chicago to inaugurate Louis Armstrong and his Hot Five, a band organized by Richard M. Jones (another New Orleans transplant) specifically to feature Armstrong as an instrumentalist and vocalist on the OKeh label. Kid Ory was recruited from California and arrived in the fall of 1925, joining Hardin, Johnny Dodds, and the guitarist Johnny St. Cyr to complete the Hot Five. When a drummer was needed, Warren "Baby" Dodds got the call, and eventually pianist Earl "Fatha" Hines and drummer Zutty Singleton became part of the extended family, known as Armstrong's Hot Seven. From November 1925 through July 1928, these bands revolutionized how jazz was played and perceived with a barrage of hits, including "Heebie Jeebies" (credited by some as the introduction of scat singing), "Cornet Chop Suey," "Potato Head Blues," "Struttin' with Some Barbecue," "A Monday Date," and the jazz masterwork "West End Blues," among dozens of others. Ory's "Muskrat Ramble" and "Savoy Blues" were recorded by the Hot Five as well, illustrating how the musicians used the New Orleans practice of "head arrangements" in the studio to collectively generate and refine ideas for the recordings, sometimes leading to a rather casual assignment of composer credits. The chemistry that existed among the musicians was what mattered most, and their ability to respond spontaneously to each other from moment to moment gave the recordings an energy that was seductive. But there was also no doubt that the dominant musical personality was Armstrong's, with his unique vocal and instrumental style creating an unmistakable sound that jazz musicians and singers have attempted to emulate ever since.

In 1926 Ory also found work recording with Jelly Roll Morton's Red Hot Peppers and playing with Joe Oliver's new band, the Dixie Syncopators, at the Plantation cabaret. Morton was the first real composer and arranger in jazz, and the solo piano and band recordings he made of his tunes, especially "Black Bottom Stomp," "Georgia Swing," "Sidewalk Blues," and "The Crave," revealed his amazing range and depth of musical vision, creating a variant of the New Orleans style that differed noticeably from Armstrong's approach while still remaining linked to it. In fact, the most singular characteristic of New Orleans style jazz recordings in the mid-1920s is the variety that was possible within the idiom. New Orleans bands such as Sam Morgan's Jazz Band, Celestin's Original Tuxedo Jazz Orchestra, and the Jones & Collins Astoria Hot Eight were each unique but nevertheless shared a stylistic affinity; likewise, the bands led by Armstrong, Morton, and Oliver in Chicago all found different ways to interpret the style, while remaining distinct from the hometown variants.

For his part, in addition to recording, Armstrong performed live with Erskine Tate's orchestra at the Vendome Theater, where he quickly established a reputation as "the world's greatest trumpet player," capable of endless high-note choruses that left audiences spellbound. He also worked with the Carroll Dickerson Orchestra at the Sunset Café, run by Joe Glaser. By 1928, the potential that was evident in his early recordings with Oliver had been fully realized. The Hot Five recordings demonstrated in detail Armstrong's mastery as an instrumentalist and vocalist, transforming the jazz template from an ensemble approach to a soloist's craft, driven almost entirely by his creative brilliance. This was the basis on which jazz came to be recognized as an American art form, and during the course of the 1930s, "hot" record collector networks gave rise to jazz critics and historians who were committed to promoting this point of view. After World War II, New Orleans adopted their agenda with enthusiasm, using jazz as the centerpiece of an increasingly prevalent economic strategy focused on cultural tourism. It is not by accident that the New Orleans airport now bears the name of Louis Armstrong.

Jazz became the city's gift to the world, but the world also knows that if it truly wants to understand the music, it must come to New Orleans.

In 1929–1930 Armstrong left Chicago to perform in theatrical productions in New York and at cabarets on the West Coast. He returned briefly in March 1931 with a new manager, Johnny Collins, to inaugurate a nightclub called The Showboat. His former manager, Tommy Rockwell, continued to book the band into venues in Harlem without Armstrong's consent, and trouble soon ensued. Armed gunmen, supposedly representing Rockwell, threatened Armstrong backstage, so Collins quickly arranged tours of the Midwest and South when the engagement concluded to remove the trumpeter from harm's way. The tour included an extended summer job at Suburban Gardens, a nightclub located in Jefferson Parish run by a bookie and bootlegger named Jack Sheehan. Sheehan gave Armstrong star billing despite objections from the white musicians union that the trumpeter's residency was costing its members lucrative work. It was Armstrong's first trip home in nearly a decade, and he received a hero's welcome from the black community, but they were not permitted to attend his performances at Suburban Gardens because of segregation. Armstrong promised a special show for "his people" at the local US Army Supply Base, which was surreptitiously cancelled at the last minute. Meanwhile, the turmoil with dueling managers continued, and in 1932–1934 Armstrong spent a considerable amount of time in Europe to get away from them, until he finally dispensed with Collins' services and successfully litigated the problems with Rockwell. In 1935 Joe Glaser became his manager, with New York ultimately serving as the base of operations. Henceforth, Louis

ABOVE Jelly Roll Morton outside the Rhythm Club in New York, 1939. Photo by Danny Barker, collection of Alyn Shipton.

Armstrong concentrated exclusively on making music, while Glaser handled the business affairs.

Armstrong's travels in England, France, Denmark, and Sweden in the 1930s set the stage for the apotheosis of jazz as a cosmopolitan music—a music belonging to the world—but he remained flexible in the face of change. Glaser provided Armstrong with big bands to keep him touring and recording throughout the next two decades, finding new ways to showcase his assets with only minimal regard for the enormous physical toll that constant travel exacted on him. For Ory and Morton, the Depression years were more difficult. By 1928, the focus of jazz activity had shifted from Chicago to New York. Ory went along when Oliver moved there in 1927, but after a brief return to Chicago, he went back to California in 1930, where he worked intermittently for the US Postal Service and dabbled in chicken farming, remaining musically inactive for more than a decade. In 1928 Morton also went to New York, where he found himself out of style, preaching the benefits of small-band, New Orleans–style jazz to consumers whose interest had been captured by the emergent big bands of Duke Ellington and Fletcher Henderson. RCA Victor, Morton's record label, dropped him in 1931, and he spent most of the rest of the decade in semi-retirement in Washington, DC, until discovered in 1938 by Alan Lomax, who was conducting interviews on folk music for the Library of Congress. Morton invaded the Archive of American Folksong and managed to convince his host that jazz was worthy of interest, despite some initial resistance on Lomax's part. Morton's extensive interviews with Lomax provide a detailed account of the history and aesthetics of New Orleans jazz—a story in which Morton assigned a major role to himself. He emphasized the importance of the "Latin tinge" in New Orleans jazz, describing clave-based rhythms (including tresillo and habanera) that can still be heard in the brass bands that play for New Orleans "second line" parades. Morton's untimely death in Los Angeles in July 1941, just as a revival of New Orleans jazz was gaining momentum, prevented him from fully capitalizing on his return to the limelight, although a series of recordings for RCA and General in 1939–1940 showed him to be in great form. Ory was there when Jelly died, and when asked if a jazz funeral would be appropriate, he reportedly replied, "We'll do it next time."

For the musicians who migrated in the years 1900–1925, when jazz was achieving its initial idiomatic coherence and spreading across the globe, all roads led to Chicago.

Thanks to the revival of interest in New Orleans–style jazz, Ory fared better and, along with trumpeter Bunk Johnson (who claimed to have mentored Louis Armstrong), returned to prominence with recordings, touring, and film appearances. In 1944 Orson Welles included him in a series of radio broadcasts, and his opinions on how to play "authentic" New Orleans–style jazz became required reading for the young adherents of the revival, who saw New Orleans style as an antidote to what they regarded as the conformism of the big swing bands and the "neurotic" impulses of bebop and modern jazz. In 1958 Ory's Creole Jazz Band toured France, where it was featured in Thomas Rowe's short documentary film, *L'homme de la Nouvelle Orléans*. In later years Ory owned music clubs in San Francisco and made regular appearances at Disneyland. In 1966 he retired to Hawaii, where he died in 1973, having outlived Louis Armstrong by about two years. Interestingly, in 1965 his "Muskrat Ramble" was given new life when Country Joe McDonald transformed it into "I-Feel-Like-I'm-Fixin'-to-Die Rag," the most famous (and lucrative) anti-Vietnam War song of the era.

Such transformations should come as no surprise. New Orleans jazz is a renewable resource. The foundation that Armstrong, Ory, and Morton built will sustain future generations because their music remains essential to the tradition and inspires innovation. Through their achievements, jazz became the city's gift to the world, but the world also knows that if it truly wants to understand the music, it must come to New Orleans. Jazz is powerful, and inherently cosmopolitan, precisely because of its ability to unite people across whatever boundaries appear to constrain them; for more than a century jazz has provided an incentive for connection that continues to grow. One could ask for no better example of this potency than the inauguration of UNESCO's International Jazz Day in New Orleans on April 30, 2012, with a sunrise concert at Congo Square, in which African drumming and a poem by Freddi Williams Evans about the square brought the jazz continuum full circle in a contemplation of African roots. On that day musicians from 190 countries performed jazz, with many included in a real-time Internet jam session with pianist Herbie Hancock, duly anchored in a New Orleans connection that speaks to both past and future.

BELOW Courtesy of the New Orleans Jazz Club Collections of the Louisiana State Museum.

BELOW Title page and sheet music for "Nuit des Tropiques, Symphonie," by Louis Gottschalk. Courtesy of the Music Division, the New York Public Library. "L. M. Gottschalk" New York Public Library Digital Collections.

Nuit des Tropiques

Symphonie

pour

Grande Orchestre

par

L. M. Gottschalk

LEFT Louis Gottschalk. Illustration by L.F. Courtesy of the Music Division, the New York Public Library. "L.M. Gottschalk" New York Public Library Digital Collections.

Louis Gottschalk

One could argue that Louis Moreau Gottschalk was New Orleans' first superstar musician. The virtuoso pianist wrote more than three hundred compositions, gained international fame entertaining royalty, staged outlandish concerts, and died relatively young. While still a teenager, he met Frédéric Chopin, who told the young man, "Give me your hand, my child; I predict that you will become the king of pianists."

Born May 8, 1929, in New Orleans to a businessman of Jewish descent from London, and a Louisiana native of Saint-Dominguan descent, Gottschalk left home at a young age to seek his musical education in Paris. The influence of his hometown remained strong in his compositions, which drew on African American, Caribbean, and South American traditions. "Bamboula," written while the nineteen-year-old Gottschalk was ill with typhoid fever, echoed the syncopation used by African slaves in New Orleans ("bamboula" is a drum of Afro-Caribbean origin.).

Some scholars cite him as a precursor to ragtime pioneer Scott Joplin, and his work is seen as uniquely danceable. The legendary choreographer George Balanchine paid him tribute with his *Cakewalk*. Gottschalk aimed for popular enjoyment over the great classics, perhaps one reason that his music is rarely performed today. According to critic Terry Teachout, "Every American composer who blends classical and popular music is following in his footsteps—though few have heard the works in which he foresaw their attempts."

Gottschalk's globetrotting included tours throughout the Caribbean, Europe, the United States, and South America, inspiring new compositions that incorporated the sounds he heard during his travels. His concerts could be bombastic, with arrangements that called for ten pianos. His romantic pursuits in the world's capitals earned Gottschalk a reputation as a ladies man. During a November 1869 in Rio de Janeiro, Gottschalk collapsed while performing his favorite number, "Morte!! (She Is Dead)." He died three weeks later in Tijuca, Brazil, at the age of 40.

-Brian W. Boyles

Cradle of Rock and Roll

Cosimo Matassa, Dave Bartholomew, and Allen Toussaint forged the future at J&M Studio

by Alison Fensterstock

September 1955: A pretty, high-haired man is pounding the piano in the back room of a little shop on Rampart and Dumaine. The studio where he's punishing the keys had been a secondary addition to the business, where its owners primarily sold and fixed radios, television sets, and record players, as well as selling worn-out discs from the jukeboxes they maintained around town. But increasingly, lately, the recording service has been drawing more and more trade, as have the records for sale. Something is simmering, and the pompadoured firecracker at the piano is at its ground zero. And in not too long, it's going to crack the world wide open—with a crash, a bang, a-wopbopaloobop, alop bam-boom.

"I'm not sure, but I'm almost positive, that all music came from New Orleans," Ernie K-Doe once declared. A flamboyant R&B star who would record his signature *Billboard* number-one hit "Mother-In-Law" at Cosimo Matassa's J&M Studio about five years after Little Richard's "Tutti Frutti" session, and with some of the same personnel, K-Doe wasn't known for understatement. But there's plenty of truth in that oft-quoted hyperbole. In a poetic coincidence of geography, the J&M Music Shop stood across from Congo Square, right in between the French Quarter and Tremé. In the eighteenth and nineteenth centuries, enslaved Africans gathered in Congo Square on Sunday afternoons to trade goods and also to dance and drum. Their polyrhythms, kidnapped from across the water to plant their seeds in fertile New Orleans soil, were the ancestors of what would become jazz, the blues, and the big beat that thumped under Little Richard's wild-man shouts at Cosimo's two hundred years later.

Cosimo Matassa grew up working in a grocery store on Dauphine Street in the French Quarter, a common family business for Sicilian immigrants like his father, who had come to America in 1910. In 1945, not quite twenty years old and a Tulane dropout, he opened the J&M Music Shop with Joe Mancuso, his dad's partner in the jukebox sideline that initially supplied the shop with records. The used-record sales were brisk enough that the partners began ordering new releases, hustling to stock the latest from the decentralized nationwide network of independent labels—Chess, King, Atlantic, Modern—that were producing jazz, jump blues, gospel, R&B, and other popular music by black artists, the sounds tracked as "race music" on the *Billboard* charts until 1949. One secret weapon was a friend of the shop who worked as a Pullman porter on the Sunset Limited, the train that ran New Orleans to Los Angeles; he was a one-man express delivery service for the latest jazz and blues records on West Coast labels.

And very soon, those labels would become J&M's clients. In 1946, Matassa bought a microphone and a disc cutter for the back room and started reading up on recording techniques. There were no other studios dedicated to recording music in New Orleans at the time, and within the year, along with the glee clubs, school bands, amateur performers, and novelty memento-seekers availing themselves of J&M's recording service, major players like RCA and Decca were dropping in on occasion to record traditional jazz groups. The city also lacked homegrown record labels; when out-of-town outfits sent representatives down to shop for new talent to wax, the pickings were rich, and it was far cheaper to record local talent at Cosimo's than to bring them to New York or Chicago or Los Angeles for a session.

A visit like that, from the New Jersey-based DeLuxe Records in 1947, was a turning point for J&M, and arguably for rock and roll itself. Over two trips that year, the label owners, brothers David and Jules Braun, collected hits from jump-blues bandleader Paul Gayten and singer Annie Laurie. They also recorded Roy Brown doing the saucy rhythm-and-blues number "Good Rockin' Tonight," a tune he'd tried, while down on his luck, to sell to the popular blues shouter Wynonie Harris. In his award-winning biography *Blue Monday: Fats Domino and the Lost Dawn of Rock 'n' Roll*, historian Rick Coleman calls the tune "the first

OPPOSITE Antoine "Fats" Domino (seated) and Dave Bartholomew, August 8, 1957. Photo by Franck - Bertacci Studio. Courtesy of the Charles L. Franck Studio Collection at The Historic New Orleans Collection.

rock n'roll anthem, leading to the use of the word 'rock' in scores of hard-partying rhythm & blues songs in the late 1940s and early 1950s and, eventually, its use in a musical context by Bill Haley, Alan Freed, and everyone." Coleman notes that the phrase "rock and roll" had been part of American slang since the 1930s, as a sexual euphemism. Though it's Alan Freed, the Cleveland disc jockey whose 1952 Moondog Coronation Ball is considered the first rock-and-roll concert, who is widely credited with popularizing the phrase in a musical context, "Good Rockin' Tonight"—released at least three years before Freed hit the airwaves—did plenty to unleash the term into the vernacular. In any case, the song was a hit. Seeing the momentum of Brown's recording, Wynonie Harris quickly backtracked on his initial decision and cut his own version in 1948, which topped *Billboard's* R&B chart. And more than that, "Good Rockin' Tonight" unleashed a sound: Brown's "passionate wailing became the basic vocal template for much of R&B, rock n'roll and soul," Coleman writes, and its rhythm and tone echoed through the R&B and early rock recordings that followed. Elvis Presley covered "Good Rockin' Tonight" as his second A-side for Sun Records in 1954; in the '50s so did Carl Perkins, Ricky Nelson, and Louisiana rock-and-roll firebrand Jerry Lee Lewis, among others.

As pivotal as "Good Rockin' Tonight" was for the birth of rock and roll, DeLuxe's relationship with Cosimo's Music Shop brought about an even more important element: it put Dave Bartholomew—and all that would come with him—into play. Bartholomew was a trumpeter and bandleader from Edgard, Louisiana, a small town upriver in St. John the Baptist Parish. In the immediate postwar years, his band was one of the most popular in town. The Braun brothers cut a few records with him at Cosimo's, including 1949's "Country Boy," which sold about 100,000 copies and remains Bartholomew's biggest hit under his own name. "I still get checks on it," he told author Jeff Hannusch in an interview for the 1985 book *I Hear You Knockin'*. Bartholomew was out on the road

Fats Domino charted more records than Little Richard, Buddy Holly, and Chuck Berry put together, and with eventual sales topping sixty-five million, he outsold every one of his contemporaries but Elvis Presley.

promoting "Country Boy" when he met Lew Chudd, owner of the Los Angeles–based Imperial Records. Bartholomew signed on with Imperial as an artist and, more importantly, as an A&R man and producer. One night, with Chudd in town and no gig of his own, Bartholomew decided to take his new boss to hear a likely prospect down in the Ninth Ward.

"I'd heard about this guy who was supposed to play pretty good boogie woogie piano down at the Hideaway Club," Bartholomew told Hannusch. "It was a Friday night, and I wasn't working, so Lew and I went down there. That was the first time we heard Fats Domino."

It's impossible to overstate the importance of the partnership between Fats Domino and Dave Bartholomew, which spawned dozens of hits—sixty-three appearances on the *Billboard* pop chart, and fifty-nine on R&B—between 1950 and 1963. The first record they cut together was "The Fat Man," a lyrically sweetened-up rewrite of the R-rated "Junker's Blues" first recorded by New Orleans boogie-woogie "piano professor" Champion Jack Dupree in 1940. Bartholomew changed the roguish blues lyrics about dope and prison to better suit the genial, cherubic Fats, as well as the wider market: "Some people call me a junker, because I'm loaded all the time" became "They call, they call me the fat man. 'Cause I weigh two hundred pounds." The song went to number two on the R&B chart. It set Fats squarely on the path to becoming, as his official Rock and Roll Hall of Fame biography notes, "a key figure in the transition from rhythm and blues to rock and roll—a transition so subtle, especially in his case, that the line between these two nominally different

BELOW Allen Toussaint in his office, ca 1993. Photo by Michael P. Smith©. Courtesy of The Historic New Orleans Collection.

ABOVE Cosimo Matassa in the recording studio. Courtesy of the Matassa Family.

forms of music blurred to insignificance." Historian John Broven agreed. "He was a rhythm and blues singer," Broven wrote in 1974, "whose music just happened to be the roots of rock n' roll." Fats charted more records than Little Richard, Buddy Holly, and Chuck Berry put together, and with eventual sales topping sixty-five million, he outsold every one of his contemporaries but Elvis Presley.

Besides steering Fats to prominence, Dave Bartholomew was busy in the studio producing artists for several labels, including Smiley Lewis' original recording of "I Hear You Knockin'" for Imperial, Shirley and Lee's "Let the Good Times Roll" for Aladdin, and Lloyd Price's influential hit "Lawdy Miss Clawdy" for the L.A.–based Specialty Records. It was for Specialty, with the J&M band, that Little Richard recorded those career-making sessions in 1955; "Little Richard had things before, but he was not successful until [sax players] Lee Allen and Red Tyler put that sound on him and put that good hard rock feel on him," Dr. John told historian John Broven in an interview for Broven's seminal 1974 book *Rhythm & Blues in New Orleans*. "It was the New Orleans sound that got Little Richard across."

That New Orleans sound was, essentially, Dave's team in Cosimo's space. Members of the Bartholomew band, including saxophonists Tyler, Joe Harris, Clarence Hall, and Herbert Hardesty, guitarist Ernest McLean, bassist Frank Fields, and, crucially, drummer Earl Palmer—formed the foundation of the J&M studio crew, along with additions like Allen. There was the "big beat"—a hard-driving backbeat with ties to parade rhythms, heard as early as 1949 on "The Fat Man," interlocking with Fats' thundering left hand on the keys. And there was Cosimo's unfussy, hands-off style as an engineer. In interviews throughout his life he used the word "transparent" most often to describe it: "I always tried to capture the dynamics of a live performance," he told Jeff Hannusch. "These guys were doing these songs on their gigs and that was the sound that I was trying to get. We didn't have any gimmicks—no overdubbing, no reverb—nothing . . . Those guys played with a lot of excitement and I felt if I couldn't put it in the groove, people weren't going to move." The magic formula made J&M a busy place, attracting labels like Chess, Atlantic, Savoy, Modern, and others to Rampart and Dumaine. By the mid-fifties, the operation had outgrown the little shop. Matassa moved up and out, into a bigger building he bought in the 500 block of Governor Nicholls Street in the French Quarter, and continued midwifing hits.

In 1949, the year of "The Fat Man," *Billboard* changed what had been its "race records" chart, a catchall title for jazz, blues, gospel, and some comedy releases by black performers, to the "rhythm and blues" chart. It was a harbinger of what was to come, fast and furious, as music hastened the integration of ears and hearts, if not yet (legally) bodies. Sounds were busting through borders of segregation, and in fact, it was the relatively nonthreatening Fats—perhaps because he was so nonthreatening—who was at the forefront. In *Rhythm & Blues in New Orleans*, John Broven, who calls him "warm, chubby, cuddly Fats," as if he were a stuffed toy or a baby animal, says, "he was rock and roll's safety valve." Coleman, in *Blue Monday*, puts a more dramatic spin on the link between Fats'—and New Orleans'—nascent sound and civil rights. He points out that the week of December 1, 1955—the winter Thursday that Rosa Parks declined to move to the back of the bus—the R&B chart's top 15 included seven songs from J&M. "With supernaturally synchronous timing," Coleman writes, "a cultural revolution brewing for centuries was channeled into music. The fusillades were rhythms. The war cries were led by Little Richard's talking drum howl—AWOPBOPALOOBOPALOPBAMBOOM!"

Market forces made rock and roll a steamroller that busted over and through the barriers of Jim Crow. As Coleman reports, white listeners were calling in to black DJ Vernon Winslow's Poppa Stoppa radio show, on WJMR-AM in New Orleans, to request "Good Rockin' Tonight" as early as 1947. (There would be several Poppa Stoppas, white and black, on New Orleans radio; Winslow, at the beginning, was taxed with feeding white DJs news from the black community, as well as the hip slang in which to deliver it. He would go on to DJ rhythm and blues and rock and roll as Dr. Daddy-O, on WYLD-FM and WWEZ-FM, as well as write an essential entertainment column in the city's black newspaper, *Louisiana Weekly*.) According to Coleman, when Cosimo Matassa learned that Winslow had to record artist interviews in a freight elevator at the New Orleans hotel because of segregation's restrictions, he offered Winslow space at J&M, where he had been quietly recording an integrated clientele as a businesslike matter of course—although the practice put him on shaky ground with the segregated local musicians' unions, not to mention socially.

Allen Toussaint grew up in the Gert Town neighborhood, in a shotgun house that would, when he reached young adulthood, become a hub for all-day hangouts, rehearsals, and writing sessions with artists like Chris Kenner, Irma Thomas, and Ernie K-Doe.

Throughout the '50s and early '60s, Cosimo's studios cranked out hits both for visiting labels from around the United States and for a new crop of locally focused enterprises, including Johnny Vincent's Ace Records, based in Jackson, Mississippi, which released music by New Orleanians including Earl King, Huey "Piano" Smith and the Clowns, Frankie Ford, Bobby Marchan, James Booker, and a young Mac Rebennack before he took on the name Dr. John. Another hometown operation to make use of the spot and its talent was Minit Records, established in 1959 by record distributor Joe Banashak in partnership with Larry McKinley, a music promoter and radio DJ whose mellifluous recorded voice can still be heard today at the gates of the New Orleans Jazz and Heritage Festival, welcoming guests for a day of music that McKinley himself—who died in 2013 at age eighty-five—likely had a lot to do with putting out into the world. Minit Records and Banashak's second label Instant, which he started up in 1961 after selling Minit off to Imperial's Lew Chudd, released pretty much every classic New Orleans rhythm-and-blues song of the '60s: Ernie K-Doe's "Mother-in-Law," Irma Thomas' "It's Raining," Chris Kenner's "Land of 1000 Dances," Jessie Hill's "Ooh Poo Pah Doo," Benny Spellman's "Fortune Teller," and more, including the earliest work of various Nevilles.

John Broven writes with well-deserved fanfare that "[t]he man responsible for dishing out the delectable sounds [at Instant and Minit] was Allen Toussaint, whose production work in New Orleans throughout the 1960s was to be equal in stature to that of Dave Bartholomew in the 1950s. Besides producing, he writes, plays piano and performs in his own right—he has not been called a genius for nothing."

Born in 1938, Toussaint grew up in the Gert Town neighborhood, in a shotgun house that would, when he reached young adulthood, become a hub for all-day hangouts, rehearsals, and writing sessions with artists like Kenner, Thomas, and K-Doe, with whom he played in the R&B group the Flamingoes, his first band. Gigging with the Flamingoes got Toussaint in with what he termed the "Dew Drop set," the older, professional musicians who played and hung out at the Uptown nightclub, hotel, restaurant, and barbershop that was the place to be for both local and touring black artists in New Orleans from the '40s through the '60s. During the Jim Crow years, marquee names like Ray Charles, Duke Ellington, and James Brown stayed there when they swung through town and enjoyed the hospitality of owner Frank Painia and the stage antics of cross-dressing emcee and singer Patsy Vidalia. Getting in with the Dew Drop set led to work, and once he was working—initially on sessions at Cosimo's or filling in on the road and in the studio for more established pianists like Huey "Piano" Smith and Harold Battiste—he impressed immediately. In 1958, he recorded his first solo album—the rollicking instrumental collection The Wild Sound of New Orleans, credited to "Tousan"—for RCA.

"From day one," Cosimo Matassa told *Gambit Weekly* in New Orleans in a 2007 interview, "in spite of his soft-spoken approach, his playing was dynamic. When he sat down and played, the level of everything jumped." His sensitive, shape-shifting skill at working with various artists also secured him the spot as Minit's premier writer, producer, and arranger, beginning in 1960. "He was able, especially so among the writers I've known, to write the songs that best fit the artists," Matassa told *Gambit*. "He'd come in with prearranged arrangements, and then adapt them based on what was going on with the musicians. He's a perfectionist. And he kept a fresh sound that was appropriate to every performer. It was astounding how he could create a song and arrange it and wrap it around a particular performer."

Toussaint was drafted into the Army in 1963, and when he returned home two years later, he struck out on his own in partnership with entrepreneur Marshall Sehorn. As the British Invasion invaded shortly after—with, ironically, bands like the Beatles and the Rolling Stones putting their stamp on the American blues, R&B, and rock-and-roll sound launched in large part at Cosimo's—the original artists lost their market primacy. But Toussaint and Sehorn, releasing songs on multiple labels that took their names from an assortment of "Sehorn/Toussaint" chimeras, such as Sansu and Tou-Sea, were at the forefront of the next rising wave: funk and soul. With a gritty house band that would later become the Meters, the team scored respectable hits with local talent like Lee Dorsey and Betty Harris, often making use of Cosimo's new studio spot Jazz City, on Camp Street, until 1973, when Toussaint and Sehorn opened their own place in Gentilly: Sea-Saint Studios, another name mash-up.

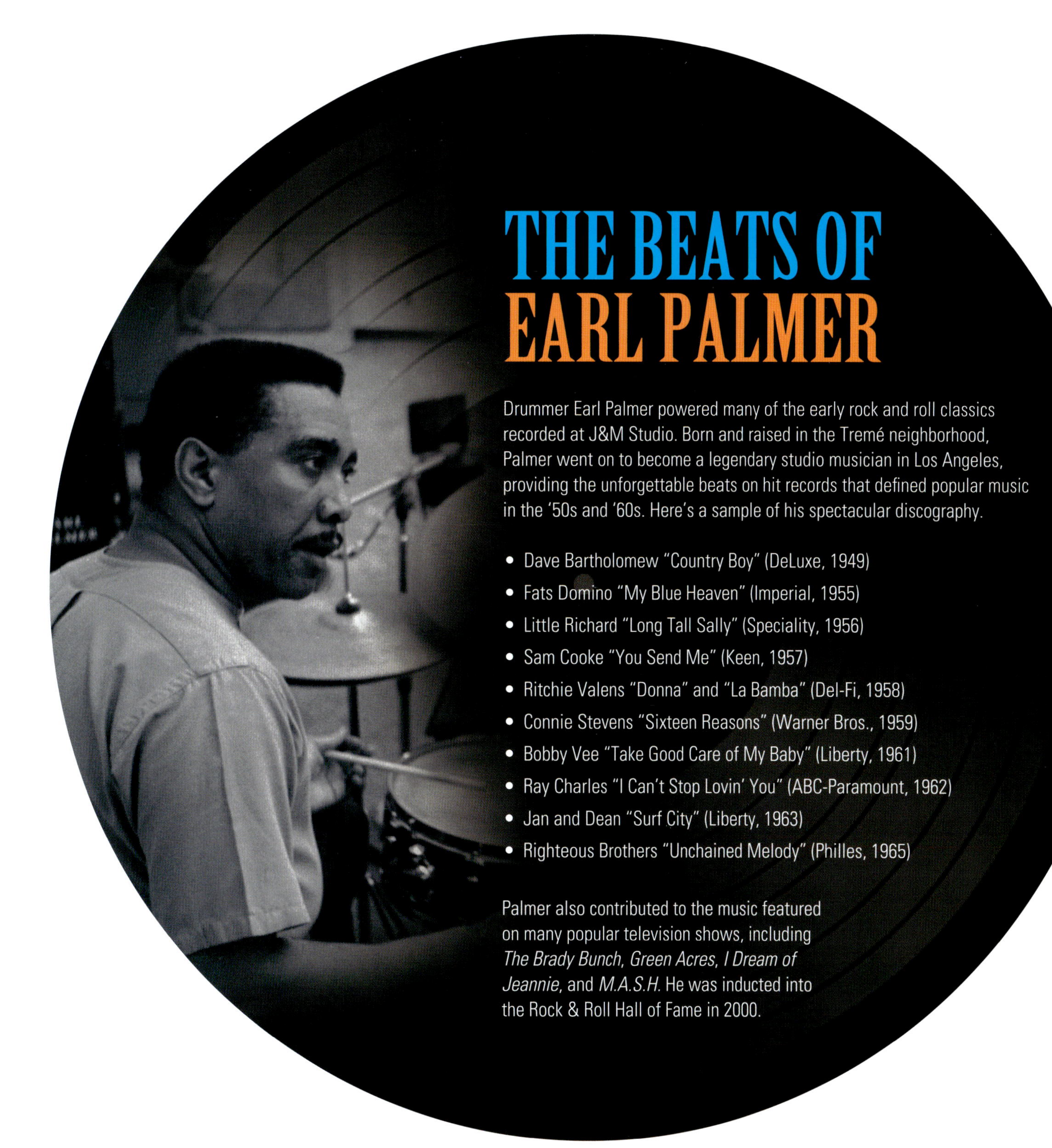

THE BEATS OF EARL PALMER

Drummer Earl Palmer powered many of the early rock and roll classics recorded at J&M Studio. Born and raised in the Tremé neighborhood, Palmer went on to become a legendary studio musician in Los Angeles, providing the unforgettable beats on hit records that defined popular music in the '50s and '60s. Here's a sample of his spectacular discography.

- Dave Bartholomew "Country Boy" (DeLuxe, 1949)
- Fats Domino "My Blue Heaven" (Imperial, 1955)
- Little Richard "Long Tall Sally" (Speciality, 1956)
- Sam Cooke "You Send Me" (Keen, 1957)
- Ritchie Valens "Donna" and "La Bamba" (Del-Fi, 1958)
- Connie Stevens "Sixteen Reasons" (Warner Bros., 1959)
- Bobby Vee "Take Good Care of My Baby" (Liberty, 1961)
- Ray Charles "I Can't Stop Lovin' You" (ABC-Paramount, 1962)
- Jan and Dean "Surf City" (Liberty, 1963)
- Righteous Brothers "Unchained Melody" (Philles, 1965)

Palmer also contributed to the music featured on many popular television shows, including *The Brady Bunch*, *Green Acres*, *I Dream of Jeannie*, and *M.A.S.H.* He was inducted into the Rock & Roll Hall of Fame in 2000.

The hyper-modern joint, with its soul-drenched New Orleans vibe, quickly became a national draw. At Sea-Saint, Toussaint produced the Pointer Sisters, Labelle's 1974 top-ten hit *Nightbirds*—with its New Orleans–flavored single "Lady Marmalade"—Paul Simon, Joe Cocker, and Wings' number-one album *Venus and Mars*, released in 1975 and tying up a rather poetic loose end; if the Brits had accidentally derailed the ascendance of New Orleans rock and roll in the early '60s, even while drinking from its well, here they were again to pay homage to its masters.

Meanwhile, several of the stars of the 1950s had ventured away to seek their fortune. Earl Palmer, the drummer whose beat anchored rock and roll, moved to Los Angeles, where he played on literally thousands of sessions. So did Harold Battiste, the extraordinary arranger and pianist who, in 1961, had co-founded New Orleans' first black-owned record label and publishing company, AFO (All For One); for fifteen years, he worked as the musical director for Sonny and Cher. And so did Dr. John, who invented a singular and timely voodoo-tinged psychedelia on a run of solo albums in the late '60s and early '70s in his Night Tripper persona. In 1972, on his fifth album, Dr. John's *Gumbo*, he reintroduced the Cosimo sound he'd cut his teeth on with a collection of loving covers of tunes popularized by Huey "Piano" Smith, Earl King, Professor Longhair, and other idols. In 2010, the Rock and Roll Hall of Fame—which had inducted Fats Domino in its inaugural class of honorees in 1986—declared the studio on Rampart and Dumaine an official landmark. By then, it was a working laundromat, which it remains at this time.

The eldest son in a musical dynasty, **Branford Marsalis** has charted his own course, collaborating with artists ranging from the Grateful Dead to hip hop emcee Guru. When Jay Leno replaced Carson in 1992, he chose Marsalis for his bandleader. But the saxophonist soon proved reluctant to scale back his adventurous musical choices, a source of friction with the show's producers. Despite a reported $1 million salary, he departed in 1995 to continue pursuing his unique sound. Photo by Darlene Susco, 2011. WIkimedia Commons.

Late Night Stars

Improvisational chops, a quick wit, and a broad musical vocabulary are all part of a New Orleans musician's toolbox. It seems, too, that those same qualities make for a great sidekick. For the better part of sixty years, a New Orleanian has served as the bandleader on a late night talk show, laughing along with the host, firing up the live audience with a top shelf band, and giving national audiences a dose of the Crescent City before they fall asleep.

LEFT Clarinetist **Pete Fountain** (1930-2016) was already a hometown favorite when Lawrence Welk lured him away to Los Angeles for a two-year stint on his weekly ABC-TV show. "Pete, are you all ready?" Welk would ask the stylish New Orleanian. "Swing right out." After Welk and Fountain parted ways over Pete's free-spirited attitude, Fountain went on to appear fifty-nine times on *The Tonight Show* with Johnny Carson. Pete Fountain see here, ca. 1968. Photo by John E. Kuhlman. Courtesy of Hogan Jazz Archive, special collections, Howard Tilton Memorial Library, Tulane University. Gift of Harry V. Souchon Jr. and Elizabeth Souchon Jahnke.

RIGHT A graduate of the New Orleans Center for Creative Arts (NOCCA), **Jonathan Batiste** comes from a storied musical family. The multi-instrumentalist studied at Julliard then cut his teeth as a touring musician before taking over as the associate artistic director at the National Jazz Museum in Harlem. When Stephen Colbert asked Batiste and his band, Stay Human, to join him on *The Late Show* in 2015, Batiste had a request: for Colbert to tour New Orleans with him. In a memorable segment, Colbert complied, walking down Frenchmen Street for another chapter in the city's late night history. Batiste is seen here performing at the 2017 Monterey Jazz Festival. Photo by David Becker. Wikimedia Commons.

Defining Jazz Fest

The history, heritage, and heirs of the festival at the Fairgrounds

by Alex Rawls

To call the relationship between New Orleans and the New Orleans Jazz and Heritage Festival complicated would be an understatement. On the surface, it seems simple. Jazz Fest is one of city's signature events, and for more than forty years it has attracted an international audience to see, hear, and taste the best of south Louisiana culture, with a heavy emphasis on its "heritage of jazz"—an umbrella phrase festival producer Quint Davis uses to characterize the jazz, R&B, funk, Cajun, zydeco, gospel, rock, and hip-hop music featured on Jazz Fest stages. But nothing becomes as big as Jazz Fest has without unforeseen, unintended consequences.

The festival started in Congo Square—then Beauregard Square—in 1970. Branford Marsalis was a decade from his professional debut with Art Blakey; Wynton Marsalis was eight years old; and Harry Connick Jr. was only two. Jean Knight's hit "Mr. Big Stuff" was a year away, Dr. John's "Right Place, Wrong Time" was three years away, and those hits represented the tail end of New Orleans R&B as a pop chart force.

Tastes had changed, and the R&B now recognized as the first blasts of rock 'n' roll had become nostalgia fodder: Fats Domino's "Ain't That a Shame" and Lee Dorsey's "Ya Ya" ended up on the soundtrack to 1973's *American Graffiti*, and the characters on the 1974 sitcom *Happy Days* sang the opening lines of Domino's "Blueberry Hill" as a coded make-out boast.

"Jazz Fest" was a misnomer from the start. The festival's complete title in 1970 was "New Orleans Jazz Festival and Louisiana Heritage Fair," so people understandably shortened it, even if the abbreviated name misrepresented the festival. That year's talent lineup followed the model that founder George Wein employed at the Newport Folk and Jazz Festivals, where he made his reputation. Jazz Fest included Cajun and zydeco artists Bois Sec Ardoin and Clifton Chenier, gospel singers The Zion Harmonizers and Sister Gertrude Morgan, blues guitarist Snooks Eaglin, as well as Pete Fountain, Ellis Marsalis, and the Olympia Brass Band and Tuxedo Jazz Band. Wein focused on music with cultural roots more than pop acumen, and by doing so, Jazz Fest began to reframe the New Orleans musical conversation. Commercial success came to mean less than an artist's ability to reflect New Orleans and the community he or she represented.

Jazz Fest situated itself in the middle of New Orleans' culture conversation even before it opened. George Wein wrote in his autobiography, *Myself Among Others: A Life in Music*, that city leaders asked him to produce a jazz festival in New Orleans in 1962 and 1964. He refused to start anything when city leaders wouldn't allow racially mixed bands and audiences in the venues together, nor would they desegregate the hotels and restaurants so that bands with black and white members could stay, eat, and drink together. In 1968, Wein reached a tentative deal to produce a jazz festival, but that fell through when Mayor Victor Schiro feared he couldn't get civic leaders to accept Wein, who had a black wife. New Orleans went ahead and staged a jazz festival without him that year, but its emphasis on national talent angered the local music community, as did the pay disparity between the visiting and local artists.

In 1969, the city met Wein's terms, and one of his first acts as the producer of a New Orleans jazz festival was to bring in Quint Davis and Allison Miner, who were young, local, and passionate about New Orleans' music. "I didn't know anything about [the culture of New Orleans]," Wein told music journalist John Swenson. "I just found Quint Davis and said, 'Let's get everybody involved.' I knew about New Orleans jazz, and a little bit about the funk, but I didn't know about the Indians and all that, so I was in a learning process the whole way." Davis would eventually take over as the festival's producer.

That first Jazz Fest introduced the Mardi Gras Indian tradition to a larger audience. Mardi Gras Indian tribes' activities had taken place on Fat Tuesday and St. Joseph's Day in the African-American neighborhoods that spawned them, so many New Orleanians had heard of Indians but had never seen them. "In the 1960s, the Mardi Gras Indians were just coming from the point of the battlefield and axes," Quint Davis told journalist David Kunian. "Frankly, they'd come down the streets and people would get their kids and go inside. It was still a little dangerous."

For that first Jazz Fest, Davis organized a Mardi Gras Indian parade, led by Big Chiefs Bo Dollis of The Wild Magnolias and Monk Boudreaux of The Golden Eagles, that went through the French Quarter en route to Congo Square. Dollis, recalling that parade, told John Swenson, "I put my suit on and started singing, leading a second line, down Canal Street all through the French Quarter, singing all the way to Congo Square and the people followed along all the way."

That parade helped to change New Orleans' relationship to Mardi Gras Indians. They have become a constant at Jazz Fest, whether performing on stage or parading through the infield of the New Orleans Fairgrounds, the festival's home since 1974. Those presentations helped to create an international awareness of New Orleans' Afro-indigenous music culture, second lines, social aid and pleasure clubs, and Mardi Gras Indians. That awareness has been a mixed blessing. It inspired David Simon and Eric Overmyer to center a major storyline on a Mardi Gras Indian Big Chief in their HBO series *Treme*, but the broader attention has led to changes in parades and second line cultural practices.

"It is often said that at the first Jazz Fest there were more performers onstage than people in the audience," the New Orleans Jazz and Heritage

OPPOSITE View of Irma Thomas performing on an outdoor stage at the New Orleans Jazz and Heritage Festival on Sunday, April 27, 1975. Photograph by Michael P. Smith©. Courtesy of The Historic New Orleans Collection.

RIGHT Trombone Shorty about to go on stage with Bo Diddley, 1990. Photo by Michael P. Smith©. Courtesy of The Historic New Orleans Collection

Foundation's website notes. Approximately 350 people attended that year, and Wein recalls in *Myself Among Others* that his wife brought kids from a nearby orphanage to the festival to eat the leftover food rather than let it go to waste. In its second year, however, with no publicity beyond word of mouth, the festival began to attract a national audience, and in 1973 it turned a profit for the first time. Attendance topped 10,000 people and forced the festival to find more space. Jazz Fest moved to the New Orleans Fairgrounds in 1974, where it drew more than 50,000 fans over four days. The festival was on a growth trajectory that would continue unchecked through the 1980s and into the '90s, aided by the festival's expansion to two weekends in 1976. Attendance reached a peak in 2001 when Jazz Fest drew 618,000 fans, 160,000 of those on the second Saturday, when the Dave Matthews Band and the rapper Mystikal brought huge crowds to the Acura and Congo Square stages.

By that point, Jazz Fest had taken the shape that it has today. For the last weekend of April and the first weekend of May, the Fairgrounds presents music in five tents and on seven stages. Restaurants from around south Louisiana sell food with a local emphasis, and some of those dishes have become as much a part of the festival as the music. For many, a day at Jazz Fest just isn't complete without Crawfish Monica, quail and pheasant gumbo, or a cochon de lait po-boy. There are no funnel cakes on the grounds, but you can get a dozen oysters on the half-shell. The food helps make it clear that music in south Louisiana is a cultural product as much as it is an entertainment commodity.

Jazz Fest helped to create an international awareness of New Orleans' Afro-indigenous music culture, second lines, social aid and pleasure clubs, and Mardi Gras Indians.

Until 1998, all of the music fit snugly on the Fairgrounds' infield. The Jazz Tent, Gospel Tent, and Blues Tent all moved to the Fairgrounds' parking lot that year—one of the signs of things going wrong by those who feel Jazz Fest has lost its way—but all three tents were able to accommodate more people in their new homes. The pavement has been hard on the sound in the Blues Tent, but the additional space allowed

ABOVE Big Chief Juan Pardo and Queen Anndrea Pardo at Jazz Fest 2017. Photo by Zack Smith.

ABOVE Clifton Chenier at the New Orleans Jazz Festival with John Hart on saxophone, April 1974.
Photo by Michael P. Smith ©. Courtesy of The Historic New Orleans Collection.

the festival to expand its food offerings and move the craft marketplace into the space around the tents.

Jazz Fest's growth made it more than just a success. The festival became an important part of New Orleans' economy, one that claims to have a greater than $300 million economic impact on the city. Jazz Fest helps fill hotel rooms, and those visitors are often fans not only of New Orleans music but New Orleans as an experience. They come to town looking to spend money eating, drinking, and buying things that are only available in the Crescent City.

Many bars and businesses claim that the money they make during Jazz Fest gets them through the lean summer months, when students and visitors are in short supply, and the festival's success made it one of the cornerstones on which New Orleans built a tourism-based economy. Its success inspired a proliferation of festivals in New Orleans, including Satchmo SummerFest, Essence Festival, Voodoo Music and Arts Experience, and the BUKU Music and Art Project. In 2014 alone, New Orleans hosted 130 festivals, which had a combined economic impact of $960,000,000 on the region, accounting for 25 percent of the visitors to the area.

Of the festivals that have followed Jazz Fest, the French Quarter Festival is unquestionably the biggest, and according to French Quarter Festival fans, their affection for it has grown because of Jazz Fest's growth. Unlike Jazz Fest's increasing emphasis on out-of-town talent, the free French Quarter Fest showcases the rank and file of the New Orleans music community—the local performers who are working in the clubs every night. In 2014, the French Quarter Fest claimed to have a $251.4 million economic impact on New Orleans.

Jazz Fest even gave rise to other festivals during Jazz Fest. In 1997, the Louisiana Music—New Orleans Pride (LMNOP) Festival premiered, presenting cutting-edge music and music industry seminars at a time when music industry professionals from around the world were in New Orleans. LMNOP took place on the weekdays between festival weekends, but it never caught on like South by Southwest—the festival it was modeled on—and only lasted four years. Chaz Fest began in 2006 in the Bywater as a place for artists who had been left out of the festival line-up that year, and it has the highest profile of the various grassroots efforts to provide additional attention and paychecks for local musicians while music fans are in town for Jazz Fest.

Over the course of the last decade, Jazz Fest scheduling has mirrored the national music marketplace more than it used to, and the egalitarian vibe that the schedule once reflected has become more hierarchical. In the festival's first two decades, emerging and established acts played sets of similar lengths, and no visiting artist played longer than any New Orleans act. Now national headliners routinely close the big stages, and national acts get longer sets than most New Orleans artists. The economic logic makes sense. No one pays Bruce Springsteen his performance fee and asks him to play for only an hour, opening for someone local. But until 2005, Jazz Fest didn't even face choices like that. In that year, AEG Live joined the production team with Festival Productions, and its deep pockets allowed Jazz Fest to reach for such artists as Neil Young, Tom Petty, Elton John, and Pearl Jam, as well as the new festgoers they bring in.

That change comes at what feels like the end of an era. Many of the New Orleans R&B artists who defined the festival passed away—Professor Longhair in 1980, Ernie K-Doe in 2001, Earl King in 2003, Snooks Eaglin and Eddie Bo in 2009, and Allen Toussaint in 2015. They were larger-than-life personas as well as talents, and without them, Jazz Fest feels a little more conventional. The Radiators and The Neville Brothers closed the festival's biggest stages for more than a decade each; their shows served as symbolic encapsulations of New Orleans' musical values. But both bands ended their runs in 2011 and 2012 respectively. And while Trombone Shorty has ably taken over the Neville Brothers' closing slot, his show doesn't yet have the same symbolic resonance.

Still, you can also point to the ways that Jazz Fest has kept the faith. Vaucresson Sausage Company sold sausages at the first Jazz Fest at Congo Square, and the family still sells them at Jazz Fest today. The festival still offers visitors an opportunity to immerse themselves in Louisiana culture as it exists today with good food, good art, and good music. Roots music continues to dominate the New Orleans and Louisiana bookings, and such artists as the Lost Bayou Ramblers, Luke Winslow-King, Tom McDermott, and Meschiya Lake and the Little Big Horns find ways to make contemporary music in traditional forms. Old skirmishes in the culture wars have died down, and the hip-hop that was so influential to a generation of brass band players is now accepted as part of the New Orleans musical story.

That story exists in new contexts though. New Orleans' music scene has inspired musicians from around the world to move to town and play their version of it, so defining "New Orleans music" is increasingly problematic. If place of birth doesn't define it, it's not clear what does, but it's reassuring that "New Orleans music" as a concept still has magic.

RIGHT James Booker and Harry Connick, Jr. at the New Orleans Jazz & Heritage Festival, April 1978. Photo by Michael P. Smith©. Courtesy of The Historic New Orleans Collection, Gift of Master Digital Corporation.

RIGHT Lil Wayne, ca. 1996. Photo by Polo Silk ©, Polo Nola Photography.

"Best Rapper Alive"

Lil Wayne revolutionized hip-hop and reenergized New Orleans' influence on popular music

by David Dennis

I was spending my summer as a cold sandwich delivery boy in Minneapolis when Lil Wayne became the best rapper in the world. The year was 2006 and Wayne had just released *Dedication 2,* a twenty-five-track maelstrom of lyrical creativity that saw the artist, raised in Hollygrove, demolish instrumentals to popular radio songs and old-school hip-hop tracks. And he gave it all away for free. The project revolutionized rap music as artists saw how *D2* propelled Wayne to the stratosphere of popularity; they started releasing their own free projects in hordes. (Yes, 50 Cent's mixtape projects predated Wayne's, but they didn't inspire nearly as many copycats.) But most importantly, the mixtape placed Wayne amongst rap's elite as a wordsmith and hit-maker. Wayne's earlier claims of "Best Rapper Alive" were coming to fruition, and he was carrying New Orleans popular music on his back in a time when the city was still reeling from Katrina and needed it most.

Lil Wayne, born Dwayne Michael Carter Jr., is rap's only child-star success story. As a squeaky-voiced preteen rapper, Carter gained the attention of Bryan "Birdman" Williams, the owner of Cash Money Records, through his rap duo with fellow teen star B.G. By the time Wayne turned fifteen, he was a full-fledged member of the label, now poised to become a rap juggernaut. Cash Money had begun to take off behind the power of Juvenile's breakout single, "Ha," from his 1998 album *400 Degreez*, and the world was clamoring for more. Cash Money delivered. New Orleans has a long history of shaping the course of American music, but Cash Money Records at the turn of the millennium helped establish the city as a place that would influence music in the twenty-first century as well. Furthering the success of their rival, Master P's No Limit Records, Cash Money put New Orleans firmly at the forefront of rap and popular music as a whole.

400 Degreez featured one of rap's most transcendent and timeless records, "Back That Azz Up." The song, a repurposed New Orleans classic, became an anthem for clubs and radio stations across the country, topping the *Billboard* Hot Rap Singles chart and peaking at 15 on the Hot 100. At the end of the song there's Lil Wayne, offering a subdued guest appearance, a simple refrain:

After you back it up, then stop
Then wha-wha-what
Drop it like it's hot

The phrase "drop it like it's hot" would become a crossover sensation, used in ad campaigns and slogans across the country for any company trying to look hip in their appeal to younger demographics. "Drop it like it's hot" demonstrated Wayne's ability to insert phrases or invent words that would become cultural milestones, as did the phrase "bling bling." While the phrase had been used a handful of times previously in rap, Wayne's usage on the hook to B.G.'s "Bling Bling" created a new entry in mainstream American vernacular. "Bling," of course a reference to shiny jewelry, is now listed in the *Merriam-Webster* dictionary. These crossover phrases demonstrated Carter's ability to create moments that resonated with larger audiences and made him a household name.

However, for most of the Cash Money Records mainstream boom, Wayne stayed in the background while Juvenile carried the flag as the label's breadwinner. Still, Wayne's talent was always evident to anyone paying attention. He spent his time at Cash Money writing and performing hooks, while also writing most of the lyrics for Mannie Fresh and Birdman's Big Tymers. But Wayne's ability to shine as a solo artist seemed questionable, especially given that he wasn't yet even old enough to vote.

In 1999 Lil Wayne dropped his debut album, *Tha Block Is Hot*—again coining a phrase that would often be used even in non-rap circles—which showed signs of an MC more sophisticated than his simple high-pitched guest appearances had revealed, a rapper who was skilled beyond his years. While Hot featured a young Lil Wayne dispensing made-up tales of street life, his revelatory "F--k Tha World" (because every rapper has a f--k-the-world song somewhere in his or her repertoire) was about being a teenage father trying to take care of his family at a young age. Wayne still had a way to go to reach Juvenile's charisma or B.G.'s control, but he showed that he could become a respected lyricist with time and find longevity in a genre where staying power is at a premium.

As he got older, Wayne demonstrated a penchant for stealing the show on songs. An original member of the Hot Boys (a Cash Money supergroup also featuring Juvenile, B.G., and Turk), he made a star-turning appearance on the Hot Boys 1999 single "I Need a Hot Girl." Early-2000s DJs were known to start Wayne's verse and mute the music while crowds rapped his entire verse a capella. His ability to shine amidst his powerhouse brethren showed a Wayne who could hold his own. Nobody could have predicted how fast he'd have to learn to carry the Cash Money flag alone.

Rap groups rarely last, and the Hot Boys were no different. By 2002, Juvenile and B.G. left Cash Money over money disputes, and Lil Wayne became the unlikely captain of the ship. Just as he'd had to support his family as an early teen, Wayne had to carry Cash Money through the slog of trying to rebuild. After his album *500 Degreez* failed to connect with audiences and critics, Wayne, now in his twenties, matured into a rapper who replaced elementary rhyme schemes with more complex metaphors and storytelling.

Hearing Wayne ascend to a new level of greatness helped me believe the city could be restored.

It was at this point that Wayne started to embrace the power of the mixtape—collections of tracks in which rappers typically rap over instrumentals from popular songs, often given away for free. These mixtapes—*Sqad Up, Da Drought 1, Dedication 1*—allowed Wayne to try out new rhyme schemes, experiment with his flow, and hone his craft. By the time he released his next album, *Tha Carter*, he'd start making claims to being the best rapper alive, and he was close to seeing those brags come true.

Then Katrina happened.

Suddenly Lil Wayne also had to carry a city on his back, preserving New Orleans's place as a rap stronghold while so many of its artists and fans were dispersed across the country. *Tha Carter II*, released three months after the storm hit, is arguably Lil Wayne's most complete album to date. Its December release didn't giving him sufficient time to address Katrina and the government debacle that followed. Yet between bars about models and cars, he inserted enough mentions of the storm and its impact to indicate that he was going to eventually weigh in on the storm in a significant way:

They tryna tell me keep my eyes open
My whole city underwater, some people still floating
And they wonder why black people still voting
Cause your president still choking
Take away the football team, the basketball team
And all we got is me to represent New Orleans

He delivered on *Dedication 2*. In "Georgia . . . Bush," he insinuated that the levees broke from a government bomb. *Dedication 2* was Lil Wayne at his most experimental, wacky, and captivating. It was also the fulfillment of his claims to be the best in the world. Hearing someone reach a goal he'd set for himself, even when it seemed fantastical at first, inspired and instilled hope in me. Hearing Wayne ascend to a new level of greatness helped me believe the city could be restored.

But herein lies the complexity of Wayne's relationship with the city: he raps like someone who loves New Orleans and the people who live in the city—but he gives interviews that are questionable at best and insulting at worst, sometimes offering odes to New Orleans and the aftermath of the storm, other times dismissing its impact. On a September 2009 VH-1 *Behind The Music* episode, Wayne claimed the storm was mostly just a nuisance: "I lost some cars. I lost a $300,000 house. I got $300,000 chains. I was in Miami. My parents weren't there. My kids weren't there. I didn't have to muster up anything." In what citizens of New Orleans considered a dramatic betrayal, Wayne actually rooted against the Saints during their magical Super Bowl year, going on the record to cheer for his childhood sports hero Brett Favre instead. In a bizarre 2009 interview with Katie Couric, in which Wayne was given a national platform to state what questions he had for George W. Bush—who was President during Katrina and who was largely blamed for bungling the recovery effort—Wayne said only, "I'm a gangster and gangsters don't ask questions." The comment was as absurd as it was disappointing. These public declarations were inconsistent with Wayne's actions in the aftermath of Katrina, as he returned to the city to donate money and time alongside his Cash Money label mates. But these actions were often ignored by his fans in lieu of focusing on his problematic statements.

Most recently, the distance between Lil Wayne's lyrics and Lil Wayne's interviews reared its ugly head on a November 2016 episode of *Dateline* in which the MC refused to validate the Black Lives Matter movement. Instead he opted to wave his red doo-rag to let the world know he's a gangster. A millionaire gangster: "I don't feel connected to a damn thing that ain't got nothin' to do with me. I'm connected to this flag right f-----g here, because I'm connected. I'm a gangbanger now." Then he made media rounds praising the white cop who saved his life when he accidentally shot himself at age twelve, claiming it as proof that racism doesn't exist. The backlash from his fans and even his peers, like Atlanta rapper T.I., who blasted Wayne on social media, was immediate and engulfing. Yet a quick perusal of Wayne's catalog shows a rapper with intimate knowledge of racial inequality and what it means to be black in America.

So fans and New Orleanians have two options: to take the whole Lil Wayne and dismiss him as an artist because of his broken spoken views, or believe that there are two Waynes and choose to like the one who makes music, who did more than his part to heal the city and its residents through sheer force of his artistic achievements.

Lil Wayne's run from 2006 to 2008 is among the most dominant in rap history. Since then, the artist who goes by "Tunechi" has had a rough life. His 2009 run to the charts, after the release of the massive commercial success *Tha Carter III*, was marred with reports of out-of-control drug use and addiction to the deadly concoction "lean." He spent eight months in 2010 in Rikers Island for gun possession. Upon his release, Wayne's struggle with sobriety affected his output; his 2011 album *Tha Carter IV* was artistically his worst album to date. Finally, a money-related dispute led to Wayne's falling out with Birdman, and *Tha Carter V* was shelved in album release purgatory.

Citing frustration with these disputes, Wayne announced his retirement from rap in September 2016, though such declarations rarely stick. But if he does decide to stay retired, it would be the end of a twenty-year career of a rapper who was the greatest in the world, even if only for a short time. We would be forced to bid farewell to the most famous, most popular New Orleans artist of the 21st century to date, someone who gave us a home when it felt like we would never have one again.

ABOVE Lil Wayne in concert, 2015. Photo by Megan Elice Meadows. Wikimedia Commons.

Drop It Like It's Hot

In February 2017, Lil Wayne broke the record for most *Billboard* Hot 100 appearances by a solo artist. With 133 credits to his name for performances on his own songs and on hits by other artists, the Hollygrove native passed his prodigy Drake on the list as well as Elvis Presley, James Brown, and Jay Z. The *Billboard* Hot 100 originated in 1958. Among the hits:

"Back That Thang Up"
Juvenile ft. Lil Wayne and Mannie Fresh, 1999
Top ranking: 19

"Tha Block is Hot"
Lil Wayne ft. Juvenile, 2000
Top ranking: 72

"Go DJ"
Lil Wayne, 2004
Top ranking: 14

"Fireman"
Lil Wayne, 2005
Top ranking: 32

"Stuntin' Like My Daddy"
Birdman and Lil Wayne, 2006
Top ranking: 21

"Swagga Like Us"
Jay-Z and T.I. ft. Kanye West and Lil Wayne, 2008
Top ranking: 5

"Lollipop"
Lil Wayne ft. Static Major, 2008
Top ranking: 1

"Down"
Jay Sean ft. Lil Wayne, 2009
Top ranking: 1

"She Will"
Lil Wayne ft. Drake, 2011
Top ranking: 3

"Believe Me"
Lil Wayne ft. Drake, 2014
Top ranking: 26

*Dates reflect entry of the single on the Top 100 Chart.

Part VII: RENEWAL

Cherice Harrison-Nelson at a memorial on the ten-year anniversary of Hurricane Katrina, August 29, 2015. Photo by Ray Laskowitz.

In Katrina's Wake

New Orleanians fought through floodwaters and uncertainty to return home

by Katy Reckdahl

As the water gushed under her front door, D'Antoinette Johnson's adrenalin spiked. Though only twenty-two years old, Johnson knew she had to act quickly. Strapping on a backpack filled with snacks and clothes, the young nursing assistant helped her preschool daughters climb from a tall dresser to the top of the refrigerator. Her brother pulled them into the attic just as the fridge floated away under their feet. They climbed onto the roof, but still the water rose. A child under each arm, Johnson jumped with her brother onto a taller house that floated past. After what seemed like forever, they were lifted from the roof into a helicopter.

The eye of Hurricane Katrina wouldn't pass east of New Orleans for a few hours. But starting in the wee hours of that Monday morning, between 4:30 and 7:30 a.m., the Industrial Canal's shoddily built east walls gave way in a few places with loud cracks, releasing twenty-foot swells of water into the city's Lower Ninth Ward neighborhood about a dozen blocks from Johnson's Charbonnet Street apartment. The water acted like a massive plow, tossing cars upside down like toys and pushing houses completely off their foundations. Throughout the day, the same scenario was repeated across the New Orleans area, with more than fifty breaks in poorly designed and constructed levees. Eighty percent of the city flooded.

As Katrina moved toward land, it pushed a funnel of storm-surge water nearly seventeen feet high from the Gulf of Mexico. Two manmade shipping channels, the Gulf Intracoastal Waterway and the Mississippi River Gulf Outlet gave the water an easy path to New Orleans, where it flowed into the area wetlands and also raised water levels in the Industrial Canal, which marks the upriver edge of the Lower Nine and connects Lake Pontchartrain to the Mississippi River.

In the Seventh Ward, Ernest Hammond, then sixty-seven, crawled into his Annette Street attic to flee the water, with an ax and a hammer in his hand, tools that had proved vital to those who'd survived the flooding that had followed Hurricane Betsy in 1965. The rough hole that Hammond chopped through his front eave allowed him to wriggle out and hail down a passing boat driven by a Good Samaritan.

About a dozen blocks away, Corey Rayford's cousin was weathering the hurricane at the family's well-known Seventh Ward house. Here, each year on Fat Tuesday, crowds gather to see Rayford emerge in a new beaded and feathered Mardi Gras Indian suit. Since each suit is a work of art, running roughly ten thousand dollars in supplies and thousands of hours of sewing time, Rayford's cousin had pledged to carry the suits upstairs if he saw signs of flooding. But at around 9 that morning, the nearby London Avenue Canal breached on both sides, sending water rushing down narrow streets. "The water rose too fast," said Rayford. "He had to save himself, and he couldn't save the suits."

In this rapidly flooding city, official rescue efforts had stalled, with the exception of some early rescuers from the US Coast Guard and Louisiana Wildlife and Fisheries. According to the official US Senate report, "A Nation Still Unprepared," FEMA drivers and vendors with vital supplies refused to enter the city without military escorts. Even city officials warned those entering the city of "lawlessness, no food and water, desperation," recalled National Guard Lt. Col. Jacques Thibodeaux.

In the resulting vacuum, a do-it-yourself atmosphere took hold. Though there was some lawlessness, to be sure, I've heard many accounts of New Orleanians, not exactly choir boys, who ended up saving themselves and their neighbors. Some families with young children or frail seniors left town in cars that weren't theirs, thanks to downtown valets who handed out keys to cars that had been parked for safekeeping by people who evacuated before the storm. In part of a well-known spate of post-storm looting, two young men rowed a boat to a Mid-City mall and loaded it up with Nike tennis shoes, then tossed most of the shoeboxes overboard to make room for an elderly couple they pulled out of the water.

Unseen by the public eye, these rescues happened in all of the worst-flooded parts of the city—Broadmoor, Gentilly, Mid-City, Pontchartrain Park, St. Roch, Gert Town, Hollygrove, eastern New Orleans, and Lakeview. In Lakeview, a white middle-class enclave, engulfed by water from the Seventeenth Street Canal, Wade Wright and his wife Barbara were rescued from a rooftop by a boat driven by a firefighter who lived on their block.

OPPOSITE *Search and Rescue on Humanity Street,* by David Rae Morris, 2005.

Jazz tuba player Jeffrey Hills, his wife Ann, and their three young children were saved around the same time. On Wednesday morning, two days after Katrina, when their kids started feeling faint from dehydration, they'd set off on foot from the Convention Center, which had become a fetid de facto shelter though it had no staff or supplies. As they trudged across the Crescent City Connection, the bridge that spans the Mississippi River, they were picked up by Gail Cotton, a bus driver. Fed up with waiting for long-promised FEMA buses, Cotton commandeered a city bus, filled it with people, and drove it all the way to a disaster shelter in Lafayette, Louisiana.

It wasn't until Friday, four days after Katrina, that evacuation efforts began to kick in on a large scale. That day, Thibodeaux was tasked with taking over the "lawless" Convention Center. Not far from City Hall, on Poydras Street, he assembled a force of one thousand National Guardsmen and 250 police officers, all armed, followed by twenty-five to thirty tractor-trailer trucks full of water and military Meals Ready to Eat. At noon, the procession traveled a dozen apprehensive blocks down Poydras Street. "We were expecting a war zone," says Mark Smith, spokesman for the Governor's Office of Homeland Security and Emergency Preparedness. But as the soldiers turned the corner, the crowd cheered. Within thirty minutes, the place was secured. Troops searched the nineteen thousand people for weapons, finding only thirteen.

Around that time, FEMA also ramped up departures of planes and buses, to virtually empty the flooded city. In all, the agency evacuated one hundred thousand stranded New Orleanians, many of whom had never before left New Orleans' city limits, to places like Dallas, Houston, and Little Rock. Some ended up as far as Alaska and Utah. Few were told their plane's final destination until they were in the air.

Professors now teach Katrina's aftermath as a civics lesson in official inaction in response to flood victims who were mostly black and poor. For D'Antoinette Johnson and others who lived through the disaster, that lesson was prolonged. During the four years that followed, Johnson and her daughters were nomads, living with an aunt in Baton Rouge, cousins in Houston and with three different relatives in New Orleans. In hindsight, their return to New Orleans may have been fraught with more difficulty than their rooftop escape, she says.

Taken as a whole, the post-Katrina tales of evacuation, relocation, and returns that I am writing about may seem like a tangle of inconsistencies. But the common thread is an unfailing passion to return home, despite bumbling and erratic housing agencies, shuttered schools, churches, and hospitals.

It's that passion to return that rebuilt New Orleans. Certainly, some evacuees happily made new homes elsewhere. But for me, the narratives most colored by sadness come from those who settled elsewhere without a choice – those who were forced to extinguish their passion to return, due to a lack of money, illness, a death in the family, or just plain hard luck.

Coming Back to Change

Sandra Gordon, then fifty-one, drove back to New Orleans a few months after the storm and pried open the doors to her flooded home. Heartbroken, she drove to St. Augustine Catholic Church in Tremé, the nation's oldest predominantly African-American Catholic parish and the place where her family has worshipped since 1865, when her enslaved great-grandmother, Mary Belle Weadd, received permission to be baptized. There, Gordon sat in a pew and cried.

Clouet, by Frank Relle, 2005.

ABOVE *Katrina's Sport Coat,* by David G. Spielman, 2005. Image taken in Lakeview after Hurricane Katrina.

Early in 2006, the Archdiocese of New Orleans announced plans to close St. Augustine and merge it with a nearby church. Efforts by Gordon and others convinced the Archdiocese to keep St. Aug open, but many New Orleans churches went through forced mergers or closed altogether.

As administrators of faltering institutions seized the moment in time to make changes, they were viewed alternately as visionaries and vultures. The state of Louisiana closed down Charity Hospital, the city's public hospital, and took over the public-school system. Federal housing officials announced plans to shutter most public housing and rebuild it as mixed-income communities. The city attempted, unsuccessfully, to jack up parade rates for the Sunday-afternoon social aid and pleasure club second lines.

While decrying the loss of the familiar and rallying around preserving what was left, New Orleanians also found themselves relying on an influx of the unfamiliar: volunteers from churches, colleges, and community groups, who bused and flew into town by the thousands to help with the city's recovery. When a crew arrived at the badly flooded Gentilly house of jazz clarinetist and historian Dr. Michael White, he told them to throw out everything. But when he returned, he found that the volunteers had carefully placed his collection of historic clarinets in his shed. "There were dozens and dozens," he said. "They looked to me like bodies. Some in tattered and water-damaged cases, which looked like coffins."

White started to think about all of the history behind those instruments and saw a parallel between them and the city's traditional culture, faced with a changing city that threatened to leave them behind. "The clarinets started to take on a persona of their own. They represented a tradition that was damaged, that was lost, that was dead, that was forgotten," he said. His friend, New Orleans photographer Eric Waters, added fresh flowers to the clarinet cases and made solemn portraits. "It became a metaphor of recovery, because it implied that, even in destruction, there is beauty," White said. "Like a jazz funeral, the end is also the beginning of something new."

Urge to Return

In the days after Katrina, a FEMA plane carried Alvin Thomas, then fifty-one, to Charlotte, North Carolina. His elderly parents had ended up in Atlanta, in a shiny new apartment complex where their lease didn't allow them to take in anyone, much less their schizophrenic son who refused to take his medication.

Separations like this were common. A RAND Corporation study found that, pre-Katrina, multi-generational families (defined as those with adult children living with parents) were "especially common"—50 percent more prevalent in the New Orleans than nationally. One year after Katrina, half of such families were no longer living together.

On his own, Thomas couldn't keep up with the paperwork needed for Katrina housing programs. In May 2007, he walked several miles holding a large yellow sign, an eviction notice that had been left on his door. When he walked into the FEMA office with the sign, his caseworker's heart fell. Thomas used the office phone to tell his younger sister Conessa that he was going back to Louisiana. The caseworker reluctantly bought him a bus ticket home.

Once back in New Orleans, Thomas usually rose before dawn and walked all day, along streets still strewn with debris from the disaster two years before. Exercising calmed his nerves, he said. When darkness fell, he returned to Lesseps Street in the city's Upper Ninth Ward. After looking both ways to make sure no one was watching, he strode up to a small porch enclosed by ornate, wrought-iron panels of scrolling oak branches and acorns.

Using keys from the lanyard around his neck, he opened the porch door's oversized padlock and then the door to the house where he'd

FEMA evacuated one hundred thousand stranded New Orleanians, many of whom had never before left New Orleans' city limits, to places like Dallas, Houston, and Little Rock.

lived with his parents. Inside, the family's narrow shotgun house was bare, having been gutted and emptied of its flooded contents by church volunteers. The house also lacked plumbing and electricity, but he created a little musty nest for himself in the front room, using a discarded mattress he'd dragged off the street, a crossword-puzzle book, and a row of off-brand canned goods from a nearby food pantry. "I just take the good with the bad, the bitter with the sweet," he said one day over a cup of coffee sweetened by about ten packets of sugar. "And I read the Word."

In the summer of 2007, his mother's best friend, Ms. Hazel Hilton, called me at *The Times-Picayune*, where I worked, and asked me to please check on Thomas because his mother was worried about her first-born son. I didn't live too far away, so I checked on him once in awhile, sometimes sitting with him at a nearby doughnut shop once winter hit and the empty house felt cold. He told me about Booker T. Washington Senior High School, where he ran track and played flute and alto sax. About his days stocking shelves at the Borden Milk warehouse. All before his "nerves got bad," as people in New Orleans say.

At night, when his beat-up gray boombox or the walls of the house spoke to him, he scrawled biblical verses in red ink on the door frame, usually about Passover and its angel of death, ready to smite the sons of those without blood on their door frames. If the weather was nice, he sat in the dark on the porch and listened to Christian radio shows or jazz music, keeping an eye out for nosy passersby through the holes between the oak-acorn scrolls. Sure, he peed in a bucket, used a neighbor's hose for water, and washed up in the bathroom at a nearby Church's Chicken. But he was home.

The following March, I wrote an elegy of sorts about Thomas, after he'd collapsed onto a cold porch floor and was found by an Episcopal Diocese volunteer who was helping his parents repair the house. Firefighters cut through his padlock and paramedics took him to a hospital, where he died of an undiagnosed brain-stem tumor.

My email and voicemail filled up with heartfelt messages from people who'd endured hardship to rebuild and others who felt stuck forever out-of-town in Katrina exile. It became clear that Thomas' insistence to return home had struck a nerve.

More Chicken Than People

For months, even years, some flooded neighborhoods were ghost towns – ghost towns dotted with chickens. Especially in the Seventh and Ninth Wards, flocks of skinny feral chickens ran the streets, clucking and crowing and scratching the ground. Many believe that some backyard chickens got loose during the flooding and multiplied.

Ed Buckner, who runs a Seventh Ward youth organization called The Porch, saw the chickens proliferate, roosting in trees and abandoned yards. "More chickens than people," he said, as he watched as the

ABOVE *Progress of Elimination*, by L. Kasimu Harris, 2009.

How it happened: HURRICANE KATRINA

by Richard Campanella

Hurricane Katrina made landfall early on Monday, August 29, 2005, and while the northward track of the weakening Category-2 system lay to the east, putting New Orleans on the "safer" side, Katrina's residual Category-5 storm surge (red arrows) would encounter major vulnerabilities in the region's defenses. For one, decades of coastal erosion, caused in part by the circa-1960s excavation of the Mississippi River-Gulf Outlet Canal (right), had the effect of minimizing terrestrial impedance, while the navigation canal's funnel-shaped confluence with the circa-1940s Gulf Intracoastal Waterway (right) maximized the ingress of the Lake Borgne surge into the eastern half of the metropolis. Similarly ungated outfall (drainage) canals in Lakeview and Gentilly enabled Lake Pontchartrain's surge to penetrate the northern flanks of the metropolis (top center). Finally, federal floodwalls and levees, which had been underfunded, scandalously under-engineered, and flippantly inspected, failed catastrophically in at least seven major locations. These and other breaches allowed storm-pushed seawater to inundate the bowl-shaped metropolis, whose sunken topography was itself produced by human action, in the form of swamp drainage. As a result, vast expanses of the East Bank flooded deeply (blue tones and hachures), in places by over ten feet, and for weeks on end—the worst catastrophe in New Orleans' history, and the first one since colonial times that called into question the very future of the city.

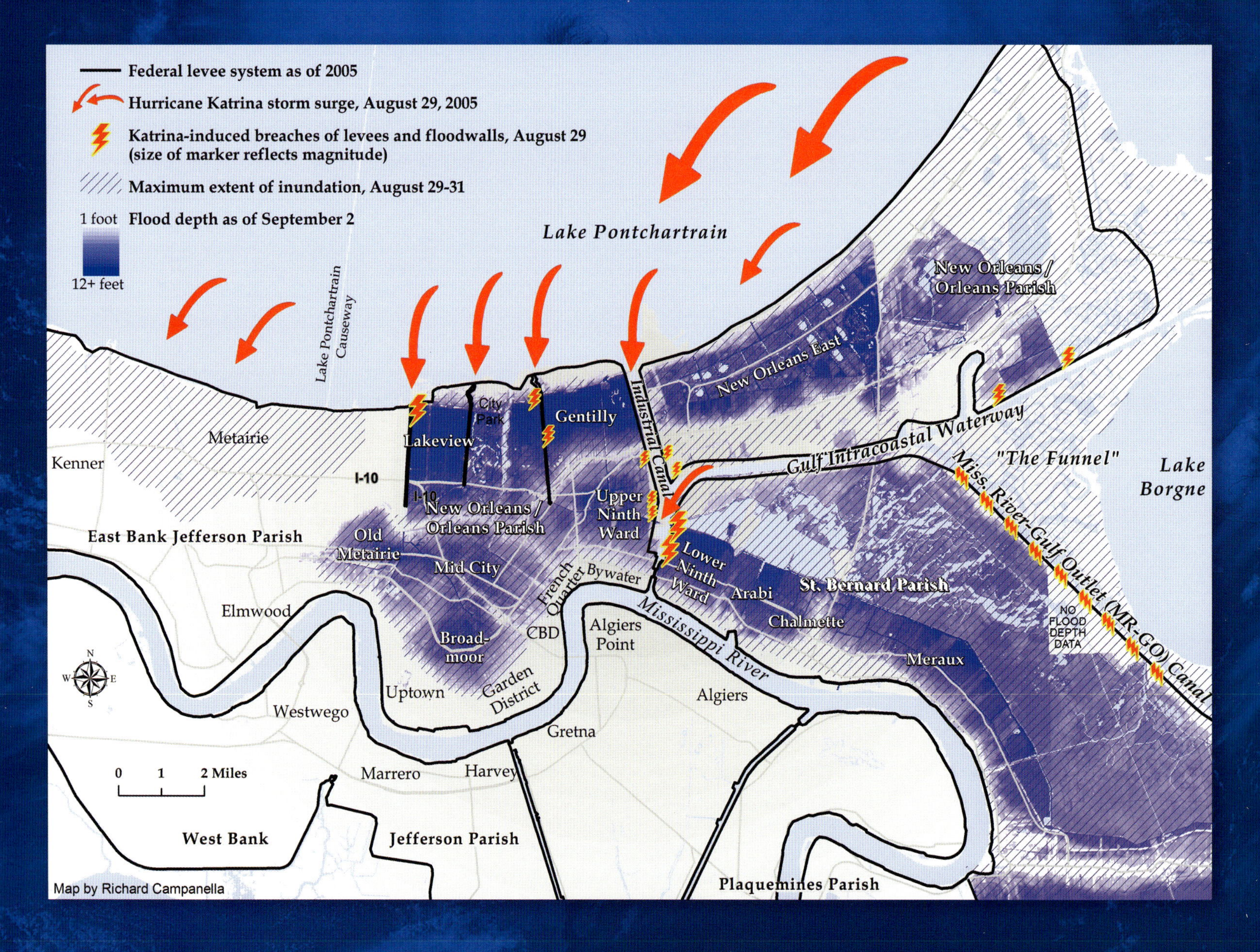

neighborhood children who sewed Mardi Gras Indian suits at The Porch become proficient at catching wild chickens—grabbing the birds over the wings, then holding them at arms' length to avoid roosters' sharp spurs.

Those who returned without a place to stay found that rents had increased exponentially. While half of New Orleans apartments had rented for five hundred dollars or less before Katrina, afterward, even modest apartments commanded monthly rents of one thousand dollars or more. In 2009, D'Antionette Johnson, the young mom who had hopped onto a roof in the Lower Nine, explained that her nursing-assistant wages hadn't risen but her rent had risen to eight hundred dollars, five times her pre-Katrina rent. Some people who returned and couldn't find affordable housing moved into vast homeless camps in the heart of the city, making national headlines. By 2007, when the first official estimation was done, the homeless population had swelled to more than 11,600, a nearly six-fold increase from the January 2005 count.

During bleak times, the stringy wild chickens provided some humor. In some ways, people saw them as fellow survivors, as neighbors who helped break the eerie quiet that took hold of the city after the flood. That idea resounded with Walter Leger, a top official at the Louisiana Recovery Authority, who became emotional at a post-Katrina groundbreaking after hearing the trill of a mockingbird perched on a nearby electric wire. Leger recalled returning to his native St. Bernard Parish, immediately downriver from the Lower Ninth Ward, which endured the same catastrophic flooding as the hardest-hit parts of New Orleans. Every home in his parish, without exception, was badly flooded. The streets were so silent that Leger found himself ecstatic at the sight of a squirrel he'd spent ten years trying to chase away. "I look forward to the day when all of our squirrels, birds, and most importantly, all of our people are back," he told the crowd.

The water acted like a massive plow, tossing cars upside down like toys and pushing houses completely off their foundations.

From the start, signs of recovery varied widely. The Lower Ninth Ward lost 80 percent of its population, while places like the Warehouse District saw a 40 percent increase. Other neighborhoods were virtually abandoned, often for reasons beyond the control of the people who once lived there.

Homecomings

Before the Industrial Canal poured into her Upper Ninth Ward neighborhood, Dorothy Scott ran Dorothy's Sno-Ball Stand. "I did very well," said Scott, an octogenarian whose stand faced the Florida public-housing projects, which had 734 apartments before Katrina.

Afterward, she had no neighbors, much less customers. The 2010 US Census, the first official post-Katrina tally, found that her census block was the city's most-emptied neighborhood, dropping from 1,604 people in 2000 to a mere 6 in 2010. The 2010 data showed that most of the city's emptiest neighborhoods had been the pre-Katrina home of public-housing projects run by the sluggish, chronically mismanaged Housing Authority of New Orleans.

In total, the city's population had dropped by 29 percent. Statistically, the least likely residents to return were African-Americans, whose numbers dropped by 118,000 people. The proportion of the city's residents that were African American dropped by 7 percent.

Black homeowners were set back by the state's Road Home program. Because of Road Home's flawed formula—which calculated the size of a grant for rebuilding a storm-damaged home based on its pre-storm value rather than the actual cost of replacing the structure—those in predominantly black neighborhoods received smaller grants that didn't come close to covering the costs of rebuilding.

In 2010, five years after the storm, I took a closer look at this, by tracking down all the residents of Ernest Hammond's block in the Seventh Ward, the 2500 block of Annette Street. With hopes of paying for a contractor, Hammond was stockpiling thousands of aluminum cans inside his brick rambler, which was rejected for a state rebuilding grant. Other neighbors weren't doing much better. A few years after the storm, they said, about half of the block's fifteen houses were occupied and the noise of power tools was in the air. But in 2010, those same houses were vacant and the block felt half empty, not half full. "Everybody's run out of money," said John Jackson, an elderly man who watched the block's progress from a well-worn porch chair.

At the time, in 2010, New Orleans had the nation's highest rate of vacant and abandoned buildings. And from that block of Annette Street, common obstacles became clear: Family members who died or took sick. Endless waits for Road Home or hazard-mitigation reimbursement money. No money to rebuild because banks took entire Road Home grants to pay off mortgages. Crooked contractors who didn't finish jobs. Thieves who stripped houses of new cabinets, plumbing, and aluminum windows. The list seemed endless.

It may seem tempting to blame officials from the Housing Authority, FEMA, or Road Home. Others may wonder whether homeowners could have done better at cutting through red tape. But in their book *Left to Chance*, University of New Orleans sociologists Pam Jenkins, Vern Baxter, and Steve Kroll-Smith found it impossible to fit the post-storm chaos into any easily discernible pattern. "For each person, it was different," Jenkins said. "It's not like you can point to one factor."

In 2005, in the immediate wake of Katrina, Emma Drayton McElveen, then eighty-eight, decided that she was too old to rebuild. So when she got her Road Home letter, she checked Option 3, selling the house to the state. "New Orleans is my home," she told her daughter Jackie Brown, with whom she lived in Houston. "But I won't be alive to see it come back. Just bring me home when I die." But because McElveen had to first resolve the estate of her late husband, the sale wasn't yet complete when McElveen died in Houston in 2009. She was ninety-two years old, and her family laid her to rest in Providence Memorial Park in New Orleans.

Her daughter, who works at the federal courthouse in Houston, struggled from afar over the next several years to get the right paperwork together and finish the sale. In 2015, as the city marked the tenth anniversary of the disaster and her date of sale with Road Home approached, Brown felt mixed emotions. She felt relief at no longer having to oversee the yardwork at her mother's former home on North Johnson Street. But signing that title away also marked the end of her family's legal ties to her home city. "Really, I'm making myself content where I'm at," Brown said. "Like my mother, when I die, I will come home."

OPPOSITE Map by Richard Campanella, 2017.

The Saints Are Coming

Super Bowl XLIV and the New Orleans comeback

by Brian W. Boyles

The New Orleans Saints' triumph in Super Bowl XLIV changed the image of the city and marked a turning point in the post-Katrina recovery. Less than five years earlier, their hometown crippled by the federal levee failures, New Orleanians listened to the doubts of talking heads and high-ranking officials. Why rebuild? Why even build in the first place? Members of Congress and even some Louisiana legislators were among a chorus of critics who used the storm as proof that New Orleans was, from its conception, a flawed, sinful place that had brought on its own demise. Better to start with "a clean slate." For people who'd lost everything, the words stung. And as they struggled to their feet, New Orleanians turned to the Saints for hope and validation.

The Saints didn't save the city, of course. The couple huddled in a FEMA trailer, the business owner who gave out free food to relief workers, and the musicians who sustained their communities—those are the heroes of the torturous years that followed the flood. The disaster affected so many lives, many of them permanently, that it's impossible to set an end date for the recovery period. And yet something changed on February 7, 2010. The championship sent a message to the nation that, yes, New Orleans was very much alive and, astoundingly, home to the best football team in the world.

As any New Orleanian can tell you, the Saints weren't always so inspirational. From their first season in 1966 to 1984, the team never finished with a winning record, going a combined 83–187–5 and driving fans to don paper bags over their heads in shame. Some predicted the franchise would relocate. Instead, Tom Benson, a New Orleans native who'd built a fortune selling cars in San Antonio, returned to purchase his hometown team in 1985. In his first victory as Saints owner, the kid from the Seventh Ward grabbed a parasol and led his own sideline parade. The "Benson Boogie" replaced the paper bag as the prominent image of the Saints for national television audiences. In 1987, the team finished 12–3 and went to its first playoff game.

Succeeding years brought peaks and valleys, occasional trips to the playoffs, and a combined 151–152 record from 1986 to 2004. In the 1990s, the team failed to sell out the Superdome for many home games, resulting in TV blackouts locally. Diehard "Who Dats" clung to hope, but for fans of the rest of the league's teams, the New Orleans franchise was little more than a loveable loser, and the city a great place to visit for a road game.

Hurricane Katrina struck just as the 2005 NFL season was about to begin. Displaced from the Superdome, the Saints went 3–13, playing "home" games in Baton Rouge, San Antonio, and New Jersey as rumors swirled that the team might permanently relocate. Tense negotiations between Benson, the NFL, FEMA, and the State of Louisiana centered on the extent of repairs needed at the Superdome. At the end of the season, NFL commissioner Paul Tagliabue expressed cautious optimism the team would come home in 2006: "We think it can, but it's not a slam-dunk." The parties eventually came to an agreement for a $336 million overhaul of the stadium.

As work began at the Superdome, the Saints set about repairing a broken team. Long plagued by a "brain drain," the perception that the best and brightest left the city for better opportunities, New Orleans fans embraced two men who chose the city despite the uncertainty: Sean Payton signed on as head coach in January 2006, and quarterback Drew Brees inked a six-year deal in March. Payton served three years in Dallas as a trusted assistant of the legendary Bill Parcells. He beat out several more experienced candidates for the opportunity to lead a team fresh off a season from hell. In Payton, Benson and general manager Mickey Loomis brought on an offensive genius who promised to focus on football as the city struggled for normalcy. In Brees, they found a folk hero.

A Texas native, Brees rejected an incentive-laden contract offer from his original franchise, the San Diego Chargers, who doubted the former Pro Bowler's ability to recover from a shoulder injury. Despite an offer from Nick Saban and the Miami Dolphins, Brees made a surprising decision: he chose New Orleans. There were, John DeShazier of *The Times-Picayune* wrote, "more reasons for Drew Brees not to be a Saint than to be a Saint, more reasons for him to have run from the team's offer than to it." Yet Brees sensed an opportunity to turn around the franchise. "I just felt that energy in New Orleans," he said. "They believe I can come back from this shoulder injury and lead them to a championship. They were as confident as I am, and that meant a lot."

"Confidence" and "championship" were not words one heard regularly on the streets of New Orleans in the spring of 2006. The basic functions of city life were unsure: Would the garbage man pick up the trash? Would the lights stay on? Federal recovery dollars hadn't reached most families, and the doorways of countless flooded homes still bore the spray-painted X mark left behind by first responders after the storm. An endless stream of volunteers from around the nation helped with the clean-up, but half of the city's residents remained displaced, unable to return home, much less buy a ticket to the Saints home opener. Most pressing for football purposes: would the Superdome be ready?

The renovation work was overseen by Doug Thornton, the longtime Superdome manager, and completed by hundreds of workers, many of them immigrants from Central and South America, part of a wave of Latinos who arrived in the city after the storm. The job demanded a herculean effort. Water damage and the subsequent months of humidity required a near total rebuild, from carpets to video monitors, seating to food stands. The roof job was the largest in the history of US construction, totaling $32.5 million for the 9.7-acre surface. The sight of men crawling around the peak of the Superdome became a strange symbol of hope. "This is our World Trade Center," said Thornton.

On September 25, 2006, the Saints came home. A national audience tuned into the *Monday Night Football* game against the rival Atlanta Falcons. For many Americans, this game provided the first images

OPPOSITE Tracy Porter of the Saints returns an interception for a touchdown in the fourth quarter of Super Bowl XLIV, February 7, 2010. Photo by Jed Jacobsohn. Courtesy of Getty Images.

RIGHT Drew Brees holds his son Baylen after his Super Bowl MVP performance. Photo by Ian Ransley.

inside the Superdome since the storm's aftermath. Onstage with locals Trombone Shorty and the Rebirth and New Birth brass bands, U2 and Green Day kicked off the festivities with a rousing, Katrina-tailored version of an old punk song, "The Saints Are Coming." The crowd went wild. A decade later, Trombone Shorty told Alex Rawls of NOLA.com, "I got chills . . . [h]earing that crowd reaction, and being a proud representative of the city on the biggest stage at the moment. It was bigger than us musicians."

Less than two minutes into the game, special teams player Steve Gleason blocked a punt, resulting in a Saints touchdown. In the annals of the recovery, that moment—and the gratified howl that erupted from the crowd—remains mythical. Finally, something went right. The Saints prevailed 23–3, and a storybook season was underway. Newly named NFL Commissioner Roger Goodell observed, "Tonight is obviously more than just a game. This means more to this community and more to this region . . . [it's] an opportunity to show the world the human spirit that exists here." The Saints finished the season 10–6, winning their division.

The next two years produced uneven results on the field, but the centrality of the team to the city's image—both for residents and for the country—was cemented in 2006. For longtime New Orleanians, the Saints jersey became a symbol of loyalty, a refusal to give up on their hometown, naysayers be damned. For new residents, the people who arrived to support the recovery, becoming a Saints fan was the first rite of belonging, a part of a growing iconography that emphasized a collective fealty to the "authentic" New Orleans. Slogans bloomed on t-shirts and bumper stickers ("Be A New Orleanian Wherever You Are," "FAITH"). The 2008 economic crisis and subsequent recession made New Orleans an attractive alternative for starting a career in education, the arts, or just finding oneself. Young newcomers flocked to traditional second-line parades and embraced local music and cuisine with gusto. Residents continued to argue about the impact of these idealistic arrivals, but on Sundays, the town came together for the Saints.

And they all agreed: one transplant was sure proving his worth. In his first three seasons paired with Payton, Brees directed a high-octane offense capable of big plays. In 2008, he threw for 5,069 yards, the second highest total in league history. The team surrounded him with explosive skilled players, including former Heisman winner Reggie Bush, wide receiver Marques Colston, tight end Jeremy Shockey, and running back Pierre Thomas. Off the field, Brees and his wife displayed a genuine love for their new city, renovating a historic house Uptown and earning praise for their civic spirit. The Saints couldn't have dreamed up a better new quarterback for the battered town.

The team entered the 2009 season with a quiet confidence. After missing the playoffs for two consecutive years, the wobbly defense was under the direction of Gregg Williams, a sought-after assistant hired to instill an aggressive style in the unit. Pre-season prognosticators remained skeptical of the Saints' championship hopes, but Brees sensed something special. "You get in July and you're working out, and you get in the best shape of your life, and especially in this stage of my career in particular, it feels like this is our time," he told *The Times-Picayune* reporter Mike Triplett. Perhaps most importantly, Benson and the state had agreed on a new deal to keep the team in the Superdome. The agreement put to bed any lingering concerns about the franchise's ties to the city and gave the NFL confidence to name New Orleans as the site of the 2013 Super Bowl, the Big Easy's ninth time hosting the big game.

But Super Bowls remained a party to host, not a realistic possibility for a home-team championship. Things began to change when the team rolled to a 13–0 start. The defense, led by linebacker Jonathan Vilma and safety Darren Sharper, morphed into a hard-hitting, turnover machine that matched the big plays of Payton's offense, giving the team an explosive quality that left opponents shell-shocked. And if the impact on the field was clear in early victories against the Philadelphia Eagles and New York Giants, the energy off the field had an economic impact in the city. Neighborhood bars were flocked with fans wearing brand-new team merchandise and celebrating long after the games ended. The Saints closed the year with a 13–3 record, their best finish in franchise history.

They stormed their way to the NFC championship game against the Minnesota Vikings, setting the stage for a classic at the Superdome. The big play defense battered Vikings quarterback Brett Favre, a future Hall of Famer and native of nearby Kiln, Mississippi, forcing two interceptions and recovering three fumbles. Tracy Porter picked off Favre's pass in the closing seconds of the fourth quarter, sending the game into overtime. When Garrett Hartley's kick split the uprights, the Superdome crowd erupted in a deafening roar. Confetti fell onto the floor where, just four years earlier, distraught New Orleanians had huddled together to wait out the storm. ""What's great about doing it here," said Payton, "is that four years ago, there were holes in this roof. The fans in this city and this region deserve it."

The two weeks leading up to the Super Bowl were consumed with giddy plans for parties. In a city obsessed with politics, the excitement overshadowed the 2010 mayoral election, scheduled for the Saturday before the game. At his victory party that evening, Mitchell J. (Mitch) Landrieu took to the stage to chants of "Who Dat!" The two-time lieutenant governor won in a landslide after a campaign that emphasized racial reconciliation and Landrieu's ample experience in government. Son of former mayor Moon Landrieu and brother of US Senator Mary Landrieu, the new mayor told the crowd that the city was ready to enter the post-recovery era. "We took a huge leap forward into the future today. The city of New Orleans showed America what it takes to rebuild a great place. We're all going together and we're not leaving anybody behind." But first, the mayor-elect added, "what we're going to do is get ready for the Saints to take it all the way and to bring the Super Bowl home for us!"

Ironically the biggest obstacle in the Saints path to victory was a native New Orleanian. Peyton Manning was a beloved figure in his hometown, a graduate of Isidore Newman School and the son of former Saints quarterback Archie Manning. Just days after the 2005 flood, Peyton and his brother Eli, quarterback for the New York Giants, mobilized a plane full of relief supplies; the brothers helped load the water, Gatorade, baby formula, and diapers bound for Baton Rouge. Manning was the reigning league MVP, and the Colts were a five-point favorite to beat the Saints and take home their second Super Bowl ring in three years.

After struggling to find their rhythm in the first quarter, the Saints began to show signs of life in the second quarter. Payton's decision to go for it on 4th-and-goal at the 1-yard line failed, but his team was energized. The defense held the Colts to just one touchdown and increasingly dictated the pace. At the half, the Saints were down 10–6.

Then something incredible happened. After planning his surprise for two weeks, Payton instructed rookie kicker Thomas Morstead to attempt an onside kick. For the first time in almost five tumultuous years, the ball bounced in New Orleans' favor, specifically off the helmet of the Colts' Hank Baskett and, amid a vicious scrum, into the arms of Saints safety Chris Reis. The tide had changed.

As signature big plays go, Payton's decision to roll the dice provided a bookend for Gleason's blocked kick in the return to the Superdome in 2006. Gleason's play showed that New Orleans was still here; the fans that night unleashed a primal scream in a city in the throes of a nightmare. Payton's gamble seemed to conjure the collective spirit of a population that took innumerable risks in resuscitating its hometown. And while Gleason did it on Monday Night Football, Payton doubled down in front of the largest television audience in history. Manning and the Colts responded with a touchdown, but the momentum—for the Saints and for their city—had changed for good. The offense took over and Brees led a drive that culminated in a 16-yard touchdown pass to Pierre Thomas. The game remained close until Tracy Porter stepped in front of a Manning pass and sprinted 74 yards for a touchdown with less than four minutes left. Final score: 31–17.

ABOVE Fans celebrate the Saints victory in the French Quarter. Photo by Cheryl Gerber.

The celebration that night in New Orleans was unlike any thrown in the city's history.

The celebration that night in New Orleans was unlike any thrown in the city's history. Impromptu parades struck out for the French Quarter. Traffic on Canal Street halted and drivers jumped out of their cars to howl at the night. Living rooms on the West Bank, barrooms in the Third Ward, bedrooms in Atlanta, Houston, Baton Rouge, wherever the displaced had landed, all filled with a feeling no one could quite describe. If we sometimes overburden sports with inferred meanings, on this night, it really was more than just football.

When the Saints visited the White House, President Obama praised the players for their leadership in the region. "Not only did the team come back—it took its city's hands and helped its city back on its feet. This team took the hopes and the dreams of a shattered city and placed them squarely on its shoulders."

New Orleanians did not wake up the next morning to streets without potholes or a new roof on every house. The challenges facing the city didn't disappear when the last seconds ticked away in Miami. Post-Katrina New Orleans was a difficult, quarrelsome place. The future of public education, the public health system, and levee protection were debated vigorously, with outside experts, state legislators, and neighborhood organizations all weighing in on the best course for the city. Whether because of a rising cost of living or better opportunities elsewhere, too many former residents never made it home to join in the conversation. Most everyone had a Katrina story to tell, a personal viewpoint that influenced their feelings on the recovery. And, New Orleanians being preservationists in spirit, they argued passionately over post-Katrina changes in architecture, food, and musical traditions. Everything, it seemed, mattered. These debates persist today, proof of a population that cares deeply about a place they almost lost. The Saints' Super Bowl victory provided a common denominator, something everyone in New Orleans could agree on: the Saints were champions and, man, was it sweet.

The rest of the country agreed. The Saints name was forever etched in the list of Super Bowl champions, joining the Steelers, the Packers, the Patriots, the rest of the country. But more important, the nation saw that New Orleans was capable of producing a winner. Maligned as ill-conceived, careless, and not wholly American, the city responded to its gravest crisis with a world championship. Experienced at celebrating each year during Carnival, where the party is a performance and everyone is a player, New Orleanians cheered their victory with an unprecedented urgency. Unlike Mardi Gras, they'd never done this before, and there was no guarantee they'd do it again. Then again, there'd been no guarantee for New Orleans since Katrina, nothing that promised that it would continue. The city had changed, but it never gave up. The Saints victory was perhaps just a symbol, but for many New Orleanians, it was a sign: they hadn't quit. They won.

For audiences around the world, the shadow cast over the city was lifted. The images that flowed from the post-Super Bowl parties and parade beckoned viewers around the globe: come to New Orleans, the city that came back.

Our Resilience

The city lays a foundation for the future

by the Honorable
Mitchell J. Landrieu

To plan for the future, we must remember where we as a city have come from. In 2018, we will celebrate the three hundredth anniversary of the founding of New Orleans, but our story starts well before Bienville gave us our name.

It was millennia ago when Chapitoulas Nation first settled on Bayou St. John in the heart of modern-day New Orleans. They called the area *Bayouk Choupic*, or Bayou Mudfish. Here, traders from the Choctaw and Chitimacha tribes could travel from the lake and portage to the river.

Imagine centuries of moonlit nights, wilderness and darkness punctuated by a fire built in a clearing, the silence being cut by laughter from a trading party resting for the night.

Then the French came, and then the Spanish. A mighty port we now know as the French Quarter was cut out of the Mississippi River bend. Cheap sugar, cotton, and indigo flowed downriver, and hundreds of thousands of African slaves were moved upriver to toil in the fertile delta soil, their free labor fueling the regional and world economy. As a result, New Orleans became a center of commerce in the new United States of America, and, until the late 20th century, the predominate capital of the South.

As a people and a city that has existed through the ages, we are known for our diverse culture and our values—faith, family, country. We are known for our way of life: slow walks on hot days, easy hellos to strangers, family reunions, hunting and fishing, music and food. But if you pull back the veil, there is something else. It is a deep resilience. Because we love this place so much we will endure anything to keep it.

Throughout our long history we endured through slavery and oppression, wars and pandemics, terrible storms and fires. Then, twelve years ago in August, again we were tested when the federal levees broke following Hurricane Katrina. It was a man-made infrastructure failure of epic proportions that resulted in floodwaters surging over the rooftops of a great American city. Eighty percent of New Orleans was under water, causing billions in damages.

In a moment, everything was gone—homes, roads, schools, hospitals, police and fire stations, grocery stores, parks, and playgrounds. As the water swallowed our neighborhoods, thousands of people trapped in the city were caught in a life or death struggle. The stories are seared into our collective memory. The rushing flood pulled people under; survivors were trapped for days with little or no help. Thousands crowded in front of the Superdome, at the Convention Center, at the Port of St. Bernard. Many more were stuck on rooftops or in attics. Bloated dead bodies floated on the streets of America. Government at every level was ill prepared and totally unable to deal with the crisis.

It was the worst disaster in American history, but as with all things that have confronted the city through the centuries, we pledged as a people to endure. Together, we started to clean up, sweating in the heat, clearing away the devastation, and putting our lives back together. We slept on floors and in tents. We cried over family photos that somehow escaped the deluge and thought about the friends and family we had lost or those who had been forced to move away.

Slowly our city has stood back up, and this comeback is one of the world's most remarkable stories of tragedy and triumph, resurrection and redemption. In one word: resilience.

We are America's comeback city, and we want to tell the whole world what we have learned from our trials by water and fire. New Orleans has taken on the toughest of challenges, resolving not to just rebuild the city that we once were, but to create the city we always dreamed we could be. Together, we have laid a solid foundation for the future and are now positioned for growth like never before.

First and foremost, we had to better protect our city from storms. None of us were prepared for Hurricane Katrina, and we suffered the terrible consequences. Now, $14.5 billion in new levees have been built, and with the BP oil spill settlement and new federal and state revenue-sharing taking effect, we finally have a partial payment on hardening key assets and rebuilding the coast, which serves as a natural buffer for storms.

In addition, our disaster preparations are both wide and deep. In partnership with a local non-profit called Evacuteer, New Orleans has developed the City-Assisted Evacuation Plan. Now during a mandatory evacuation, local, state, and federal officials, along with faith and community-based organizations, provide transportation to residents and tourists unable to self-evacuate. If you drive around New Orleans, you will see sixteen large public art displays scattered around the city. We call these landmarks "Evacuspots," and they serve as gathering sites during an evacuation. These are physical symbols of our preparedness.

However, to be truly resilient we have to go further. We must combat other chronic stresses like poverty, inequality, violence, and racism. So now we're in the midst of historic reforms that will strengthen the New Orleans Police Department and the Orleans Parish Prison. We're improving the health care delivery system, so instead of sitting in an emergency waiting room, now people can get primary care at one of our seventy neighborhood health clinics, many of which were developed after Katrina, or at our new world-class hospitals—one for our veterans at the new VA hospital, as well as our new University Medical Center and another new hospital in New Orleans East. We've also redeveloped nine public housing developments offering residents updated amenities like swimming pools and fitness centers.

We also have our Economic Opportunity Strategy and STRIVE programs, which help ensure broad-based economic growth, where there is a pathway to prosperity anyone can follow and no one is left behind. And we're creating thousands of new jobs while cultivating a new, vibrant entrepreneurial ecosystem for promising industries like water management, digital media, and bioscience.

New Orleans has taken on the toughest of challenges, resolving not to just rebuild the city that we once were, but to create the city we always dreamed we could be.

And we need to improve our schools. The work that has been done in recent years by thousands of parents, teachers, students, administrators, policy makers, and advocates is the most important development in New Orleans since Hurricane Katrina. We are using more than $1.8 billion to rebuild, renovate, or refurbish every school in the city, reversing decades of divestment. No other city in America has nicer schools, and no other city school system in America is improving faster. We have created a new way of school governance guided by results and defined by choice, equity, and accountability, where nearly 100 percent of students attend public, not-for-profit charter schools. The results are impressive—dropouts are down, graduation rates are up, and we're closing the achievement gap. Our kids are more prepared for the future.

Overall, the goal is nothing less than to create a city of peace, opportunity, and responsibility for all people—a city for the ages. We're not there yet. We are far from perfect. But the people of New Orleans are committed to our city and know we are on the right path. Indeed, this is what we do, not just as New Orleanians, but also as Americans—work hard and dream of something more, something better.

So, as we turn the corner on the twelfth anniversary of Katrina and begin looking forward to New Orleans' three hundredth anniversary, we have shown what is possible. Together, we have laid a solid foundation for the future, and we are now positioned for growth like never before.

We are an ascendant city.

We have come back strong when no one thought it was possible. And as we close out one century, we can feel confident that, no matter what the next century will bring, we will be still standing—resilient, unbowed and unbroken, and optimistic about tomorrow.

OPPOSITE Mayor Landrieu joins the St. Augustine High School Band at the ribbon-cutting celebration for the Loyola Avenue streetcar line, January 28, 2013. Courtesy of the Regional Transit Authority.

The Soul of New Orleans

A lifetime of second lines and jazz funerals

by Dr. Michael White

On a hot Sunday morning in May 1975, I found myself in front of a small black Baptist church. I had on a black suit and a white band cap, and I held a clarinet. A sea of uniformly dressed church members poured out and lined up behind me and the other nine musicians. A few faint trumpet notes were followed by three thunderous bass drum beats to begin a song. I panicked. There was no song title given, no written music, no indication of key or structure. No one had told me what I was supposed to do. As the melody of the hymn "Lord, Lord, Lord" became recognizable, I fumbled around to find a few good rhythmic figures and high notes to fill in empty spaces. For the next ninety minutes we paraded through the neighborhood. A crowd gathered, dancing alongside the procession while we jazzed up several other up-tempo hymns. At the end of the procession, the white-haired mahogany-complexioned bandleader, trumpeter Ernest "Doc" Paulin, frowned and shook his head as he handed me a small roll of dollars. It seemed obvious to me that, at twenty years old, I had just had my first and last job as a "professional" musician.

I was never more wrong. For the next four years I was a regular member of Doc Paulin's Brass Band. We played in neighborhoods all over New Orleans about once a week, mainly in black community parades and funeral processions. This was my introduction to "second line" culture, then an almost underground phenomenon, which many decades before had given birth to America's greatest original artistic contribution—jazz. Black community parades were rarely ever discussed in the media and remained relatively unknown to a large segment of locals. That Sunday in 1975 was the beginning of a lifelong career in jazz and my becoming part of a tradition that had served as a symbol of black freedom and the American democratic ideal. Every job with Doc was an eye-opening experience revealing a jazz culture that had little to do with the loud, fast, commercialized music of Bourbon Street or the corny stereotypes of early jazz music and musicians.

Brass bands have been an important part of New Orleans' unique musical history since the eighteenth century, when European style military bands played for parades, funerals, and other ceremonies. Brass bands gained greater popularity during and after the Civil War, so that by the late nineteenth century a number of brass bands had been established in New Orleans. This included several African-American bands, which prided themselves on their musical training and skill at reading difficult music scores.

The post-Reconstruction years were turbulent for African Americans in the South, due to new Jim Crow laws that limited their freedom and civil rights, as well as the rise of violent white supremacy groups. The highly spirited black population of New Orleans responded with protests, demonstrations, and legal action. During the 1890s, an intense desire for freedom and equality and resentment towards increasing racism, combined with the traditional local obsession with celebration, formed a musical revolution (later called "jazz") that would influence the direction of American culture. It began when legendary uptown cornet player Charles "Buddy" Bolden and others started to improvise popular dance and parade music, using bent tones and other effects from the black blues and hymn-singing style on horns. This loose, personal, and exciting sound was marked by instrumental "conversations" and driving steady rhythms. Early New Orleans jazz was a style or approach that incorporated and transformed songs from ragtime, marches, hymns, blues, and other popular music. Jazz was an exciting dance music that soon spread outside of the black community, where it could be heard throughout the city and surrounding areas in nearly every location and type of event.

Though jazz was often played by the five-to-seven-member combos that introduced it to the world on recordings made in the North, its longest lasting popularity and most important social function in its birthplace remained with brass bands that played in black community processions. Just as the style of society dance orchestras, which only read music, was overshadowed by hot improvised jazz, the same thing happened as brass bands also began to improvise. The typical New Orleans brass band had ten or eleven

OPPOSITE Lois Andrews dancing on coffin at a second line in 2006. Photo by Eric Waters.

ABOVE *Family Ties Social Aid and Pleasure Club, 2011.* Photo by Eric Waters.

musicians who improvised musical conversations within the basic roles of their instruments: trumpets played melodies in harmony; trombones gave rhythmic punctuations and sliding growls; a clarinet danced freely around the melody and gave high-note harmonies; a baritone and an alto horn (later replaced by saxophones) played rhythmic and harmonic phrases; and a snare drum played press rolls and accents. The characteristic New Orleans brass band sound was especially marked by a unique rhythmic pulse created by the tuba's two-beat based "oom-pah" against rousing syncopated bass drum beats.

The most common brass band activities throughout the twentieth century were black social club parades, church parades, and funerals with music—later known as "jazz funerals". Dozens of black benevolent societies and social aid and pleasure clubs that became popular after the Civil War were the main sponsors of brass band activities. The largest and most socially significant events were the clubs' annual anniversaries and holiday parades, held on Sundays. Very different from the city's internationally famous Mardi Gras parades, the black social club events had no floats, maskers, throws, or other carnival staples. Several aspects of the black community parades were reminiscent of West African processions. They were an evolved, linear and mobile continuation of the popular African circle dances of nineteenth-century Congo Square. During my years in Doc Paulin's band, we played parades for nearly every club: the Young Men's Olympians, the Money Wasters, the Jolly Bunch, the Lady Zulus, the Scene Boosters, and several others. Social club parades had three main parts. Divisions of club members uniformly dressed in loud, sometimes contrasting colors, creating a visual unity that redefined acceptability. Club members carried colorful umbrellas, a symbol of royalty or social status in West African processions, and waved handkerchiefs, an African gesture to purify the air. Between club divisions were one or more brass bands wearing dark band uniforms, later changed to black suits. The club and band formed the "first line" by walking in the street. An important part of these parades was the "second line"—a crowd of thousands of anonymous faces, people who seemed to appear from nowhere and hypnotically dance alongside the band throughout the entire hours-long route.

When the music began a magical transformation took place. Club members and second liners did a free-form West African–derived dance, which was also known as the "second line." As intensity would build from the interaction between hot jazz music and dancing, a collective euphoria could transform the event into an almost spiritual dimension, in which a sense of total freedom, equality among all people, limitless power, and a redefinition of earthly reality prevailed. Second liners, not limited to the street, danced on top of, under, around, and through anything or anyone in their path. Normal obstacles simply became dance partners in the celebration: cars, fences, stop signs, trees, trash cans, stairs, houses. I remember many times seeing old people whose bodies had bent and withered with age suddenly straighten up and dance as if they were young again, with canes high in the air. There was one guy who defiantly cheated death by dancing on rooftops of houses, pretending to stumble but never losing step with the music. I could never understand how he was always on a rooftop next to the band, no matter how many streets we crossed. There were handicapped and mentally challenged people who would dance freely and happily with strangers or blend into the crowd. I've seen babies too young to walk wiggle in time to the music in their mothers' arms. Sometimes the magical intensity and spiritual harmony made it seem as if the second liners' movements created the rhythmic phrases that came from my clarinet, or that the notes would leap from the bell of my horn and assume wildly moving human form.

That Sunday in 1975 was the beginning of a lifelong career in jazz and my becoming part of a tradition that had served as a symbol of black freedom and the American democratic ideal.

While on the surface, social club parades were an exciting and fun means of celebration, release, and bonding, their social significance went much deeper. These large gatherings were also a show of unity and strength in the struggle for freedom and equality. The bold colors of the club, the conservative band uniforms, the improvised jazz, and the wild movements of the second liners were a celebration of a diverse heritage and a model of a desired democratic existence. Normal concepts of reality, social order, rules, and acceptability were constantly challenged, redefined, and blended in endless symbolic gestures. Club members, musicians, and ordinary followers coexisted and freely and equally participated in the mass creative celebration. The brass band's jazz style was also a democratic exercise. Individual musicians took pride in having their own highly personal and unique instrumental sound and expression within an ensemble approach. This open and public musical display of an individual's emotions, voice, and spirit rejected the feelings of invisibility that came with the indifference and limitations of society's imposed second-class citizenship. With a nod toward social change, even the complex European-derived marches, while maintaining the basic melody and structure, were relaxed and reconceived to allow for improvisation and the incorporation of diverse musical ideas from various individual and cultural sources.

A scaled-down, tamer variation of social club parades was the tradition of church parades, which existed throughout much of the twentieth century. It was common for small black Baptist churches to have Sunday morning parades with brass bands to celebrate religious holidays, pastors' anniversaries, or the founding of a new church. As a show of strength, pride, and religious conviction, one or more churches would parade through nearby neighborhoods for an hour or two in divisions separated by gender and age. Church members dressed conservatively in white dresses and black suits. At the ministers' insistence, brass bands would only play up-tempo hymns, but in the same jazzed-up style as in social club parades. During my years with Doc Paulin, we played for dozens of church parades in the New Orleans area. It was always amusing to see church members strutting gracefully and proudly in rank to the music,

ABOVE *Original Nine Social Aid and Pleasure Club, 2012.* Photo by Eric Waters.

ABOVE *Gip and Son, 2006.* Photo by Eric Waters.

trying hard not to break out in a raucous second-line dance that the music invited them to do. Church parades never drew the large crowds or had the intensity of social club events, but they did allow the music to echo sweetly through alleyways and neighborhood streets. The increasing cost of musician fees, parade permits, and police escort fees, as well as the decline in traditional-style bands, all contributed to the demise of this once-noble New Orleans tradition.

The best-known brass-band functions outside of the black community have been funerals with music, or jazz funerals. This unique practice appeared along with early jazz and was born from a blend of African and European burial customs and concepts. Although funerals for deceased musicians have been highly publicized and well attended, the majority of jazz funerals were given for members of social and benevolent organizations. The jazz funeral celebrates a deceased person with both somber and joyous expression. As the coffin is carried out of a church or funeral home, the band plays slow dirges and sad hymns. The moaning bass drum beat, soft long tuba and trombone notes, sweetly singing trumpet melodies, and weeping high-note wailing of a clarinet parallel the grief and sense of loss felt by the deceased's family members and friends. The band lines up in front of the hearse, the motorcade, and the club members dressed in black suits, and the group slowly proceeds toward the cemetery playing more dirges. If the cemetery is far away, the band opens up into two lines and plays a final song as the procession passes through, "cutting the body loose." After burial, or when the motorcade moves a distance away, there is up-tempo music and second-line dancing by some family members, friends, and onlookers that can last for several blocks or longer. This joyous celebration explores the old concept of "rejoicing at death." The deceased is free of suffering and earthly burdens and is now with the Creator, a cause for joy. I have played in over one hundred fifty jazz funerals during my career, but none made a more lasting impression than the first one with Doc Paulin in Hahnville, LA. It was at a small Baptist church along the Mississippi River levee with a nearby cemetery. The funeral was for a member of a very old benevolent society. Members were dressed in Napoleonic type navy blue uniforms with admirals' hats and carried shiny swords. Their stone solemn faces, strict ceremonial decorum and the old hymns of our band fit descriptions of early jazz funerals. It seemed like I participated in a lost part of history that never quite sounded, looked or felt the same in other funerals.

The community processions continued into the 1950s and beyond by a small number of long-established, newly formed, or pick-up groups, including the Eureka, Young Tuxedo, George Williams, Doc Paulin, and E. Gibson Brass Bands. There have been many changes in second line culture since my mid-1970s entry, when traditional-style jazz dominated brass bands, social club parades, and jazz funerals. During that time the Fairview Brass Band, a youth group founded by legendary musician Danny Barker, as well as Doc Paulin's Band, nurtured and developed a generation of young musicians who would either continue in the traditional vein or foster the evolution of brass bands into a new modern style. In the 1960s and '70s, Harold Dejan's popular Olympia Brass Band moved outside of community events to perform in concerts, international tours, festivals, tourism promotion, films, and sports events. This was a major change in the image and visibility of brass bands that led to colorful uniforms, a smaller band size, limited repertoire, singing, solo playing, and other commercial concessions. Olympia also began to perform songs with a dominant rhythm-and-blues influenced sound. Olympia's success opened the door for major revisions in the nature of brass band appearance, style, and types of work. In 1977 the Dirty Dozen Brass Band appeared in community parades with a new sound, which blended contemporary and traditional jazz, rhythm and blues, Caribbean music, and other styles. This revolutionary approach, marked by faster tempos, prominent tuba lines, modern jazz solos, and original songs, started a new phase of modern brass bands that gave rise to the funky, rap-influenced Rebirth Brass Band in the 1980s and has continued inspiring dozens of newly formed bands into the present. The Dirty Dozen, Rebirth, and several other groups have mainly moved beyond performing in community parades in favor of stage concerts and concert tours. The new types of performances and major label recordings,

I remember many times seeing old people whose bodies had bent and withered with age suddenly straighten up and dance as if they were young again, with canes high in the air.

including Rebirth's hit song, "Do Whatcha Wanna," have helped to give New Orleans street culture a popular visible presence around the world.

Today the term "second line" still refers to a crowd of parade followers, but it is also commonly used to mean a social club parade, a jazz funeral, or any event with brass bands. Scaled-down versions with brass bands, umbrellas, and handkerchiefs have become common at local weddings, festivals, parties, conventions, sports contests, graduations, and other events. Like brass bands, the once-declining black social clubs have not only persisted but also grown tremendously in number, even after Hurricane Katrina. The appearance of authentic New Orleans street culture in movies, documentaries, and on television shows has created interest and participation in the black community parades and funerals by numbers of white people, who follow and joyously dance among a sea of black faces. Today's social club parades focus on having fun, bonding with the community, expressing a common heritage, and defying conformity. In the spirit of friendly competition, some clubs spend considerable money on elaborate custom-made outfits. Some contemporary jazz funerals avoid slow dirges and mournful expression in favor of fast-paced funk-style songs played throughout processions that more closely resemble regular second lines than the traditional dual-perspective ceremonies. It is also common today for funerals to be given for anyone in or outside of the black community, including mock and commemorative celebrations for non-local major celebrities.

As a jazz musician for more than forty years I have performed hundreds of jobs with more than a dozen brass bands, including my own Liberty Brass Band. I am proud to have witnessed and participated in the tradition and evolution of brass bands, which includes several of my relatives who played in parades and funerals since the earliest days of jazz. Although uniquely local in its origin, brass band music exudes a timeless, universal joy that invites all to join in and share the spirit of New Orleans music. Today there are traditional and modern-style brass bands and followers of all ages at home and around the world. As the city reaches its tricentennial it has become increasingly common to have mini-parades with brass bands and second line dancing indoors or in the street for events like weddings, music festivals, sporting events, conventions, airport greetings and graduations. Recent mock jazz funerals in honor of non-local major musical celebrities, like Prince and Michael Jackson, and a growing number of short second line parades along French Quarter and Uptown streets have become a common sight. Since a number of these events are organized by people outside of the black community and often consist of non-locals and musicians that have never been involved in authentic neighborhood based functions, they have become the subject of controversy and criticism in the local media and among some who are concerned with authenticity, purity and preserving the original meaning and sacredness of unique African American traditions. But with endless excuses for having a parade, and the continuous number of young musicians forming brass bands, it appears that the unique sound and spirit of New Orleans and its parade traditions will continue as long as the city exists.

BELOW *Tuba, 2011.* Photo by Eric Waters.

Suggested Reading List

Introduction

"The Land Is of Peculiar Formation"
How the Mississippi River created New Orleans' dynamic deltaic environment
By Richard Campanella

Campanella, Richard. *Bienville's Dilemma*. Lafayette: University of Louisiana Press, 2008.
Colten, Craig E. *An Unnatural Metropolis: Wresting New Orleans from Nature*. Baton Rouge: Louisiana State University Press, 2005.
McPhee, John. *The Control of Nature*. New York: Farrar, Straus and Giroux, 1989.
Saucier, Roger T. *Geomorphology and Quaternary Geologic History of the Lower Mississippi Valley*. Vicksburg: U.S. Army Engineer Waterways Experiment Station, 1994.

Promethean Ambition
How an imperial backwater entered world history
By Lawrence N. Powell, PhD

Hall, Gwendolyn M. *Africans in Colonial Louisiana: The Development of Afro-Creole Culture in the Eighteenth Century*. Baton Rouge: Louisiana State University Press, 1992.
Powell, Lawrence N. *The Accidental City: Improvising New Orleans*. Cambridge: Harvard University Press, 2012.
Usner, Daniel H. *Indians, Settlers, & Slaves in a Frontier Exchange Economy: The Lower Mississippi Valley Before 1783*. Chapel Hill: University of North Carolina Press, 1992.

People

Introduction: Two Jacksons, Andrew and Mahalia
By Brian W. Boyles

Brock, Jerry. "Hallelujah, Mahalia!" *Louisiana Cultural Vistas*, Summer 2012.
Whitman, Alden. "Mahalia Jackson, Gospel Singer, And a Civil Rights Symbol Dies." Obituary
reprint. *On This Day. New York Times*, January 28, 2010.

American Indians in New Orleans
Native American communities were integral to the city's foundation
By Daniel H. Usner, PhD

Usner, Daniel H. "American Indians in Colonial New Orleans." In *Powhatan's Mantle: Indians in the Colonial Southeast*. Edited by Greg A. Waselkov, Peter H. Wood, and Tom Hatley. Lincoln: University of Nebraska Press, 2006.
Usner, Daniel H. *American Indians in the Lower Mississippi Valley: Social and Economic Histories*. Lincoln: University of Nebraska Press, 1998.

Home for a Healthy Mind in a Healthy Body: Germans in New Orleans
By Brigitta Malm

Hoffman, Annette, R. *The American Turner Movement: A History from its Beginnings to 2000*. Edited by Giles Hoyt. Translated by Ernestine Dillon and Phillip Reid. Purdue: Max Kade German-American Center at IUPUI and the Indiana German Heritage Society, 2011.
Merrill, Ellen. *Germans of Louisiana*. Gretna: Pelican Publishing Company, 2004.
Mehrlaender, Andrea. *The Germans of Charleston, Richmond and New Orleans during the Civil War Period*, 1850–1870. Berlin: De Gruyter, 2011.
Reeves, Sally. "The LEH's Home at Turner Hall." *Louisiana Cultural Vistas*, Summer 2001.

Vietnamese Make their Mark on New Orleans Culture and Cuisine
By Nancy Dixon, PhD

Vanlandingham, Mark J. "Post-Katrina, Vietnamese Success." *Sunday Review. New York Times*, August 14, 2015.
"Vietnamese History in New Orleans." *New Orleans Official Guide*, July 2017.

Spaces and Places

Introduction: Pythian Temple
By Brian W. Boyles

"From Common and Basin to Tulane and Loyola: 150 Years of Change in Our Neighborhood" New Orleans Public Library exhibition, curated by Wayne Everard, 2015.
Hamilton, Green P. *Beacon Lights of the Race*. Memphis: F.H. Clarke & Brother, 1911.

"A Graceful Curve of the River"
Urbanism, Architecture, and the Emergence of a Built Environment
By Richard Campanella

Campanella, Richard. *Cityscapes of New Orleans*. Baton Rouge: Louisiana State University Press, 2017.
Edwards, Jay D. "The Origins of Creole Architecture." *Winterthur Portfolio: A Journal of American Material Culture*, 29, nos. 2–3, Summer/Autumn 1994.
Friends of the Cabildo. *New Orleans Architecture, Vol. I–IX*. Gretna: Pelican Publishing Company, 1971–1997.
Heard, Malcolm. *French Quarter Manual: An Architectural Guide to New Orleans' Vieux Carré*. New Orleans: Tulane School of Architecture, 1997.

World Expositions

"Audubon Park History." *Audubon Nature Institute*, July 2017.
Fairall, Herbert S. *The World's Industrial and Cotton Centennial Exposition, New Orleans, 1884–1885.* Iowa City: Republican Publishing Co., 1885.
Laborde, Peggy Scott, and Steven Tyler. *A World's Fair to Remember*, WYES-TV, 2003.
O'Brian, Bridget, and Dean Bacquet. "Going Broke: Troubled Story of a World's Fair." *New Orleans Times-Picayune*, November 11, 1984.

Conflict and Freedom

Introduction: Jordan Noble
By Brian W. Boyles

Brock, Jerry. "Jordan Noble: Drummer, Soldier, Statesman" *Louisiana Cultural Vistas*, Winter 2014.

New Orleans and the Civil War
The conflict transformed the city from Cotton Kingdom to frontier of emancipation
By Lawrence N. Powell, PhD

Bell, Caryn. Revolution, *Romanticism, and the Afro-Creole Protest Tradition in Louisiana, 1718–1868.* Baton Rouge: Louisiana State University Press, 1997.
Johnson, Walter. *Soul By Soul: Inside the Antebellum Slave Market.* Cambridge: Harvard University Press, 1999.
Tregle, Joseph. *Louisiana in the Age of Jackson: A Clash of Cultures and Personalities.* Baton Rouge: Louisiana State University Press, 1999.

Engine of Equality
New Orleans was a frontier for legal battles and protests that fueled the Civil Rights Movement
By Kara Tucina Olidge, PhD

Douglas, Davidson M. *Bush v. Orleans Parish School Board and the Desegregation of New Orleans Schools. Great Debates in United States History.* Federal Judicial Center: Federal Judicial History Office, 2005.
Morial, Sybil Haydel. *Witness to Change: From Jim Crow to Political Empowerment.* Winston-Salem: John F. Blair Publisher, 2015.

Spirituality and Sin

Models of Piety
The Ursuline nuns and the roots of New Orleans Catholicism
By Emily Clark, PhD

Clark, Emily. *Masterless Mistresses: The New Orleans Ursulines and the Development of a New World Society: 1727–1834.* Chapel Hill: Omohundro Institute of Early American History and Culture by the University of North Carolina Press, 2007.
Clark, Emily, ed. *Voices from an Early American Convent: Marie Madeleine Hachard and the New Orleans Ursulines, 1727–1760.* Baton Rouge: Louisiana State University Press, 2007.
Emily Clark and Virginia M. Gould. "The Feminine Face of Afro-Catholicism in New Orleans, 1727-1852." *William and Mary Quarterly*, 3d ser. 59:2 (April 2002): 409–448.
Heaney, Jane Frances. *A Century of Pioneering: A History of the Ursuline Nuns in New Orleans, 1727–1827.* New Orleans: Ursuline Sisters of New Orleans, Louisiana, 1993.

Shalom, New Orleans
Jewish roots date back to city's founding
By Nancy Dixon, PhD

Cohen, Rich. *The Fish That Ate the Whale: The Life and Times of America's Banana King.* New York: Cohen Farrar, Straus & Giroux, 2012.
"Encyclopedia of Southern Jewish Communities - New Orleans, Louisiana." *Goldring/Woldenburg Institute of Southern Life*, July 2017.
Levitas, Susan. "Gefilte Fish in the Land of the Kingfish: Jewish Life in Louisiana." *Louisiana Folklife Festival Booklet, 2004. Folklife in Louisiana: Louisiana's Living Traditions*, 2015.

Cities of the Dead
New Orleans cemeteries evolved out of necessity and diversity
By Sally Asher

Asher, Sally. *Stories From The St. Louis Cemeteries Of New Orleans.* Charleston: History Press, 2015.
Christovich, Mary Louise, Leonard V. Huber, and Peggy McDowell. *New Orleans Architecture. Volume III: The Cemeteries*, Edited by Mary Louise Christovich. Gretna: Pelican Publishing Company, 2004.
Huber, Leonard V. *Clasped Hands: Symbolism in New Orleans Cemeteries.* Lafayette: University of Southwestern Louisiana, 1982.

Cuisine and Culture

"Wettest City on Earth"
New Orleans' love affair with the cocktail
By Allison Alsup

Alsup, Allison, Elizabeth Pearce, and Richard Read. *The French Quarter Drinking Companion: A Guide to Bars in America's Most Eclectic Neighborhood*, Second Edition. Gretna: Pelican Publishing Company, 2017.
Pearce, Elizabeth. *Drink Dat New Orleans: A Guide to the Best Cocktail Bars, Neighborhood Pubs, and All-Night Dives.* New York: Countryman Press, 2017.
Williams, Elizabeth M., and Curtis McMillian. *Lift Your Spirits: A Celebratory History of Cocktail Culture in New Orleans.* Baton Rouge: Louisiana State University Press, 2016.
McCaffety, Kerry. *Obituary Cocktail: The Great Saloons of New Orleans.* Gretna: Pelican Publishing Company, 2001.
Wohl, Kit. *New Orleans Classic Cocktails.* Gretna: Pelican Publishing Company, 2012.

Carnival Time
Mardi Gras celebrations in New Orleans date back to eighteenth century
By Brian Costello

Hardy, Arthur. *Mardi Gras in New Orleans, An Illustrated History,* 5th edition. Mandeville: Arthur Hardy Enterprises, 2014.

Golden Crown
Tootie Montana revolutionized the art of Mardi Gras Indian suits.
By Brian W. Boyles

"Allison 'Tootie' Montana." *NEA National Heritage Fellowships*, 1987.
Salaam, Kalamu ya. "Mardi Gras Indians and Tootie Montana." *Louisiana Cultural Vistas*, Spring 1998.

Throw Me Something, Sister!
By Nancy Dixon, PhD

Hardy, Arthur. "Krewe of Venus led the way for women's parading organizations in 1941." *New Orleans Advocate*, February 17, 2015.

The Sporting Life
Boxing, baseball, and horse racing thrived during New Orleans' gilded age
By S. Derby Gisclair

Coleman, Ricardo. "Fisticuffs and Firsts: A Timeline of Boxing in New Orleans" *Louisiana Cultural Vistas*, Spring 2016.

Bohemian Revival
Artists and writers led the French Quarter renaissance of the 1920s
By John Shelton Reed, PhD

Anderson, Elizabeth, and Gerald R. Kelly. *Miss Elizabeth: A Memoir.* Boston: Little, Brown and Company, 1999.
Harvey, Chance. *The Life and Selected Letters of Lyle Saxon*. Gretna: Pelican Publishing Company, 2003.
Littleton, Taylor Dowe. *William Spratling: His Life and Art.* Baton Rouge: Louisiana State University Press, 2014.

Sounds

Cradle of Rock and Roll
Cosimo Matassa, Dave Bartholomew, and Allen Toussaint forged the future at J&M Studio
By Alison Fensterstock

Berry, Jason, Jonathan Foose, and Tad Jones. *Up from the Cradle of Jazz: New Orleans Music since World War II*. Second Edition. Lafayette: University of Louisiana at Lafayette Press, 2009.
Broven, John. *Rhythm and Blues in New Orleans*. Gretna: Pelican Publishing Company, 1978.
Coleman, Rick. *Blue Monday: Fats Domino and the Lost Dawn of Rock n Roll.* Cambridge: Da Capo Press, 2006.
Hannusch, Jeff. *I Hear You Knockin: The Sound of New Orleans Rhythm and Blues*. Ville Platte: Swallow Publications, 1985.

Earl Palmer's Soundtrack of the Twentieth-Century
By Brian W. Boyles

Scherman, Tony. *Backbeat: Earl Palmer's Story*. Washington DC: Smithsonian Institution Press, 1999.

Louis Gottshalk , New Orleans' First Rock Star
By Brian W. Boyles

Collins, Peter. "Louis Moreau Gottschalk." *Knowlouisiana.org Encyclopedia of Louisiana*, Edited by David Johnson. Louisiana Endowment for the Humanities, April 3, 2013.
Teachout, Terry. "Our Gottshalk." *Commentary Magazine*, September 1, 2006.

Biographies

Publisher
Brian W. Boyles is Vice President of the Louisiana Endowment for the Humanities and Publisher of *Louisiana Cultural Vistas* magazine. His first book, *New Orleans Boom & Blackout: One Hundred Days in America's Coolest Hotspot*, was selected by the Young Leadership Council of New Orleans as the 2015 One Book One New Orleans citywide read.

Executive Editor
Nancy Dixon, PhD is the Program Coordinator and professor of English at Dillard University. She has written several articles and two books on New Orleans literature and culture and received a National Endowment for the Humanities grant to continue her research, "Defining, Documenting, and Teaching Creole Culture." Her first book, *Fortune and Misery: Sallie Rhett Roman*, won the Louisiana Endowment for the Humanities Book of the Year Award in 2000, and her most recent book is *N.O. Lit: 200 Years of New Orleans Literature* (Lavender Ink, 2013).

Managing Editor
Romy Mariano, is the managing editor of *Louisiana Cultural Vistas* magazine and KnowLouisiana.org, the encyclopedia of Louisiana history and culture. She earned degrees in English and studio art practices from Lafayette College and completed her MFA in Painting from the San Francisco Art Institute. She has spent 13 years working closely with national as well as international artists, and has worked as a fine art buyer and consultant for multi-million dollar design projects in the New Orleans metropolitan area. Mariano maintains her art practice and exhibits on a regional and national level.

Assistant Editor
Ann Glaviano edits the Louisiana Endowment for the Humanities magazine *Louisiana Cultural Vistas*. For the past decade she has provided editing support to authors in a wide range of disciplines, including law, medicine, social science, history, literary scholarship, fiction, nonfiction, and poetry. A New Orleans native, she holds an MFA from The Ohio State University; her writing has appeared in *Tin House, Ninth Letter, Prairie Schooner*, and *Antigravity*, among other publications.

EDITORIAL BOARD
Richard Campanella, professor and geographer with the Tulane School of Architecture, is the author of ten books and more than two hundred articles on the history, geography, architecture, and culture of New Orleans. The only two-time winner of the Louisiana Endowment for the Humanities Book of the Year Award, he has also received the Louisiana Literary Award, the Williams Prize, and the Tulane Honors Professor of the Year Award. In 2016, the Government of France named Campanella *Chevalier dans l'Ordre des Palmes Académiques* (Knight in the Order of the Academic Palms).

Robert L. Dupont, PhD, is Chair of the Department of History and Philosophy at the University of New Orleans, where he teaches urban history. He is the author of *UNO at Fifty*, a history of the university, and co-editor of *Cities as Multiple Landscapes - Investigating the Sister Cities Innsbruck and New Orleans.*

Freddi Williams Evans is the author of *Congo Square: African Roots in New Orleans*, the 2012 Louisiana Endowment for the Humanities Book of the Year, which influenced the New Orleans City Council to officially name the world-famous location "Congo Square" in 2011. Evans co-chairs the New Orleans Committee to Erect Historic Markers for the Transatlantic Slave Trade to Louisiana and the Domestic Slave Trade to New Orleans and serves on the New Orleans Tricentennial Subcommittee on Domestic Slave Trade Markers.

Alecia P. Long, PhD, is the Paul W. and Nancy Murrill Professor of History at Louisiana State University and author of *The Great Southern Babylon: Sex, Race, and Respectability in New Orleans, 1865-1920* (2004). Her current project, *Crimes Against Nature: New Orleans, Sexuality, and the Search for Conspirators in the Assassination of JFK*, connects Clay Shaw's 1969 trial for conspiracy to its overlooked role in the national movement for gay civil rights.

Kara Tucina Olidge, PhD, is the Executive Director of Tulane University's Amistad Research Center, the nation's oldest and most comprehensive independent archive specializing in the history of African Americans and other ethnic communities. Her scholarly work focuses on the intersection of art, critical cosmopolitanism, and community activism.

Lawrence N. Powell, PhD, currently serves as chair of the Louisiana State Museum Board and the Southern Institute for Education and Research. He previously held the James H. Clark Endowed Chair in American Civilization at Tulane University. His most recent book is *The Accidental City: Improvising New Orleans.*

CONTRIBUTORS

Award-winning author **Allison Alsup** lives, writes, and drinks in New Orleans. She teaches fiction classes via the New Orleans Writers Workshop.

Sally Asher is the author of *Hope & New Orleans: A History of Crescent City Street Names, Stories From the St. Louis Cemeteries of New Orleans*, and an upcoming book about Prohibition in New Orleans from Louisiana State University Press. She holds two master's degrees from Tulane University in English and Liberal Arts, with a concentration in history.

C. W. Cannon, PhD, is the author of three novels—*Soul Resin, Katrina Means Cleansing*, and *French Quarter Beautification Project*. He won the 2014 New Orleans Press Club Award for best column for his work at *The Lens*. He teaches writing and New Orleans Studies at Loyola University New Orleans.

Emily Clark, PhD, is Clement Chambers Benenson Professor of American Colonial History at Tulane University. She has authored several books and articles, including the prize-winning *Masterless Mistresses: The New Orleans Ursulines and the Creation of a New World Community* (2007), and serves as co-editor of *New Orleans and Saint-Louis Senegal: Mirror Cities of the Atlantic World*, forthcoming from Louisiana State University Press.

Brian J. Costello is the author or co-author of more than twenty books. For thirty years he has written feature articles on Louisiana and European history and culture. He is founding historian, archivist, and genealogist of the Pointe Coupee Parish Historic Materials Collection and a lifetime advocate of and participant in Louisiana Carnival.

Jack Davis lives in New Orleans where he was a reporter and editor in New Orleans from 1972 to 1983, at *Figaro, The States-Item* and *The Times-Picayune*. At Tribune Company 1983–2007, he was metropolitan editor of the *Chicago Tribune*; CEO/publisher of the *Hartford Courant* in Connecticut and of *The Daily Press* in Virginia; and president of Tribune Interactive.

David Dennis is a writer and adjunct professor of journalism at Morehouse College. He was born in Lafayette, Louisiana.

New Orleans music writer **Alison Fensterstock** has worked as a staff critic and reporter for the New Orleans *Gambit* and the daily *Times-Picayune*. Her work has also appeared in *Pitchfork*, Rolling Stone, *NPR Music*, and the *Oxford American*, and she writes a quarterly column for the Louisiana Endowment for the Humanities magazine *Louisiana Cultural Vistas*.

Helen Freund is a freelance reporter, the Food and Dining Reporter for the New Orleans *Gambit*, and Crime and Courts Reporter for The *New Orleans Advocate*.

New Orleans native **S. Derby Gisclair** is a retired investment consultant who now has more time to devote to researching and writing about sports history—particularly baseball, boxing, and horse racing.

Erin M. Greenwald, PhD, is curator of programs at the New Orleans Museum of Art and previously served as curator of The Historic New Orleans Collection's award-winning exhibition Purchased Lives: New Orleans and the Domestic Slave Trade, 1808-1865. She holds a PhD in History from The Ohio State University.

Rodger Kamenetz, who lives in New Orleans, is an award-winning poet, author and teacher. His best known book, *The Jew in the Lotus* is the story of rabbis on a holy pilgrimage through India to meet with the Dalai Lama. More recently, he has developed a new approach to dreams he calls "natural dreamwork".

Laura D. Kelley, PhD, is a historian at Tulane University and the Program Director for Tulane's Summer in Dublin program. She wrote *The Irish in New Orleans* and is currently completing her second manuscript, *Erin's Enterprise*.

Historian **Jon Kukla, PhD,** author of *A Wilderness So Immense: The Louisiana Purchase and the Destiny of America* (2003), lives in Richmond, Virginia. His other recent books include *Mr. Jefferson's Women* (2007) and *Patrick Henry: Champion of Liberty* (2017).

Brigitta Malm moved from Germany to New Orleans to work at the German Consulate until its closure in 1973. She has since written and presented papers on many aspects of German history and culture in New Orleans.

Keith Weldon Medley is the author of *We as Freemen—Plessy v. Ferguson and Black Life in Old New Orleans*. He has compiled hundreds of articles on Louisiana culture and history in *Smithsonian Magazine* and *American Legacy* and has appeared in the documentaries *Faubourg Tremé: The Untold Story of Black New Orleans, Tremé: Beyond Bourbon Street*, and *How the World Got Mixed Up* (BBC).

Justin Nystrom, PhD, is an associate professor of history and directs the Center for the Study of New Orleans at Loyola University New Orleans. He is the author of *New Orleans after the Civil War: Race, Politics, and a New Birth of Freedom* and the forthcoming *Creole Italian: How Sicilian Immigrants Shaped the Culture of America's Most Interesting Food Town*.

Zella Palmer, educator, food historian, author and filmmaker, serves as the Chair of Dillard University Ray Charles Program in African-American Material Culture, where she is committed to preserving the legacy of African-American and Latino culinary history in New Orleans and the South.

Bruce Boyd Raeburn, PhD, is Director of Special Collections and Curator of the Hogan Jazz Archive at Tulane University. He is a historian specializing in jazz origins and historiography.

Alex Rawls has written about music and culture in New Orleans for almost thirty years. He currently covers the city at his website *MySpiltMilk.com.*

Katy Reckdahl is a New Orleans-based news reporter who writes frequently for the *New Orleans Advocate* and has written for *The Times-Picayune, The New York Times, The Atlantic,* and *Christian Science Monitor.* She has received first-place awards from the New Orleans Press Club and national awards including a James Aronson Award and a Casey Medal for Meritorious Journalism.

John Shelton Reed, PhD, is William Rand Kenan Jr. Professor Emeritus at the University of North Carolina, Chapel Hill. His many books about the South include *Dixie Bohemia: A French Quarter Circle in the 1920s.*

A lifelong New Orleanian, **Sally K. Reeves** is supervising archivist at the Notarial Archives division of the Orleans Parish Clerk of Civil District Court's Office and was the first woman president of the Louisiana Historical Society. She is the author of *Legacy of a Century: The Academy of the Sacred Heart in New Orleans* (1997) and co-author of *New Orleans Architecture* (8 volumes, 1971–1997) and *Historic City Park, New Orleans* (1983).

Maurice Carlos Ruffin has written essays for *Virginia Quarterly Review, LitHub,* and *Unfathomable City.* His first novel, *We Cast A Shadow,* will be published by One World Random House in 2019.

Jerry Strahan is the author of *Andrew Jackson Higgins and the Boats that Won World War II.* He is a longtime volunteer at the National World War II Museum and has participated in both the building of its Higgins-designed LCBP and the restoration of the Higgins LCPL and a PT boat.

Pamela Tyler, PhD, lives in New Orleans and earned her PhD in History at Tulane University. She is the author of *Silk Stockings and Ballot Boxes: Women and Politics in New Orleans, 1920–1963* (1996) and *New Orleans Women and the Poydras Home: More Durable than Marble* (2016).

Daniel H. Usner, PhD, a native of New Orleans, is the Holland N. McTyeire Professor of History at Vanderbilt University. His most recent book is *Weaving Alliances with Other Women: Chitimacha Indian Work in the New South.*

Reverend Dwight Webster, PhD, is the Senior and Founding Pastor of Christian Unity Baptist Church and Co-Moderator of the Justice and Beyond Community Coalition in New Orleans. He is on the faculty of the Institute for Black Catholic Studies at Xavier University of Louisiana and the Sankofa Institute of the Oblate School of Theology in San Antonio, Texas.

Dr. Michael White is a professor of Spanish and African American music at Xavier University of Louisiana, where he holds the Keller Endowed Chair in Humanities. He is an internationally acclaimed jazz clarinetist, composer, producer, and historian who continues to bring the exciting spirit of his ancestral New Orleans jazz tradition to the world through numerous recordings and performances.

Leadership of Partners

New Orleans Convention and Visitors Bureau

J. Stephen Perry
President/CEO

Cara Banasch, MBA
Senior Vice President of Business
Development & Strategy

Kristian Sonnier
Vice President of Communications
& Public Relations

Board of Directors

Michael Smith, Chairman
Greg Rusovich, Chair-Elect
Jim Cook, Past Chair
Steve Pettus, Treasurer
Darryl Berger, Secretary

Ex Officios:
Darryl Berger
Jim Cook
Ron Forman
Stan Harris
Melvin Rodrigue
Doug Thornton

Members at Large

Mickal Adler
Don Allee
Bonnie Boyd
Robert Bray
Steve Caputo
Katy Casbarian
Kathie Jacobs
Diane Lyons
Octavio Mantilla
Quentin Messer
Amy Reimer
Paul Scott
Susan Taylor
David Teich
David Villarrubia
Camille Whitworth

New Orleans Tourism and Marketing Corporation

Board of Directors

Mark Romig, President and CEO
Board of Directors
Mr. Darryl Berger, Chairman
Nick Mueller, PhD, Vice-Chairman
Mr. Octavio Mantilla, Treasurer
Naydja Bynum, DNS, Secretary
Sheila Burns
Hon. LaToya Cantrell
Mr. Jim Cook
Flozell Daniels, Jr.
Hon. Stacy Head
Mr. Mohan Koka
Hon. Nadine Ramsey
Mr. Dan Real
Mr. Ted Selogie
Mr. Michael Smith
Mr. David Teich
Hon. Jason Williams

2018 NOLA Foundation

Executive Committee

Louisiana Endowment for the Humanities

Board of Directors

Index

YMPIA